THE OTHER SIDE OF THE SKY

Borgo Press Books by GARY WESTFAHL

Islands in the Sky: The Space Station Theme in Science Fiction Literature
The Other Side of the Sky: An Annotated Bibliography of Space Stations in Science Fiction, 1869-1993

Other Books by GARY WESTFAHL

Cosmic Engineers: A Study of Hard Science Fiction
Foods of the Gods: Eating and the Eaten in Fantasy and Science Fiction (co-edited with George Slusser and Eric S. Rabkin)
The Greenwood Encyclopedia of Science Fiction and Fantasy: Themes, Works, and Wonders (edited)
Hugo Gernsback and the Century of Science Fiction
Immortal Engines: Life Extension and Immortality in Science Fiction and Fantasy (co-edited with Slusser and Rabkin)
The Mechanics of Wonder: The Creation of the Idea of Science Fiction.
No Cure for the Future: Disease and Medicine in Science Fiction and Fantasy (co-edited with Slusser)
Nursery Realms: Children in the Worlds of Science Fiction, Fantasy, and Horror (co-edited with Slusser)
Science Fiction and Market Realities (co-edited with Slusser and Rabkin)
Science Fiction and the Two Cultures: Essays on Bridging the Gap between the Sciences and the Humanities (co-edited with Slusser)
Science Fiction, Canonization, Marginalization, and the Academy (co-edited with Slusser)
Science Fiction, Children's Literature, and Popular Culture: Coming of Age in Fantasyland
Science Fiction Quotations: From the Inner Mind to the Outer Limits (edited)
The Science of Fiction and the Fiction of Science: Collected Essays on SF Storytelling and the Gnostic Imagination, by Frank McConnell (edited)
Space and Beyond: The Frontier Theme in Science Fiction (edited)
Unearthly Visions: Approaches to Science Fiction and Fantasy Art (co-edited with Slusser and Kathleen Church Plummer)
World Weavers: Globalization, Science Fiction, and the Cybernetic Revolution (co-edited with Wong Kin Yuen and Amy Chan Kit Sze)
Worlds Enough and Time: Explorations of Time in Science Fiction and Fantasy (co-edited with Slusser and David Leiby)

THE OTHER SIDE OF THE SKY

AN ANNOTATED BIBLIOGRAPHY OF SPACE STATIONS IN SCIENCE FICTION, 1869-1993

by

Gary Westfahl

THE BORGO PRESS

An Imprint of Wildside Press LLC

MMIX

Borgo Literary Guides
ISSN 0891-9623

Number Five

www.wildsidebooks.com

FIRST EDITION

CONTENTS

To my daughter,

ALLISON WESTFAHL KONG,

who will be totally uninterested
in the contents of this book,
but may recognized the obsessive
energy which went into its creation
as her inheritance.

INTRODUCTION

The following is an annotated bibliography of 975 science fiction works—561 novels, 297 short stories, and 117 films or television programs—which feature, involve, or mention a space station. The earlier figure of 948 works given in my accompanying critical study, *Islands in the Sky: The Space Station Theme in Science Fiction Literature* (first published in 1996 and now revised and republished by Wildside Press), did not reflect some late additions. Although the language describing the study's parameters and a few passages involving individual works are identical in both books, *Islands in the Sky* is otherwise substantially different from this bibliography in its intent, structure, and content, and each work may be read and consulted without reference to the other.

The bibliography was originally completed in 1991 and prepared, like *Islands in the Sky*, for publication shortly thereafter by Borgo Press. Three years later, with publication still far from imminent, I updated the bibliography one more time to include works published through 1993 before necessarily turning my attention to other projects. After the closure of Borgo Press in 1999 seemingly eliminated any prospects for publication, the manuscript sat untouched until 2003, when Wildside Press agreed to publish the bibliography alongside a Second Edition of *Islands in the Sky*. Because of an increasingly busy schedule and other reasons to be explained, I have made no systematic attempt to further update the bibliography, limiting my recent work to correcting some errors, writing in more detail about some works I have recently read, and adding a number of pre-1994 works to the bibliography.

PARAMETERS OF THE BIBLIOGRAPHY

The parameters of this bibliography were both broad and narrow. First, believing that even stories with brief references to space stations might serve as worthwhile data, I resolved to include virtually every single story in which space stations figured, even if they were only fleetingly mentioned. In dealing with texts written before 1980, this did not cause major problems, since science fiction then was not dominated by stories about space travel, and such stories only occasionally dealt with space stations. In turning to the literature of the last two decades, however, I found both a numerical and a proportional increase in the number of stories involving space travel, since virtually every story set in the future, even those mostly set on Earth, included discussions of or episodes of space travel. And virtually every one of those stories envisioned space stations as elements of humanity's inhabited space. This is why any effort to extend the bibliography beyond 1993 seemed such a daunting task, and why any other researcher studying this topic in recent science fiction will be obliged to establish a policy of including only those works in which space stations play a major role.

On the other hand, I tried to limit the scope of my research by establishing a strict and narrow definition of a space station: "an artificial structure designed to remain permanently in the vacuum of outer space, either in a fixed position or a fixed orbit, and designed for permanent human habitation." The most familiar type of space station is the large spinning wheel or torus built of metal, ranging in size from an office building to a city block, though such facilities may come in many shapes and sizes.

I also included four related types of structures:

1) *Spaceships* which are parked in a permanent position or a permanent orbit to serve as space stations, like the *S. S. Randolph* in Robert A. Heinlein's *Space Cadet* or the "Dead Star Station" in Jack Williamson's story of that name;

2) *Space stations which are transformed into spaceships*, a development seen in works like Frank Belknap Long's *This Strange Tomorrow*, Ben Bova's *Exiled from Earth* and Thomas N. Scortia's *Earthwreck!*;

3) *Inhabited asteroids*, when those asteroids have been hollowed out, tunneled through, or otherwise built on or modified to the point where they may be considered artificial structures, like the asteroid in Robert A. Heinlein's "Misfit" which is "converted" into a space station; and

4) *Space habitats*, enormous enclosed spheres or cylinders which have earthlike landscapes and structures on their interior surfaces.

I excluded stories like Michael McCollum's "A Greater Infinity" which refer to previous or existing space stations—Skylab, Salyut,

Mir—without adding any speculative material about them. I also excluded three types of structures, for these reasons:

1) *Generation starships*, vessels which takes hundreds of years, and several generations, to reach another star, first seen in Don Wilcox's "The Voyage That Lasted 600 Years"—because, despite the fact that most of their residents will spend their entire lives in space, these enclosures still maintain a sense of traveling and have as their goal an eventual landing on a planet, not permanent life in space;
2) *Flying cities*, large inhabited platforms within a planet's atmosphere, like the "vacation city" visited in Hugo Gernsback's *Ralph 124C 41+*—because, despite their similarities to space stations, these communities are not truly isolated from the planet's surface and lack any contact with the environment of space; and
3) *Artificial worlds*, huge artificial constructs of planetary dimensions like Larry Niven's *Ringworld*—because these places offer no sense of living in space and completely mimic a natural world in their environment and the problems they present.

For the record, I distinguished a space habitat from an artificial world by this criterion: a person who suddenly found herself in a space habitat would immediately realize that she was in an artificial structure in space—by seeing landscapes curving up into the sky, or large windows filled with stars; but a person who suddenly found herself on an artificial world would have no immediate way of knowing that it was not a natural world.

Needless to say, these guidelines were not without gray areas and ambiguities—at what point does an inhabited asteroid become a space station and at what point does a space habitat become an artificial world?—so I tended to include borderline works. I further strayed from my own criteria in some cases to include prominent works whose structures have consistently been, or could logically be, regarded as "space stations": the "space station" in Stanislaw Lem's *Solaris*, although that structure—in the novel, at least—would be better described as a flying city; the Death Stars of George Lucas's *Star Wars* and *Return of the Jedi*, although I would classify them simply as large armed spaceships; the "Ship" of Alexei Panshin's *Rite of Passage*, which remains permanently in space although its residents continue, paradoxically, to think and act like starship passengers; and the "Cities in Flight" of James Blish's four novels, which look like cities in space but actually function as spaceships, occasionally landing on a planet's surface. Many readers browsing through this bibliography would expect to find those works, so I included them to meet their expectations.

This bibliography focuses on novels, short stories, films, and television programs. The full title of the first section is "Novels and Longer Works" because it includes a few works—imagined histories of or documents from the future, like Stewart Cowley's *Starliners: Commercial Spacetravel in 2200 A.D.* and Franz Joseph's *Star Fleet Technical Manual*—which are undeniably fictional but which could in no way be described as "novels"; and the full title of the second section is "Short Stories and Shorter Works" because it includes a few poems, song lyrics, and extremely short stories that might be better described as extended jokes. Generally, I excluded works of nonfiction involving space stations with a few exceptions: significant early pieces by Konstantin Tsiolkovsky that are little more than extended lectures with examples, and a few nonfictional works that incorporate fictional passages, like Gerard O'Neill's *2081*, Arthur C. Clarke's *The Lost Worlds of 2001*, and Fredric Golden's *Colonies in Space: The Next Giant Step*.

At one point I started work on a fourth section devoted to "Comic Books, Artwork, and Visual Displays" but soon concluded both that this would not be a fruitful line of research and that I lacked the background and interest to do a thorough job in this area; so I omit these references, though I retain a copy for any scholar who would like to work in this area. In a way, it is a shame to omit from this bibliography the Justice League Satellite, the space station headquarters of the Justice League of America, which, after appearing in over 150 adventures, is surely the most thoroughly described and frequently visited space station in science fiction. In addition, there is an interesting story explaining how Superman's Fortress of Solitude, now at the North Pole, was originally located in Earth orbit, and Captain Kirk and his crew visited a beautiful and unique "Space Mausoleum" in one *Star Trek* comic book. One area I did not even begin to examine was television cartoons, although simply by sharing in my children's youthful television viewing, I have noted visits to space stations by the Care Bears, Inspector Gadget, Barbie and the Rockers, and Charlie Brown and his friends. Science fiction art, video games, and toys are other unexplored areas; I remember as a child building a Revell model of a space station, in the familiar doughnut design, and regret that it was lost long ago. All in all, there is no doubt plenty of available material for a bibliography focusing on *images* of space stations in addition to *stories* about them.

How the Bibliography Was Compiled

I originally worked for five years on researching space stations in science fiction, roughly from 1986 to 1991, and while the available resources for scholars may be vastly improved today—most spectacularly by the addition of access to the Internet—a brief account of my experiences still may be helpful to anyone contemplating a similar project.

I found general bibliographical information about space stations to be limited at best. Sam Moskowitz's "The *Real* Earth Satellite Story" in *Explorers of the Infinite* listed several important works, and Norman Spinrad's essay "Dreams of Space" cited a number of recent novels. Books like Peter Nicholls's *The Science in Science Fiction*, Robert Malone's *Rocketship*, and Harry Harrison's *Spacecraft in Fact and Fiction* also mentioned a few relevant texts, but there was nothing resembling a thorough survey of the literature involving space stations.

To locate the novels listed in the first section, I first read in their entirety two massive bibliographical compilations, Donald Henry Tuck's *The Encyclopedia of Science Fiction and Fantasy through 1968* and I. F. Clarke's *The Tale of the Future, from the Beginning to the Present Day*, which contain brief entries on virtually all science fiction novels and anthologies in English published up to 1970. In a way, these works were complementary: Tuck emphasizes American works and lists them alphabetically by authors' last names; Clarke emphasizes British works and lists them in chronological order. Together, Tuck and Clarke provided me with scores of relevant novels, even though their brief descriptions of novels sometimes failed to note space stations as elements, so that relevant texts needed to be identified by other means. I also read through Neil Barron's more selective bibliography, *Anatomy of Wonder*, and though it only provided a few more sources, at least one of them—Charles L. Harness's *The Paradox Men*—proved a significant addition to the bibliography. Lillian Biermann Wehmeyer's bibliography of children's science fiction, *Images in a Crystal Ball*, also added a few items.

My efforts to locate other relevant works, particularly those published in the last twenty years, were necessarily less systematic. Friends and colleagues were helpful, and a thorough listing of those who assisted or encouraged me is provided in *Islands in the Sky*. In addition, I repeatedly looked through new and used book stores to find titles, and I finally decided to browse through the entire J. Lloyd Eaton Collection of Science Fiction and Fantasy Literature at the University of California, Riverside, the largest institutional collection of science fiction in the world, and I examined every work whose title or cover suggested a reference to space stations. I stumbled upon several books purely by accident; at one early point, for instance, I deliberately took a break from space stations and decided to finally read that novel that everyone was talking about, William Gibson's *Neuromancer*—only to discover, as no colleagues or critical sources had mentioned, that the entire second half of the novel took place in a space habitat. Much later, my final burst of space station research involved helpful contact with the knowledgeable George Zebrowski when I was preparing a bibliography on space habitats for his and Gregory Benford's anthology *Skylife: Space Habitats in Story and Science* (2000), although Zebrowski's definition, unlike mine, included generation starships.

When one is driven to haphazard research methods, the results are likely to be haphazard; and while I can reasonably claim to have a virtually complete listing of science fiction novels prior to 1970 which involve space stations, I have surely missed scores of more recent works in this category.

I initially wanted to read every single novel that I located, but there were in the end simply too many titles, and I was forced to read selectively, concentrating on novels written before 1970 and novels where space stations played a major role. As a result, there are large numbers of "Unseen" novels. In listing the novels that I have not read, my primary concern was to avoid presenting errors: I was irritated when I found references to stories about "space stations" that actually concerned spaceships or asteroid outposts, and I did not want to give other researchers similarly incorrect information. For that reason, despite suggestive titles or illustrations, I included only three types of "Unseen" novels: works specifically described by a reliable bibliographical source as involving a space station; works I personally examined in which I found a reference to a space station, either in the cover blurb or the text itself; and works that were part of a trilogy or series in which another work I had read featured a space station. (If I had read a related work and knew that it had no references to space stations—such as Arthur C. Clarke's first sequel to *2001: A Space Odyssey*, *2010: Odyssey Two*—I noted that fact and omitted it.)

The second section, "Short Stories and Shorter Works," is shorter, and was harder to compile, because available lists of short science fiction works provide only authors and titles; thus, while looking for key words in Donald B. Day's *Index to the Science Fiction Magazines 1926-1950* and its successors did lead me to John Norment's "Space Platform Xz204c Does Not Answer" and Kris Neville's "Satellite Secret," I also wasted time tracking down stories like "Prison in the Sky" or "Promotion to Satellite" that turned out to have nothing to do with space stations. My next step was to look at short story collections focused on space, and I did manage to find several space station stories in anthologies like Jerry Pournelle's three *Endless Frontier* volumes, Susan Shwartz's *Habitats*, and Isaac Asimov, Martin H. Greenberg, and Charles G. Waugh's *Space Shuttles*; Bruce Sterling's *Mirrorshades: The Cyberpunk Anthology* also included several relevant works. At one point I looked through several books of science fiction art like *DiFate's Catalog of Science Fiction Hardware*, hoping to find illustrations of space stations that would identify stories, but the process proved essentially unproductive.

Finally, I began to thumb through issues of old science fiction magazines, paying special attention to *Astounding Science Fiction* and its successor, *Analog Science Fiction/Science Fact*, since it was a major magazine that regularly emphasized hard science fiction; this explains why there are so many stories from that publication in my bibliography. I also completely examined several short-lived magazines with suggestive titles, like *Orbit Science Fiction, Satellite Science Fiction*, and *Space Adventures*, and other magazines that I happen to have easy access to, such as *Galileo*. One serendipitous discovery came when I was looking for a possible source in an old issue of *Wonder Stories Quarterly* shelved in the Eaton Collection and happened to notice a stack of *Fantastic* magazines from the 1950s sitting out to be moved to another shelf; for no particular reason, I picked up the top issue and found a space station story, Lee Grant's "Signal Thirty-Three." Still, since I was not obsessed enough to examine every issue of every science fiction magazine ever published—the only way I can think of to achieve a complete bibliography—I am sure I have omitted a number of relevant short stories.

At a very late stage in my research, I started consulting sources that I should have looked at earlier—the regular book and magazine reviews in *Analog Science Fiction/Science Fact* and *Locus*—and found a few additional novels and stories there. A more systematic look through these and other reviews would have undoubtedly yielded more items.

For the third section, "Films and Television Programs," I began by reading through several reference works on science fiction films; by far the most useful was Phil Hardy's *Encyclopedia of Science Fiction Movies*, which offered unusually detailed descriptions and mentioned a number of foreign-language films not cited in other references. In addition, John Stanley's *Revenge of the Creature Features Movie Guide*, while opinionated and often silly, was extremely thorough in its coverage. The other film books that I examined, unfortunately, were not especially helpful.

For information on television series, I relied on a number of reference books, notably including *Starlog TV Episodes Guide, Volume 2*, which described, among other things, all episodes of the series *Buck Rogers in the Twenty-Fifth Century*; Jean-Marc Lofficier's *Doctor Who: The Programme Guide*, which offered detailed information on a major television series that I knew little about; David J. Schow and Jeffrey Frentzen's *The Outer Limits Companion*, which devoted several pages to the relevant episode "Specimen: Unknown"; David Gerrold's *The Trouble with Tribbles*, which provided more than enough information on the one episode of the original *Star Trek* series that took place in a space station; and Lee Goldberg's *Unsold TV Pilots*, which listed two relevant pilot episodes that had not been discussed in other sources.

The third section includes a high proportion of "Unseen" works for the obvious reason that many of these films and television programs are rarely shown on television and are not readily available on videocassettes or DVDs. For this reason, I have sometimes been obliged to rely on vague memories and outside references.

For the record: I examined a total of 236 novels, 288 short stories, and 77 films or television programs, for a total of 601 examined works; left unseen were 325 novels, 9 short stories, and 40 films or television programs, for a total of 374 unexamined works.

I conclude with two warnings for other science fiction researchers. First, there is an awful lot of science fiction out there. I considered myself well acquainted with the field, but when I began this project, I could list off the top of my head only about 30 to 35 relevant works; when I had finished, I had found almost 1,000 relevant works. Reviewing the bibliography one more time before sending it off to the publisher, I am again struck by how many of the cited texts have been completely overlooked by other scholars and researchers. Based on my own experience, I therefore propose Westfahl's Rule of 30: if a knowledgeable reader of science fiction begins a focused research project by listing all of the related works she can think of, she will ultimately find about 30 times that number of texts. I applied this rule when I was told that a scholar was seeking some help in compiling a bibliography of science fiction works about time travel and other phenomena involving time. Since I could easily think of at least 100 relevant works, I estimated that a reasonably thorough bibliography on that subject would include at least 3,000 works. I declined to participate in the project.

My second warning is that it will not be easy to find all of those science fiction works. Perhaps I gave up on the secondary sources too soon; perhaps I should have looked more at histories, bibliographies, and other reference works on science fiction. But I suspect that I still would not have found revealing references to large numbers of the works in my bibliography. In preparing my book and this bibliography, I asked a simple question—which science fiction works involve space stations?—and found there was no reasonable or systematic way to obtain a thorough answer; and researchers who approach any other science fiction topic will be similarly handicapped. One can hope for vast improvements in the bibliographical apparatus for science fiction, but using only the resources now available, it remains true that a science fiction researcher will necessarily have to locate most of the relevant sources by locating them on her own and by looking at them with her own eyes.

FORMAT OF THE BIBLIOGRAPHY

In each entry, the first paragraph provides a summary of the work; the second paragraph offers commentary; and in some cases, there is a third paragraph with textual notes or cross-references. The only exceptions occur when I am listing a number of related, unseen works; these are simply preceded by general introductory comments.

In cases where the story is well known, proceeded along familiar lines, or was not especially important to the subject at hand, the summaries may be brief; in cases where the story is obscure, complicated, or important, the summaries may be longer. Commentaries tend to focus on the relevance of the work to the topic of space stations, though in a few cases I stray into unrelated subjects. For example, those who still believe that no science fiction story ever predicted a televised moon landing will find one interesting item in this bibliography. Textual notes and cross-references are there when I happened to have information or happened to think of some connection; I would not claim that they are complete, or always available when needed.

As I put the bibliography together, there were a few cases where I had difficulty deciding whether to list a lengthy work as a novel or short story; I ultimately used the criterion that if a work had ever been separately published as a novel, or if it had appeared in a magazine labeled as a novel, I would list it as a novel, and if it had only been published in magazines or anthologies, and if it had never been described as a novel, I would list it as a short story. Therefore, Poul Anderson's *Hunters of the Sky Cave*, Robert A. Heinlein's *Waldo*, and C. L. Moore's *Judgment Night* are included in the first section because they were once published as paperback novels, while Joan Vinge's "The Crystal Ship," roughly the same length, is included in the second section because it has only been published as part of an anthology and has never to my knowledge been identified or published as a novel.

Another ambiguity involved novels originally published in shorter versions in magazines, and related short stories later published together as a novel or connected work—a "fix-up"; should I simply list the books, or should I also list all the shorter works later incorporated into the books as separate short stories? In most cases, I listed the final work as a novel without padding the bibliography by individually listing all the excerpts, stories, or shorter versions that had been previously published, on the theory that other researchers would be most interested in reading the final product, not the rough drafts. Exceptions to this policy were those cases where I read one of the constituent stories without reading the later novel; for example, I examined only two of the five stories—"Itch on the Bull Run" and "Switch on the Bull Run"—that later contributed to Sharon Webb's *The Adventures of Terra Tarkington*, and I read only one story, "All the Colors of the Vacuum," that later contributed to Charles Sheffield's *The McAndrew Chronicles*. In these cases, I listed the story or stories in Part B and the novel in Part A. In addition, since the first, shorter versions of Spider and Jeanne Robinson's *Stardance* and Gregory Benford and Gordon Eklund's *If the Stars Are Gods* both won Nebula Awards, I thought it important to list those two works both as novellas and as novels.

In alphabetizing authors and works, I have followed a few irregular policies. First, I have listed all works by the name of the author which is most familiar to readers, whether that is a real name or a pseudonym; thus, there are listings under Hal Clement, not Harry Clement Stubbs, and under Murray Leinster, not Will Jenkins. Second, in the cases of single sequels or related works which do not assume the character of a series, I have placed titles in normal alphabetical order, with cross-references; but in the cases of definite series of three works or more, I usually list them according to internal chronological order, not alphabetically by title, and list them as a group alphabetically by the title of the entire series; when no overall name for the series is provided in individual works, brackets after the title name the series and give the number of that particular work in the series. Finally, as a personal rebellion against confusing and inconsistent guidelines involving the alphabetical order of names beginning with "Mc" or "Mac," I have alphabetized these names naïvely: Katherine MacLean, George R. R. Martin, and Dean McLaughlin, in that order.

As one indication of how frequently space stations have appeared in fiction at various times, I next offer a compilation of "Works Listed in Chronological Order, 1869-1993," although the statistical picture that emerges is best described as suggestive, not definitive, since there are, as I have warned, many unrepresented works. This section lists slightly more works—987—because I decided to indicate the individual publication dates of all portions of two early and important works: Edward Everett Hale's "The Brick Moon" and George O. Smith's *Venus Equilateral*, adding a total of 12 items to the survey.

Finally, a "Timeline" graphically illustrates the frequency and distribution of space station stories from 1869 to 1993. In general, the picture provided is what one might expect: only scattered items before World War II; a growing amount of interest in the decade following World War II, as America's incipient space program publicized the concept of the space station; a decline in attention to the subject during the 1960s, as the actual triumphs of the space program and the New Wave movement diminished interest in space adventures; and a new growth in the late 1970s and 1980s, as proposals for space habitats brought new life to the subject. The large number of more recent works—altogether, more than half of the items in my bibliography were published in the last twelve years—is due, as I have suggested, not to any unusual new interest in the subject, but only to the explosive growth in the entire field of science fiction, and to the noted contemporary consensus that future space travel, and space stations as one aspect of that travel, are inevitable.

I concluded the original version of this introduction with language suggesting that I might someday return to this research and inviting readers to provide me with names of additional works involving space station for a potential expanded version of this bibliography. In light of everything that has occurred to me since completing these books, however, such a development now seems virtually impossible; thus, any further progress in researching and understanding space stations in science fiction will have to be achieved by another obsessive scholar. Until that person comes to the forefront, this book and its companion, *Islands in the Sky*, will have to suffice as the best available sources of information on the subject.

—Gary Westfahl
Riverside, California
September, 2009

ACKNOWLEDGMENTS

Most of the work of thanking those individuals who assisted in my space station research, and those individuals who have provided assistance and encouragement over the years, has been accomplished in the two sets of "Acknowledgments" in *Islands in the Sky*, so my comments here will be brief. Ivan Adamovic, Richard Bleiler, George F. Butler, Amy Chan Kit Sze, John Clute, Martin Coleman, Arthur B. Evans, Joan Gordon, John Grant, Donald M. Hassler, Veronica Hollinger, Fiona Kelleghan, Mark R. Kelly, David Langford, Rob Latham, Farah Mendlesohn, Kathleen Church Plummer, David Pringle, Robert Reginald, Andy Sawyer, Darrell Schweitzer, David Seed, George Slusser, Fred Shapiro, and Wong Kin Yuen are among the many colleagues who deserve a second round of applause, and of course I must thank Robert Reginald of Borgo Press and John Gregory Betancourt of Wildside Press for agreeing to publish this book after all these years, and I must again thank Reginald for his assistance in preparing this book for publication. Finally, I must as always gratefully acknowledge the support of my wife, Lynne Lundquist Westfahl, my children Allison Westfahl Kong and Jeremy Westfahl, and my son-in-law Steven Kong.

—Gary Westfahl
Riverside, California
September, 2009

PART A.

NOVELS AND LONGER WORKS

A1. Abels, Harriette S. [Sheffer] *Meteor from the Moon.* 1979. Mankato, MN: Crestwood House, 1980. 47 p.

As spaceship EM-88 returns to space station Astro-Orb, the crew observes a meteor brush against the station and disrupt its spin and position. After helping residents cope with the changed gravity, they travel to the Moon, where a power station broadcasts beams of "solar power" to restore the station to its original position.

Even in a book aimed at young readers, the scientific illiteracy here is inexcusable: the author does not seem to understand the difference between a space station's orbit and its spin, and the notion that beams of "solar power" (does she mean laser beams?) could move a space station is absurd. Needless to say, there are no insights about space stations to be found here.

Note: this is one of nine short novels involve Astro-Orb and spaceship EM-88. The others, all unseen, are:

A2. Abels, Harriette S. [Sheffer] *Forgotten World.* 1979. Mankato, MN: Crestwood House, 1980. 47 p.

A3. Abels, Harriette S. [Sheffer] *Green Invasion.* 1979. Mankato, MN: Crestwood House, 1980. 47 p.

A4. Abels, Harriette S. [Sheffer] *Medical Emergency.* 1979. Mankato, MN: Crestwood House, 1980. 47 p.

A5. Abels, Harriette S. [Sheffer] *Mystery on Mars.* 1979. Mankato, MN: Crestwood House, 1980. 47 p.

A6. Abels, Harriette S. [Sheffer] *Planet of Ice*. 1979. Mankato, MN: Crestwood House, 1980. 47 p.

A7. Abels, Harriette S. [Sheffer] *Silent Invaders*. 1979. Mankato, MN: Crestwood House, 1980. 47 p.

A8. Abels, Harriette S. [Sheffer] *Strangers on NMA-6*. 1979. Mankato, MN: Crestwood House, 1980. 47 p.

A9. Abels, Harriette S. [Sheffer] *Unwanted Visitors*. 1979. Mankato, MN: Crestwood House, 1980. 47 p.

A10. Aldiss, Brian W. *Helliconia Spring*. New York: Atheneum, 1982. 361 p.

This novel about an intricately realized planetary ecology includes scenes of people in a space station overhead.

Unseen; this is the first book in a trilogy. The other two volumes, both unseen, are:

A11. Aldiss, Brian W. *Helliconia Summer*. New York: Atheneum, 1983. 398 p.

A12. Aldiss, Brian W. *Helliconia Winter*. New York: Atheneum, 1985. 281 p.

A13. Allen, Roger MacBride. *Farside Cannon*. New York: Baen, 1988. 406 p.

This near-future tale of conflict between Earth and space colonies includes a visit to New Goddard Station in Earth orbit.

Unseen.

A14. Allen, Roger MacBride. *The Ring of Charon*. New York: Tor, 1990. 500 p.

This novel about gravity research near Pluto mentions space stations and space habitats.

Unseen.

A15. Anderson, Kevin J., and Doug Beason. *Assemblers of Infinity*. New York: Bantam, 1993. 355 p.

This story about the discovery of an alien artifact on the surface of the Moon has as one setting Collins L-1 Waystation.

Unseen.

A16. Anderson, Kevin J., and Doug Beason. *Lifeline*. New York: Bantam, 1990. 460 p.

When Earth is destroyed, only three space colonies from the United States, the Soviet Union and the Philippines survive to keep the human race alive.

Unseen.

A17. Anderson, Poul. *Hunters of the Sky Cave*. In *Agent of the Terran Empire*. New York: Ace, 1980. Originally published in shortened form in *Amazing Stories* (June, 1959). Also published as *We Claim These Stars!* New York: Ace, 1960. 125 p.

While enjoying an evening on the Crystal Moon, a beautiful, jewel-like satellite orbiting Jupiter, Ensign Flandry meets a telepathic alien and rushes to Earth to argue for his capture. However, he is sent on another assignment instead.

While the interior of the Crystal Moon is barely described, its multi-colored crystalline exterior makes it seem quite attractive. The creation is reminiscent of Smith and Starzl's Pleasure Bubble in "The Metal Moon" (q.v.)—another crystalline pleasure satellite orbiting Jupiter.

Note: this is one of several Anderson novels and stories that feature Ensign Flandry, but I have chosen not to list them here, since I believe that references to space stations in other Flandry stories are at best peripheral.

A18. Anderson, Poul. *The Long Way Home. Astounding Science Fiction*, 55 (April, 1955, through July, 1955). Also known as *No World of Their Own*. Later republished as *The Long Way Home*. New York: Ace, 1978. 245 p.

This far-ranging space adventure briefly looks back at the early days of space travel when "The space stations were useful" with a specific reference to "a space station near Earth" (*Astounding*, April, 1955, 13).

Unseen.

A19. Appleton, Victor. [pseudonym] *The City in the Stars. A Tom Swift Adventure [#1]*. New York: Wanderer, 1981. 191 p.

Living in the space habitat New America, Tom copes with the villainous attacks and acts of sabotage of the evil station director Grotz and his henchmen, while hurrying to perfect a new fusion drive in time for a spaceship race. Eventually, Grotz is exposed, Tom completes his invention, and he wins the race—after which he delivers a ringing speech calling for continued planetary exploration.

Just as this novel's 1955 counterpart, *Tom Swift, Jr., and His Outpost in Space* (q.v.), summarized then-current ideas about space stations, this first novel in the updated series is a useful compendium of the features and possibilities of a space habitat. Like the heroes of other stories, however, Tom is not content to live in such a habitat, preferring to venture forth to other worlds.

Note: this is the first of eleven books in this third Tom Swift series; the other volumes to my knowledge do not seem to involve space stations or space colonies. A fourth Tom Swift series focuses only on earthbound adventures.

A20. Appleton, Victor, II. [pseudonym] *Tom Swift and His Outpost in Space*. [*Tom Swift, Jr. #6*] New York: Grosset & Dunlap, 1955. 210 p.

Broadcasting companies finance Swift Enterprise's construction of the world's first space station; Tom figures out the technical problems and supervises its building while fending off saboteurs.

In between the juvenile heroics, the novel offers a reasonably good listing of the various problems of building a space station, and possible solutions to them—oxygen, weightlessness, heating and cooling, etc. An interesting bit of prophecy is the station's "staggering" cost.

Note: along with *Tom Swift and the Cosmic Astronauts* (discussed below), other books in the Tom Swift, Jr., series which feature or mention Tom's Outpost in Space, all unseen, include:

A21. Appleton, Victor, Jr. [pseudonym] *Tom Swift on the Phantom Satellite*. [*Tom Swift, Jr. #9*] New York: Grosset & Dunlap, 1956. 214 p.

A22. Appleton, Victor, Jr. [pseudonym] *Tom Swift in the Race to the Moon*. [*Tom Swift, Jr. #12*] New York: Grosset & Dunlap, 1958. 180 p.

A23. Appleton, Victor, Jr. [pseudonym] *Tom Swift and His Space So-lartron*. [*Tom Swift, Jr. #13*] New York: Grosset & Dunlap, 1958. 183 p.

A24. Appleton, Victor, Jr. [pseudonym] *Tom Swift and the Asteroid Pirates*. [*Tom Swift, Jr. #21*] New York: Grosset & Dunlap, 1963. 178 p.

A25. Appleton, Victor, II. [pseudonym] *Tom Swift and the Cosmic Astronauts*. [*Tom Swift, Jr. #16*] New York: Grosset & Dunlap, 1960. 184 p.

While trying to figure out a new method of space travel—research which twice takes him to his outpost in space—Tom Swift, Jr., fights against an Oriental villain named Li Ching, who at one point seizes control of the station before Tom defeats him.

Like other space stations, Tom's outpost in space seems rather vulnerable—to mechanical accidents (a rocket from Tom's "space friends" inadvertently hits the station, disrupting its orbit); to "cosmic radiation" which interferes with the station's mechanism and causes wild spinning; and to armed takeover by a small band of a dozen men.

A26. Ash, Alan. *Conditioned for Space*. London: Ward, Lock & Co., Limited, 1955. 192 p.

A man from 1954, accidentally frozen in ice, is revived one hundred years later and equipped with new powers, including super-strength and the ability to survive in a vacuum, to be the prototype of a new type of human truly suited to travel in space. After visiting the British and Commonwealth Space Station, he is recruited to journey to another planet which is bombarding Earth with radioactive dust as a prelude to an invasion; he and his crew are imprisoned, but he later succeeds in escaping and destroying the planet, though at the cost of his own life.

There are four Space Stations in the year 2055—British, American, Russian, and Chinese—though only the American station "had almost reached the proportions of a complete town...movies and saloons and so on" (48, 51). The British station is in the familiar "cart-wheel" shape (48) and is noteworthy only for its emphasis on color-coding in decor.

A27. Asimov, Isaac. *The Caves of Steel*. 1954. New York: Pyramid, 1962. 189 p.

The people of the overpopulated future Earth live in huge domed cities under the domination of human space colonists called Spacers. When a Spacer is mysteriously killed, an Earth detective teams up with a Spacer robot to solve the crime.

In one of the many conversations that fill this (and every) Asimov novel, plans are mentioned to build "space stations inside Mercury's orbit to act as energy accumulators" to replace Earth's dwindling supply of uranium (131); but the idea is rejected because of "the impossibility so far of projecting a beam tight enough to reach fifty million miles without dispersal to uselessness" (132). This is odd, since a previous story in Asimov's robot series, "Reason" (q.v.), features exactly such a space station—one of the numerous inconsistencies in Asimov's future history.

A28. Asimov, Isaac. *Foundation and Earth*. Garden City, NY: Doubleday, 1986. 356 p.

While searching for the mythical homeworld of humanity, Earth, space travelers stop at an "entry station" orbiting the planet Comporellon before landing on its surface.

This is, I believe, the first time that space stations have played a conspicuous role in Asimov's *Foundation* series, although there are several such structures orbiting Comporellon, and a traveler's comment about them suggests that these are very common in the Foundation universe: "Some might be orbiting factories or laboratories or observatories, or even populated townships. Some planets prefer to keep all orbiting objects outwardly dark, except for the entry stations. Terminus does, for instance" (56).

Note: space stations do not appear in the original trilogy, and I do not recall any in the fourth book in the series *Foundation's Edge* (1981).

There are, however, brief references in the sixth book, *Prelude to Foundation* (q.v.) and one would assume there are similar references in the seventh and final book, currently unseen:

A29. Asimov, Isaac. *Forward the Foundation*. Garden City, NY: Doubleday, 1993. 417 p.

A30. Asimov, Isaac. *Prelude to Foundation*. Garden City, NY: Doubleday, 1988. 403 p.

This novel chronicles the early career of Hari Seldon, the man who would later establish the two Foundations dedicated to restoring order to the galaxy. He arrives at Trantor, announces the theoretical possibility of a mathematical system to predict the future of humanity, and he attempts to evade capture in various sections of Trantor while being assisted by a mysterious figure who turns out to be the robot R. Daneel Olivaw.

The novel includes three brief references to space stations, the lengthiest reference being a comparison of the world of Trantor to a space station: "Trantor is very much like an enormous and overgrown space settlement.... Space settlements are essentially enclosed cities, with everything artificially cycled, with artificial ventilation, artificial day and night, and so on" (51)

A31. Asimov, Isaac. *Nemesis*. Garden City, NY: Doubleday, 1989. 364 p.

Seeking to build a new civilization free from Earth's influence, inhabitants of a space colony use a limited form of faster-than-light travel to move out to a newly discovered brown dwarf star called Nemesis—where they find an earthlike planet with primitive life forms. It is discovered that Nemesis is going to pass near the Sun in five thousand years and make Earth uninhabitable, but when Earthmen fly to investigate Nemesis, the planet's life forms—now revealed as a single intelligent being—suggest a way to move Nemesis out of the Sun's way.

The desire to "build our new society" in space (22) is hardly new, but Asimov offers this criticism: while the large population of Earth has struggled toward acceptance of human diversity, space colonies reestablish old patterns of selectivity: "What all the Settlements fear and hate most is variety. They don't want differences in appearance, tastes, ways, and life. They select themselves for uniformity and despise everything else" (118). There is also the suggestion that people may carry "some dim atavistic memory of Earth...a feeling for a huge endless world in [one's] genes; a longing that a small, artificial turning city-in-space could not fulfill" (271). In addition to his space colony, Asimov's expedition to Nemesis leaves from a more conventional space station, Station Four: "The early stations had been Earth's launching pads for the construction of the first Settlements" (247).

A32. Baker, Pip and Jane Baker. *Doctor Who—Terror of the Vervoids*. London: W. H. Allen and Co., 1988. 144 p.

A novel based on a portion of a televised *Doctor Who* adventure involving a space station.

Unseen; for a more complete plot summary, see "The Trial of a Time Lord" in Part C.

A33. Baker, Pip and Jane Baker. *Doctor Who—The Ultimate Foe*. London: W. H. Allen and Co., 1988. 126 p.

A novel based on a portion of a televised *Doctor Who* adventure involving a space station.

Unseen; for a more complete plot summary, see "The Trial of a Time Lord" in Part C.

A34. Ball, Brian N. *Singularity Station*. New York: DAW, Inc., 1973. 176 p.

Haunted by the loss of his spaceship in the mysterious Jansky Singularity, Al Buchanan gets the job of occupying the one-man Jansky Station set up to monitor the phenomenon. Against orders, he decides to move the station into the Singularity; and with the help of a maniacal escaped criminal, he discovers the Singularity harbors a Sargasso Sea of lost ships suspended in time and that it functions as a gateway to another universe.

Obsessed with the Singularity, Buchanan never seems to respond to living in the station itself, which is largely controlled by robots. In refusing to respond to Buchanan's sightings of the lost ships, the robot controlling the station appears to be going mad, but Buchanan finally decides that it was deliberately suppressing information, to protect humanity from a phenomenon it was not ready for. Jansky Station is similar to the stations near strange regions of space in Martin's "The Second Kind of Loneliness" and Gibson's "Hinterlands" (q.v.).

A35. Ballou, Arthur W. *Bound for Mars*. Boston: Little, Brown, and Company, 1970. 218 p.

After the first mission to Mars departs from space station OFTEL (Orbital Facility for Space Exploratory Travel), a crewman becomes obsessed with stopping the mission at all costs. He fabricates a supposed message from aliens warning humans to stay away from Mars, but the hoax is revealed, the crewman is accidentally killed, and the ship begins the process of landing.

Almost nothing is said about the space station, and Ballou's only real contribution may be the singular name he devises for his space station—OFTEL—which, in addition to its acronymic meaning, may be a clipped version of "Off-Tellus," or off-Earth.

Note: there is a preceding novel with some of the same characters called *Marooned in Orbit* which apparently does not involve space stations.

A36. Banks, Iain M. *Consider Phlebas*. New York: Bantam, 1991. 497 p. Originally published in 1987.

This novel of life in space includes an adventure in a doomed space habitat.

Unseen. This is the first of seven novels to date set in the same universe; *The State of the Art* is an anthology including at least one Culture story. *Excession* (1996), *Inversions* (1998) *Look to Windward* (2000), and *Matter* (2008) appeared after 1993. The two early novel and anthology are unseen:

A37. Banks, Iain. *The Player of Games*. 1988. New York: St. Martin's Press, 1989. 309 p.

A38. Banks, Iain. *The State of the Art*. Willimantic, CT: M. V. Ziesing, 1989. 122 p.

A39. Banks, Iain. *Use of Weapons*. 1990. New York: Bantam, 1992. 389 p.

A40. Barnes, John. *The Man Who Pulled Down the Sky*. 1986. Chicago: Congdon & Weed, Inc., 1988. 256 p.

A novel about conflict between Earth, the Orbital Republics, and the independent asteroids.

Unseen.

A41. Barnes, John. *Orbital Resonance*. New York: Tor, 1991. 214 p.

An adventure novel involving space colonies.

Unseen.

A42. Barr, Tyrone C. *The Last Fourteen*. [Also known as *Split Worlds*] 1959. New York: Chariot, 1960. 156 p.

Nine men and five women on a space station are the only survivors when a global nuclear war devastates Earth. Returning after five years in orbit, they attempt to establish a new utopian society, but their checkered pasts and jealousies soon lead to murder, dissension, and dictatorship.

After the disaster (and it was amazingly coincidental that the war broke out during the three hours [!] the space station was scheduled to be in orbit), Captain Adams avoids disharmony on board by, among other things, keeping the men and women separate, foreshadowing NASA's equally prudish attitudes towards cohabitation in space. A generally silly novel focusing on personalities and mild prurient interest, it nevertheless reinforces the point that a manned (and womanned) space station might be the only way to ensure the survival of the human race.

A43. Baxter, Stephen. *Raft*. 1991. New York: Penguin, 1992. 303 p.

In an alternate universe where gravity is extraordinarily strong, the survivors of a crushed spaceship from Earth live either on the "Raft" constructed from the ship, or in shacks orbiting a small object.

Unseen.

A44. Bayley, Barrington J. *Collision Course*. New York: DAW, 1973. 175 p.

A novel about the home of the Interstellar Space Society, called Retort City—a gigantic city in a bottle in deep space.

Unseen.

A45. Bear, Greg. *Eon*. New York: Bluejay, 1985. 504 p.

A novel about the strange discovery of a hollowed-out asteroid that enters Earth orbit from another universe.

Unseen. There have been three sequels to date: *Legacy* (1995) and *The Way of All Ghosts* (1999) appeared after 1993; the other, also unseen, is:

A46. Bear, Greg. *Eternity*. New York: Warner, 1988. 399 p.

A47. Bear, Greg. *Hegira*. New York: Dell, 1979. 240 p.

A novel involving a massive artificial world.

Unseen.

A48. Beebee, Chris. *The Hub*. London: Macdonald & Co., 1987. 249 p.

A novel about the Cipola space habitat.

Unseen. To date, one sequel, also unseen, has appeared:

A49. Beebee, Chris. *The Main Event*. London: Macdonald & Co., 1989. 202 p.

A50. Beliayev, Aleksandr. *The Struggle in Space*. 1928. Translated by Albert Parry. Washington, DC: Arfor Publishers, 1965. 116 p.

A Muscovite from 1928 wakes up in the future realm of Radiopolis, part of a communist utopia that now extends throughout Europe, Asia and Africa. As he learns about this new world, its harmonious social order, and its many scientific marvels, there looms the prospect of a final confrontation with America, the last bastion of evil capitalism in the world. He participates in an apparently successful assault on America, but he and a friend are captured by a remaining capitalist baron who takes them on board "a large airship...a veritable flying city," which can "go above the atmosphere to navigate in airless space" (114). The capitalists hope to "last an indefinitely long time away from this planet" (114), but the need for periodic supplies from Earth means they "are doomed" (115); instead, they decide to blow up the airship with atomic power and, in that way, destroy the entire planet Earth as well. As the protagonist and his friend are blowing up the airship with other explosives before atomic energy can be used, he wakes up, back in 1928.

The episode involving an early space station actually only involves the last three pages of the novel, which is otherwise an uninteresting combination of the scientific utopia and the future war novel. Still, Beliayev is noteworthy as the first author directly inspired by Konstantin Tsiolkovsky (Parry's introduction says that Beliayev was a great admirer of Tsiolkovsky), and his book stands with Kurd Lasswitz's *Two Planets* (q.v.) as an anticipation of the military possibilities of a space station. Beliayev also differs from Tsiolkovsky in seeing some difficulty in maintaining life in space without regular supplies from Earth.

A51. Benford, Gregory. *Great Sky River*. New York: Bantam, 1987. 326 p.

On the planet Snowglade near the center of the galaxy, ragtag bands of humans try to survive against the powerful Mechs (mechanical intelligences) gradually taking over their world. Finally, however, aided by a mysterious voice from the galaxy's center and a strangely sympathetic Mech, the people are allowed to board a starship and travel to another world.

In Benford's future history, humanity at one stage lived in huge space cities called Chandeliers before being reduced to pathetic scavengers by the Mechs. At one point, his hero Killeen sees a remaining Chandelier through a telescope and is inspired by the sight—"There's one still left!... A city. Human city!" (170) People abandoned them and moved to planetary settlements called Citadels because the Chandeliers were too vulnerable to Mech attacks: "Mechs hit the Chandeliers too last I heard.... You stayed there you'd likely be suredead" (171-172).

Note: *In the Ocean of Night* and *Across the Sea of Suns* are loosely linked to this work; its later sequels are *Tides of Light* (q.v.), *Furious Gulf* (1994), and *Sailing Bright Eternity* (1995).

A52. Benford, Gregory, and Gordon Eklund. *If the Stars Are Gods*.

1977. Updated Edition. New York: Bantam, 1989. 229 p.
Based on a novella of the same name originally published in
1974.

During his long life, a man is repeatedly involved with the discovery
of alien life forms: as part of the first manned mission to Mars, he uncovers evidence of Martian life; while on the Moon, he is assigned to
meet visiting aliens who worship stars as sentient gods; in response to
a mysterious radio message apparently from a gas giant planet around
another star, he heads a satellite outpost studying Jupiter for clues to
the message and discovers life in its atmosphere; and in examining a
strange crystal lattice on Titan, he finally dies—though his essence is
trapped and preserved by the alien builders of the lattice.

The space station around Jupiter, called the Orb, is much like the facility in Benford's *Jupiter Project* (q.v.), with a similar structure and
purpose. There are familiar complaints about its decor—"In a largely
futile attempt at coziness, the room had been decorated in a spiral rainbow swirl...a welcome contrast to the womb whiteness of most of the
Orb" (114)—its tension—"This cramped Orb breeds much hostility"
(114)—and its dullness—"Out here everything becomes so similar,
monotonous" (151).

A53. Benford, Gregory. *Jupiter Project*. 1975. New York: Berkley,
1980. 182 p. An earlier version appeared in *Amazing Science
Fiction* (September-November, 1972).

Young Matt Bohles lives with his parents in JABOL (the Jovian As-
tronautical-Biological Orbital Laboratory), a "big tin can" in orbit
around Jupiter (6). Citing financial problems, Earth orders the space
cylinder abandoned, but Matt discovers a form of alien life when he
repairs an observation satellite, and his father finds evidence of an
alien vehicle, apparently ensuring JABOL's future—and Matt's continued residence there.

Benford makes a number of good points about life in a space station,
the most important being that the cramped and restricted life style
would breed conformity and rigidity, particularly in its younger residents: "That was the danger of compression, of packing people so
close together they *had* to get along. In those circumstances, everybody had to back down, live life according to the concensus [sic] rules.
That might be okay if you were already an adult.... But to grow up you
had to take *risks*" (166). More familiar complaints are the lack of pri-

vacy and space (26, 27), the need for colorful decor (8), and the stupidity of using hand weapons (120).

A54. Benford, Gregory. *Tides of Light*. New York: Bantam, 1989. 362 p.

Driven by a mysterious message from the center of the galaxy, a group of humans last seen in *Great Sky River* (q.v.) travel to a distant planet, where they find and occupy a space station of the malevolent machine intelligences called Mechs. There they encounter a strange and menacing race of cyborgs who can live in the vacuum of space and join an army battling against them on the planet's surface; ultimately, however, the army's leader is revealed as a Mech and the humans and cyborgs become allies in the quest to reach the galactic center.

With a large space station as the initial scene of the action, and references to vast space cities called Chandeliers where humans once lived before the Mechs appeared, this novel certainly warrants a place in my bibliography; but Benford recommended the book to me for a different reason—the cyborgs, who are "amphibious" in their ability to move in and out of space, could be seen, he argued, as "living space stations," an outgrowth of simple dwellings in space. (For a different sort of "living space station," see Fritch's "Many Dreams of Earth.")

A55. Bernard, Rafe. *The Wheel in the Sky*. London: Ward, Lock, & Co., 1954. 192 p.

An International Space Commission launches materials and crewmen into space to build the world's first space station, which, after some minor problems, is completed and occupied.

Bernard's novel, somewhat similar to Castle's *Satellite E One* (q.v.), offers more color and excitement—some saboteurs, the solemn ceremony of the lighting of the first cigarettes—but less real emotion. Earth bureaucrats and their petty concerns are repeatedly cited as an irritant.

A56. Bester, Alfred. *The Demolished Man*. 1953. New York: Vintage, 1996. 245 p.

In a world of mind readers, an unscrupulous businessman schemes to successfully commit a murder, but he is ultimately captured and "demolished"—his personality restructured.

Although most of Bester's novel takes place on Earth, there is an interesting visit to the space community of Spaceland—a "flat plate of asteroid rock" with protective domes over various settlements that grew into "an irregular table in space, extending hundreds of miles" (154).

A57. Bischoff, David F., and Thomas Monteleone. *Day of the Dragonstar*. New York: Berkley, 1983. 291 p.

A novel about what John Clute in *The Encyclopedia of Science Fiction* described as an "artificial-world-cum-zoo in space" (125).

Unseen. This is the first book in the Dragonstar trilogy; the other two, also unseen, are:

A58. Bischoff, David F., and Thomas Monteleone. *Night of the Dragonstar*. New York: Berkley, 1985. 264 p.

A59. Bischoff, David F., and Thomas Monteleone. *Dragonstar Destiny*. New York: Ace, 1989. 216 p.

A60. Bishop, George. *The Shuttle People*. New York: Bantam, 1983. 210 p.

Detective Ted Royce investigates the murder of an astronaut near Edwards Air Force Base and discovers an elaborate plot involving the so-called "Shuttle People"—astronauts permanently adjusted to zero gravity who have developed delusions of grandeur and a desire to control the world. A substance accidentally discovered in Space Station 11 seems to promise eternal life, so the renegades seize control of the station and conceal its whereabouts from the United States government. They plan to use the substance to make themselves immortal while blackmailing the government with a nuclear bomb. However, Royce finds out who is behind the plot and helps the government defeat the rebels.

The novel provides another warning about psychological problems developing in space residents—"You know how these shuttle people are," one character says, "Emotionally and mentally unstable" (69)—and another criticism of the concept of military space stations. Here, the author presents the standard argument—"As we now know, space stations command the world" (82)—but his story undermines it: the renegade astronauts find it easy to take over one station, bring an H-bomb to it, and pose a credible threat to the authorities who set up the system.

A61. Blackburn, John. *A Scent of New-Mown Hay*. New York: M. S. Mill, Co., 1958. 224 p.

A story about a biological disaster on Earth begins with the Russians apparently planning to build and launch a satellite station.

Unseen.

A62. Blish, James. *They Shall Have Stars*. [also published as *Year 2018*] [*Cities in Flight #1*] 1957. New York: Avon, 1967. 159 p.

Scientists work with robots and machinery to build a bridge on Jupiter as a means of studying gravity, while other scientists on Earth are researching methods of indefinitely prolonging human life.

The novel mentions one conventional space station in Earth orbit. "Satellite Vehicle One" (129), evidently a regular stopover for spaceships—a character refers to "the regular SV-1-Mars-Belt-Jupiter X cruiser" (135). However, the focus is on the development of the two inventions—anti-gravity "spindizzies" and life-prolonging "anti-agathic drugs"—which will make possible the flying cities featured in the other three novels in the series, all discussed below.

A63. Blish, James. *A Life for the Stars*. [*Cities in Flight #2*] 1963. New York: Avon, 1968. 143 p.

A young Earth boy, kidnapped and taken aboard the city of Scranton when it flies off into space, is transferred to the flying city of New York, where he learns about the background and culture of the Okie cities and eventually qualifies to become a citizen, receive the life-prolonging drugs, and serve as the new city manager.

With its viewpoint character a young newcomer, this is really the only novel in the series that provides some glimpse of what daily life in a city flying through space would be like. The true space stations in the novel are the Vegan "orbital forts" (58), attacked and destroyed by Earthmen, although legend has it that one escaped to become a roving marauder (as seen in the series' next novel, *Earthman, Come Home* [q.v.]).

A64. Blish, James. *Earthman, Come Home.* [*Cities in Flight #3*] 1958.
New York: Avon, 1968. 253 p.

The resourceful mayor of the flying city of New York, John Amalfi,
seeks work on the planets of Utopia and He, but the collapse of the
galactic monetary system finally strands New York in a vast jungle of
desperately poor flying cities. The cities embark on a caravan to Earth,
to petition their home planet for assistance, but a Vegan orbital fort
sneaks into the convoy to carry out a final assault on Earth; however,
Amalfi detects the intruder and manages to destroy it. Finally, Amalfi
decides to move out to the Greater Magellanic Cloud, where they defeat an old renegade city and settle on their planet.

This novel is disappointing, for Blish seems to squander the enormous
potential of the concept of Cities in Flight by opting for improbable
adventures tightly focused on the characters of Amalfi and his city
manager, Hazelton; the other inhabitants, and the city of New York
itself, are barely seen at all. And the analogy between the flying cities
and Okie migrant workers, as other commentators have noted, becomes an increasingly illogical constraint on the narrative. The legendary Vegan orbital fort does finally make an appearance, only to be
blasted out of existence by Amalfi and friends.

A65. Blish, James. *The Triumph of Time.* [*Cities in Flight #4*] 1958.
New York: Avon, 1968. 158 p.

The traveling planet of He reappears to inform John Amalfi and the
other residents of New Earth that the destruction of the entire universe
is imminent. After studying matters, they decide to travel to the center
of the universe, where, at the moment of the universe's end, they
might be able to survive briefly to influence the development of future
universes. Fending off a last-minute attack from the oppressive empire
of the Web of Hercules, they succeed in doing so.

Oddly, long after Blish's Cities in Flight have stopped flying, we finally get a comment on what life in those cities was like, when a character exclaims, "I hate that damned town.... I was a prisoner on board
it far too long" (118). In contrast, Amalfi himself longs to get the city
flying again, but he seems motivated more by the desire to face and
solve problems than by any genuine love for life in space.

A66. Bisson, Terry. *Voyage to the Red Planet.* New York: William
Morrow, 1990. 224 p.

This satirical novel about a trip to Mars includes a stopover at an orbital station.

Unseen.

A67. Bloom, Britton. *Matrix Cubed.* [*Buck Rogers: Inner Planets Trilogy #3*] New York: TSR, 1991. 288 p.

The third volume in a trilogy of Buck Rogers space adventures.

Unseen; the first volume in the trilogy is *First Power Play*, by John Miller, and the second is *Prime Squared*, by M. S. Murdock. I list all these recent Buck Rogers adventures because of one of them refers to a space elevator. Others to date include: *Arrival*, by M. S. Murdock *et al.*; the three volumes in the *Martian Wars Trilogy*, all by Murdock—*Rebellion 2456*, *Hammer of Mars*, and *Armageddon off Vesta*; and the three volumes of the *Invaders of Charon* series—*The Genesis Web* by J. H. Brennan, and *Nomads of the Sky* and *Warlords of Jupiter*, both by William H. Keith, Jr.

A68. Blumberg, Rhoda. *The First Travel Guide to the Moon.* New York: Scholastic, Inc., 1980. 83 p.

This step-by-step description of a trip to the Moon includes a description of a stop at Space Base, "the human-made satellite used as a way station to the Moon" (21).

Unseen.

A69. Bova, Ben. *Colony.* New York: Pocket, 1978. 470 p.

A genetically manipulated superior man, born and bred in space habitat Island One, escapes to Earth and becomes involved in a three-way struggle for control of the planet between the World Government, multinational corporations, and underground revolutionary movements.

Bova's novel includes both one of the best realized space habitats—strongly influenced by O'Neill, whose habitat name he borrows—and a glimpse at a standard space station used as a way station between Earth and Island One. While corporations finance the space habitat, largely as a refuge for company presidents when Earth explodes into violence, the hero persuades all that it should be used to provide wealth for planet Earth and to serve as a steppingstone to new communities in space.

Note: this novel is a continuation of sorts to Bova's Kinsman saga in *Kinsman* and *Millennium* (q.v.).

A70. Bova, Ben. *Exiled from Earth*. New York: Dutton, 1971. 202 p.

When the World Government decides that genetic engineering will be too disruptive to the world, they round up all its scientists and exile them to a space station. A few scientists do escape but get involved with a dangerous political activist, suggesting that the World Government's concern might be legitimate. When all scientists arrive at the station, there is an initial period of depression, but they soon decide that instead of staying in orbit like a "merry-go-round" (198), they should turn their station into a starship and explore the universe.

Much of Bova's novel involves adventure and intrigue on Earth, but a brief and convincing picture is given of a space station as prison. The final decision to turn the station into a starship—seen also in Duncan's *Dark Dominion* and Long's *This Strange Tomorrow* (q.v.)—suggests that a space station might be seen as a spaceship going nowhere.

Note: this is the first novel in a trilogy; the other two volumes, *Flight of Exiles* and *End of Exile*, are discussed below.

A71. Bova, Ben. *Flight of Exiles*. 1972. In *The Exiles Trilogy*. By Ben Bova. 1980. New York: Berkley, 1983, p. 153-288.

As the traveling space station approaches Alpha Centauri, residents must decide whether to stay in that system and prepare genetically altered humans to live on one of its planets, or to travel to another star with a more Earthlike planet. After the leading advocate of staying is revealed as a murderer, they decide to move on to the other star.

There are scattered references to the starship's previous role of space station, notably when people discuss whether it is sturdy enough to last through another stellar voyage.

A72. Bova, Ben. *End of Exile*. 1975. In *The Exiles Trilogy*. By Ben Bova. 1980. New York: Berkley, 1983, p. 293-441.

The space station—now about to fall apart—is nearing its destination, but its young residents no longer understand the station's mission. But the last survivor from the previous generation instructs one young man, who recruits helpers and manages to get the station residents teleported to their new world before the station is destroyed.

Here, there are no explicit references to the station's original function—"The origins of the ship were shrouded in mystery" (356)—and the story is basically a rewrite of Robert A. Heinlein's "Universe."

A73. Bova, Ben. *Kinsman*. New York: Dial Press, 1979. 245 p.

Obsessed by a desire to live in space, Chet Kinsman joins the Air Force to become an astronaut, flies some orbital missions, works with NASA on lunar expeditions, and finally engages in a series of political maneuvers—including meetings on Space Station Alpha—to achieve his goal of living on the Moon.

This novel clearly suggests that humanity's primal desire to explore space will not be satisfied by space stations, or even space habitats; despite his obsession with space, Kinsman seems bored during his visit to Space Station Alpha, and he openly ridicules a Professor Alexander who espouses visionary plans for space colonies. Only life on the Moon arouses his interest.

Note: the sequel to this novel is *Millennium*; *Colony* (q.v.) is loosely linked to these two novels; and Bova's story "Isolation Area" (q.v.) also takes place on Space Station Alpha.

A74. Bova, Ben. *Mars*. New York: Bantam, 1992. 502 p.

This novel about the exploration of Mars includes a reference to "space stations in Earth orbit" (160).

Unseen.

A75. Bova, Ben. *Millennium: A Novel about People and Politics in the Year 1999*. 1976. New York: Del Rey/Ballantine, 1977. 294 p.

Chet Kinsman, now commander of the American Moonbase next to the Russian Lunagrad, observes with dismay preparations for nuclear war on Earth. He decides to join the Russians, declare the Moon an independent nation, seize control of the American and Russian space stations, and use their facilities to take over the antiballistic missile satellites in place around the Earth, so that he can enforce peace on Earth. He ultimately succeeds while losing his own life.

It seems rather implausible that Earth governments would place all controls of space weapons systems on a space station, especially given their vulnerability, which is noted in the novel: the captain of Space Station Alpha exclaims, "Look at this place! It's made of straw! A single grenade exploded in co-orbit with us would shred us like goat's cheese" (123). And while that doesn't occur, Kinsman is able to seize control of a station with several hundred people on board with a force of twenty-six men.

A76. Bova, Ben. *Peacekeepers*. 1988. New York: Tor, 1989. 337 p.

After a devastating war, the nations of Earth create the Peacekeepers— an international force designed to monitor military activities and take action to prevent any war. One faction of the Peacekeepers tries to seize control of the Peacekeeper space stations watching Earth and use them to take over the world; but a loyal station commander successfully resists their attacks until the coup attempt fails. Unfortunately, one crazed terrorist with six nuclear bombs remains at loose, delaying progress towards world peace; but a lone fanatic, with occasional— and unofficial—help from the Peacekeepers, finally tracks him down and destroys him, though the result is a ruinous nuclear explosion.

Again, a space facility designed to ensure peace instead almost provokes a disastrous war—although that is certainly not Bova's message. His space station is likened to a submarine (87, 88) and a "sitting duck" as in Saari's story of that name (q.v.). Overall, the space station battle is the most convincing part of the novel; elsewhere, Bova's characters—from the cliché-spouting cigar-store Indian to the implacably evil Arab terrorist—simply fail to ring true.

Note: the part of this novel dealing with the attack on the space station has been published as a short story, "Battle Station."

A77. Bova, Ben. *The Weathermakers*. New York: Holt, Rinehart, and Winston, 1967. 249 p. A portion of the novel was published as "The Weathermakers" in *Analog Science Fiction/Science Fact* in 1966.

Using such tools as lasers from space stations and planes with powerful chemicals, the man in charge of project THUNDER prevents hurricanes from striking America's East Coast. Eventually, he leads to the establishment of a system of complete weather control under international supervision.

Unseen, but see comments on "The Weathermakers" in Part B.

A78. Bova, Ben, and Bill Pogue. *The Trikon Deception*. New York: Tor, 1992. 309 p.

This near-future suspense novel involves a scientific research station in Earth orbit.

Unseen.

A79. Brack, Vcktis. [pseudonym; possibly Leslie Humphrys, also known as Bruno C. Condray] *Odyssey in Space*. London: Gannet Press, 1953. 127 p.

A space adventure involving space stations.

Unseen.

A80. Brennan, J. H. *The Genesis Web*. [*Buck Rogers: Invaders of Charon #1*] New York: TSR, 1992. 278 p.

The first volume in a new Buck Rogers trilogy.

Unseen; the second and third volumes are *Nomads of the Sky* and *Warlords of Jupiter*, both by William H. Keith, Jr.

A81. Brin, David. *Earth*. New York: Bantam, 1990. 601 p.

A novel about a future disaster on Earth that includes references to space stations.

Unseen.

A82. Brin, David. *Startide Rising*. New York: Bantam, 1983. 462 p.

A crew of humans and "uplifted" dolphins finds a fleet of ancient abandoned spaceships, and because of their discovery they are pursued by several alien races to a distant water world. There, they repair their craft and devise an escape plan, while coping with internal dissension and evidence of planetary life forms.

The novel refers to "orbit cities" around Jupiter (81).

Note: this is a loose sequel to *Sundiver* (q.v.). To date, four additional novels in the series have appeared: *Brightness Reef* (1995), *Infinity's Shore* (1996), *Heaven's Reach* (1998), and this unseen novel:

A83. Brin, David. *The Uplift War*. West Bloomfield, MI: Phantasia Press, 1987. 506 p.

A84. Brin, David. *Sundiver*. New York: Bantam, 1980. 340 p.

A novel about vehicles called "sunships" that hover close to the Sun.

Unseen. See comments on *Startide Rising*.

A85. Brown, Dale. *Silver Tower*. New York: Berkley, 1989, 1988. 384 p.

When the Soviet Union launches an invasion of Iran in 1992, Armstrong Space Station maneuvers to monitor all hostile activities; seeing its importance, the Soviets send two armed space shuttles to attack it. After it is crippled, the Americans reoccupy the station, finally get its laser defense system working, and use it to fend off a second attack and disintegrate large numbers of Soviet cruise missiles.

This novel is best characterized as an unknowing rehash of stories of military space stations in the 1950s: launched for defensive purposes, the station becomes the object of attack and increases tension; and like Kornbluth's *Not This August* (q.v.), the novel ends with a dark warning of further escalation: "too much success, like Skybolt has had now, can breed a need for more and more.... I wanted to develop it for defensive reasons only. But now...." (379; author's ellipses).

A86. Brown, Fredric. *The Lights in the Sky Are Stars*. 1953. New York: Bantam, 1963. 149 p.

An ex-spaceman, desperately anxious to see humanity continue space exploration, helps elect a woman senator who has promised to support a manned expedition to Jupiter. They become lovers, and she arranges to put him in charge of the project. However, when it is discovered that he lied about his space travels—he actually never left Earth—he loses the job, but is still happy when he finally witnesses the launch of the Jupiter mission.

In Brown's future history, the early space program focused on space stations, and two of them—one for meteorology, one for broadcasting—were actually built (33-34). But the invention of nuclear rockets made further space stations unnecessary. There were plans for "The G-Station," "A super-luxury space station to be put in the seven hundred mile orbit by a cartel of the biggest of the gambling syndicates, a super-duper gambling club for millionaires," but "the project folded" (119), though its site was used for Project Jupiter. This novel about a man obsessed with space travel can be compared to Dean McLaughlin's *The Man Who Wanted Stars* (q.v.), though Brown's hero is considerably more sympathetic.

A87. Brown, Fredric. *Martians, Go Home!* New York: E. P. Dutton and Co., 1955. 174 p. A shorter version was originally published in *Astounding Science Fiction* in 1954.

Martians come to Earth and make pests of themselves until someone figures out how to get rid of them. In the Prologue, while discussing the state of scientific progress at the time the Martians arrived, the narrator mentions plans to build a space station (ix).

Unseen.

A88. Brown, Slater. *Spaceward Bound.* New York: Prentice-Hall, Inc., 1955. 213 p.

A group of young space enthusiasts, financed by a millionaire from India, set up the city of Astropolis in the West Indies to educate future spacemen and prepare for space flight. However, their plans are threatened by Professor Homberg, who opposes space flight and instead urges the construction of a space station to establish "orbital dictatorship" (68). He eventually tries to destroy Astropolis, but despite some damage, the work will continue.

While space stations are usually seen as a way to carry on the exploration of space, here they are seen as an alternative: "the whole question of space station versus space flight" (138) is a matter of continuing controversy at Astropolis. Although Homberg's plans for "the largest and most deadly flying fortress the world has ever seen" (118) are described as evil, Brown endorses the logic behind the idea; Homberg says, "What was it Archimedes said about the lever? Give me a lever and a point to rest it on and I will move the world. Well, give me a space station and an orbit for it to move in and I will rule [the world]" (82). With Homberg's defeat, the idealistic young men of Astropolis apparently rededicate themselves to space exploration, with only minimal plans for a space station as "a fuel dump in space" (66).

A89. Brunner, John. *The Crucible of Time*. New York: Del Rey/Ballantine, 1983. 288 p. Novel originally published in *Isaac Asimov's Science Fiction Magazine* in 1982 and 1983.

During the course of their history, an alien race gradually realizes that its planet lies in a turbulent region of space, which has brought a number of disastrous climatic changes and meteorites, and which will eventually destroy their world. Their racial goal becomes to move into and live in outer space to escape the coming catastrophe; and having done so, they sit in their new home, a "vast artificial globe" (5), and retell the stories of their ancestors' struggles.

Konstantin Tsiolkovsky originally warned that inhabiting space was the best way to preserve the human race from planetary disaster; here, an alien race is driven by obvious, impending doom to achieve that result. It is unclear whether these aliens plan to live in space indefinitely or eventually seek another planetary home their plans at one point are "to link a group of orbiting ecosystems into what might become a colony, a settlement, and finally a vehicle, a junq [sic] to sail the interstellar sea" (247)—but at the end of the novel they seem settled in space: in "the safe dark deeps that they were steering for...they were certain of energy, and the means to feed themselves and grow more drifting globes, choosing what they wanted from the resources of the galaxy" (287).

Note: an unseen sequel to this novel is:

A90. Brunner, John. *The Tides of Time*. New York: Del Rey/Ballantine, 1984. 235 p.

A91. Brunner, John. *Sanctuary in the Sky*. New York: Ace, 1963. 122 p.

A neutral race, the Graithes, has occupied the abandoned space station Waystation to serve as a meeting place and home for refugees between the empires of two warring races, the Pags and the Cathrodynes. A mysterious visitor, Lang, is finally revealed as a member of the race which built Waystation to serve as a starship to seed the Galaxy with humanoid life. He evacuates the station and returns it to its original mission, this time pointed to other galaxies.

While other space stations have been turned into starships, Waystation is actually a starship temporarily serving as a space station. While controlled by the Graithes, it serves a variety of purposes: trading post, sanctuary, vacation spot, and brothel.

A92. Brunner, John. *The Shock Wave Rider*. New York: Harper & Row, Publishers, 1975. 246 p.

A computer-wise fugitive in a repressive future America contacts a utopian community in California and figures out how to release all concealed information to the general public, thus bringing an end to corruption and oppression.

The company that Brunner's hero works for is in the business of building orbital factories; and while none are visited in the novel, there are transcripts of television commercials featuring such factories.

A93. Bujold, Lois McMaster. *Falling Free*. 1988. New York: Baen, 1991. 307 p.

In a space habitat orbiting a distant planet, a large corporation has created a genetically engineered race of "quaddies"—people with two additional hands instead of legs—to be space workers. When new developments seem to make these workers economically unfeasible, the company decides to sterilize them and house them on a planet. However, a sympathetic engineer organizes the quaddies and they seize control of the habitat, transform it into a space vehicle, and move the habitat through a wormhole to a hoped-for new home in an unknown solar system.

Frankly, it is surprising that this novel won a Nebula Award. Bujold has a fascinating concept: building on the logic of other novels which depict legless and handicapped people happily living in weightlessness, she posits that a race of people with four hands would be ideally suited for such an environment. But surprisingly little is said about the quaddies' psychology and lifestyle, the other characters are underdeveloped, and the melodramatic plot is a compendium of clichés: space residents oppressed and exploited by a cruel Earth corporation, and a space habitat transformed into a starship as a way of breaking free from Earth control.

Note: this is one of a number of novels and story collections set in the same future universe. Published after 1993 were *Mirror Dance* (1994), *Cetaganda* (1995), *Dreamweaver's Dilemma* (stories, 1996), *Memory* (1996), *Komarr* (1998), *A Civil Campaign* (2000), *Diplomatic Immunity* (2002), and *Winterfair Gifts* (2008, first published as a novella in 2002). Published before 1993, all unseen, are in order of publication:

A94. Bujold, Lois McMaster. *Ethan of Athos*. New York: Baen, 1986. 237 p.

A95. Bujold, Lois McMaster. *Shards of Honor*. New York: Baen, 1986. 313 p.

A96. Bujold, Lois McMaster. *The Warrior's Apprentice*. New York: Baen, 1986. 315 p.

A97. Bujold, Lois McMaster. *The Borders of Infinity*. [short stories] New York: Baen, 1989. 311 p.

A98. Bujold, Lois McMaster. *Brothers in Arms*. New York: Baen, 1989. 338 p.

A99. Bujold, Lois McMaster. *The Vor Game*. New York: Baen, 1990. 345 p.

A100. Bujold, Lois McMaster. *Barrayar*. New York: Baen, 1991. 389 p.

A101. Bulmer, Kenneth. [as Tully Zetford] *Star City. Hook #3*. 1974. New York: Pinnacle, 1975. 154 p.

The "star-spanning man of the future" has an assignment on Stellopolis, a huge pleasure city in space.

Unseen.

Note: this is the third of four Hook novels. The others, all unseen, are:

A102. Bulmer, Kenneth. [as Tully Zetford] *Whirlpool of Stars. Hook #1*. 1974. New York: Pinnacle, 1975. 151 p.

A103. Bulmer, Kenneth. [as Tully Zetford] *The Boosted Man. Hook #2*. 1974. New York: Pinnacle, 1975. 148 p.

A104. Bulmer, Kenneth. [as Tully Zetford] *The Virility Gene. Hook #4*. 1975. New York: Pinnacle, 1976. 146 p.

A105. Byers, Edward A. *The Babylon Gate*. New York: Baen, 1986. 246 p.

An obsessive millionaire recruits and trains a few people with teleki-netic powers and takes them to an Earth-orbiting space station called Up-Top, where their powers are amplified by a device called the Babylon Gate. From orbit, these so-called "Gods" intervene to stop a war and gradually assume *de facto* control of the entire Earth. But Gil Warden, who has the power to mysteriously remove and retrieve small objects, sets out to oppose them; he kills two of them, and after being captured and having his memories removed, he recovers, travels to Up-Top, and finally manages to kill them all and end the threat to Earth.

Byers combines two familiar themes: an armed space station as a way to militarily control the Earth, and a space station as the ideal place to study and improve psychic powers. His novel is impelled by the same sense of hallucinogenic illogic found in Gordon R. Dickson's *The Pritcher Mass* (q.v.), another work involving space stations and strange mental abilities. There are also numerous references to Greek mythology which seem to add little to his story.

A106. Caidin, Martin. *Four Came Back*. New York: D. McKay, 1968. 275 p.

A mysterious plague kills four of the eight crewmen on board a joint American-European space station, provoking panic and rioting on Earth until the solution is found.

To my knowledge, this novel presents the most accurate prediction of the space station that is currently being planned and funded—a small, primarily scientific outpost, under international control but dominated by NASA. Caidin's contention that a new disease in space would lead to violent rioting and mass hysteria directed at the space program is neither persuasive nor persuasively presented.

A107. Caidin, Martin. *Killer Station*. New York: Baen, 1985, 1984.

370 p.

A gigantic American space station, ostensibly for research but carrying a secret nuclear reactor, is sabotaged and sent plunging toward Earth on a collision course with New York City.

Frankly inspired by the concern over Skylab's untimely fall, Caidin's novel begins well but ultimately stumbles over the implausibility of its main crisis. In both his novels, by the way, Caidin asserts that the Americans, no matter what they say to the world, will inevitably sneak military projects onto their stations—hardly a reassuring message to our European allies.

A108. Cameron, Berl. [house pseudonym] *Solar Gravita*. London: Curtis Warren Ltd., 1953. 159 p.

A desperate flight to the Sun is launched from Earth-orbiting manned Satellite 14.

Unseen.

A109. Card, Orson Scott. *Ender's Game*. New York: Tor, 1985. 357 p.

From an early age, a boy is trained to play various battle games, moving to a space station for advanced training. When he wins a final game, he is told that his recent games have all been actual battles with aliens, and that he has now defeated the aliens once and for all.

The expanded version of the novel follows the same story, and adds little information about the space station, since most of the new material involves the activities of Ender's brother and sister on Earth.

Note: this is the first of several related novels. Two sequels published before 1993 are listed below; the original Ender series concluded with *Children of the Mind* (1996), though Card more recently returned to the character with *A War of Gifts* (2007) and *Ender in Exile* (2008). A related series focusing on Ender's companion Bean has four novels to date: *Ender's Shadow* (1999), *Children of the Hegemon* (2001), *Shadow Puppets* (2002), and *Shadow of the Giant* (2005).

A110. Card, Orson Scott. *Speaker for the Dead*. New York: Tor, 1986. 415 p.

Years after destroying the Bugger race, Ender secretly carries a surviving queen, hoping to find the aliens a new home world, while serving as someone who speaks on behalf of the dead. On a Portuguese-speaking planet, he finds a suitable home for the Bugger queen, as well as a wife.

This was originally included in the bibliography simply because of its connection to *Ender's Game* but might arguably be removed, given that its references to space stations are minimal at best.

A111. Card, Orson Scott. *Xenocide*. New York: Tor, 1991. 394 p.

While traveling through the cosmos, Ender now focuses his attention on two new problems—his efforts to prevent the impending destruction of another mysterious alien race, and his relationship with a developing computer intelligence named Jane.

Again, this is a novel originally included in the bibliography though it has little to say about space stations.

A112. Castle, J. [Jeffrey] Lloyd. *Satellite E One*. 1954. New York: Bantam, 1958. 164 p.

The story of how the European Federation (with primarily British participation) constructed the first space station, beginning with the first two solo flights, then picturing the large station that was ultimately built around the early spaceships.

Despite awkward construction, stereotypical characterization, and a leaden pace, Castle's novel sporadically evokes some of the real awe and mystery of space life—especially in the story of the first space traveler, trapped in his primitive "mummy suit," desperately flailing about in his craft. Castle's station, like Russia's Mir and Space Station Freedom, is built out of modules—cylindrical structures that first serve as spaceships and then are left in orbit to be attached to other modules; eventually six of them are joined to form a ring. Castle thus qualifies as the most accurate prophet of the actual means employed to build a space station.

A113. Charbonneau, Louis. *Down to Earth*. [Also known as *Antic Earth*] London: H. Jenkins, 1967. 221 p.

After the apparent destruction of Earth in a war, a distant and isolated "emergency landing station," constructed in a hollowed-out asteroid, is menaced by a mysterious intruder.

This suspenseful novel offers one striking image: to help the family in this station cope with the isolation and alienness of space, they are continually surrounded by realistic holographic projections of ordinary Earth street scenes; but to defeat the intruder, they must decide to turn off the comforting illusions and confront the reality of space.

A114. Cherryh, C. J. [Carolyn Cherry] *Downbelow Station*. New York: DAW, 1981. 432 p.

Pell, a large space station circling a planet in a distant solar system, struggles to preserve its neutrality—and ultimately, its very existence—against a host of problems: representatives from Earth, eager to bargain away its minimal control over space; the Earth's Company Fleet, belligerent and no longer controlled by Earth; the Union, a sinister government of faraway space stations; Jon Lukas, a Pell resident conspiring with the Union to wrest control of the station from the popular Konstantin family; and an overcrowded, rebellious group of refugees.

The *Gone with the Wind* of space station novels, Cherryh's massive epic, despite its *deux ex machina* happy ending—Pell's neutrality is preserved by an unlikely alliance of merchanter ships and a mutinous Company warship—repeatedly suggests how vulnerable a space station, even a large one like Pell, is to sabotage, treachery, attack, accidents, and popular discontent. While William John Watkins's novels (q.v.) suggest that station residents may develop a reckless, devil-may-care attitude towards life, Cherryh argues that stationers will be passive in the face of danger; the common denominator in both attitudes is a sense of fatalism in regards to the hazards of space life.

Note: Cherryh has written numerous novels taking place in the same future universe as *Downbelow Station*. Two of them—*Merchanter's Luck* and *Voyagers in Night*—are discussed below, and three others were published after 1993—*Tripoint* (1994), *Finity's End* (1997), and *Regenesis* (2009). Three related novels—*Gate of Ivrel* (1976), *Well of Shiuan* (1977), and *Fires of Azeroth* (1978)—are not listed since they do not appear to involve space stations. All other novels in this universe are listed immediately below. A space station story unrelated to these novels, "Wings," is discussed in Part B.

A115. Cherryh, C. J. [Carolyn Cherry] *Angel with the Sword*. New York: DAW, 1985. 293 p.

A116. Cherryh, C. J. [Carolyn Cherry] *Brothers of Earth*. New York: DAW, 1976. 254 p.

A117. Cherryh, C. J. [Carolyn Cherry] *The Pride of Chanur*. [*Chanur #1*] New York: DAW, 1982. 224 p.

A118. Cherryh, C. J. [Carolyn Cherry] *Chanur's Venture*. [*Chanur #2*] New York: DAW, 1984. 312 p.

A119. Cherryh, C. J. [Carolyn Cherry] *The Kif Strike Back*. [*Chanur #3*] New York: DAW, 1985. 299 p.

A120. Cherryh, C. J. [Carolyn Cherry] *Chanur's Homecoming*. [*Chanur #4*] New York: DAW, 1986. 398 p.

A121. Cherryh, C. J. [Carolyn Cherry] *Chanur's Legacy: A Novel of Compact Space*. [*Chanur #5*] New York: DAW, 1992. 386 p.

A122. Cherryh, C. J. [Carolyn Cherry] *Cuckoo's Egg*. New York: DAW, 1985. 319 p.

A123. Cherryh, C. J. [Carolyn Cherry] *Cyteen*. New York: Warner, 1988. 680 p.

A124. Cherryh, C. J. [Carolyn Cherry] *The Faded Sun: Kesrith*. Garden City, NY: Doubleday, 1978. 248 p.

A125. Cherryh, C. J. [Carolyn Cherry] *The Faded Sun: Shon'jir*. 1978. New York: DAW, 1979. 253 p.

A126. Cherryh, C. J. [Carolyn Cherry] *The Faded Sun: Kutath*. 1979. New York: DAW, 1980. 256 p.

A127. Cherryh, C. J. [Carolyn Cherry] *Forty Thousand in Gehenna*. New York: DAW, 1983. 445 p.

A128. Cherryh, C. J. [Carolyn Cherry] *Heavy Time*. New York: Warner, 1991. 330 p.

A129. Cherryh, C. J. [Carolyn Cherry] *Hellburner*. New York: Warner, 1993. 393 p.

A130. Cherryh, C. J. [Carolyn Cherry] *Hunter of Worlds*. New York: DAW, 1977. 254 p.

A131. Cherryh, C. J. [Carolyn Cherry] *Port Eternity*. New York: DAW, 1982. 191 p.

A132. Cherryh, C. J. [Carolyn Cherry] *Rimrunners*. New York: Warner, 1989. 327 p.

A133. Cherryh, C. J. [Carolyn Cherry] *Serpent's Reach*. New York: DAW, 1980. 287 p.

A134. Cherryh, C. J. [Carolyn Cherry] *Merchanter's Luck*. New York: DAW, 1982. 208 p.

The down-and-out owner of a space freighter joins forces with a member of a powerful Merchanter family to carry cargo to Venture Station, near the Sun; however, the ship turns out to be a pawn in a complex struggle between space factions.

Three large space stations are visited here: Viking Station, where ship owner Sandor Kreja meets Allison Reilly; Downbclow Station, also seen in Cherryh's *Downbelow Station* (q.v.), where they meet again and agree to a deal; and Venture Station, where the ship is seized by enemy forces. What stays in one's mind about this novel is an overwhelming feeling of despair among spacefaring people, with life a constant struggle against bureaucratic interference and powerful alliances. As in *Downbelow Station*, the happy ending here seems forced, a contradiction of the gloom and spirit of helplessness that accompanies the protagonist throughout the book. One might argue that these people lack the stability of life on a planet, and that there is something intrinsically fragile and threatening about a life spent entirely in space.

A135. Cherryh, C. J. [Carolyn Cherry] *Voyager in Night*. New York: DAW, 1984. 221 p.

Three independent miners, after leaving Endeavor Station, are captured by a strange alien vehicle; two of them die, while the other experiences bizarre adventures with the aliens and various computer-created "doppelgängers" of himself and his crewmates.

In this Cherryh novel, there is little activity on board the station itself, but the character of one protagonist, a "stationer," is worth noting; born on a space station, he now has agoraphobia and a fear of being alone.

A136. Claremont, Chris. *FirstFlight*. New York: Ace, 1987. 243 p.

Despite a crucial mistake in a simulation flight, a female space pilot, Nicole Shea, is assigned to her first mission. When her ship is attacked and crippled, she and her crew detect and reach an alien spacecraft; after her friend is partially transformed into an alien with vast knowledge and psychic powers, he and the aliens help Shea track down and defeat her attacker, a bitter grounded pilot with grandiose schemes for revenge and power.

Shea's simulated mission is a flight from Earth to a space station, Hightower, at the L-5 point, but problems are programmed to occur that virtually ensure that the ship will hit and damage the station. Other space stations mentioned in the novel are Gagarin (24), Wolfe Station (90), and Pico Station (105). There is also a brief reference to a unique zero-gravity sport called SkyBall (24).

Note: there have been two sequels to this novel, *Sundowner* (1994) and this unseen novel:

A137. Claremont, Chris. *Grounded!* New York: Ace, 1991. 323 p.

A138. Clarke, Arthur C. *Arthur C. Clarke's July 20, 2019: Life in the 21st Century*. An *Omni* Book. New York: Macmillan Publishing Company, 1986. 281 p.

This book contains nonfictional discussions of future possibilities interspersed with fictional vignettes of future life; one chapter, "A Day in the Life of a Space Station," includes a letter discussing present-day astronaut Bonnie Dunbar, now envisioned as a resident of space station Magellan in 2019, and her complaints about prepared soup packets that burst in zero gravity; the text then describes her typical daily schedule.

Most of the relevant chapter is a straightforward account of logically imagined daily life in a space station, touching on matters like meals, exercise, work (Bonnie does materials research, other work on biomedicine), and personal hygiene. The most interesting observation is that space station residents—at least in the kind of near-Earth facility depicted here—won't socialize much in the usual way: "for those working in space, most discussions are with people hundreds or thousands of miles away, rather than with the person floating nearby. It's as if each astronaut is standing at the top of a pyramid, apart from his fellows" (118-119).

A139. Clarke, Arthur C., with Gentry Lee. *Cradle*. New York: Warner, 1988. 293 p.

One hundred thousand years ago, alien probes visited Earth, took samples of life forms, including humans, studied them, and genetically improved them. When a ship lands on Earth to plant the "seeds" of these improved forms, three humans who contact the aliens persuade them that humans should be left alone to develop in their own way, and the "cradle" containing the life forms is not left on Earth.

A space station figures in a subplot of the novel: one character, Troy Jefferson, creates a video game called "Alien Adventure" where the player begins on a space station in another solar system. Before he sets out on his mission, he must first consult the library in the station to get needed information. Thus, once again, a space station functions as a place to begin an adventure.

A140. Clarke, Arthur C. *A Fall of Moondust*. New York: Harcourt Brace Jovanovich, Inc., 1961. 243 p.

A cruiser on a routine tour across the surface of the Moon is buried underneath fifty feet of moondust, and the problem is to locate the ship and bring it to the surface before its passengers die.

A key role in the drama is played by Tom Lawson, an astronomer in the Lagrange observatory overlooking the Moon; he is the one who first finds a trace of the missing vehicle by using his infrared detector, and he later goes to the Moon to assist in the search.

A141. Clarke, Arthur C. *The Fountains of Paradise*. 1979. New York: Ballantine, 1980. 297 p.

After building the Gibraltar Bridge, engineer Vannevar Morgan launches his next project: a "space elevator" which will use super-strong cable to link a mountain in Taprobane through a Midway Station to an Upper Terminal in geosynchronous Earth orbit—a cheap and efficient way to travel from Earth to space. First, he must dislodge the monks occupying the mountain and later must lead an attempt to rescue scientists working along the incomplete structure.

In addition to the intricacies of the Space Elevator, Clarke describes a number of geosynchronous satellites, with colorful names appropriate for the region of Earth they oversee: Kinte Station, Columbus Station, Ashoka, Imhotep, Confucius, and Kamehamela. In an epilogue set farther in the future, Clarke envisions a number of such satellites linked to the ground and to each other which form a gigantic Ring City, "a whole world in itself, where half a billion humans had opted for permanent zero-gravity life" (296). Another element in the future skies is orbiting fortresses armed with laser beams, later converted to be used to control the weather.

A142. Clarke, Arthur C. *The Ghost from the Grand Banks*. New York: Bantam, 1990. 253 p.

In the early twenty-first century, two rival groups plan to raise the two broken halves of the *Titanic* and exhibit them; but a massive earthquake in 2010 disrupts the efforts and irretrievably buries the sunken ship under a wave of undersea mud.

There are two minor references to space stations: in discussing "the most important lesson the *Titanic* can teach—the dangers of overconfidence, of technological hubris" (36), Clarke elaborates, "Chernobyl, Challenger, Lagrange 3 and Experimental Fusor One have shown us where *that* can lead" (37). And it is mentioned that a sponsor of one salvage effort has "booked space on Skyhab 3" to "set[ ] up a weightless lab" (167). Such activity in space does not seem in keeping with the general level of technological advances otherwise shown in the novel, however. And in keeping with the theme of "technological hubris," perhaps, Clarke describes the laying of a trans-Arctic cable as an advance over the communications satellites he once championed: "By eliminating the long haul up to the geostationary orbit, and its slight but annoying time delay, the global phone system had been noticeably improved" (153); so space stations are not the ideal answer to improved communication on Earth.

A143. Clarke, Arthur C. *The Hammer of God*. New York: Bantam, 1993. 226 p.

In the year 2110, an asteroid named Kali is discovered that is moving on a collision course with the Earth. A mission to Kali sets up a mass driver to change the asteroid's orbit; when that is sabotaged, the spaceship that delivered the mass driver tries to do the work. When the spaceship also fails, a nuclear bomb is fired at the asteroid which fails to explode; but the impact splits the asteroid in two, and both pieces miss the Earth at the last minute.

Only an obsessive completist would include this novel because of its brief references to "great observatories...in orbit" (72) and "the tank farm orbiting Europa" (131). Indeed, after devoting much attention to space stations, Clarke here displays a renewed interest in planetary settlements—on the Moon, on a Mars that is being terraformed, and on the Jovian moon Europa.

A144. Clarke, Arthur C. *Imperial Earth*. New York: Ballantine, 1976. 301 p.

Duncan Makenzie, cloned "grandson" of the ruler of the Titan colony, travels to Earth to give a speech at America's Quincentennial and to arrange for the creation of his own cloned "son." While there, he becomes committed to building a massive device for detecting very long radio waves to learn more about the universe and its alien life.

Before reaching Earth, Duncan stops at Port Van Allen, a massive space station orbiting Earth "whose commerce it directed and controlled" (93). There are also brief references to "fueling stations" (5-6) and "zero-gravity orbiting factories" (242). Finally, Clarke's narrator mentions proposals to transform Saturn's smaller moons into "orbital zoos," "private pleasure domes," or "islands in space for experiments in super-technology life styles," but dismisses these plans as "Utopian" (18-19).

A145. Clarke, Arthur C. *Islands in the Sky*. 1952. New York: Signet, 1960. 157 p.

By winning a contest, a young man gets to visit the orbiting Inner Station; because of an emergency, and human and mechanical problems, he also ends up going to the Hospital Station, orbiting the Moon, and stopping by a Relay Station before returning to Earth.

Clarke pictures a total of eight space stations circling a future Earth, with different locations and functions: an Inner Station, a refueling stop, hotel, and school for apprentice spacemen; three Meteorological

Stations, for Earth observation and astronomy; a Space Hospital, with medical research facilities; and three Relay Stations, for Earth and interplanetary television, radio, and telephone. In describing these stations' engineering and functioning, Clarke is technically sound and sometimes prophetic. The story in the foreground seems like a typical, cliché-ridden West-Point-in-space adventure, complete with firm but kindly commander, rival cadets, practical jokes and hijinks, and a final crisis in which the cadets must help out in a real emergency. However, each time Clarke seems about to lapse into the worst sorts of space melodrama—meteor collisions, space pirates, alien invaders—he coyly saves face with a prosaic explanation. Thus, the meteor ripping through the station's hull turns out to be a staged training exercise in emergency repair; the space pirates are merely a film crew shooting a movie in space; and the tentacled alien is simply a hydra artificially enlarged in weightlessness. Clarke can be said to be both emulating and deconstructing the genre of juvenile space opera; still, since these contrivances provide about the only excitement the novel has to offer, the practical message is that life in a space station will basically be uneventful.

A146. Clarke, Arthur C. *The Lost Worlds of 2001*. New York: Signet, 1972. 240 p.

While describing the process of creating the film *2001: A Space Odyssey* (q.v.), Clarke provides in narrative form some of the materials that were prepared for—but never used in—either the film or the novel of that name (q.v.)

Two passages in the book are relevant here: Chapter 13, "From the Ocean, from the Stars," describes where the six crewmen of the spaceship *Discovery* were when they received orders to join that mission. Astronomer Victor Kaminski was serving on Cytherean Station One, a space station orbiting Venus, observing that planet; and Jack Kimball was enjoying a sexual interlude on Intelsat VIII, a communications satellite orbiting Earth. And Chapter 21, *"Discovery,"* portrays the launch of that vessel from the vicinity of Space Station One—a fact which changes somewhat one's view of the entire story. That is, the film features steady outward movement—to the space station, to the Moon, to Jupiter, to the cosmos; but in light of this work, one sees two successive missions launched from the space station—one to the monolith on the Moon, one to the monolith near Jupiter. Thus the station serves twice as the point of departure toward the unknown.

A147. Clarke, Arthur C. *Prelude to Space*. 1951. [This edition published as *The Space Dreamers*; also published as *Masters of Space*] New York: Lancer, 1969. 158 p.

While a corporation sponsored by the British government prepares to launch the first flight to the Moon from a base in Australia, a visiting historian observes the people involved in the project, including its administrators, scientists, and pilots.

Clarke briefly mentions space stations while discussing plans for the militarization of space:

> The United States Army's belated discovery, at the end of the Second World War, of [Hermann] Oberth's twenty-year-old plan for "space-stations" had revived ideas which it was a gross exaggeration to call "Wellsian."
>
> In his classic book, *Wege zur Raumschiffahrt*, Oberth had discussed the possibility of great "space-mirrors" which could focus sunlight upon the Earth, either for peaceful purposes or for the incineration of enemy cities. Oberth himself never took this last idea very seriously, and must have been surprised at its solemn reception two decades later. (87)

However, Clarke's overall focus in this novel, as in other works of the era, is on exploring and colonizing other planets.

A148. Clarke, Arthur C., with Gentry Lee. *Rama II*. New York: Bantam, 1989. 420 p.

In this sequel to *Rendezvous with Rama* (q.v.), a second Raman starship enters the Solar System and a second expedition goes to explore it; but this ship behaves in a different way, and when it turns and heads for Earth, it is decided to destroy the ship with atomic missiles. However, sympathetic crew members inside of Rama II manage to warn the ship, which generates a defense against the missiles, and the ship starts to leave the Solar System with three people still on board.

After the visit of the first Raman craft, Excalibur Station is set up to watch for the approach of a second ship; although it is at one time abandoned, it is reoccupied in time to detect the coming of Rama II. Also, the ship that takes the crew to Rama II is assembled in space near space stations LEO-2 (Low Earth Orbit) and LEO-3, although no scenes take place in those stations.

Note: this was the first of a trilogy of novels based on the original novel. The other two, both unseen, are:

A149. Clarke, Arthur C., and Gentry Lee. *The Garden of Rama*. New York: Bantam, 1991. 441 p.

A150. Clarke, Arthur C., and Gentry Lee. *Rama Revealed*. New York: Bantam, 1994. 466 p. Originally published in London in 1993.

A151. Clarke, Arthur C. *Rendezvous with Rama*. 1973. New York: Ballantine, 1974. 274 p.

A spaceship crew lands on and explores the interior of Rama, a massive cylindrical biosphere which flies near the Sun, performs a series of mysterious, apparently automatic activities, then heads back into deep space, its makers and purpose still unknown.

Though Clarke's Rama, with interior plains and a cylindrical sea, resembles the space habitats of recent science fiction, it would be better described as a spacecraft—or "space ark" as postulated by J. D. Bernal (who is mentioned in the novel). There are space stations in Clarke's future world, briefly mentioned at times, but they are small—"The largest...Syncast Five, was less than two hundred meters in diameter" (36)—and insignificant— inhabited planets and moons dominate Solar politics.

Note: a trilogy based on this novel is discussed above.

A152. Clarke, Arthur C. *Sands of Mars*. 1951. New York: Pocket, 1959. 217 p.

A science fiction author travels to Mars after a stopover at Space Station One; he witnesses the discovery of Martians and the transformation of the Martian moon Phobos into a miniature sun, which promises to make Mars more habitable.

Space Station One in fact turns out to be the Inner Station seen in Clarke's *Islands in the Sky* (q.v.); the Outer Station is also mentioned. Here once again a space station is a brief interlude on a voyage to another world.

A153. Clarke, Arthur C. *The Songs of Distant Earth*. New York: Ballantine, 1986. 253 p.

Long after the Earth was destroyed by the Sun's explosion, a generation starship from Earth arrives at the water world Thalassa to replenish its ice shield and continue its cosmic voyage.

There are a few references to space stations in Earth's past: the "Louis Pasteur satellite hospital" (35), the "Lagrange One zero-gravity research satellite" (42), and the "first Space Elevator" (162).

A154. Clarke, Arthur C. *2001: A Space Odyssey*. Based on a screenplay by Stanley Kubrick and Arthur C. Clarke. New York: Signet, 1968. 221 p.

On the way to the Moon to investigate the mysterious monolith, Dr. Heywood Floyd stops at Space Station One to transfer to another spaceship; there, he phones home and meets—warily—an inquisitive old friend from Russia.

Clarke's novel provides more details about the station which is seen in the film (q.v.): Floyd is met and escorted by a man from "Station Security"; incoming passengers have to go through separate barriers for "U.S. Section" and "Soviet Section" but are afterwards free to mingle—making for a "rather pleasant symbolism" of the station's international character; and a detailed list of station facilities is offered.

Note: Clarke wrote three sequels to the novel: *2010: Odyssey Two*, which features no space stations, *2061: Odyssey Three* (q.v.), and *3001: The Final Odyssey* (1997). The film sequel *2010: The Year We Make Contact* (q.v.) does briefly mention space stations. For more information on the original story, see Clarke's *The Lost Worlds of 2001*.

A155. Clarke, Arthur C. *2061: Odyssey Three*. New York: Ballantine, 1987. 276 p.

Happily living in a space station in his declining years, Heywood Floyd is persuaded to join an expedition to Halley's Comet as it approaches Earth in the year 2061. But because of a crash landing on the forbidden world of Europa, the ship is diverted there to perform a rescue mission.

As he has argued elsewhere, Clarke sees the weightlessness of outer space as a highly desirable environment, particularly for the elderly. Floyd loves his space station home, has no desire to return to Earth, and only reluctantly agrees to venture back into space.

A156. Cohen, Barney, and Jim Baen. *The Taking of Satcon Station.* New York: Tor, 1982. 287 p.

An adventure involving the rundown Satcon Station, described on the cover as an "orbiting Chinatown."

Unseen.

A157. Cole, Allan, and Chris Bunch. *Sten.* [*Sten #1*] New York: Del Rey/Ballantine, 1982. 279 p.

Apparently trapped forever in the huge, repressive factory in space called Vulcan, a worker named Sten helps an agent from the Emperor investigating its abuses and is rewarded with a chance to leave Vulcan and join the Emperor's forces. After becoming part of the elite force of undercover operatives, Sten and his team return to Vulcan to inspire and lead a successful rebellion.

Vulcan is the flip side of Basil E. Wells's benevolent "Factory in the Sky" (q.v.)—a nightmarish factory town in space where men and women work in dangerous and oppressive conditions and are in effect permanently indentured to the company. Despite the power of its controllers, however, Vulcan is ultimately susceptible to infiltration and revolution. In its scope and multiplicity of environments, Vulcan compares to Sector Twelve General Hospital in the stories of James White (q.v.).

Note: This is the first of eight Sten adventures. The others, all unseen, are:

A158. Cole, Allan, and Chris Bunch. *The Wolf Worlds.* [*Sten #2*] New York: Del Rey/Ballantine, 1984. 304 p.

A159. Cole, Allan, and Chris Bunch. *The Court of a Thousand Suns.* [*Sten #3*] New York: Del Rey/Ballantine, 1986, 1985. 275 p.

A160. Cole, Allan, and Chris Bunch. *Fleet of the Damned.* [*Sten #4*] New York: Del Rey/Ballantine, 1988. 340 p.

A161. Cole, Allan, and Chris Bunch. *Revenge of the Damned*. [*Sten #5*] New York: Del Rey/Ballantine, 1989. 354 p.

A162. Cole, Allan, and Chris Bunch. *The Return of the Emperor*. [*Sten #6*] New York: Del Rey/Ballantine, 1990. 371 p.

A163. Cole, Allan, and Chris Bunch. *Vortex*. [*Sten #7*] New York: Del Rey/Ballantine, 1992. 373 p.

A164. Cole, Allan, and Chris Bunch. *Empire's End*. [*Sten #8*] New York: Del Rey/Ballantine, 1993. 439 p.

A165. Cooper, Edmund. [writing as George Kinley] *Ferry Rocket*. London: Curtis, 1954. 158 p.

A journalist, a scientist, and a psychiatrist, each assigned to investigate mysterious deaths at the lunar colony, fly with the daughter of the colony's leader, Fabian Scott, from a spaceport in Australia to the Commonwealth Space Station, where they transfer to a moonship. When they arrive, they discover that Scott has gone mad and is planning to detonate atomic bombs and transform the Moon into a vast spaceship under his control. They manage to thwart his plans and safely return to Earth, again stopping at the Space Station.

In this novel, what was later employed as the serious premise of the television series *Space: 1999* is more logically presented as a madman's scheme. The Station itself is of standard design—"a large silvery car tyre, or a heavy wheel, joined by a spherical hub by two tubular spokes" (55)—and shares space with an unseen American Space Station on the other side of the Earth. Equipped with missiles, these stations serve two purposes: "to act as celestial policemen, and to function as springboards for man's long leap into space" (56).

A166. Cooper, Edmund. *Seed of Light*. New York: Ballantine, 1959. 159 p.

When the Commonwealth launches a missile-laden satellite to achieve world peace, two scientists who visit the station before it is regularly manned—one deranged, the other traitorous—start an attack on Earth bases which leads to a devastating nuclear war. One surviving city on Earth manages to send off a generation starship, hoping to give humanity a new start.

Although with excessive sermonizing, the first part of the novel makes the point that a space station armed with weapons is more likely to incite war than to ensure peace. Cooper states that life aboard such a station would induce paranoia and, eventually, a desire to destroy life on Earth. Gunn's *Station in Space* (q.v.) provides another pessimistic assessment of armed space stations and the effects of space life on their inhabitants.

A167. Cooper, Tom. *War Moon*. New York: Worldwide, 1987. 381 p.

A novel about a Russian "orbiting battle station" (cover blurb).

Unseen.

A168. Correy, Lee. [G. Harry Stine] *Manna*. New York: DAW, 1983. 293 p.

A former American astronaut joins forces with the United Mitanni Commonwealth, an African nation committed to personal freedom and space development, in its struggles—on land and in space—against the conservative financial cartels that still dominate the Earth.

Correy's novel presents as good a picture as any of the crowded skies in recent science fiction; the space around Earth is so cluttered with power satellites, military bases, observation stations, and commercial facilities that simply flying from Earth to L-5 without incident is a major chore. Primarily devoted to making the argument that space development will solve all human problems by providing "manna from Heaven" and presenting his utopian nation, Correy spends little time describing the two space stations visited in the novel; one character comments that "when you've seen one space station you've seen them all" (66).

A169. Correy, Lee. [G. Harry Stine] *Space Doctor*. 1981. New York: Ballantine, 1985. 245 p.

A rural doctor is hired by an old friend, a politician-businessman in charge of building a solar power space station, to set up and run a hospital for the construction workers in space.

Stine updates the attitude toward building space stations common in 1950s novels like del Rey's *Step to the Stars* and Leinster's *Space Platform* (q.v.): it's just another big construction job, so you hire some savvy businessman to run it and get some construction workers to build it. Like Heinlein and Pournelle, Stine complains about government bureaucrats, regulations, and red tape; unbridled free enterprise and space colonies are the keys to reestablishing individual freedom. However, only those men and women who have a self-reliant frontier spirit can cope with the psychological problems of life in space.

A170. Coulson, Juanita. *Tomorrow's Heritage. Book One of the Series Children of the Stars.* New York: Del Rey/Ballantine, 1981. 372 p.

In a future Earth recovering from a devastating war, members of the powerful Saunders family struggle: matriarch Jael works to get her oldest son Patrick elected Chairman of the planet on a platform of "Earth First"; daughter Mariette is married to the head of the rebellious Goddard Space Colony; and younger son Todd, whose communications company's headquarters is Geosynch space station, strives to keep family peace while awaiting the arrival of an alien spaceship whose signals he has picked up.

Science fiction readers may be depressed to find the grand themes of the genre—space exploration, contact with alien life, and the search for immortality (a complex at the South Pole keeps people frozen for future revival)—trivialized as pawns in an absurd, soap-opera family power struggle. Interestingly, inhabitants of the space colony are devoting all their energies to setting up a Mars base, showing the continuing force of planetary exploration—not space colonies—as the focus of future human effort.

Note: this is the first of four Children of the Stars novels. The other three, all unseen, are:

A171. Coulson, Juanita. *Outward Bound. Book Two of the Series Children of the Stars.* New York: Del Rey/Ballantine, 1982. 371 p.

A172. Coulson, Juanita. *Legacy of Earth. Book Three of the Series Children of the Stars.* New York: Del Rey/Ballantine, 1989. 357 p.

A173. Coulson, Juanita. *The Past of Forever. Book Four of the Series Children of the Stars.* New York: Del Rey/Ballantine, 1989. 327 p.

A174. Cover, Arthur Byron. *Stationfall*. A Byron Preiss Book. An In-
focom Book. New York: Avon, 1989. 297 p.

Seeking information about his dead robot companion Floyd, who
keeps sending him messages, hapless hero Homer Hunter arrives at
Aurelian space station and has a series of adventures involving religious cults, warring factions, demons, vampires, time travelers, and
ancient gods.

With a population dedicated to bizarre religious rituals, drugs, and violence, Aurelian might be listed as an example of the space station as
madhouse; however, the entire fabric of Cover's future universe seems
mad, with various strange occurrences and mysterious beings. Cover
does contribute a few new ideas in space station design—
"pyramids...webs of double helices, a wide variety of polyhedrons"
(39)—a unique type of space station school—the puritanical Divinity
School—and at least one new industry for space stations—"the choco-
late factory" (279).

Note: this is the sequel to Cover's *Planetfall*, which does not involve
space stations; the projected third volume, *Futurefall*, has apparently
never appeared. Both novels are related to interactive computer games
with the same names, although the Stationfall game seems to have a
scenario significantly different from the novel—the advertisement in
this volume mentions arriving at "a strangely deserted space station"
(300).

A175. Coville, Bruce. *Space Station ICE-3*. [Also known as *Murder in
Orbit*] New York: Scholastic, 1987. 188 p.

A juvenile novel about a space station.

Unseen.

A176. Cowley, Stewart. *Spacebase 2000*. New York: St. Martin's
Press, 1984. 192 p. Previously published as two books: *Space-
craft 2000 to 2100 A.D.* By Stewart Cowley. Secaucus, New
Jersey: Chartwell Books, Inc., 1978. And *Great Space Battles*.
By Stewart Cowley and Charles Herridge. Secaucus, New Jer-
sey: Chartwell Books, Inc., 1979.

Told from the viewpoint of a future historian, this book first lists and
describes various space vehicles of the twenty-first century, then tells

the story of the human race's wars in space.

Two of the vehicles described could be considered space stations: "Skybases," types of "General Purpose Depot" which are used as "maintenance depots...rest centres, hospitals, and regional command posts," and nicknamed "Letterboxes" (27, 26); and "Astrolabs," types of "Class II Mobile Laboratory" which are used as "mobile research stations" (82).

A177. Cowley, Stewart. *Starliners: Commercial Spacetravel in 2200 A.D.* New York: Exeter, 1980. 90 p.

A guidebook for the future space traveler, listing the companies that offer flights to various locations.

The book mentions "AC Terminal Beta" or "the Doughnut," a space station in the Alpha Centauri system, which is now being considered for "conversion into a holiday complex" because it is rarely used (18, 19), and a type of space station called the "Traffic Control Station...which monitors and directs all movement in the busiest of space-lanes"—their "wheel-like forms are familiar to anyone who has boarded a liner" (90).

A178. Crandall, Melissa. *Shell Game. Star Trek #63.* New York: Pocket, 1993. 277 p.

Captain Kirk and the crew of the *Enterprise* encounter a deserted Romulan space station.

Unseen.

Note: other works taking place in the *Star Trek* universe which feature or mention space stations, all discussed or mentioned below, are: the *Star Trek* episode, "The Trouble with Tribbles" (and the short story version by James Blish); a number of novels based on the original series—J. M. Dillard's *Star Trek: The Lost Years*, Diane Duane's *Spock's World*, L. A. Graf's *Death Count*, Jean Lorrah's *The Vulcan Academy Murders*, and Vonda N. McIntyre's *Enterprise: The First Adventure*; three "reference books" about the *Star Trek* universe— Stan and Fred Goldstein's *Star Trek Spaceflight Chronology*, Franz Joseph's *Star Fleet Technical Manual*, and Jeff Maynard's *Introduction to Navigation: Star Fleet Command*; the film and Gene Roddenberry's novelization *Star Trek: The Motion Picture*; the film and

Vonda N. McIntyre's novelization *Star Trek II: The Wrath of Khan*; the film and Vonda N. McIntyre's novelization *Star Trek III: The Search for Spock*; the films *Star Trek IV: The Voyage Home*, *Star Trek V: The Final Frontier*, and *Star Trek VI: The Undiscovered Country*; four episodes of the series *Star Trek: The Next Generation*—"The Measure of a Man," "A Matter of Perspective," "The Best of Both Worlds," and "Birthright"; all 1993 episodes of the series *Star Trek: Deep Space Nine*—"Emissary," "Past Prologue," "A Man Alone," "Babel," "Captive Pursuit," "Q-Less," "Dax," "The Passenger," "Move Along Home," "The Nagus," "Vortex," "Battle Lines," "The Storyteller," "Progress," "If Wishes Were Horses," "The Forsaken," "Dramatis Personae," "Duet," "In the Hands of the Prophets," "The Homecoming," "The Circle," "The Siege," "Invasive Procedures," "Cardassians," "Melora," "Rules of Acquisition," "Necessary Evil," "Second Sight," and "Sanctuary"; and the four 1993 novels based on *Star Trek: Deep Space Nine*—Peter David's *The Siege*, J. M. Dillard's *Emissary*, K. W. Jeter's *Bloodletter*, and Sandy Schofield's *The Big Game*. There are no doubt other references to space stations in the many *Star Trek* novels I have not examined, as well as numerous *Star Trek* novels published since 1993 that include space stations—including a long series of novels set on Deep Space Nine—but since these are described in other references, I have not bothered to list them all in this Bibliography.

A179. Cross, John Keir. *The Stolen Sphere*. [Also known as *The Flying Fortunes in an Encounter with Rubberface*] 1952. New York: Dutton, 1953. 220 p.

A family of acrobats battles a criminal who has stolen a small-scale model of the space station being built by Britain and other western governments.

The novel basically demonstrates that the idea of a space station was common enough at the time to become the McGuffin for an otherwise routine juvenile adventure book. A curious framing device has the story being written by men of the future, when the space station has become a reality.

A180. David, Peter. *The Siege. Star Trek: Deep Space Nine #2*. New York: Pocket, 1993. 272 p.

An original novel featuring Deep Space Nine space station.

Unseen; this novel is apparently unrelated to the episode of *Star Trek: Deep Space Nine* also called "The Siege."

A181. Davis, Margaret. *Mind Light*. New York: Del Rey/Ballantine, 1992. 343 p.

An independent starship that needs a pilot finds one at a space station called Demarker Station.

Unseen.

A182. Dawson, Basil. *Dan Dare on Mars*. London: Hulton Press, 1956. 176 p.

Dan Dare gets a message about a disaster on Mars sent from the Mars Satellite.

Unseen.

A183. Del Rey, Lester. [Walter Alvarez del Rey] *Mission to the Moon*. New York: Holt, Rinehart and Winston, 1956. 207 p.

Jim Stanley, hero of *Step to the Stars* (q.v.), returns to the space station he helped build, hoping to participate in the first lunar landing. When young Fred Halpern rashly flies to the Moon on his own, Jim gets the lunar mission ready ahead of schedule and rushes to the Moon to rescue Fred and establish a moon base.

A continuing subplot involves rising world tensions about the American military station and the enemy construction of a rival station—tensions resolved when the World Congress votes to internationalize space beyond Earth's orbit. When Jim first arrives at the station, he likens it to "home," but at the end of the novel he takes up residence on the Moon.

Note: another del Rey novel, *Moon of Mutiny*, deals with Fred Halpern's further adventures on the Moon, as described below.

A184. Del Rey, Lester. [Walter Alvarez del Rey] *Moon of Mutiny*. New York: Holt, Rinehart and Winston, 1961. 217 p.

Expelled from Goddard Space Academy for rebelliousness, Fred Halpern visits his father on Stanley Station, where he is recruited as a last-minute replacement for the injured co-pilot of the third lunar expedition. On the moon, he rebels again to attempt a rescue of men in a wrecked spaceship, but after succeeding he is rewarded by an offer to become a lunar colonist.

Stanley Station—apparently renamed to honor Jim Stanley, hero of *Step to the Stars* and *Mission to the Moon* (who appears briefly as a lunar miner)—stays afloat financially because of its weather predictions. Like Stanley in *Mission,* Fred is at first happy to be back on the Station—it "smelled like home" (53)—but a couple of paragraphs later he is already "bored with it" (53).

A185. Del Rey, Lester. [Walter Alvarez del Rey] *Prisoners of Space.* Philadelphia: Westminster, 1968. 142 p.

Two children born on the Moon cannot live in Earth's gravity, and when there are plans for abandoning the moonbase, it appears that the children will be forced to live in an orbiting space station. However, the discovery of aliens on the Moon keeps the moonbase functioning and inspires plans for a manned base on Mars.

Unseen.

A186. Del Rey, Lester. [Walter Alvarez del Rey] *Siege Perilous.* [Actually written by Paul Fairman, based on detailed outlines by del Rey] New York: Lancer, 1966. 157 p.

A spaceman, after a crippling accident that exposed his inner organs to the vacuum of space, is forced to become the only permanent resident of a space station. However, after he and two crewmen successfully overcome a group of Martian humanoids who seize control of the station in an effort to conquer the Earth, he hopes that he can return to Earth.

Only one man is allowed to stay on the station because "space gnawed at men's minds" (6)—a previous commander had gone mad and tried to bomb Earth. The fact that the Martians, who learned English by watching old movies beamed from Earth, speak and act like characters from westerns, war movies, and gangster movies provides ironic commentary on how those genres have contributed to naïve space opera.

A187. Del Rey, Lester. [Walter Alvarez del Rey] *Step to the Stars.*

1954. New York: Paperback Library, 1966. 160 p.

Jim Stanley, a construction worker, is sent up to help build "Big Shush," a military space station which the Major Electric Company is contracted to complete.

A typical space station construction story of its day—there is tension between the military and civilian commands, sabotage rears its ugly head, but ultimately the station is finished and filled with bombs, so that world peace is assured.

Note: This novel is the first of a loose trilogy, the other two being *Mission to the Moon* and *Moon of Mutiny*, discussed above.

A188. Dick, Philip K. *The Crack in Space*. New York: Ace, 1966. 190 p. Originally published in shortened form as "Cantata 140" in *The Magazine of Fantasy and Science Fiction* (July, 1964).

In a series of elaborate intrigues involving a presidential election campaign in 2080, the problem of millions of unemployed people in cold storage, and the discovery of a parallel Earth inhabited by apemen, one participant is George Walt, the mutant with one head and two bodies who runs the Golden Door Moments of Bliss Satellite, a 5,000-room brothel in Earth orbit.

Aside from its large size and its moving holograms of inviting females on the doors of each room, Dick's satellite seems much like a terrestrial house of ill repute; the author's creative energies are here directed more at describing the future Earth and the strange parallel world.

A189. Dick, Philip K. *Dr. Bloodmoney [or How We Got Along after the Bomb]*. 1965. New York: Carroll & Graf, 1988. 298 p. Originally published by Ace in 1965.

After a nuclear war, Walter Dangerfield, an astronaut originally destined for Mars, remains in Earth orbit, broadcasting news and music to the devastated Earth, thus maintaining communication and morale. As various residents of the San Francisco area struggle to rebuild their lives, their "handy"—an armless, legless mutant with great psychic powers—conspires to kill and replace Dangerfield, but another mutant invisibly living in his sister's stomach manages to stop him and take over his body.

There were efforts to inhabit space before the war—a "space platform" in 1967 (29) and a ten-man "Soviet space station" whose residents quickly starve to death (118); but only Dangerfield is able to survive because his Mars mission provided him with years and years of supplies. He was originally accompanied by his wife, but she succumbed to "suicidal depression" (118) and killed herself. The way he is attacked—the mutant uses mental power to squeeze his heart from a great distance—represents a novel method of attacking a space station. Essentially, Dangerfield functions as a disc jockey in space, a pattern also seen in the film *Thunderbirds in Outer Space* (q.v.), and becomes crucially important to the recovering Earth: people gather around the radio every night as a ritual to hear his reassuring voice and listen to his music and helpful information. When he seems to be dying, everyone is deeply concerned, though there is no way to reach him and help. This inadvertent space station thus demonstrates how important a space-based communication system might be.

A190. Dicks, Terrance. *Doctor Who and the Revenge of the Cybermen*. 1976. London: W. H. Allen and Co., 1978. 128 p.

Returning to the space station seen in Ian Marter's *Doctor Who and the Ark in Space* (q.v.), Who and his friends find they have come to it at an earlier time when it was "doing the kind of job it was originally meant for—a beacon to guide and service space freighters" (3-4). But almost all of the crew has been killed by a mysterious plague—actually a poison injected by the Cybermats, small ratlike creatures controlled by the evil Cybermen, who are plotting to use the station to destroy Voga, the asteroid of gold—a substance that kills them. But a group of Vogans is plotting to lure the Cybermen to the station and destroy them. After a series of adventures, the Doctor must finally foil the Cybermen's scheme to have the station fall on Voga and destroy the asteroid with cobalt bombs—which he succeeds in doing.

The complete plot, which includes the machinations of a human double-crosser named Kellman, defies summary; what should be noted is that the novel offers yet another example of a station invaded by aliens, and a station which threatens to fall disastrously on a planetary surface.

Note: this novel is based on the *Doctor Who* serial, "Revenge of the Cybermen," discussed in Part C below; the serial and novel are loose sequels to "The Ark in Space" and "The Sontaran Experiment," also discussed in Part C.

A191. Dicks, Terrance. *Doctor Who—The Faceless Ones*. London: W. H. Allen and Co., 1987. 144 p.

A novel based on a televised *Doctor Who* adventure involving a space station.

Unseen; for a more complete plot summary, see "The Faceless Ones" in Part C.

A192. Dicks, Terrance. *Doctor Who—The Mysterious Planet*. London: W. H. Allen and Co., 1988. 144 p.

A novel based on a portion of a televised *Doctor Who* adventure involving a space station.

Unseen; for a more complete plot summary, see "The Trial of a Time Lord" in Part C.

A193. Dicks, Terrance. *Doctor Who—The Space Pirates*. London: W. H. Allen and Co., 1990. 132 p.

A novel based on a televised *Doctor Who* adventure involving a space station.

Unseen; for a more complete plot summary, see "The Space Pirates" in Part C.

A194. Dicks, Terrance. *Doctor Who—The Wheel in Space*. London: W. H. Allen and Co., 1988. 144 p.

A novel based on a televised *Doctor Who* adventure involving a space station.

Unseen; for a more complete plot summary, see "The Wheel in Space" in Part C.

A195. Dickson, Gordon R. *The Pritcher Mass*. 1972. New York: Tor, 1983. 251 p.

A future Earth is dying because of a strange plague that will eventually kill all humans; in response, the government has set up a metal platform beyond Pluto, where people with paranormal powers are building a psychic construct called the Pritcher Mass to search for worlds where people could migrate. Chaz Sant goes to work on the Mass after being threatened by mysterious forces and saved by a woman with unusual powers who calls herself a witch. He finds he can use the Mass to teleport himself back to Earth, where he learns that a group of criminals called the Citadel is controlling the building of the Mass for its own ends. He organizes a revolt with the few people who are immune to the plague and a coven of witches, announces that anyone with a little will power can resist the infection, and is told by an alien he is in mental contact with that the Mass is actually on Earth and powered by the people of Earth. The Citadel is destroyed, and humans can continue to live and progress on Earth.

This less-than-clear summary results from a less-than-clear novel, which is built on the surrealistic illogic of nightmares, not the scientific logic of extrapolation. In the tradition of van Vogt, Dickson's hero continually discovers that everything he has been told is false: for example, when he arrives at the Mass, he is told that he and the others working there can never return to Earth, but one chapter later, he has teleported himself back to Earth, and the Deputy Director of the Mass then returns to Earth to capture him. And the reasonable premise in the novel that a space facility far away from Earth might be the best place to develop mental powers is finally thrown away when it is revealed that the Mass is actually located on the planet Earth.

A196. Dietz, William C. *Drifter*. New York: Ace, 1991. 200 p.

This space opera includes a visit to a "planet-sized laboratory" (as described by Joseph M. Dudley in *The Science Fiction Research Association Newsletter*, No. 199 [July/August, 1992], p. 58).

Unseen; two sequels, also unseen, were:

A197. Dietz, William C. *Drifter's Run*. New York: Ace, 1992. 196 p.

A198. Dietz, William C. *Drifter's War*. New York: Ace, 1992. 230 p.

A199. Dillard, J. M. *Emissary*. *Star Trek: Deep Space Nine #1*. Based on a teleplay by Michael Piller. Story by Rick Berman and Michael Piller. New York: Pocket, 1993. 274 p.

The novelization of the first episode of *Star Trek: Deep Space Nine*, "Emissary" (q.v.).

Unseen.

A200. Dillard, J. M. *Star Trek: The Lost Years*. New York: Pocket, 1989. 307 p.

After completing its five-year mission, the starship *Enterprise* arrives at Spacedock in Earth orbit to be refitted, and Kirk, Spock, and McCoy go their separate ways; however, they all become involved in thwarting a Romulan plot to take over the planets Djana and Vulcan.

Apparently, the committees that now govern the Star Trek universe have decided that the Earth-orbiting facility of the film and Vonda N. McIntyre's novel *Star Trek III: The Search for Spock* (q.v.), with its large enclosed structure, is the canonical facility. The only detail added here is a description of a large viewing port, where crowds gather to welcome the *Enterprise* home.

A201. Donaldson, Stephen R. *The Gap into Conflict: The Real Story*. New York: Bantam, 1991. 210 p.

The first in a series of novels involving stations in the asteroid belt.

Unseen; there were four other novels in the series, *The Gap into Madness: Chaos and Order* (1994), *The Gap into Ruin: This Day All Gods Die* (1996), and these two unseen novels:

A202. Donaldson, Stephen R. *The Gap into Vision: Forbidden Knowledge*. New York: Bantam, 1991. 407 p.

A203. Donaldson, Stephen R. *The Gap into Power: A Dark and Hungry God Arises*. New York: Bantam, 1992. 473 p.

A204. Downing, Paula E. *Fallaway*. New York: Del Rey/Ballantine, 1992. 242 p.

The story of an asteroid hollowed out and occupied first by an alien race, then by humans.

Unseen.

A205. Drake, David, and Bill Fawcett, editors. *Battlestation, Book 1*. New York: Ace, 1992. 258 p.

Far in the future, a race of implacable aliens called the Ichtons is ravaging through the worlds of the Galactic Core, killing all life forms and reducing planetary surfaces to barren wastelands. In response to requests for help from four afflicted races, the worlds of the Alliance construct a massive mobile space station called the Stephen Hawking and send it to the Core, along with many spaceships of the Fleet, to battle against the Ichtons. There are many stories to tell about the Fleet's first encounters with the Ichtons, efforts to infiltrate the Ichton ranks, and the daily lives of the many residents of the space station.

This "braided" anthology primarily consists of ten individual stories and one poem involving aspects of this scenario, which are discussed separately below; these are "Gung Ho," by Judith R. Conly (poem); "Facing the Enemy," by David Drake; "Killer Cure," by Diane Duane; "The Eyes of Texas," by S. N. Lewitt; "A Transmigration of Soul," by Janet Morris; "Star Light," by Jody Lynn Nye; "Blind Spot," by Steve Perry; "Trading Up," by Mike Resnick and Barbara Delaplace; "The Stand on Luminos," by Robert Sheckley; "Globin's Children," by Christopher Stasheff; and "Comrades," by S. M. Stirling. The storyline is also advanced by a number of brief passages before and between the stories written by Bill Fawcett: "Prologue," p. 1-3; "Indies," p. 26; "Battle Station," p. 36-37; "The Stephen Hawking," p. 81-82; "The First Weeks," p. 107-108; "The Ichtons," p. 131-132; "Civilians," p. 152; "The Edge," p. 179; "Origin of the Species," p. 210; and "No Win," p. 230. Of these, the one of greatest interest to space station scholars would be "The Stephen Hawking," which describes the station in detail:

> The station itself was a globe over five kilometers in diameter. It left Alliance space with a mixed crew of over ten thousand Fleet and civilian personnel...the walls of every deck were color-coded beginning at the top with red and descending through the spectrum to violet. Each color contained five major levels and up to three times that number of subdecks.... The central core of the Hawking was a three-hundred-meter tube running along the decks containing the massive warp drive and magnetic engines. Entrance ports were located all along the hull. (81)

Notes: this was projected as the first of several braided anthologies to follow the Stephen Hawking and its adventures, but only one additional volume appeared: *Battlestation, Book Two: Vanguard* (q.v.).

This series is the successor to a previous series of six anthologies, *The Fleet*, which involved the same general background (though about fifty years earlier) and some of the same characters featured here. To my knowledge, the stories in *The Fleet* did not significantly involve space stations.

A206. Drake, David, and Bill Fawcett, editors. *Battlestation, Book 2: Vanguard*. New York: Ace, 1993. 264 p.

While the Fleet and the battle station Stephen Hawking have had some successes in their skirmishes with the Ichtons attacking the worlds of the Galactic Core, they are gradually realizing just how massive the Ichton threat is, and they begin to search for new information that might help to defeat them. In the meantime, levels of stress are increasing on board the Stephen Hawking, and there are Ichton attempts to destroy or infiltrate the station.

Like its predecessor, *Battlestation, Book One* (q.v.), this braided anthology primarily consists of eleven stories and one poem involving aspects of this scenario which are discussed separately below; these are: "Imperatives," by Judith R. Conly (poem); "Failure Mode," by David Drake; "The Handmaiden," by Diane Duane; "Joint Ventures," by Don John Dugas; "You Can't Make an Omelet," by Esther M. Friesner; "Battle Offering," by Katherine Kurtz; "Medic," by Mercedes Lackey and Mark Shepherd; "Charity," by S. N. Lewitt; "Deadfall," by Scott MacMillan; "Taken to the Cleaners," by Peter Morwood; "Shooting Star," by Jody Lynn Nye; and "Hearing," by Christopher Stasheff. Bill Fawcett wrote "Prologue," p. 1-2, and these "Interludes": "Old Grudges," p. 31; "Weapon of War," p. 63-64; "RX," p. 84; "Reinforcements," p. 115-116; "Counterintelligence," p. 127; "Net Profit," p. 147; "Stern Chase," p. 176-177; "In Danger's Way," p. 195-196; "The Last Reserve," p. 214-215; and "Bequest," p. 240-241.

A207. Drake, David. *Fortress*. New York: Tor, 1987. 311 p.

In an alternate universe, a President Kennedy who avoids assassination orders the creation of a space defense system which includes space stations.

Unseen.

A208. Duane, Diane, and Peter Morwood. *Space Cops: Mindblast*. New York: Avon, 1991. 256 p.

The first book in a projected series about space policemen in the solar system.

Unseen; two sequels to this novel, both unseen, are:

A209. Duane, Diane, and Peter Morwood. *Space Cops: Kill Station.* New York: Avon, 1992. 279 p.

A210. Duane, Diane, and Peter Morwood. *Space Cops: High Moon.* New York: Avon, 1992. 256 p.

A211. Duane, Diane. *Spock's World.* New York: Pocket, 1988. 310 p.

This *Star Trek* novel about the planet Vulcan refers to the *Enterprise* stopping at a spacedock in Earth orbit (5).

Unseen.

A212. Duncan, David. *Dark Dominion.* New York: Ballantine, 1954. 206 p.

Fending off external threats and internal suspicions of treachery, the researchers working on the secret "Magellan Project" discover a remarkable new propulsion system that enables them to launch the first space station; but instead of entering orbit, the station commander, aware of all the discord the station launching has caused, decides it would be better to fly off to the stars.

I believe this is the first story in which a space station is converted into a spaceship (see also Long's *This Strange Tomorrow*, Bova's *Exiled from Earth*, and Scortia's *Earthwreck!*). In this novel, a military space station designed to preserve peace finally has to leave Earth in order to prevent war.

A213. Dwiggins, Don. *The Asteroid War.* Chicago: Children's Press, 1978. 63 p.

A juvenile novel about a 10,000-person space station that is mining the asteroid belt while fending off alien attacks.

Unseen.

A214. Elliot, E. C. [Reginald Martin] *Kemlo and the Crazy Planet.*

[*Kemlo #1*] London: Thomas Nelson & Sons Ltd., 1954. 200 p.

A space adventure featuring the young residents of space station Satellite Belt K.

Unseen. This was the first of fifteen novels featuring Kemlo. Three of these—*Kemlo and the Martian Ghosts, Kemlo and the Sky Horse*, and *Kemlo and the Zones of Silence*—are discussed below; the other eleven, all unseen, are:

A215. Elliot, E. C. [Reginald Martin] *Kemlo and the Craters of the Moon.* [*Kemlo #5*] London: Thomas Nelson & Sons, 1955. 200 p.

A216. Elliot, E. C. [Reginald Martin] *Kemlo and the Space Lanes.* [*Kemlo #6*] London: Thomas Nelson & Sons, 1955. 200 p.

A217. Elliot, E. C. [Reginald Martin] *Kemlo and the Star Men.* [*Kemlo #7*] London: Thomas Nelson & Sons, 1955. 193 p.

A218. Elliot, E. C. [Reginald Martin] *Kemlo and the Gravity Rays.* [*Kemlo #8*] London: Thomas Nelson & Sons, 1956. 202 p.

A219. Elliot, E. C. [Reginald Martin] *Kemlo and the Purple Dawn.* [*Kemlo #9*] London: Thomas Nelson & Sons, 1957. 200 p.

A220. Elliot, E. C. [Reginald Martin] *Kemlo and the End of Time.* [*Kemlo #10*] London: Thomas Nelson & Sons, 1957. 196 p.

A221. Elliot, E. C. [Reginald Martin] *Kemlo and the Zombie Men.* [*Kemlo #11*] London: Thomas Nelson & Sons, 1958. 202 p.

A222. Elliot, E. C. [Reginald Martin] *Kemlo and the Space Men.* [*Kemlo #12*] London: Thomas Nelson & Sons, 1959. 186 p.

A223. Elliot, E. C. [Reginald Martin] *Kemlo and the Satellite Builders.* [*Kemlo #13*] London: Thomas Nelson & Sons, 1960. 186 p.

A224. Elliot, E. C. [Reginald Martin] *Kemlo and the Space Invaders.* [*Kemlo #14*] London: Thomas Nelson & Sons, 1961. 214 p.

A225. Elliot, E. C. [Reginald Martin] *Kemlo and the Masters of Space.*

[*Kemlo #15*] London: Thomas Nelson & Sons, 1963. 194 p.

A226. Elliot, E. C. [Reginald Martin] *Kemlo and the Zones of Silence.* [*Kemlo #2*] London: Thomas Nelson and Sons Ltd., 1954. 201 p.

Flying from Satellite Belt K to Satellite Belt S to visit relatives, Kemlo and his friends Krillie and Krinsetta are assaulted by young men from Belt S, who fight them and take Krinsetta away with them. When all ships get off course, they are forced to land in the Zones of Silence, strange little worlds in space inhabited by creatures with telepathic powers.

This novel establishes the main purpose of the Satellite Belts as traffic control—they "sent out the controlling waves to keep the giant space and rocket ships on their true courses" (8). It is also mentioned that "the living environment could be cramped unless all people living there...made an effort to get on together" (6).

A227. Elliot, E. C. [Reginald Martin] *Kemlo and the Sky Horse.* [*Kemlo #3*] London: Thomas Nelson & Sons Ltd., 1954. 189 p.

When an arrogant Earth visitor to Satellite Belt K belittles the station's mechanical horse in the recreation room, Kemlo, some friends, and a sympathetic teacher decide to build a sophisticated mechanical horse that could actually be ridden in outer space. They succeed in building one, although there is momentary trouble when the Earth lad takes the horse on an unauthorized flight and gets lost in space.

This is certainly the most literal vision of space as the New Frontier, complete with cowboy suits for space boys to wear while riding their sky horses. One interesting idea is that the youngsters born in space are acclimatized to space life, while their parents have to wear special suits or stay in separate compartments; the concepts of parents and children inhabiting different environments could generate intriguing conflict, though none is found here—"Life was organized very similarly to that on Earth, apart from the restrictions forced upon them by living in space" (55).

A228. Elliot, E. C. [Reginald Martin] *Kemlo and the Martian Ghosts.* [*Kemlo #4*] London: Thomas Nelson & Sons Ltd., 1954. 202 p.

After winning a space scooter race, Kemlo and two other young men from Satellite Belt K are chosen to be part of an expedition to the Martian moon Deimos, where they are attacked by mysterious invisible beings.

After living on the space station, residents of Satellite Belt K are said to have lost "the spirit of adventure" (16); planetary exploration is the implied answer to the problem.

A229. Fancher, Jane S. *Groundties*. New York: Warner, 1991. 376 p.

A novel involving conflict between Earth and the space colonies.

Unseen; its two sequels, also unseen, were:

A230. Fancher, Jane S. *Uplink*. New York: Questar, 1992. 378 p.

A231. Fancher, Jane S. *Harmonies of the 'Net*. New York: Questar, 1992. 378 p.

A232. Farren, Nick. *The Long Orbit*. New York: Del Rey/Ballantine, 1988. 264 p.

A novel of intrigue involving struggles for the control of space development in a future era when large space stations already exist.

Unseen.

A233. Farren, Nick. *Vickers*. New York: Ace, 1988, 1986. 263 p.

A story about a soldier turned assassin includes a visit to one of the large manned satellites orbiting Earth called "donuts."

Unseen.

A234. Fear, W. H. *Lunar Flight*. London: Badger, 1958. 160 p.

The book includes a description of life on Space Station One.

Unseen.

A235. Feeley, Gregory. *The Oxygen Barons*. New York: Ace, 1990. 264 p.

This near-future space adventure involves an orbital factory and space habitat.

Unseen.

A236. Forstchen, William R. *Into the Sea of Stars*. New York: Del Rey/Ballantine, 1986. 231 p.

When Earth fought a devastating war, over seven hundred space colonies elected to leave the Solar System. When a history professor sets out in a starship to relocate them, he finds a primitive tribal culture, a sepulchral race of immortals, a society of radical feminists, and a former penal colony now set to attack Earth.

Like others, Forstchen sees space colonies as a way for any group to establish its own culture and develop in its own way. And as in other novels, the eventual mobility of these colonies is the key to their freedom.

A237. Foster, Alan Dean. *The Black Hole*. Based on the Walt Disney Productions film; screenplay by Jeb Rosebrook and Gerry Day; story by Jeb Rosebrook and Bob Barbash and Richard Landau. New York: Del Rey/Ballantine, 1979. 213 p.

A spaceship crew discovers a mad scientist hovering near a huge black hole, preparing to enter it.

Unseen, but see comments on the film of the same name which this novel is based on.

A238. Forward, Robert L. *Timemaster*. New York: Tor, 1992. 274 p.

This novel describes a number of massive structures in space.

Unseen.

A239. Gail, Otto. *The Stone from the Moon*. 1926. Translated by Francis Currier. *Science Wonder Quarterly*, 1 (Spring, 1930), p. 294-359, 418-419.

While unraveling a mystery concerning a Mayan girl with strange psychic powers and space travel by ancient Earth civilizations, an archaeologist visits Astropol, a dumbbell-shaped space station constructed by the Gorf Company.

Gail anticipates several themes of later science fiction stories: a space station as a "platform in space" from which to launch interplanetary missions; building a gigantic mirror near that station to provide heat and weather control for Earth; and the military potential of that mirror, making secrecy necessary, lest some nation try to destroy the station. The magazine it appeared in featured a striking cover illustration by Frank Paul.

Note: this is a sequel to an earlier novel about a flight to the Moon, *The Shot into Infinity*, which apparently does not involve space stations.

A240. Gear, W. Michael. *The Artifact*. New York: DAW, 1990. 526 p.

This novel about the discovery of an alien artifact includes references to space stations.

Unseen.

A241. Gear, W. Michael. *Starstrike*. New York: DAW, 1990. 540 p.

To combat alien invaders, human soldiers train on a distant space station.

Unseen.

A242. Gear, W. Michael. *The Warriors of Spider*. New York: DAW, 1988. 367 p.

A novel about the Directorate, a galactic empire of the future which includes both planetary colonies and space stations.

Unseen. This is the first novel in a trilogy; the other two novels, both unseen, are:

A243. Gear, W. Michael. *The Way of Spider*. New York: DAW, 1989. 408 p.

A244. Gear, W. Michael. *The Web of Spider*. New York: DAW, 1989. 648 p.

A245. Gernsback, Hugo. *Ultimate World*. Edited, and with an introduction, by Sam Moskowitz. 1971. New York: Avon, 1975.
187 p.

In 1996, mysterious insect-like aliens called Xenos arrive on Earth,
capture people to observe their sex habits, genetically transform children into telepathic, super-intelligent beings, and move the asteroid
Eros into Earth orbit and hollow it out to serve as the "Xenos' City in
the Sky" (125). However, a year later they are apparently wiped out by
an attack of their enemies, and Earth moves towards eliminating war
and turning the transformed Eros into "a permanent space laboratory"
and a "super space-hotel" (180, 181).

There were apparently other space stations in existence before the
Xenos arrived, but the only reference to them is one question about
Eros: "Was the new moon another space station that dwarfed all human-built ones?" (111) The unseen Xenos excavate the asteroid to en-
close "a vast metropolis" with hexagonal buildings and rooms (120),
making it big enough for 400,000 to 600,000 occupants. Earth scientists speculate that the Xenos were changing Eros to serve as a gigantic
spaceship, but when they are wiped out, the people of Earth happily
plan to employ it as a space station.

A246. Gibson, Edward. *In the Wrong Hands*. New York: Bantam,
1992. 362 p.

A future space adventure involving Space Station Equality.

Unseen.

A247. Gibson, Edward. *Reach*. Garden City, NY: Doubleday, 1989.
334 p.

A manned space mission to the Wayfarer Objects—small bodies passing the Solar System outside the orbit of Pluto—is attacked and absorbed by a mysterious being known as Choke, apparently residing in
an alternate universe where matter repels matter, and brought into contact with our universe by the tiny black hole accompanying the Objects. A follow-up mission also encounters Choke, but three crewmen
manage to drive it away before being absorbed, and a third mission is
then planned.

This is an obvious item of interest, as the first science fiction novel by a former resident of a space station (in addition to shuttle missions, Gibson spent 84 days in Skylab). But space stations are only a minor part of the novel, though many are mentioned as part of Gibson's future world, including Space Station Kennedy (16), Savitskaya (36), Gagarin (60), Goddard (63), Nagami (67), and Tsien (81). The mission does launch from Space Station von Braun, and upon arriving, Gibson's hero feels a surge of warm feelings: "this part of the space station seemed the same. Each shape, each color, each shading of the sun-drenched surfaces had a familiarity to it, an open friendliness and warmth, like the well-worn footpath to home's back door" (174). Of course, the mission quickly leaves the station, as in many earlier novels employing the space station as a starting place.

A248. Gibson, William. *Count Zero*. New York: Ace, 1987, 1986. 246 p.

In this loose sequel to *Neuromancer* (q.v.), an ailing billionaire named Virek schemes to obtain immortality and struggles with the gods and artificial intelligences who now inhabit cyberspace. Involved in their machinations are Turner, a mercenary hired to arrange for the defection of a biochip engineer who ends up protecting his daughter; Count Zero, a would-be computer cowboy accidentally exposed to powerful experimental software; and Marly, an art dealer hired by Virek to search for the creator of mysterious sculptures who turns out to be an artificial intelligence working in an abandoned space station.

When Marly goes into space to look for the sculptor, she stops first at the "Japan Air's orbital terminus," whose interior was "so bland, so unremarkable, so utterly like any crowded airport, that she felt like laughing" (176). She then goes to the Place, a discarded fragment of Freeside, the Tessier-Ashpool space habitat seen in *Neuromancer* which, after the adventures in that novel, was sold and taken apart. There she finds Wigan Ludgate, a former computer cowboy who has become deranged and inclined to see visions of God—another instance of madness abetted, if not induced, by life in space. There is also a brief reference to "an orbital branch of the Nederlands Algemeen Bank" (25).

Note: Gibson wrote one additional novel set in the universe of *Neuromancer*: *Mona Lisa Overdrive* (q.v.).

A249. Gibson, William. *Mona Lisa Overdrive*. Toronto and New York: Bantam, 1988. 260p.

3Jane, the cloned member of the Tessier-Ashpool family last seen in *Neuromancer* (q.v.), launches an elaborate revenge scheme that including killing Molly (now known as Sally) and kidnapping Angie Mitchell, a popular simstim star. Others that get involved include Bobby Newmark (from *Count Zero* [q.v.]), now living in his own private cyberspace; Kumiko, the daughter of a powerful Japanese businessman; and Mona, a confused young woman who has plastic surgery to make her look exactly like Angie Mitchell and who eventually takes her place. In the end, Angie joins Bobby to live in Cyberspace, where they undertake an expedition to the other, alien-generated computer realm previously reported by Neuromancer.

While this third novel in Gibson's Sprawl trilogy includes no trips into space, it does supply the information that the Tessier-Ashpool family split off their family headquarters from Freeside, renaming it Straylight, and sold the rest of the station to another company, which now calls it Mustique II (81-82). One interesting scene in Newmark's private world involves a walk through long dark passages which represent a space station, and there is a reference to an advertisement for an "orbital spa" (71).

A250. Gibson, William. *Neuromancer*. New York: Ace, 1982. 271 p.

A computer "cowboy" adept in traveling in and manipulating Cyberspace—an illusory world shared by computer users—is recruited to help bring to life an Artificial Intelligence; the mission involves a dangerous trip to the Freeside space colony.

In addition to the space habitat, which occupies half of the novel, there is also mention of a Rastafarian space colony. Of interest is the attitude ascribed to the family which built the habitat: "Tessier and Ashpool climbed the well of gravity to discover that they loathed space.... We [are] growing inward, generating a seamless universe of self" (173). This hatred and avoidance of outer space is seen less explicitly in other depictions of space habitats.

A251. Gilliland, Alexis A. *Long Shot for Rosinante*. [*Rosinante #2*] New York: Del Rey/Ballantine, 1981. 181 p.

On Earth, the North American Union schemes to maintain control of Mexico in the face of increasing resistance; one problem is a computer construct called Corporate Susan Brown, now living in the space habitat Rosinante in the asteroid belt, who has information that might damage the NAU. As revolt spreads, a disgruntled officer launches an atomic missile at Rosinante, but residents manage to avoid destruction. Fearing another attack, the habitat's leader, Charles Cantrell, finally decides to develop a powerful laser weapon and declares independence; eventually, he forms an alliance with the restructured NAU.

Gilliland's novel is more focused on political intrigue on Earth than the life of his space habitat, which is hardly mentioned at all in the first half of the work. A long final chapter, describing the ceremonial announcement of independence, lacks any power at all because readers know almost nothing about Rosinante and its inhabitants. At least Gilliland can be praised for devising unique names for his space habitats: the names of the three in the asteroid belt (two of them unfinished) were taken from Cervantes—Sancho Panza, Rosinante, and Don Quixote—and the name of an "orbital city" (2)—Laputa, from Book Three of Swift's *Gulliver's Travels*—is an inspired choice.

Note: this is the second of three books about space habitat Rosinante; the other two, both unseen, are:

A252. Gilliland, Alexis A. *The Revolution from Rosinante*. [*Rosinante #1*] New York: Del Rey/Ballantine, 1981. 185 p.

A253. Gilliland, Alexis A. *The Pirates of Rosinante*. [*Rosinante #3*] New York: Del Rey/Ballantine, 1982. 216 p.

A254. Golden, Frederic. *Colonies in Space: The Next Giant Step*. New York: Harcourt Brace Jovanovich, 1977. 131 p.

This nonfiction book about space colonies includes a fictional "Space Colonist's Journal" (p. 8-22) describing a future engineer's journey from Earth first to the Orbital Transfer Station in Earth orbit, then to the gigantic, wheel-shaped Beta Colony at the L5 point.

The space station is likened to "a busy metropolitan hotel" (10) and Beta Colony is "a bustling, thriving community lined with flowers and trees, almost a gardenlike setting" (17). There are thus no surprising features about these structures. In this future world, there are also space habitats shaped like wheels, cylinders, or spheres; "the variety of designs adds interest to life in space" (14). The rest of the book has a cursory survey of older science fiction about space stations and a description of the full system envisioned by Gerard O'Neill in the 1970s: a base on the Moon hurling materials to the L5 point, where they are used to build space habitats.

A255. Goldstein, Stan, and Fred Goldstein. *Star Trek Spaceflight Chronology*. Illustrated by Rick Sternbach. A Wallaby Book. New York: Pocket, 1980. 192 p.

An imaginary history of spaceflight, beginning with the actual vehicles of the 1960s and 1970s, and proceeding onward until the 23rd-century world of the starship *Enterprise*. Tsiolkovskygrad, "the first L-5 city in space," is completed in 2005, followed by several more; "spacefarms" in orbit are built in 2037; large Starbases are built beginning in 2092; Delta Research Station is completed in 2132; and the 25th Starbase is completed in 2195.

An ingenious conceit, one in which the few mentions of space stations are overshadowed by reports of planetary exploration, scientific discovery, and space war and diplomacy. Note: while this book describes Starbases as gigantic space stations, this is not clearly established in the *Star Trek* series, and the only type of space station mentioned in that series, the small Space Station K-7, is not referred to here.

A256. Goulart, Ron. *Everybody Comes to Cosmo's. The Exchameleon Book Three*. New York: St. Martin's Press, 1988. 184 p.

An adventurer has a mission on a huge "orbiting spa/casino/ nightclub/hotel satellite" (cover blurb).

Unseen; this is the third adventure of the Exchameleon. The other two, both unseen, are:

A257. Goulart, Ron. *Daredevils, Ltd. The Exchameleon Book One*. New York: St. Martin's Press, 1987. 185 p.

A258. Goulart, Ron. *Starpirate's Brain. The Exchameleon Book Two*. New York: St. Martin's Press, 1987. 184 p.

A259. Goulart, Ron. *Star Hawks: Empire 99*. Illustrations by Gil Kane. New York: Playboy Press, 1980. 192 p.

The Star Hawks, top interstellar agents, embark on a mission to Empire 99 from their headquarters called the Hoosegow, a satellite orbiting the planet Esmeralda.

Unseen; the novel is based on the comic strip by Gil Kane and Ron Goulart, some of which was reprinted in two books: *Star Hawks* (1979) and *Star Hawks II* (1981). A second novel, also unseen, is:

A260. Goulart, Ron. *Star Hawks: The Cyborg King*. Illustrations by Gil Kane. New York: Playboy Press Paperbacks, 1981. 192 p.

A261. Graf, L. A. *Death Count. Star Trek #62*. New York: Pocket, 1992. 276 p.

This *Star Trek* adventure includes an assignment to Space Station Sigma One, and at one point a near collision between the *Enterprise* and the station.

Unseen.

A262. Greenhough, Terry. *Thoughtworld*. 1977. London: New English Library, 1978. 144 p.

A hollow artificial planetoid—Tynar's Hypothesis Experimental Environment One, or Theeo, or Thoughtworld—has been constructed to test Tynar's Hypothesis: that human mental powers will increase in the absence of gravity. There, qualified people called Thinkers work on problems on their own, and for hire. But Thoughtworld is plagued by minor sabotage, attempts to kill one apparently insane Thinker, and efforts of an alien empire to hijack the planetoid. Finally, the tyrant is killed, the rebels against him who hijack Thoughtworld are reasoned with, and the remaining Thinkers can contemplate the limitless possibilities of improved thought.

There is unusual variety in the assaults upon Thoughtworld—a traitor in their midst, explosions, decompression, gunshots, armed attackers, a sudden spinning of the little world, and finally moving it away in tow with tractor beams. In addition to the idea that human brain power would increase in the absence of gravity, Greenhough also offers "Vitch's corollary: That the failings of cellular brains, such as delusions, madness, neuroses, obsessions and hatred, must also increase in potency in no-grav" (79)—meaning that living in a space station would effectively induce insanity.

A263. Groom, Pelham. *The Purple Twilight*. London: T. Werner Laurie, Ltd., 1948. 281 p.

A group of British pilots, recruited by an American businessman to build a number of Terminals in Space to beam concentrated sunlight to barren regions of Earth, persuade their employer to let them take a trip to Mars after building the first Terminal. There, they discover an ancient and dying civilization which once mentally traveled to Earth and dominated the continent of Atlantis until they were driven out; afterwards, they made their race sterile after an atomic war on Mars between men and women. The Earthmen return to Earth determined to continue building Terminals in Space to ensure peace on Earth; but they discover their employer is in prison, and all space activities have been halted while nations construct atomic weaponry for war.

The strange novel combines the dreamy atmosphere of a turn-of-the-century "scientific romance" like Munro's *A Trip to Venus* (q.v.) with up-to-date scientific information about space travel and space stations taken directly from recent books by Willy Ley and Wernher von Braun. It is interesting that unlike later books, which envisioned space stations armed with atomic weapons, Groom sees the two forces as stark alternatives: either man will build space stations and achieve peace, or will build atomic weapons and wage war. And even though the Terminals in Space here have strictly peaceful purposes, fearful people on Earth spread "propaganda" about their dangers: "the general line is going to be that Terminals will produce a threat to world security...[there is talk of] the Heinies' plan to frizzle the towns of the Allied Nations by just such stations in space" (102-103). One fascinating moment comes when the narrator is experiencing life in weightlessness and envisions strange creatures evolving in such an environment: "without gravity muscles would eventually weaken and waste away.... I saw huge shapeless jellyfish-like creatures which wobbled about in space" (80).

A264. Gunn, James. *Station in Space*. New York: Bantam, 1958. 156 p.

The public rallies to support building two space stations after a fraudulent, fatal space flight is staged by desperate space workers. However, the space stations turn out to be basically useless, and life in space seems to inevitably drive people crazy—indeed, the very ability of man to live permanently in space is called into question.

Gunn's novel is a striking answer to the idealistic, humanity's-next-bold-step-into-the-unknown space station novels that were so common in the 1950s (Castle, Bernard, del Rey, Leinster, Wyndham, Clarke, *et al.*). According to Gunn, it will take a moving hoax to build any support for space travel; space stations will be built essentially as a way to spend money and employ people—making them WPA projects on a cosmic scale; and life in space causes people to go insane—in fact, a manned mission to Mars proves impossible because every crew sent invariably goes mad and slaughters each other before reaching Mars!

A265. Gunnarsson, Thorarinn. *The Starwolves.* New York: Warner, 1988. 281 p.

This novel of space adventure includes a "free-orbiting station" (10).

Unseen; three sequels to this book, all unseen, are:

A266. Gunnarsson, Thorarinn. *Starwolves: Battle of the Ring.* New York: Questar, 1989. 240 p.

A267. Gunnarsson, Thorarinn. *Starwolves: Technical Error.* New York: Questar, 1991. 231 p.

A268. Gunnarsson, Thorarinn. *Starwolves: Dreadnought.* New York: Questar, 1993. 234 p.

A269. Haldeman, Jack II, and Jack Dann. *High Steel.* New York: Tor, 1993. 252 p.

An adventure involving orbiting industrial facilities.

Unseen.

A270. Haldeman, Jack C., II. *Vector Analysis.* 1978. New York: Berkley, 1980. 183 p. A portion of the novel appeared in *Analog Science Fiction/Science Fact* in 1977.

A young expert on parasites goes to work on Delta III, an orbiting station "for biological and medical research" (7) with a special focus on the study of alien creatures brought back by space probes. One of these creatures unleashes a strange "dream plague" on the station, which causes a strange madness and eventual death. Discovering that a few people seem to have the ability to produce antibodies, he deliberately infects the woman he loves, and she and the others soon make enough antibodies to save the surviving diseased people.

The novel is a grander version of the story of Martin Caidin's *Four Came Back* (q.v.)—a mysterious space disease begins killing the crew of a space station, and survivors struggle to figure out a cure while Earth watches with grave concern. A subplot involves a visiting senator's scheme to shut down the research on the station.

A271. Haldeman, Joe, and Jack C. Haldeman II. *There Is No Darkness*. New York: Ace, 1983. 245 p. Portions of the book were previously published in *Isaac Asimov's Science Fiction Magazine* in 1979.

A young man from the harsh planet of Springworld enrolls in Starschool—a spaceship that travels to various worlds while educating its charges. On Earth, he engages in gladiatorial work to pay back a tax imposed at the Customs Satellite orbiting Earth; on Hell, he and some friends are kidnapped and forced to join a mercenary army on the planet; and on the artificial world of Construct, they encounter mysterious beings called Lobsters who probe their minds and accidentally provide them with valuable information.

In a spacefaring civilization, a space station to receive and inspect visitors is virtually inevitable, complete with long waits, red tape, and high charges. The most interesting feature of the novel, though, is Construct—built by aliens, it consists of spheres within spheres, with various chambers duplicating the conditions on every known inhabited world. Its avowed purpose is to provide facilities for different species to meet and communicate—all visitors are always allowed to visit other areas, even those which are dangerous to them.

A272. Haldeman, Joe. *Worlds: A Novel of the Near Future*. 1981. New York: Pocket, 1982. 239 p.

Marianne O'Hara, a young woman who has grown up in one of the forty-one space habitats orbiting Earth, visits the planet for the first time, generally finding it chaotic, violent, and unpleasant. She becomes involved with a revolutionary group and is kidnapped, only to be rescued by an FBI agent named Jeff Hawkings that she has fallen in love with. When she manages to get back into space, unseen machinations result first in a surprise nuclear attack on the space habitats; then there is a war on Earth which releases a devastating plague. With Earth apparently dying, the space habitats are now humanity's only hope.

Essentially, there are two stories here: a well-developed and modest tale of a girl from a space habitat who visits and learns about her home planet; and an unconvincing apocalyptic story involving corrupt, evil schemers who bring about the death of planet Earth. It seems a rather overemphatic way to bring home Haldeman's familiar point that "The Earth is closed space; history's mistakes endlessly repeating. The future belongs to the Worlds" (169). Interesting aspects of the novel include: Jacob's Ladder, an orbiting church; a visit to Devon's World, home to a religion dedicated to sexual excess; and the observation that "You don't meet many real political dissidents in the Worlds; too easy to go someplace else if you don't like it at home" (63).

Note: this is the first volume in a trilogy; the third, unseen volume is listed below, followed by an entry for the second volume, *Worlds Apart*.

A273. Haldeman, Joe. *Worlds Enough and Time*. 1992. New York: Avon, 1993. 318 p.

A274. Haldeman, Joe. *Worlds Apart: A Novel of Future Survival*. 1983. New York: Ace, 1984. 227 p.

In this sequel to *Worlds* (q.v.), Jeff Hawkings, stranded on Earth, struggles to help humanity suffering from the effects of a nuclear war and a devastating plague which kills all people past the age of twenty, and he finally manages to set up a new society in the Florida Keys. Meanwhile, Marianne O'Hara in the space colony New New York participates in the planning and building of a starship, which eventually takes off with O'Hara and her husbands as part of the crew.

Although people on Earth remain hostile to the space-dwellers, the residents of New New York are vital to humanity's survival: they develop and deliver an antidote to the deadly plague, and O'Hara joins a mission to Earth to help some survivors develop agriculture. In space, there are repeated references to feelings of "paranoia" (52, 108, 141) and there are reports of an "epidemic" of suicides, "an alarming sag in New New's morale," and increasing "Drug addiction and alcoholism" (55)—which all may be more a response to Earth's devastation than to life in space. Still, the decision to build and launch a starship, also seen in space habitat novels like Mack Reynolds's *Chaos in Lagrangia* (q.v.), suggests there is something unsatisfactory about permanent life in space, and O'Hara suspects that the starship project was originally undertaken "for obvious morale purposes" (139).

A275. Hand, Elizabeth. *Icarus Descending*. New York: Bantam, 1993. 334 p.

A devastated future Earth is ruled by aliens in orbiting HORUS space stations.

Unseen.

A276. Harness, Charles L. *The Paradox Men*. [*Flight into Yesterday*] 1953. Revised Edition. New York: Crown Publishers, Inc., 1984. 202 p. Originally published in a shorter magazine version in *Startling Stories* (May, 1949), as "Flight into Yesterday."

The future Earth is controlled by a repressive imperial government which has reintroduced slavery; but a group of rebels called Thieves steal from the rich to buy the freedom of slaves. One Thief called Alar seems to be uniquely powerful and important and is both sought after and protected in unusual ways as he travels from Earth to the Moon to "solar stations" close to the Sun. He is finally revealed as a man called Muir mutated by time travel into an advanced form, and the novel ends with the launching of the spaceship that arrives five years in the past to begin the action.

Despite critical comment, this "extensively recomplicated plot" (James Blish's words) really does not make any more sense than an A. E. van Vogt or Frank Belknap Long epic. Its point of interest here is the solarions—stations hovering near the Sun where insanity is the rule: "every one of these creatures was stark mad" (146). As Alar later explains,

> "Let us examine a society of some thirty souls, cast away from the mother culture and cooped up in a solarion. Vast dangers threaten on every side...it is the normal lot of people who live this life to be—by terrestrial standards—insane. Insanity under such conditions is a useful and logical defense mechanism, an invaluable and salutary retreat from reality.
> "Until the crew makes this adjustment—'response challenge to environment' as we Toynbeeans call it— they have little chance of survival. The will to insanity in a sunman is as vital as the will to irrigate in a Sumerian...."

Shey smirked.... "Would you say, then, that the *raison d'être* of a solarion psychologist is to drive the men toward madness?" (155-156)

A277. Harper, Tara K. *Lightwing*. New York: Del Rey/Ballantine, 1992. 261 p.

This novel involves telepathy experiments conducted in space at Corson Station.

Unseen.

A278. Harris, Raymond. *Shadows of the White Sun*. New York: Ace, 1988. 230 p.

A novel involving seven space habitats orbiting the Sun.

Unseen.

A279. Harrison, Harry. *Skyfall*. 1976. New York: Ace, 1978. 378 p.

The first in a planned series of U.S.-Soviet solar power stations, the Prometheus One, is unwisely launched due to political pressure despite technical problems; as a result, a faulty rocket places it in a decaying orbit, an errant booster smashes into a small English city, and the whole station itself threatens to crash like an atomic bomb on an American city.

Although never fully operational, the Prometheus One, in its brief life, manages to experience the whole gamut of space station problems: bureaucratic infighting and politics on Earth, mechanical failures, accidents, personal problems and a nervous breakdown in space, a missile attack, and finally, sabotage—a crewman turns the station into an atomic bomb so it will explode before impacting Earth. All this is truly a space station designer's nightmare. A novel with a similar scenario is Caidin's *Killer Station* (q.v.).

A280. Harvey, Frank. *Air Force!* New York: Ballantine, 1959. 142 p.

This book includes stories about manned Earth satellites.

Unseen.

A281. Heinlein, Robert A. *Between Planets*. 1951. New York: Ace, 1969. 190 p.

A young man, traveling from Earth to Mars to see his parents, arrives at Circum-Terra space station just after it has been taken over by Venusian rebels seeking independence. Before blowing up the station, the rebels send some passengers to Earth and others—including the hero—to Venus. There, he joins the rebellion and learns he has been unknowingly used as a courier.

Although Heinlein's other space stations are primarily transportation centers, Circum-Terra is also armed with missiles aimed at Earth to keep the peace. This is precisely why it is the only Heinlein space station to be attacked and destroyed!

A282. Heinlein, Robert A. *The Cat Who Walks through Walls*. New York: Putnam, 1985. 382 p.

Heinlein's hero, fed up with the increasingly over-regulated life at the "Golden Rule" space habitat, and apparently being pursued by mysterious enemies, elects to travel to the Moon, where he eventually meets up with and joins Lazarus Long's force of time-space soldiers.

Expanding his "Future History" to include space habitats for the first time (although one is mentioned in the non-Future History novel *Friday* [q.v.]), Heinlein reiterates the theme that any place that becomes civilized becomes unlivable, and that the intelligent man will always want to live on the frontier. Along with this comes the suggestion that people living in a space station or habitat will not want to be reminded of Earth and will want new and novel environments, not "familiar" ones.

A283. Heinlein, Robert A. *Friday*. New York: Holt, Rinehart, and Winston, 1982. 368 p.

Returning from a mission that took her to the space habitat Ell-Five and Stationary Station, attached to the Kenya Beanstalk which she rides down to Earth, special courier Friday is attacked by enemies; after being rescued, she stays alive during a time of extreme political disturbance on Earth and, after finding out that a new outbreak of the Black Death will soon devastate Earth, she emigrates to live on a planet in another solar system.

Heinlein's heroine/narrator makes several disparaging references to residences in space: Ell-Five "looks like a junkyard from outside and has only one arc that looks good from inside" (44), and "Aside from its spectacular and always changing view of Earth," Stationary Station "has nothing to offer but high prices and cramped quarters" (294). There is also the element of danger: another space elevator, the Quito Skyhook, is said to have been destroyed by sabotage, and Friday speculates that if the Black Death ever reached Ell-Five, it "would be a ghost town in a week" (236).

A284. Heinlein, Robert A. *The Rolling Stones*. 1952. New York: Ace, 1969. 253 p. Originally published as "Tramp Space Ship" in *Boys' Life* (September, October, November, and December, 1952).

The Stones, a family living on the Moon, decides to venture out into space, traveling first to Mars, then to the asteroid belt, and finally toward the outer planets.

When the Stones are maneuvering to leave the Earth-Moon system, they are concerned about a possible collision with "Earth's three radio satellites and her satellite space station" (87), and the novel has other brief references to space stations (94, 132). In the asteroid belt, the Stones visit "Rock City"—a collection of discarded space ships which stay together to form a community—which, it could be argued, represents a type of space station.

A285. Heinlein, Robert A. *Space Cadet*. 1948. New York: Ace, 1969. 221 p.

Space Cadet Matt Dodson and his classmates receive advanced training on board the S. S. Randolph, an old spaceship now in permanent Earth orbit 10 miles from Terra Station. While on leave, they visit the nearby space station.

Although it is strictly a background element—as is often the case in Heinlein's works—the briefly glimpsed Terra Station seems a true satellite city, with a "Paradise Walk" of restaurants and shops.

A286. Heinlein, Robert A. *Stranger in a Strange Land*. 1961. New York: Avon, 1962. 414 p.

This famous novel chronicles the adventures of Valentine Michael

Smith, a human born on Mars and raised by Martians who brings his unique knowledge and abilities to Earth and establishes a new religion before his martyrdom.

The first page of the novel mentions that "Only by refueling at a space station could the *Envoy* make the trip [to Mars]" (9); and a later overview of the future comments that "Federation defense stations swung in the sky, promising death to any who disturbed the planet's peace; commercial space stations disturbed the peace with endless clamor of endless trademarked trade goods" (71).

Note: the "Complete and Uncut" version of this novel published in 1990 contains no additional references to space stations.

A287. Heinlein, Robert A. *To Sail beyond the Sunset*. 1987. New York: Ace, 1988. 434 p.

Heinlein relates the adventures of Maureen Smith, mother of Lazarus Long, as she raises a large family in early twentieth-century America, lives through American life during the early days of space travel, and eventually joins up with the time-space warriors who are fighting mysterious foes.

Heinlein uses the novel to clear up an old mystery in his "Future History": the end of "Blowups Happen" (q.v.) clearly states that the dangerous nuclear power plant will be relocated in Earth orbit, but there is no mention of that space station in other stories. In this novel, Maureen learns, when her son visits her from the future, that the station will soon blow up and all its inhabitants will be killed; she briefly attempts to prevent this disaster, but fails.

A288. Heinlein, Robert A. *Waldo*. In *Waldo and Magic, Inc.* By Robert A. Heinlein. 1950. New York: Pyramid, 1963, p. 9-103. Story originally published in *Astounding Science-Fiction* (August, 1942). Published separately as *Waldo: Genius in Orbit* in 1950.

A brilliant engineer suffering from myasthenia gravis must live in a private space station in Earth orbit, where weightlessness will not tire his frail muscles. When he is asked to solve a problem involving failing engines energized by broadcast power, he finds the answer lies in a mystical "Other World" which produces energy that can repair the machines. When he learns how to draw upon this energy, he is cured, and Waldo becomes a skilled dancer.

Heinlein has some interesting notes about the design of a space station—no floors, flimsy, "fairylike" furniture, and special arrangements for indirect lighting and smoking. The idea that individuals with physical impairments might survive in weightless conditions appears in other stories like del Rey's *Siege Perilous* (q.v.); and the concept of weak station residents occurs in Leiber's *A Specter Is Haunting Texas* (q.v.), where people living in space have evolved physical frailty.

A289. Hinz, Christopher. *Liege-Killer*. New York: St. Martin's Press, 1988. 458 p.

A novel about a post-Holocaust world dominated by space habitats.

Unseen; this is the first novel in the Paratwa trilogy. The other two, both unseen, are:

A290. Hinz, Christopher. *Ash Ock: The Paratwa Saga, Book Two*. New York: St. Martin's Press, 1989. 308 p.

A291. Hinz, Christopher. *The Paratwa*. New York: St. Martin's Press, 1991. 404 p.

A292. Hitchcock, Raymond. *Venus 13: A Cautionary Space Tale*. London: W. H. Allen, 1972. 160 p.

According to John Clute in *The Science Fiction Encyclopedia*, this is a "story of complications surrounding a eugenic mating in a space satellite" (287).

Unseen.

A293. Hodgman, Ann. *Galaxy High School*. New York: Bantam Skylark, 1987. 96 p.

The adventures of two teenagers from Earth at Galaxy High School, a high school in space for a variety of alien beings.

Unseen; the stories are based on episodes of the Saturday morning cartoon series on CBS.

A294. Hogan, James P. *Endgame Enigma*. 1987. New York: Bantam,

1988. 436 p.

Suspecting that a Russian space habitat described as "an innocuous social experiment in space-living" is actually designed to launch a military attack, two American agents are sent to investigate the station; but they are caught and placed in a prison city in the habitat. Taking advantage of curiously lax security, they establish a communications link with Earth and explore the station, finding nothing unusual or suspicious. They finally discover, though, that they are actually on Earth, in an underground rotating platform, and their investigations were allowed in order to reassure the West about the station's military nature. A few prisoners escape from the mock-up, tell the American government what is going on, and prevent world war.

This novel illustrates the extreme vulnerability of space stations, in that the Russians are driven to truly Byzantine measures to forestall an armed attack on their space fortress, which would apparently be easy to accomplish. Since Hogan's heroes have actually been taken from the real station and placed in a phony station on Earth, the novel is a strange variation on the usually dark scenario of a space station returning to Earth; but the optimistic ending has the Russian government overthrown and humanity about to move out in vast numbers to occupy space: "The human race would soon explode outward across the Solar System. Real colonies were taking shape in the Earth-Moon system.... The late twentieth century...with its endless pessimisms about imminent doom and declining everything, seemed a long way away" (429-430).

A295. Hogan, James P. *The Two Faces of Tomorrow*. New York: Ballantine, 1979. 392 p.

An experiment to test the behavior of a massive computer system takes place in a space station.

Unseen.

A296. Holmes, Robert. *Doctor Who—The Two Doctors*. London: W. H. Allen and Co., 1985. 159 p.

A novel based on a televised *Doctor Who* adventure involving a space station.

Unseen; for a more complete plot summary, see "The Two Doctors" in

Part C.

A297. Hoover, H. M. *Away Is a Strange Place to Be*. New York: E. P. Dutton, 1990. 167 p.

An innkeeper's niece, Abby Tabor, is kidnapped along with a spoiled rich boy and transported to a space habitat under construction named VitaCon. There, she and many other children are forced to work on preparing the facility for human habitation. After some months, she and the boy run away, manage to get on board an outgoing spaceship, and get to a space habitat named Port Rolf, where they contact their parents; and after a visit to the boy's home, a habitat named Triark, Abby goes home. Later, the other children are taken away from Vita-Con, and Abby uses the money from a financial settlement involving her kidnapping to help those children start new lives.

This juvenile novel has a few interesting observations about people living in a space habitat: "Colonial people...were fond of colors, perhaps because of the cold blackness of space outside their homes"(15); "Habitat people were not quite her idea of *human*. Why else could this man give them hope and then tell them something like the crispy-critter story when they were so scared already?" (100) "She wondered if the size of the planet was why some people preferred living in habitats, where everything was geared to a human scale and, unless one stopped to think, nothing overwhelmed" (157). VitaCon itself is a raw, unfinished habitat, though it will eventually house 10 million people. Abby's problem is that in the habitat, "the only law here or in any corporate habitat is corporate law" (74); hence, outsiders have no right to interfere with its business, and it is only by an illegal raid that the other children working as forced labor are eventually rescued.

A298. Hubert, Jean-Pierre. *Mort à l'étouffée*. Paris: Kesselring, 1978. Page numbers unknown.

This novel with political themes describes a city floating in space.

Unseen.

A299. Hunt, Gill. [house pseudonym; this novel written by John Jennison] *Station 7*. London: Curtis Warren, Ltd., 1951. 112 p.

A convoy of ship travels to Station 7, orbiting the planet Jarda in the Alpha Centauri system; but when alien spaceships appear, the station is abandoned and the crewmen captured and taken to an alien planet where beautiful women are in control, and only a few men are allowed to live to keep the race going. Aided by a sympathetic woman, the crewmen attempt to escape from a reservation for men, but they are stopped.

In this future world, the first six major space stations were built to orbit the outer planets: Mars, Jupiter, Saturn, Uranus, Neptune, and Pluto; there are also "numerous small [stations] orbiting round Terra. These were used for communication and television relays, for weather observation and control, and even as entertainment centers" (25). Station 7 is described as having a "weird, umbrella-like shape gleaming brassily" (24), with an interior lounge that "was as luxuriously appointed as any in the most expensive of Terran hotels" (29); it generates power with mirrors that concentrate heat on water which is converted into steam. When the alien spaceships appear, the convoy commander announces that "The station itself was too vulnerable to attack" (37), orders it abandoned, and sends the crew to a base on the surface of Jarda—where they are captured anyway. And despite the novel's title, the station is then completely forgotten about one-third of the way through the book.

A300. Ingrid, Charles. [Rhondi Vilott] *Radius of Doubt. The Patterns of Chaos #1*. New York: DAW, 1991. 348 p.

This novel about the pilot of a faster-than-light starship includes a stop at a space station.

Unseen. Three sequels have appeared: *The Downfall Matric* (1994), *Soulfire* (1995), and this unseen novel:

A301. Ingrid, Charles. [Rhondi Vilott] *Path of Fire. The Patterns of Chaos #2*. New York: DAW, 1992. 349 p.

A302. Innes, Evan. [Zach Hughes] *America 2040. [America 2040 #1]* New York: Bantam, 1986. 344 p.

This novel about the first starship refers to orbiting space stations with weapons and includes a visit to the space station President Healy.

Unseen. This is the first of five related novels; the others, all unseen, are:

A303. Innes, Evan. [Zach Hughes] *The Golden World*. [*America 2040 #2*] New York: Bantam, 1986. 373 p.

A304. Innes, Evan. [Zach Hughes] *City in the Mist*. [*America 2040 #3*] New York: Bantam, 1987. 374 p.

A305. Innes, Evan. [Zach Hughes] *The Return*. [*America 2040 #4*] New York: Bantam, 1988. 374 p.

A306. Innes, Evan. [Zach Hughes] *The Star Explorer*. [*America 2040 #5*] New York: Bantam, 1988. 322 p.

A307. Janifer, Laurence M. [formerly Larry Mark Harris], and J. L. Treibich. *Target: Terra*. New York: Ace, 1968. 149 p.

The Intelligence Officer on a missile-laden space station must cope with his slightly addled crewmates and an increasing variety of unexplained problems and mishaps, culminating in one crewman's attempt to blow up the world.

This novel has the flavor of *Catch-22*, with the protagonist putting in absurd requests for "travel pay" and "flight pay" while on the station, the by-the-book commander, the drunken cook, the sex-crazed ecologist, and the protocol-bound navigator; the space station as madhouse. The crewman who tries to destroy Earth—accidentally under the influence of LSD—has developed a hatred for Earth because his three-month stay was indefinitely extended due to anti-missile missiles.

Note: this was the first volume of a trilogy. The other two volumes, both unseen, were:

A308. Janifer, Laurence M. [formerly Larry Mark Harris], and S. J. Treibich. *The High Hex*. New York: Ace, 1969. 112 p.

A309. Janifer, Laurence M. [formerly Larry Mark Harris], and S. J. Treibich. *The Wagered World*. New York: Ace, 1969. 79 p.

A319. Jeter, K. W. *Bloodletter. Star Trek: Deep Space Nine #3*. New York: Pocket, 1993. 276 p.

An original novel involving space station Deep Space Nine.

Unseen.

A311. Jones, Raymond F. *The Alien. Galaxy Novel #6*. New York: World Editions, 1951. 160 p.

This novel begins with the "laboratory ship" of the "permanent Smithson Asteroidal Expedition" (7) studying remains of an ancient alien civilization. They discover a dead alien, preserved as protoplasm, with instructions on how to revive him; when they do it, they discover the being is a mad dictator who quickly takes over the Earth and launches plans for space conquest. The scientists travel to the world which once defeated the space dictator, and an alien there gives one scientist three organs with amazing psionic powers which enable him to defeat the dictator.

The laboratory ship, permanently stationed in the asteroid belt, is a space station of sorts, though no attention is paid to its appearance or lifestyle in this fast-moving and illogical adventure.

A312. Jones, Tupper. *The Building of the Alpha One*. [poems] New York: Exposition Press, 1956. 80 p.

Tales in verse about the first space station.

Unseen.

A313. Joseph, Franz. *Star Fleet Technical Manual*. New York: Ballantine, 1975. [unpaginated; 194 p.]

This is purportedly a copy of the training manual used by cadets at the Star Fleet Space Academy of the *Star Trek* universe, accidentally transmitted to present-day Earth. It includes treaties, navigational charts, and diagrams of various vehicles, uniforms, and weapons.

The book contains a diagram of Star Fleet Academy, here pictured as an immense space station consisting of six connected Earth-like habitats arranged in a circle.

A314. Kahn, James. *Return of the Jedi*. Based on a story by George Lucas; screenplay by Lawrence Kasdan and George Lucas. New York: Del Rey/Ballantine, 1983. 213 p.

The third adventure in the *Star Wars* saga, including a new and even more powerful Death Star.

Unseen, but see comments on the film of the same name this novel is based on.

A315. Kato, Ken. *Yamato—A Rage in Heaven, Part One*. New York: Questar/Warner, 1990. 336 p.

The first volume in an epic space opera; its second volume, listed below, includes an orbiting space fortress.

Unseen. The sequel, also unseen, is:

A316. Kato, Ken. *Yamato—A Rage in Heaven, Part Two: The Way of the Warrior*. New York: Questar/Warner, 1992. 297 p.

A317. Keith, William H., Jr. *Nomads of the Sky*. [*Buck Rogers: Invaders of Charon #2*] New York: TSR, 1992. 280 p.

The second volume in a new Buck Rogers trilogy.

Unseen; the first volume is *The Genesis Web*, by C. M. Brennan; the third volume, also unseen, is:

A318. Keith, William H., Jr. *Warlords of Jupiter*. [*Buck Rogers: Invaders of Charon #3*] New York: TSR, 1993. 278 p.

A319. Kelleam, Joseph E. *Overlords from Space*. New York: Ace, 1957. 146 p.

Aliens who have taken over the Earth are opposed by a scientific underground hiding in an abandoned space satellite.

Unseen.

A320. Killough, Lee. *Spider Play*. New York: Warner, 1986. 232 p.

This adventure novel involves the Lanour Space Platform.

Unseen.

A321. Kingsbury, Donald. *The Moon Goddess and the Son*. 1986. New York: Baen, 1987. 471 p.

The adventures of a young woman named Diana who is determined to live in space.

Unseen, but see comments in Part B on Kingsbury's novelette of the same name, which this novel is based on.

A322. King, T. Jackson. *Retread Shop*. New York: Warner, 1988. 276 p.

A novel about growing up in a space habitat.

Unseen.

A323. Kirby, William S. *Iapetus*. New York: Ace, 1993. 243 p.

On his way to Saturn's moons, a man stops over at Elf Hive, a space station at the L-5 point.

Unseen.

A324. Kornbluth, C. M. *Not This August*. [Also known as *Christmas Eve*] Garden City, NY: Doubleday, 1955. 190 p.

When the United States is defeated and occupied by the Russians and Chinese, its only hope is a secretly built "bombardment satellite," armed with H-bombs, and almost ready to launch. When members of the underground manage to get the satellite into orbit, the success of their rebellion is assured.

For once, a space station armed with missiles has a definite good result—America is rescued from Communist tyranny. However, at the end of the novel, Kornbluth's hero points out that this "Military Satellite One" will bring no lasting peace, only a new cycle of escalation and conflict; and the story concludes with him joining in a pacifistic prayer for peace.

A325. Kotani, Eric, [Yoji Kondo] and John Maddox Roberts. *Act of God*. New York: Baen, 1985. 282 p.

A renegade group in the Soviet government is planning to cut huge chunks of ice off comets and hurl them to Earth as the ultimate explosive weapon. However, American agents figure out the scheme and send an expedition out to intercept the Russian spaceship and prevent the launching of the ice; but a political solution on Earth ultimately eliminates the threat.

There are numerous references to permanent space stations in the novel, and both the Russian and American expeditions to the comet set off from a station. As in Hogan's *Endgame Enigma* (q.v.), the end of the military problem brings an optimistic conclusion, with visions of energetic and extensive space habitation.

A326. Kotani, Eric, [Yoji Kondo] and John Maddox Roberts. *The Island Worlds*. New York: Baen, 1987. 279 p.

A novel about space habitats.

Unseen.

A327. Langford, David. *The Space Eater*. New York: Pocket, 1983. 224 p.

A novel involving space stations and teleportation.

Unseen.

A328. Lasswitz, Kurd. *Two Planets*. [*Auf zwei Planeten*; also known as *Twin Planets*] 1897. Abridged by Erich Lasswitz. Translated by Hans H. Rudnick. Afterword by Mark Hillegas. Carbondale, Illinois: Southern Illinois University Press, 1971. 405 p.

Two explorers discover a community of humanoid Martians on an island near the North Pole and learn that the Martians have also placed two ring-shaped space stations above both poles. When they learn about the human race, the Martians issue ultimatums, then attack and attempt to establish control over the Earth. However, the Americans counterattack and take over the two space stations, which forces the Martians to surrender and reach a peaceful settlement.

Lasswitz remarkably anticipates many of the themes of later space station stories: the station in the shape of a ring; the station as an observation post—in what is obviously intended as an awe-inspiring set-piece, the explorers on the station get a breathtaking look at the Earth, first with the unaided eye, then with a powerful telescope; the station as an invaluable element in space travel—in addition to the stations above Earth, the Martians have a spaceport above their own south pole, capable of receiving up to 70 spaceships; and the station as a military base—while no space weapons are involved, the two stations are depicted as essential to the Martian conquest of Earth, and the American seizure of them dooms their efforts.

A329. Lattimer, Dick. *Space Station Friendship: A Visit with the Crew in 2007*. Foreword by Eugene A. Cernan. Harrisburg, PA: Stackpole, 1988. 239 p.

Evidently a fact-based description of a space station in the near future.

Unseen.

A330. Leiber, Fritz. *A Specter Is Haunting Texas*. New York: Walker and Co., 1968. 245 p.

In the Sack, a free-fall section of space station Circumluna, inhabitants can choose to become either tall, frail Thins or gigantic Fats. One of the Thins—wearing an exoskeleton to support his weak body—visits Earth to investigate an old mining claim and becomes involved in a revolutionary movement against Texas, now an independent nation dominating North America.

Except for a brief postscript, Leiber's novel takes place entirely on Earth; still, there are a few interesting thoughts about long-range developments in space station life. Society in Circumluna is dominated by scientists and technicians; the protagonist, an actor by trade, offers some comments on the conventions of weightless theater; and the novel boldly postulates that inhabitants in a weightless environment will be virtually immortal.

Note: a "prequel" of sorts to this novel is Leiber's "The Beat Cluster" (q.v.).

A331. Leiber, Justin. *Can Animals and Machines Be Persons? A Dialogue*. Indianapolis, IN: Hackett Pub. Co., 1985. 76 p.

This nonfiction discussion of future legal problems features an imagined scenario of a monkey and computer on a space station.

Unseen.

A332. Leinster, Murray. [Will Jenkins] *City on the Moon*. New York:

Avalon, 1957. 224 p.

In the midst of dealing with numerous attempts to sabotage Civilian City on the Moon, Joe Kenmore flies to the Space Laboratory, stationed far beyond the Moon, where scientists are conducting dangerous research to control atomic energy. Maddened by stress, and mistakenly believing their knowledge could destroy the universe, the scientists blow up the Laboratory; Joe barely escapes, returns to the Moon, and kills the saboteurs, while another scientist solves the problem of harnessing atomic power.

Though most of the action takes place on the Moon, the Space Laboratory is in some ways the focus of the novel; Civilian City exists solely to support its work, which is described as essential to humanity's further conquest of space. In this story, all occupants of a space station go mad, but this is attributed to the nature of their work, not the environment they are living in.

Note: This is the third and last story in a loose trilogy featuring Joe Kenmore, the others being *Space Platform* and *Space Tug* (q.v.).

A333. Leinster, Murray. [Will Jenkins] *Men into Space*. New York: Berkley, 1960. 142 p.

Military man Colonel Edward McCauley participates in a number of adventures involving the exploration of space: the first manned launch into space, the first orbital flight, the building of the Space Platform, problems on the Moon, a flight around Venus, and an expedition to Mars.

Leinster makes the interesting point that the Space Platform, no matter how important and wonderful it is considered at the time of its construction, will eventually have to be junked as a hazard to further space flight (66-67). After it is built, it is referred to as a way station and space observatory when the Venus flight stops there for refueling.

Note: this book is based on the 1959-1960 CBS television series, *Men into Space*. See also discussions in Part C of these individual episodes of the series which involved space stations: "Asteroid," "Building a Space Station," "Dark of the Sun," "Edge of Eternity," "Mission to Mars," "Quarantine," "Sea of Stars," "Verdict in Orbit," and "Voice of Infinity."

A334. Leinster, Murray. [Will Jenkins] *Space Platform*. 1953. New York: Belmont, 1966. 157 p.

A young factory engineer, Joe Kenmore, helps build and launch a gigantic American space station, fighting off repeated efforts to sabotage the project.

Another 1950s novel claiming that the way to achieve world peace is for Americans to put nuclear weapons in orbit. In this novel, Leinster's hero and his friends are not allowed to actually go into space, but they will reach space in the sequels, *Space Tug* and *City on the Moon* (q.v.).

A335. Leinster, Murray. [Will Jenkins] *Space Tug*. 1953. New York: Belmont, 1965. 157 p.

While the Space Platform continues to battle repeated attempts to destroy it, Joe Kenmore and his friends prepare for the first flight to the Moon.

Leinster brings back the main characters from *Space Platform*, and they get to not only visit the space station, but also accompany the first flight to the Moon. Read today, these novels are striking for their failure to acknowledge that other nations might legitimately resent an American space station armed with nuclear weapons.

Note: there is one further book in this series, *City on the Moon* (q.v.).

A336. Leinster, Murray. [Will Jenkins] *The Wailing Asteroid*. 1960. New York: Avon, 1966. 143 p.

In response to a strange message, a scientist and his friends build a spaceship and travel to a small asteroid, which they discover has been rebuilt as a space fortress by a long-vanished race of aliens. They were summoned, they learn, to use its weapons to fend off a coming attack by another alien race. They manage to figure out its weapons and, discovering a matter transporter, plan to explore and inhabit the new world it leads to.

This alien space fortress, unlike those built by humans, manages to successfully serve its purpose, although the novel's conclusion emphasizes that the enemy aliens are not fully defeated. One passage suggests that the aliens who built the fortress were the ancestors of humanity.

Note: the novel was later filmed as *The Terrornauts* (q.v.).

A337. Lem, Stanislaw. *Solaris*. 1961. Translated from the French by Joanna Kilmartin and Steve Cox. London: Faber & Faber, 1971. 216 p.

In a space station hovering above, scientists study and attempt to understand a mysterious creature, a large, constantly changing oceanic being, which creates illusions of departed loved ones for each resident.

Technically, this is not a true space station, since it is within the planet's atmosphere, but it is repeatedly called a space station and, despite the uncertainties of the double translation, one must assume that is what Lem wanted it regarded as. And, in fact, there are similarities between it and the space stations of lesser writers, notably the air of incipient insanity that haunts its inhabitants.

Note: see comments on the 1971 film version of this novel.

A338. Leonard, J. L. *Flight into Space*. New York: Signet, 1953. 190 p.

At first glance, this seems to be more of a nonfictional essay about possibilities for space travel and exploration, including space stations; yet the Library of Congress has classified it as a work of fiction.

Unseen.

A339. Lerner, Edward M. *Probe*. New York: Warner, 1991. 314 p.

This suspense novel involving a deep-space probe refers to plans for expanding space station Freedom (10).

Unseen.

A340. Long, Frank Belknap. *The Martian Visitors*. New York: Avalon, 1964. 192 p.

John Ridgeway, in charge of constructing the largest Space Station yet attempted, visits a circus with his children, where he sees an amazingly realistic picture of a Martian landscape projected on a screen by a clairvoyant. Because of that man's subsequent threats, Ridgeway and others are lured back to the screen, which teleports them to Mars, where they meet a robot who wishes to learn if men on Earth are as grand as the extinct men of Mars, and to cooperate with them if they are.

This is a delightfully incoherent novel, with an attempted realistic portrayal of the construction of a space station intermingled with the illogical antics of apparently malevolent Martians. Given the enormous pressure that Ridgeway is said to be feeling as the station nears completion, his visit to Mars and encounters with aliens there might be better explained as a lunatic's hallucinations.

A341. Long, Frank Belknap. *Space Station #1*. New York: Ace, 1957. 157 p.

A space policeman searches for a despised millionaire's kidnapped daughter while on a space station, a task complicated by the practice of wearing strange masks.

As is the case in other Long works, the story here does not make a great deal of sense, and, despite the title, there is virtually no sense of what the station looks like or how it functions. The adventure is played out in a dream-like mood, incident succeeding incident with no feeling of overall coherence or control.

A342. Long, Frank Belknap. *This Strange Tomorrow*. New York: Belmont, 1966. 158 p.

Earth "Coordinators" diagnosed as having mental problems are sent to space station Molidor to undergo "space therapy," but the method is a failure and a revolt results in the station traveling to and landing on Mars.

in this unintentionally hilarious novel, the idea behind "space therapy" is that "remoteness from Earth and a drastic environment change would diminish [patients'] anxiety and their inability to cope with the harsher aspects of reality"; however, in practice, the method seems to consist of: constant mistreatment by brutal "clinicians," long hours spent staring out into space, and periodic staged "entertainments" featuring ballet dancers and clowns designed to recapture the spirit of childhood. Little wonder that most patients end up worse than they started, and that one character finally admits that "Space Therapy has failed."

A343. Lorrah, Jean. *The Vulcan Academy Murders*. New York: Pocket, 1984. 280 p.

Kirk, Spock, and McCoy travel to the planet Vulcan to arrange for an injured crewman to undergo an experimental healing process—which is also being used on a Vulcan scientist and Spock's mother, Amanda. When the scientist and the crewman mysteriously die, Kirk suspects murder, and he eventually identifies the murderer as an Earth woman working on Vulcan who hoped to kill Amanda and marry Spock's father herself.

This clumsy mystery, in which the identity of the murderer is virtually announced in the second chapter, establishes that there are two space stations orbiting Vulcan (34); there is also a brief reference to Space Station K-7 (278), the setting for the *Star Trek* episode and story "The Trouble with Tribbles" (q.v.).

A344. Low, A. M. [Archibald Montgomery Low] *Satellite in Space*. London: H. Jenkins, 1956. 191 p.

This novel describes interactions between Earth satellites, including one controlled by a German Nazi.

Unseen.

A345. Lucas, George. [actually written by Alan Dean Foster] *Star Wars: From the Adventures of Luke Skywalker*. New York: Del Rey/Ballantine, 1976. 220 p.

The adventures of Luke Skywalker, including an encounter with the massive space fortress called the Death Star.

Unseen, but see comments on the film of the same name.

A346. Lupoff, Richard A. *The Forever City*. Illustrated by Bob Eggleton. A Byron Preiss Book. New York: Walker and Company, 1987. 230 p.

Three people—an astrophysicist, a cybernetics expert, and a cameraman for holographic films—leave from the space city Yukawa in search of a lost comrade somewhere in the Oort Cloud. They recover a strange piece of matter with the power to send people into strange dimensions. The astrophysicist is hurled into a blissful vision of the entire cosmos—and to her death; the cybernetics expert Mariel travels to another space city, Hawking, which she experiences in four different eras—its present, a future when there is war between ordinary humans and weird genetic experiments, a further future where a bizarre form of group intelligence has taken over, and a final future where the city is dead and deserted; and the cameraman Alfonso travels to the nineteenth-century Earth of the science fiction film he was working on, where he finds the missing person. Using an alien teleporter, they travel to Mariel and together make their way back to Yukawa, to study the strange piece of matter.

It is oddly appropriate that one of the last novels I read as part of a project that threatened to last forever should be called *The Forever City*, and that it is one of the rare novels that offers a glimpse of the entire history of a space habitat, with a final vision of a cold, empty cylinder still orbiting Jupiter. It is not an optimistic projection: even at the present time the space city Hawking is in the grip of "paranoia and tyranny" (199); their efforts to improve the human race through genetic manipulation only produce monsters; the group intelligence that finally emerges is not some grand construct, as in Zebrowski's *Macrolife* (q.v.), but manifests itself as tiny whispering voices, weak and pathetic; and the ultimate prognosis for human life in space colonies is grim, as represented by the deserted city she finally reaches. The final oddity is that this novel is apparently designed for juvenile readers; like Stone's *Green is for Galanx* (q.v.), it seems rather serious, even gloomy, for that genre. Surprisingly, the space city where the protagonists live, Yukawa, is hardly described at all, although it is interestingly located far above the plane of the Solar System at about the same distance from the Sun as the Earth.

A347. Lupoff, Richard A. *Sun's End*. New York: Berkley, 1984. 280 p.

While working on constructing the first space habitat, a computer technician named Buchanan is gravely injured in an accident. After eighty years of work, he reawakens as a brain and nervous system encased in an artificial body. Now a wealthy and influential figure, Buchanan soon learns that the Earth is rapidly becoming intolerably hot, and in a century or so only those living in space habitats will survive; seeking an answer, he investigates signs of intelligent life on Mercury, Titan, and the newly discovered planet Zimarzla, but he finally decides that he is no longer a human being and has no interest in their problems.

This book, unusually, describes the construction of a space habitat, however briefly. The future world he awakes to features familiar themes: numerous space habitats which promote "cultural diversity" (73), including one modeled on medieval Japan; space elevators which travel from Earth's surface to space; one or two space habitats which have elected to travel to another star; and hostility between Earth dwellers—"Planet-lubbers"—and habitat dwellers—"Tin canners" (193).

Note: the sequel to this novel, unseen, is:

A348. Lupoff, Richard A. *Galaxy's End*. New York: Berkley, 1988. 236 p.

A349. Lydecker, John. [Stephen Gallagher] *Doctor Who—Terminus*. 1983. London: W. H. Allen and Co., 1984. 128 p.

A novel based on a televised *Doctor Who* adventure involving a space station.

Unseen; for a more complete plot summary, see "Terminus" in Part C.

A350. MacGregor, Ellen, and Dora Pantell. *Miss Pickerell and the Weather Satellite*. 1971. New York: Pocket, 1980. 165 p.

The indefatigable Miss Pickerell is concerned when a weather satellite's incorrect predictions threaten to cause a flood, so she flies up to a space station, goes into space to give the satellite a good cleaning, and discovers that a laser beam from Earth has been causing the problem.

The space station is apparently one of many—a character mentions that "Some of the larger space stations have both zero and artificial gravity" (74). The station includes "meteorological and life science laboratories" (77) and a number of animals: "dogs, two goats, several white rabbits, a small pig, at least a dozen mice, monkeys, rats, and pigeons, and a baby lamb" (82).

Note: this is one of many Miss Pickerell adventures, including some other space adventures, but none of the other books apparently involve space stations.

A351. Maddox, Tom. *Halo*. New York: Tor, 1991. 288 p.

A novel about a dying man who is mentally linked to the artificial intelligence in charge of a space colony.

Unseen.

A352. Marsten, Richard. [Evan Hunter, formerly known as S. A. Lombino] *Rocket to Luna*. New York: Winston, 1952. 211 p.

A young space cadet, visiting the Space Station as part of his final year of schooling, ends up participating in the first mission to the Moon due to a crewmember's accident—which is unfairly blamed on him. However, he proves his worth by helping make the problem-plagued mission a success.

The Space Station here is simply a stepping stone to the stars, sketched in perfunctorily before the author gets down to the real excitement of going to the Moon.

A353. Marter, Ian. *Doctor Who and the Ark in Space*. London: W. H. Allen and Co., 1977. 140 p.

In the future, when solar flares make the Earth uninhabitable, all the surviving people are placed in suspended animation and stored in a space station until conditions improve. Unfortunately, as Doctor Who and his friends discover when they arrive there, a race of wasp-like aliens called the Wirrn, who can survive in the vacuum of space, have invaded the station and plan to feed upon the humans, absorb their knowledge, and make themselves masters of the universe. Luckily, the Doctor discovers a way to destroy the aliens, and he and his companions then travel to the Earth's surface to prepare for the planet's resettlement.

As in other works, a space station here becomes the means for the human race to survive catastrophe on Earth; however, since humanity seems to have become rigid and overspecialized, only the Doctor's intervention can help them overcome the alien invasion. To illustrate how melodramatic the story is, I need only point out that one scene involves the Doctor's friend crawling through a ventilation shaft—a space station cliché also found in works like del Rey's *Siege Perilous* and C. J. Cherryh's *Downbelow Station* (both q.v.).

Note: this novel is based on the *Doctor Who* serial "The Ark in Space," discussed in Part C below. Loose sequels to this serial and novel are "The Sontaran Experiment" and "Revenge of the Cyber-men," also discussed in Part C.

A354. Marter, Ian. *Doctor Who and the Sontaran Experiment*. London: W. H. Allen and Co., 1978. 128 p.

A novel based on a televised *Doctor Who* adventure involving a space station.

Unseen; for a more complete plot summary, see "The Sontaran Experiment" in Part C.

A355. Martin, Philip. *Doctor Who—Mindwarp*. London: W. H. Allen and Co., 1989. 142 p.

A novel based on a portion of a televised *Doctor Who* adventure involving a space station.

Unseen; for a more complete plot summary, see "The Trial of a Time Lord" in Part C.

A356. Mason, Anne. *The Dancing Meteorite*. New York: Harper & Row, Publishers, 1984. 214 p.

Kira Warden, a teenager living on a station in a distant solar system, is an "e-comm"—a specialist in translating alien languages and understanding alien cultures. One of her jobs is communicating with a group of aliens called Thagnians who are forced to stay at the station because their home world was destroyed. When she observes a meteorite moving strangely, she deduces that one of the Thagnians is using magnetic powers to manipulate the meteorite so as to damage the station and enable the Thagnians to leave. After a crisis involving two other alien races, Kira reveals the situation, absolving two officers who had been blamed for negligence in not dealing properly with the meteorites, and arranges for the Thagnians to join some of their people now living on a nearby world with other aliens.

The station Kira lives in floats within the atmosphere of a planet, so it is technically not a space station; still, since the planet is uninhabited, and since the facility otherwise has all the attributes of a space station, I have included the novel. Interestingly, one of Kira's problems is that she is labeled "earthbound"—trapped in old ways of thought characteristic of planet dwellers. There is another station manned by aliens in another part of the planet's atmosphere; apparently, such facilities are common throughout the known galaxy.

A357. Mason, Douglas R. *Satellite 54-Zero*. New York: Ballantine, 1971. 185 p.

A government agent is sent to investigate the Director of Satellite 54-Zero, a weather-monitoring space station; he discovers a bizarre plot to create a new life form based on ancient alien transmissions from Jupiter.

Mason envisions a large network of weather stations in space as necessary for large-scale agriculture on Earth. In his future world, space activities were first undertaken primarily by wealthy individuals and corporations, then later taken over by the government.

A358. Maynard, Jeff. *Introduction to Navigation: Star Fleet Command*. Packaged with *Star Trek Maps*. By Jeff Maynard. New York: Bantam, 1980. 31 p.

Another imagined document from the *Star Trek* universe of the future, "this manual is an introductory text designed to give the reader a thorough understanding of the basic principles and techniques of navigation in space" (5).

A section on "Support Facilities" describes two types of space stations: "Deep space stations," which are "major civilian repair, resupply, and refueling facilities," and "K-class space stations," which "are intended for the support of colonization efforts on the Federation frontier" (17). Space station K-7, of course, was the setting for the *Star Trek* episode, "The Trouble with Tribbles" (q.v.), and the maps which accompany this manual show a number of other K-class stations in Federation space.

A359. McCaffrey, Anne. *Pegasus in Flight*. New York: Del Rey/Ballantine, 1990. 290 p.

The woman in charge of Earth's developing psychic Talents must cope with the woman in charge of building a large space platform in Earth orbit, who is demanding over a hundred Kinetics to help in construction tasks. She also faces the responsibility of training two newly discovered Talents, one with enormous kinetic abilities, the other with a flair for languages.

Although the space platform is never visited in the novel, it is repeatedly mentioned, and there is one unique problem facing the Talents who must work there: loud mental "noise" caused by the thoughts of the many other workers in the confined quarters of the platform. There are also many accidents killing and injuring construction workers, although the Talents arrange a system for rescuing them and reducing the dangers.

Note: this is one of a series of novels involving powerful mental Talents assisting in the conquest of space. Peter Riedinger, the young boy with kinetic powers, reappears at the head of the space teleportation system in *The Rowan* (q.v.). An earlier novel in the series, *To Ride Pegasus*, does not involve space stations.

A360. McCaffrey, Anne. *The Rowan*. New York: G. P. Putnam's Sons, 1990. 335 p.

On an alien planet, an orphan girl with amazing psychic powers is trained to be a Prime—one of the handful of advanced Talents whose mental abilities transport people and goods across the stars. She meets and falls in love with another powerful Talent, and together they fight off an alien attack.

Most of the Stations in this novel, used for teleportation, are on planetary surfaces; however, there are brief but unambiguous references to "space stations" (47, 163) and people's "orbital homes" (148).

Note: there were five additional novels involving the Talents: *Lyon's Pride* (1994), *The Tower and the Hive* (1999), *Pegasus in Space* (2000), and these unseen novels:

A361. McCaffrey, Anne. *Damia*. New York: Ace, 1992. 336 p.

A362. McCaffrey, Anne. *Damia's Children*. New York: Ace, 1993. 272 p.

A363. McCaffrey, Anne, and S. M. Stirling. *The City Who Fought*. New York: Baen, 1993. 436 p.

Space station SSS-900 is a "living" space station, controlled by a human brain, in the same manner as the spaceship in McCaffrey's *The Ship Who Sang*.

Unseen.

A364. McCollum, Michael. *The Sails of Tau Ceti.* New York: Del Rey/Ballantine, 1992. 261 p.

This space adventure refers to space habitats Lagrange Three and Four (11).

Unseen.

A365. McCutchan, Philip. *Skyprobe.* A Commander Shaw Novel. New York: John Day Company, 1967, 1966. 208 p.

A secret group of sinister Communist scientists has planted a traitor on board Skyprobe IV, a 21-day American mission in high Earth orbit, and plans to divert it and force it to land in Soviet territory. Meanwhile, Commander Shaw works to find their secret base and ultimately foils the plot—but also accidentally destroys the spacecraft.

Despite its short stay in space, Skyprobe IV develops some typical space station problems—boredom, a saboteur, and "incipient madness" (192). There are a few references to actual manned space stations, which cannot help Skyprobe IV because they are fixed in near-Earth orbit.

Note: this is one of several Commander Shaw novels; the others do not seem to involve space travel or space stations.

A366. McDevitt, Jack. *A Talent for War.* New York: Ace, 1989. 310 p.

This space adventure includes a visit to the "orbiting station at Abonai" (19).

Unseen.

A367. McDonough, Thomas. *The Architects of Hyperspace.* New York: Avon, 1987. 265 p.

A novel about an artificial world.

Unseen.

A368. McIntyre, Vonda N. *Barbary*. Boston: Houghton Mifflin Company, 1986. 192 p.

An orphan girl travels to live with an old friend of her mother's in the Einstein space station, a research facility in a large elliptical orbit around Earth. She arrives at a time of great tension, since an alien vessel has been detected in the solar system. When the cat she smuggled aboard accidentally ends up on an unmanned probe sent towards the alien ship, she and her new sister go out in a space raft to rescue the cat; they are picked up by the aliens, who explain their peaceful intentions, and brought back to the space station.

In a way this is a distaff version of Ted White's *Secret of the Marauder Satellite* (q.v.)—the story of a confused teenager who finds a home at a space station: as soon as she arrives, she thinks, "For the first time in as long as she could remember, Barbary began to believe she really belonged somewhere" (75), and her last line in the novel is, "We're with the—beings in the starship.... They're bringing us home" (192). Her cat is originally going to be confiscated and removed, but when the cat kills a rat, the station personnel realize that their station is infested with rats, and cats seem to be the best solution to the problem.

A369. McIntyre, Vonda N. *Enterprise: The First Adventure*. New York: Pocket, 1986. 371 p.

The young James T. Kirk, just promoted to be captain of the *Enterprise*, goes to the earth-orbiting Spacedock and meets his new crew. They then embark on a mission which involves traveling vaudevillians, a Klingon privateer, and an encounter with a strange race of ethereal aliens.

The early parts of the novel include several references to Spacedock, including a scene in the Spacedock bar. One interesting point is that the new helmsman, Sulu, finds it rather difficult to maneuver the *Enterprise* out of Spacedock and almost collides with the structure; evidently, this facility is not designed very well.

A370. McIntyre, Vonda N. *Starfarers*. New York: Ace, 1989. 280 p.

This novel about the launching of the first interstellar spaceship includes a reference to the "deserted Soviet space station" (55).

Unseen; there were three sequels to this novel, *Nautilus* (1994), and these unseen novels:

A371. McIntyre, Vonda N. *Transition*. New York: Bantam, 1991. 290 p.

A372. McIntyre, Vonda N. *Metaphase*. New York: Bantam, 1992. 353 p.

A373. McIntyre, Vonda N. *Star Trek III: The Search for Spock*. Based on a Screenplay by Harve Bennett. New York: Pocket, 1984. 297 p.

Though Spock has died, his body has been rejuvenated on the experimental Genesis planet and his mind has been placed into that of Dr. McCoy. To bring Spock's mind and body together, Kirk and his *Enterprise* crewmates fly to the Genesis planet, defeat a Klingon expedition, and bring McCoy and Spock's new body to Vulcan, where they are reunited to make Spock live again.

The abandoned Spacelab, scene of much mayhem in *Star Trek II: The Wrath of Khan* (film and McIntyre's novel q.v.) is briefly glimpsed: Kirk's son David thinks, "If haunts were possible, it must be haunted" (35-36). There is also some description of Spacedock, the huge enclosed structure in Earth orbit seen in the film (q.v.) where starships can be refurbished in a shirtsleeve environment.

A374. McIntyre, Vonda N. *Star Trek II: The Wrath of Khan*. Based on a Screenplay by Jack B. Sowards and a Story by Harve Bennett and Jack B. Sowards. New York: Pocket, 1982. 223 p.

On the Spacelab space station orbiting Regulus 1, Captain Kirk's ex-wife and his son are working on Project Genesis, a method for transforming lifeless worlds into paradises. The starship *Reliant*'s search for a suitable planet finds the twentieth-century superman Khan, who takes over the ship and seizes control of Spacelab; Kirk and the *Enterprise* fly to Spacelab and succeed in killing Khan and foiling his plans; but Spock sacrifices his life to save his friends.

There is a little more detail given about the "Laboratory Space Station" Spacelab (33) seen in the film (q.v.), including the information that it can house several hundred people and is "the Federation's least exciting entertainment spot" (110). As in Leinster's *City on the Moon* (q.v.) and other stories, a space station functions as a good place for dangerous scientific experiments—and as a easy target for armed takeover. Also described is the Spacedock where the *Enterprise* is repaired—"the angular chaos of the space station" (61)—but this facility differs radically from the Centroplex spacedock of the film and novel *Star Trek: The Motion Picture* (q.v.) and from the enclosed Spacedock found in the film and novel *Star Trek III: The Search for Spock* (q.v.).

A375. McKillip, Patricia A. *Fool's Run*. New York: Warner, 1987. 221 p.

Seven years ago, a woman was possessed with a vision of a mysterious alien seeking light in order to be transformed and to live; under its influence, she massacres fifteen hundred people and is sentenced to the orbiting prison, the Underworld. When a group of musicians including her sister visit the Underworld, the band's leader is also possessed by the vision and helps the woman escape from the prison. As they are pursued, the alien seen in the vision apparently achieves its goal, and freed from her obsession, the woman instantly dies, and the others return to their previous lives.

In a time when prisons are horribly overcrowded, and funds for building new prisons are hard to come by, it remains startling that science fiction writers regularly assume that some future government will be willing to spend large sums of money to construct and maintain huge space prisons. Then again, logic does not seem to be fantasy writer McKillip's strong suit, as her novel is long on atmosphere and short on logic; the method by which this universally despised criminal is rescued by musicians lacking any plan or special devices is particularly unclear. There are also references to other habitations in space and to a space station orbiting the Moon, New Horizon, "a quiet place...for the study of the criminally insane" (17)—the only space asylum in science fiction except for Molidor in Long's *This Strange Tomorrow* (q.v.), although its business seems to be conducted a little more logically than in Long's novel.

A376. McKillip, Patricia A. *Moon-Flash*. New York: Atheneum, 1984. 150 p.

This juvenile novel features people on a planet who see strange flashes in the sky; they turn out to be exhausts from rockets leaving a space station.

Unseen.

A377. McLaughlin, Dean. *The Man Who Wanted Stars.* New York: Lancer, 1965. 222 p. Different versions of Parts I and II were published as "The Last Thousand Miles" in *Astounding Science Fiction* (February, 1956), and "Welcome Home" in *Infinity* (October, 1957).

America has abandoned its space program, leaving the space station Orbitbase deserted and thus not giving a manned mission returning from Jupiter a way to land on Earth. A daring attempt to land their spaceship ends with a crash and only one survivor. The experience galvanizes Joe Webber, a tireless promoter of space flight, who desperately tries to obtain funding for space projects. A friend's accidental discovery of an immortality treatment gives Webber and his cohorts time to accomplish their goals, and eventually they build a moon colony and a starship. However, Webber's obsessions have made him more and more unlikable, and when he persuades people to go on the starship with a false promise of a faster-than-light drive, his friends decide to replace him as commander of the craft.

This novel provides only a few details about Orbitbase—that its primary business was weather observation (66-67) and that after being abandoned, it fell to Earth and "turned into a meteor" (149). Webber is a thoroughly unsympathetic and obnoxious character—selfish, bullying, deceitful—and his decision to lure people onto a starship without telling them the trip will take 50 to 75 years is psychotic and irrational. McLaughlin's point, presumably, is that it will take unpleasant and obsessive people to accomplish the worthwhile goal of space travel; more valuable is the notion that it will take virtual immortality to make a true commitment to space possible.

A378. Merak, A. J. [John S. Glasby] *Barrier Unknown.* London: Badger, 1960. 142 p.

A space station confronts danger from radiation and aliens.

Unseen.

A379. Michaels, Melisa. *First Battle.* [*Skyrider #2*] New York: Tor, 1985. 253 p.

Eager to provoke a war between Earth and the space colonies, an Earth agency has men posing as colonials take hostages at a peace conference in space and imprison them in an abandoned space station. Melacha Rendell, the fiercely independent "Skyrider," leads a mission to rescue them; though captured herself, she eventually escapes and manages to prevent the war, at least temporarily.

This is an example—and not a particularly distinguished one—of the new space western, with anarchistic space colonies struggling against the oppressive Earth.

Note: this is the second of five Skyrider novels. The others, all unseen, are:

A380. Michaels, Melisa. *Skirmish*. [*Skyrider #1*] New York: Tor, 1984. 252 p.

A381. Michaels, Melisa. *Last War*. [*Skyrider #3*] New York: Tor, 1986. 219 p.

A382. Michaels, Melisa. *Pirate Prince*. [*Skyrider #4*] New York: Tor, 1988. 254 p.

A383. Michaels, Melisa. *Floater Factor*. [*Skyrider #5*] New York: Tor, 1988. 281 p.

A384. Michener, James A. *Space*. New York: Random House, 1982. 622 p.

This massive fictional history of the American space program, from World War II to the space shuttle, focuses on four men: a German rocket scientist who comes to America; a senator who supports the space program; a NASA official; and an astronaut who flies on the Gemini 13 and Apollo 18 space flights.

The novel includes scattered references to space stations: the scientist supporting a plan to assemble the moon rocket in Earth orbit says, "in addition, it erects a platform from which all the universe can be explored later on. Will we want a space station in permanent orbit?...Do we want to explore Mars and Venus?...Mine the asteroids? Put great telescopes in space? Establish settlements on the Moon? All these things can be done if we start with a solid space platform" (302). Later, the astronaut reads a book by Gerard O'Neill called *The Colonization of Space* (though O'Neill actually never wrote a book with that title) and predicts that soon, some nation will scale down O'Neill's proposal and build a solar power space station for 80 to 100 residents

(534-535). And, after the Apollo mission shuts down, one proposal is for "the establishment of a permanent station in space" (610).

Note: the television miniseries based on this novel is not listed in Part C, because it includes no references to space stations.

A385. Miller, John. *First Power Play*. [*Buck Rogers: Inner Planets Trilogy #1*] New York: TSR, 1990. 320 p.

The first volume in a trilogy of Buck Rogers space adventures.

Unseen; the second volume is *Prime Squared*, by M. S. Murdock, and the third is *Matrix Cubed*, by Britton Bloom.

A386. Miller, Walter M., Jr. *A Canticle for Leibowitz*. 1959. New York: Bantam, 1961. 278 p. Some parts of the book appeared in different form in *The Magazine of Fantasy and Science Fiction* in 1955 and 1956.

After a devastating nuclear war, members of a monastic order struggle to preserve documents from before the "Flame Deluge" and revive interest in science. When this occurs, the advances are greater—space stations and travel to the stars—but the results are the same—a nuclear war. This time, however, churchmen from the order escape to the stars to continue their ancient mission.

This famous science fiction novel qualifies for inclusion because there are a few scattered references to space stations in the final part describing the new technological age: "One enemy space station" (229), "missions to...space installations and/or planetary outposts" (246) and "observation satellites" (213).

A387. Mixon, Laura J. *Astropilots*. New York: Scholastic, Inc., 1987. 236 p.

Space pilots are trained at a station in the asteroid belt called the Collegium.

Unseen.

A388. Moon, Elizabeth. *Hunting Party*. New York: Baen, 1993. 364 p.

This novel about a female space adventurer begins with her spaceship docked at Rockhouse Station.

Unseen.

A389. Moorcock, Michael. *The Fireclown.* [also known as *The Winds of Limbo*] Compact SF. London: Richmond Hill Publishing Works, Ltd., 1965. 189 p.

While searching for the mysterious revolutionary known as the Fireclown, Alan Powys and Helen Curtis visit the Monastery of St. Rene Lafayette, a space station run by monks "who practiced a form of scientific mysticism" (92).

The Monastery is Moorcock's joking reference to Scientology, since "Rene Lafayette" was one of L. Ron Hubbard's pseudonyms and the monks are intent on "clearing" other monks so that they can become "Auditors." As the book points out, a "space station monastery circling in space, away from the things of Earth" (98) is a logical enough idea, but this is apparently the only station of its kind in science fiction (although there is an orbiting church briefly mentioned in Joe Haldeman's *Worlds* [q.v.]).

A390. Moore, C. L. *Judgment Night.* In *Judgment Night.* By C. L. Moore. New York: Gnome Press, 1952, p. 3-156. Story originally published in two parts in *Astounding Science-Fiction* (August, 1943), p. 9-52, and (September, 1943), p. 110-161. Also published as *Judgment Night.* New York: Paperback Library, 1965. 156 p.

Circling the capital world of a threatened galactic empire is Cyrille, an artificial "pleasure world" which provides a dazzling variety of environments and activities for the wealthy and privileged. It is first the place where the militant heroine, daughter of the current emperor, enjoys a brief vacation; later, when the enemy converts the world into a weapon, it is the scene for a tense duel between her and two of the enemy leaders.

Cyrille and its incredible facilities are described in lush prose, praised by Sam Moskowitz in his *Seekers of Tomorrow.* In the realm of pleasure stations, Cyrille occupies the same position that James White's Sector Twelve (see his *Hospital Station*) has for hospital stations: a vision of ultimate possibilities.

A391. Moore, Patrick A. *Wheel in Space*. London: Lutterworth, 1956. 152 p.

This novel, one of many juveniles by the author, describes a space station.

Unseen.

A392. Morris, Janet, and David Drake. *Kill Ratio*. New York: Ace, 1987. 268 p.

This action adventure in space involves space habitats.

Unseen.

A393. Morris, Janet, and Chris Morris. *Medusa*. New York: Baen, 1986. 343 p.

This near-future suspense tale includes a visit to Skylab 2 in Earth orbit.

Unseen.

A394. Morris, Janet, and Chris Morris. *Outpassage*. New York: Pageant, 1988. 368 p.

This novel about rebellion and alien contact in space includes references to "orbital stations based around Io" (33) and the "Lunar Orbital Station" (37).

Unseen.

A395. Morris, Janet, and Chris Morris. *Threshold*. New York: Roc, 1991. 250 p.

An adventure involving a space hotel called Threshold.

Unseen; there were two sequels to this book, also unseen:

A396. Morris, Janet, and Chris Morris. *Trust Territory*. New York: Roc, 1992. 261 p.

A397. Morris, Janet, and Chris Morris. *The Stalk*. New York: Roc,

1994. 268 p. [actually in bookstores by December, 1993]

A398. Munro, John. *A Trip to Venus*. London: Jarrold & Sons, 1897. 254 p.

A marvelous invention enables a group of adventurers to fly to the planet Venus, where they encounter a gentle utopian civilization; after a stopover on Mercury and a nearly fatal encounter with the Sun, they return to Earth, though they plan to return to Venus someday.

What interests the modern reader is not this routine space adventure but the speculative discussions that precede it. Although Munro never really hits upon the idea of a motionless or static structure in space, he does see the possibility of observatories in space—"One of these days, I suppose, we astronomers will be packed in bullets and fired into the ether to observe eclipses and comets' tails" (43)—and he envisions "artificial planets" traveling through the cosmos:

> "Independent, free of rent and taxes, these hollow planetoids would serve for schools, hotels, dwelling-houses—"
> "And lunatic asylums."
> "They would relieve the surplus population of the globe." (61)

A399. Murdock, M. S. *Prime Squared*. [*Buck Rogers: Inner Planets Trilogy #2*] New York: TSR, 1990. 276 p.

The second volume in another Buck Rogers trilogy.

Unseen; the first and third volumes are *First Power Play*, by John Miller, and *Matrix Cubed*, by Britton Bloom. There are four other Buck Rogers adventures by M. S. Murdock, unseen, listed below. I include these novels because one of them, *Rebellion 2456*, begins with a ride on a space elevator.

A400. Murdock, M. S. *Rebellion 2456*. [*Buck Rogers: Martian Wars Trilogy #1*] New York: TSR, 1989. 281 p.

A401. Murdock, M. S. *Hammer of Mars*. [*Buck Rogers: Martian Wars Trilogy #2*] New York: TSR, 1989. 288 p.

A402. Murdock, M. S. *Armageddon off Vesta*. [*Buck Rogers: Martian*

Wars Trilogy #3] New York: TSR, 1989. 288 p.

A403. Murdock, M. S., Flint Dille, Robert Sheckley, Abigail Irvine, Ulrike O'Reilly, and Jerry Oltion. *Arrival.* [*A Buck Rogers Book*] New York: TSR, 1988. 320 p.

A404. Naha, Ed. *The Paradise Plot.* New York: Bantam, 1980. 340 p.

A murder mystery that takes place on a space station.

Unseen; the sequel, also unseen, is:

A405. Naha, Ed. *The Suicide Plague.* New York: Bantam, 1982. 279 p.

A406. Neville, Kris. *The Mutants.* New York: Belmont, 1966. 158 p.

The expanded version of "Earth Alert!" (q.v.)

Unseen.

A407. Newman, Richard Louis. *Siege of Orbitor.* New York: Leisure, 1980. 254 p.

Plagued by mysterious acts of sabotage, the space freighter Orbitor is forced to land on Solbase 8, a hollowed-out asteroid orbiting Jupiter. There, the crew is unknowingly recruited to transport a dangerous weapon to Pluto, to be used by disgruntled criminals to take over the Solar System.

If the above plot summary doesn't really make sense, neither, ultimately, does the novel, which leaves many unanswered questions, including why anyone would build an artificial planet with an atmosphere as a home for fifteen criminals. There is one interesting observation about Solbase 8: "The whole concept of placing man in a captive state, and making him feel comfortable and happy, was new—and it was working" (49).

A408. Nighbert, David F. *The Clouds of Magellan: A Science-Fiction Novel.* New York: St. Martin's Press, 1991. 308 p.

A novel about the discovery of a huge alien artifact called the Wheel.

Unseen. This is the sequel to an earlier novel, *Timelapse* (1988), which apparently does not involve space travel.

A409. Niven, Larry [Laurence van Cott Niven], with Stephen Barnes. *The Descent of Anansi*. New York: Tor, 1982. 278 p.

Falling Angel Enterprises, a ragtag collection of old shuttle tanks and other "space junk" orbiting the Moon, declares its independence from America and arranges to sell a shipment of its new super-strong cable to a Japanese company. The space shuttle *Anansi*, carrying the cable to Earth, is sabotaged by a competing Brazilian company which plans to commandeer the shuttle and claim the cable as salvage. However, thanks to the ingenuity of *Anansi*'s crew, the Brazilians are defeated and crew and cable make it safely to Earth.

The novel points out that an independent nation in space, lacking a military ally on Earth, would be highly vulnerable to acts of piracy. Another of its observations: because men will outnumber women in space, infidelity will be a fact of life—"infidelity so rampant that it transcended the abnormal" (66).

A410. Niven, Larry [Laurence van Cott Niven], Jerry Pournelle, and Michael Flynn. *Fallen Angels*. New York: Baen, 1991. 391 p.

A novel involving colonies in space called Space Habs.

Unseen.

A411. North, Rick. [House pseudonym] *The Young Astronauts. The Young Astronauts #1*. New York: Zebra, 1990. 158 p.

A group of young people begin their training for an eventual manned mission to Mars.

Unseen; since this first novel takes place on Earth, references to space stations are no doubt tangential. However, the second and third books, both unseen and listed below, involve, respectively, the youngsters' training on an "orbital platform" circling Earth, and the building of the Mars ship near that platform. There are also three additional volumes in the series, all unseen. These five books are:

A412. North, Rick. [House pseudonym] *Ready for Blastoff. The Young Astronauts #2*. New York: Zebra, 1990. 156 p.

A413. North, Rick. [House pseudonym] *Space Blazers*. *The Young Astronauts #3*. New York: Zebra, 1990. 156 p.

A414. North, Rick. [House pseudonym] *Destination Mars*. *The Young Astronauts #4*. New York: Zebra, 1991. 172 p.

A415. North, Rick. [House pseudonym] *Space Pioneers*. *The Young Astronauts #5*. New York: Zebra, 1991. 174 p.

A416. North, Rick. [House pseudonym] *Citizens of Mars*. *The Young Astronauts #6*. New York: Zebra, 1991. 158 p.

A417. Nourse, Alan E. *Scavengers in Space*. New York: David McKay Co., 1959. 180 p.

After representatives of an evil conglomerate kill an asteroid miner, his two sons and a friend return to his claim site in the asteroids to look for what he found there. They are captured by the conglomerate and taken to their orbit ship headquarters, but, using an amazing weapon found in their father's pack, they manage to escape and return to Mars. A return trip reveals that their father found a cache of ancient alien artifacts, suggesting that an intelligent race once lived on a vanished planet in the asteroid belt.

The only genuine space station in the novel is the Star-Jump satellite station orbiting Mars, briefly seen in the opening chapter, where one son is preparing for the first expedition to the stars. Still, the orbit ship which serves as the conglomerate's headquarters functions as a space station, and the adventures there feature one device—heroes crawling through the ventilator shafts—frequently seen in space station stories ranging from del Rey's *Siege Perilous* to Cherryh's *Downbelow Station* (q.v.).

A418. O'Neill, Gerard K. *2081: A Hopeful View of the Human Future*. New York: Simon and Schuster, 1981. 268 p.

Amidst a great deal of nonfictional discussions of future possibilities, O'Neill offers the first-person narrative of Eric C. Rawson, who travels from a distant space colony to Freeport Seven, a space station orbiting Earth, and then down to the surface of the planet, where he sees progress on various fronts.

Although it qualifies as a work of fiction—barely—O'Neill is basically presenting the same type of bland utopianism found in his *The High Frontier*. Strangely, given his known interests, the space colony and space stations are only minor elements in his narrative, which focuses on future conditions on the planet Earth.

A419. Packard, Edward. *Space Vampire. Choose Your Own Adventure #71*. New York: Bantam, 1987. 118 p.

In this book where readers repeatedly must choose between alternate story continuations, the adventures involving an alien vampire begin on a space station orbiting Mars.

Unseen; since many books in the *Choose Your Own Adventure* series involve outer space settings, there may be other books which refer to space stations. It does not seem to be an avenue of research worth pursuing.

A420. Panshin, Alexei. *Rite of Passage*. New York: Ace, 1968. 254 p.

After establishing colonies of people transported from a devastated Earth, huge inhabited Ships continue to patrol the skies, maintaining control over the colony planets. To limit population, the residents force all young people to land on a planet and survive for thirty days before being accepted as adults. When one young woman on her "rite of passage" visits a planet plotting against the Ships, the residents decide to exterminate the planet—against the wishes of the woman, who hopes that someday attitudes will change.

While I have been familiar with this novel since reading it in 1968, I include it belatedly—and reluctantly—on the grounds that it does indeed involve a community of people permanently living in space. It is difficult to approach this novel in that way, however, because its residents resolutely refuse to accept that they are living permanently in space. That is, although Panshin speaks of the ship being converted into a city, they still refer to it as "the Ship"; their efforts to rigorously limit population makes perfect sense for a spaceship on a long voyage, but little sense for a true space colony, which should seek to expand and nurture offshoots; and their determination to maintain strict control over the colony planets reflects a twisted dedication to their original mission—to set up planetary colonies—instead of a more reasonable resolve to leave the planets alone and build a space civilization. In particular, the final decision to destroy a planet for not-particularly-provocative activities suggests that residents of the Ship are truly becoming irrational. The paradox of the novel is thus that the residents of the Ship are not in a state of "passage"—but they continue to act as if they were.

A421. Patchett, Mary E. *Adam Troy: Astroman*. London: Lutterworth, 1954. 189 p.

This juvenile space adventure includes a visit to a space station, E.E. 1.

Unseen.

A422. Pedler, Kit [Christopher Magnus Howard Pedler], and Gerry Davis. *The Dynostar Menace*. London: Pan, 1975. 191 p.

To solve Earth's energy problems, a harried crew works to make the Dynostar Spacelab into a functioning giant reactor.

Unseen.

A423. Perry, Steve. *The 97th Step*. New York: Ace, 1989. 294 p.

A novel about "orbit worlds."

Unseen.

A424. Place, Marian T. *The First Astrowitches*. New York: Avon Camelot, 1984. 155 p.

This fantasy about young witches includes a visit to a spacelab in Earth orbit.

Unseen.

A425. Pohl, Frederik. *Gateway*. [*Book One of the Heechee Saga*] 1977. New York: Del Rey/Ballantine, 1978. 313 p.

Talking to his computer psychiatrist, Robinette Broadhead recalls his experiences at Gateway—an asteroid spaceport built by ancient aliens known as Heechees. There, "prospectors" board spacecraft which automatically travel faster than light to unknown destinations; some ships never return, some return with dead crewmen, and a few return with valuable artifacts or scientific data. After two uneventful trips, Broadhead's third mission traps his crew near a black hole—but he escapes when the other crewmen are jettisoned and left suspended in time.

Gateway is essentially an asteroid converted into a space station, riddled with tunnels constructed by the Heechee. Among its few permanent residents are a man without legs and a very fat woman—occupants best suited to very low gravity. Pohl describes the special type of walk needed for such an environment: "she sort of pushed herself up on the ball of each foot in turn, and let herself float to the next step...it turned out to be a pretty efficient way of walking in near-zero gravity, but my reflexes kept lousing it up. I suppose you have to be born on Gateway to come by it naturally" (88, 90). He also comments that "Gateway was kind of a trashy place; any scrap of paper or bit of featherweight plastic that was thrown away was likely to float anywhere inside the asteroid" (188), and "It is difficult being drunk in nearly zero gravity. You long for the reassurance of a hundred kilos of solid weight to hold you to the ground" (220).

Note: this is the first of six works to date in the Heechee series: *The Boy Who Would Live Forever: A Novel of Gateway* (2004) and four earlier sequels discussed below.

A426. Pohl, Frederik. *Beyond the Blue Event Horizon*. [*Book Two of the Heechee Saga*] New York: Del Rey/Ballantine, 1980. 309 p.

Millions of years ago, alien Heechee landed on Earth, captured some australopithecines, and placed them on a huge spacecraft later named Heechee Heaven, where they survived. When humans from Gateway arrive, they are killed and turned into computer programs; one explorer gives birth to a child, who grows up roaming through Heechee Heaven and often visiting another Heechee structure, the Food Factory, which flies through the Solar System's Oort Cloud harvesting materials and changing them into foodstuffs. Robin Broadhead finances an expedition to the Food Factory and they meet the child, who takes them to Heechee Heaven where they are captured by the surviving australopithecines; Robin goes there to rescue them and obtains vast new amounts of artifacts and information about the mysterious Heechee.

Both the Food Factory and Heechee Heaven are essentially spacecraft temporarily serving as space stations, and Heechee Heaven is renamed and used as a vehicle in *Heechee Rendezvous* (q.v.); nevertheless, the Food Factory provides an interesting model for a space station which produces food in an unorthodox manner. There is one reference to true space stations; talking about the possible benefits of obtaining "Heechee technology," Robin exclaims, "we can take all the asteroids in the solar system and turn them into Gateways. Build space habitats" (110).

A427. Pohl, Frederik. *Heechee Rendezvous*. [*Book Three of the Heechee Saga*] 1984. New York: Del Rey/Ballantine, 1985. 331 p.

While the Earth suffers through terrorist acts and the prospect of renewed warfare, Robin Broadhead and his wife go off in search of his missing lover, Klara, who is found by Juan (the child of *Beyond the Blue Event Horizon* [q.v.]) and taken with him on his obsessive search for his father, who might be stranded in a black hole. Meanwhile, the alien Heechee are hiding in a black hole to avoid mysterious, powerful aliens called the Assassins who seem to be intent on reversing the expansion of the universe and destroying it in order to recreate it with different physical laws. When their survey ship discovers that humans are traveling and broadcasting their presence throughout the Galaxy, the Heechee intervene to stop Juan and regulate human travel so as to avoid detection.

This third novel in the series reflects the growing military tensions of the 1980s and introduces for the first time genuine, human-built space stations, used for military purposes, of course. The major facility is the High Pentagon, five American space stations in tandem, which Robin visits to obtain information about the missing Klara. In providing background information on these stations, Pohl makes the familiar point that military space stations can only lead to the building of similar facilities by the enemy and an increased chance of war: "At one time, they said, [the High Pentagon] had been the very latest in defense. Its huge nuke-fueled missiles were supposed to be able to zap any enemy missile from fifty thousand miles away. Probably they indeed could—when they were built—and maybe three months after that, until the other fellows began using the same pulse-hardening and radar-decoy tricks and everybody was back to Go. Unfortunately they all 'went,' but that's a whole other story" (234).

A428. Pohl, Frederik. *The Annals of the Heechee*. [*Book Four of the Heechee Saga*] 1987. New York: Del Rey/Ballantine, 1988. 341 p.

Both humans and the alien Heechee are now aware that mysterious malevolent aliens called the Assassins are plotting to destroy and re-create the universe while they hide in an immense, energy-filled black hole called a kugelblitz. They cooperate to construct a space station called the Watch Wheel near the kugelblitz, to look for any alien activity. When a message is sent from Earth to the kugelblitz, Robin Broadhead—now dead and transformed into a computer program—discovers that two Assassins have penetrated human defenses and accompanied two children to Earth. After a brief encounter with them, he is recruited to travel to the kugelblitz and confront the aliens. There, he learns that the Assassins are really not malevolent; they are similar computerized constructs like Robin—now seen as a superior form of life—and their efforts to reshape the universe will ultimately be beneficial to all such beings.

In this fourth novel in the series, two structures seen previously are renamed and given new functions: the Gateway asteroid is now Wrinkle Rock, "converted into an old folks' home" (8-9); and the High Pentagon, now focused on the alien threat, is now the JAWS satellite—for Joint Assassins Watch Services. And we learn that the High Pentagon was once infiltrated by terrorists, another argument against military space stations. There are apparently other occupied structures in space, based on one reference to humans going back "to one of the habitats" (29). As human life seems to evolve toward disembodied, computerized intelligence, space stations become more important reflecting, perhaps, the fact that such beings have no need for terrestrial homes.

A429. Pohl, Frederik. *The Gateway Trip: Tales and Vignettes of the Heechee.* [*Book Five of the Heechee Saga*] New York: Del Rey/Ballantine, 1990. 241 p.

This book retells the central events in the first four books in the series, without specifically naming any of the characters; it includes one extended story about a Heechee prospector on Venus and a number of briefer accounts of explorers from the Gateway asteroids.

Except for the Venus story, Pohl here adds very little to the Heechee series; regarding space stations, there is a brief reference to "astronomical observatories in orbit" (140) and the comment that Heechee Heaven, first seen in *Beyond the Blue Event Horizon* (q.v.) was "not simply a space station" (201).

A430. Pohl, Frederik. *Man Plus*. 1976. New York: Bantam, 1977. 246 p.

As part of a plan by computers to ensure the survival of humanity—and their own survival—an astronaut, Roger Tallaway, is bioengineered to become a cyborg capable of living on the surface of Mars. Despite some preliminary problems and a critical malfunction on Mars, the experiment works, and Tallaway will be the first of a new human race on Mars.

There are several references to space stations in the novel—"the second-generation space station" (4) where Tallaway stayed and where he rescued some cosmonauts, "Space Station Three" (145), and "Space Station Betty" (187); but the novel essentially argues against space stations as a home for man: when the computer analyze the problem of "extraterrestrial colonization" (197) they do not even consider habitations on space—changing people to live on other planetary surfaces is the only hope.

A431. Pohl, Frederik. *Mining the Oort*. New York: Del Rey/Ballantine, 1992. 264 p.

In this novel about mining resources from comets in the Oort Cloud, there are references to "orbital farm habitats" (dust jacket blurb).

Unseen.

A432. Pohl, Frederik, and Jack Williamson. *The Reefs of Space*. [*Starchild #1*] New York: Ballantine, 1964. 188 p. Also in *The Starchild Trilogy*. Garden City: Doubleday, n.d. Novel originally published in *Worlds of If Science Fiction* in 1963.

Under the repressive control of the Plan of Man computer government, a scientist struggles to devise some means of escaping to the Reefs of Space—land masses far beyond Pluto created by tiny organisms called Fusorians. His invention of the "jetless drive" finally persuades the Plan of Man to free him and loosen its grip on humanity.

There is one reference to inhabited "orbiting stations around Mercury" (20)—and a curious one, since some of the action in the sequel, *Starchild* (q.v.), takes place on the surface of Mercury, with no mention of space stations. Then again, little that happens in this entire trilogy bears close examination.

A433. Pohl, Frederik, and Jack Williamson. *Starchild*. [*Starchild #2*]
New York: Ballantine, 1965. 191 p. Also in *The Starchild
Trilogy*. Garden City: Doubleday, n.d. A shorter version of this
novel originally published in *Galaxy Magazine* in 1964.

To protect against rebellious people living in the Reefs of Space, the
Plan of Man government has built a "Spacewall" of space stations beyond Pluto. A spy is sent to one of these facilities, Polaris Station, to
investigate possible treason; but he is instead teleported first to the
Reefs, and then to Earth, as part of the scheme of an intelligent star to
contact humanity and overthrow the Plan of Man.

The idea of a "Spacewall" of space stations is interesting, but the novel
itself is not—an incoherent and illogical sequence of events in which
the visit to the space station is just one poorly sketched episode.

Note: the third novel in the Starchild trilogy, *Rogue Star*, contains no
references to space stations.

A434. Pournelle, Jerry. *Exiles to Glory*. New York: Ace, 1978. 216 p.

A novel featuring characters from the stories "Consort" and "High Justice" (q.v.).

Unseen.

A435. Preuss, Paul. *Breaking Strain. Arthur C. Clarke's Venus Prime
#1*. New York: Avon, 1987. 265 p. Based on "Breaking
Strain." By Arthur C. Clarke.

As part of the work of an ancient society dedicated to perfecting the
human race, a young woman is bioengineered to have enhanced sensory capabilities and has three years of her memory erased. Recovering, she escapes from a treatment facility and starts a new life working
as a Space Board inspector. She is assigned to investigate a mysterious
accident on a cargo ship from Earth to Port Hesperus, the immense
space station orbiting Venus, and uncovers a complex plot involving
the ancient society, a wealthy Earth woman, and the surviving crewman.

This novel is based on and partially incorporates Clarke's 1948 novella, "Breaking Strain," which features no space stations; but Preuss
significantly expands on and updates the story to serve as the basis for

a series of novels. In particular, while Clarke's cargo ship was headed for the surface of Venus, Preuss creates Port Hesperus, a reasonably well realized and described space habitat with a number of insights into the life and problems of such a structure, especially the mood in the station that the heroine senses of "tension in reserve...a certain resentment, the half-conscious undercurrent of brewing discontent" (166), and the flat statement that its policemen were "used to dealing with drunkenness and homicidal rage and other forms of insanity that commonly afflict the human residents of space stations" (230).

Note: this is the first of six Venus Prime novels; the next five, unseen, are listed below.

A436. Preuss, Paul. *Maelstrom. Arthur C. Clarke's Venus Prime #2.* New York: Avon, 1988. 268 p. Based on "Maelstrom II." By Arthur C. Clarke.

A437. Preuss, Paul. *Hide and Seek. Arthur C. Clarke's Venus Prime #3.* New York: Avon, 1989. 281 p. Based on "Hide and Seek." By Arthur C. Clarke.

A438. Preuss, Paul. *The Medusa Encounter. Arthur C. Clarke's Venus Prime #4.* New York: Avon, 1990. 304 p. Based on "A Meeting with Medusa." By Arthur C. Clarke.

A439. Preuss, Paul. *The Diamond Moon. Arthur C. Clarke's Venus Prime #5.* New York: Avon, 1990. 278 p. Based on "Jupiter V." By Arthur C. Clarke.

A440. Preuss, Paul. *The Shining Ones. Arthur C. Clarke's Venus Prime #6.* New York: Avon, 1991. 261 p. Based on "The Shining Ones." By Arthur C. Clarke.

A441. Randall, Marta. *Dangerous Games.* New York: Pocket, 1980. 499 p.

An interstellar space adventure which includes a stopover at a space station.

Unseen, but see comments on the original novella of this name. There was one previous novel with the same setting, also unseen:

A442. Randall, Marta. *Journey.* New York: Pocket, 1978. 324 p.

A443. Randle, Kevin, and Richard Driscoll. *Star Precinct*. New York: Ace, 1992. 185 p.

The adventures of space policemen in the 107th Precinct, "A city drifting in space" (37).

Unseen; this is the first of three books involving this setting. The others, unseen, are:

A444. Randle, Kevin, and Richard Driscoll. *Star Precinct 2: Mind Slayer*. New York: Ace, 1992. 183 p.

A445. Randle, Kevin, and Richard Driscoll. *Star Precinct 3: Inside Job*. New York: Ace, 1992. 182 p.

A446. Reed, Van. [house pseudonym] *Dwellers in Space*. London: Curtis Warren, Ltd., 1953. 159 p.

To preserve peace in the Solar System, a spaceship with crewmen from all planets endlessly patrols space, on the lookout for any signs of dissension.

Unseen.

A447. Resnick, Mike. *Eros Ascending. Tales of the Velvet Comet #1*. New York: Signet, 1984. 254 p.

An accountant, sent to the orbiting brothel the Velvet Comet to doctor the books so as to create fictional mammoth losses and thus close it down, instead falls in love with the madam in charge and works to keep the Velvet Comet in business. Ultimately, the madam is killed and he commits suicide, but the security chief he befriended vows to ensure the brothel's survival.

Despite its stationary orbit, the Velvet Comet is often referred to as a "spaceship" (and only once as a "space station") and there are various plans afloat to give it "motive power." The people living and working there seem reasonably well adjusted, but no one seems to regard it as a permanent home—the accountant and the madam dream of retiring to a rural planet.

Note: this is the first of four Velvet Comet novels. The third, *Eros Descending*, is discussed below; the other two, both unseen, are:

A448. Resnick, Michael. *Eros at Zenith. Tales of the Velvet Comet #2.* New York: Signet, 1984. 255 p.

A449. Resnick, Michael. *Eros at Nadir. Tales of the Velvet Comet #4.* New York: Signet, 1986. 252 p.

A450. Resnick, Michael. *Eros Descending. Tales of the Velvet Comet #3.* New York: Signet, 1985. 250 p.

A crusading preacher, determined to shut down the space brothel Velvet Comet, instead develops a lustful attraction for an alien prostitute there and is disgraced. His son and successor goes to the Velvet Comet and threatens to destroy it with a nuclear bomb unless it closes—and his demand is fulfilled.

The novel comments, "It has often been said that no man is safe from an assassin who is willing to sacrifice his own life. The same is true of the *Comet*" (244)—and, presumably, of any space station. The novel event in this third Velvet Comet adventure is a horse race in space between the recreated Secretariat and Seattle Slew.

A451. Reynolds, Mack. *Chaos in Lagrangia.* Edited by Dean Ing. New York: Tor, 1984. 256 p.

Apparently a utopia, the L-5 space habitat Grissom is actually beset by boredom and a declining birth rate, and threatened by a totalitarian coalition of native malcontents, Soviet agents, and Elitists from a dictatorial space habitat in the asteroid belt. The crisis is averted when it is proposed that the colonists build starships instead of new habitats, so the sense of boredom and lack of purpose can be alleviated by the exploration of deep space.

In its way, the book is a striking indictment of the whole idea of space habitats: they become boring to younger residents, are vulnerable to all types of attack, are highly susceptible to dictatorial takeover, and can only be revitalized by devoting themselves to space exploration, not space habitation. Another Reynolds novel in a similar critical vein is *Trojan Orbit* (q.v.).

A452. Reynolds, Mack. *Lagrange Five.* New York: Bantam, 1979. 227 p.

A novel featuring a space habitat at the L-5 position in space.

Unseen.

A453. Reynolds, Mack. *Satellite City*. New York: Ace, 1975. 238 p.

A government agent investigates the "hotel wheel" of Satellite City, a freewheeling haven for gambling, prostitution, and other illicit activities which he discovers is actually under Mafia control.

Satellite City is said to have three wheels—an additional "science wheel" for research and a "hospital wheel"—but only the hotel wheel is visited or described. The novel is an interesting picture of the ultimate free enterprise in space—a satellite outside the control of any terrestrial government. For another scenario involving a Mafia-controlled space station, see Reynolds and Ing's *Trojan Orbit*.

A454. Reynolds, Mack, with Dean Ing. *Trojan Orbit*. New York: Baen, 1985. 374 p.

A journalist, an American spy, and a jewel thief on the lam, simultaneously arriving at space colony Island One, gradually discover that the whole project is a gigantic racket run by the Mafia—a plan to milk billions of dollars from innocent investors, deliberately let the project fail, and then take it over and turn it into a freewheeling "sin city" in space. After the criminals are exposed and removed, they and others decide to remain in Island One and dedicate themselves to creating a viable space colony.

This can be viewed both as an updating and a "prequel" to Reynolds's *Satellite City* (q.v.), explaining how and why the Mafia might get involved in building a space station (and, in an interesting sidelight, how and why they might also get involved with running a university). While the final revelation of deliberate sabotage weakens the case somewhat, Reynolds and Ing go out of their way to show how unrealistic and visionary planners of space colonies are—how they are ignoring innumerable unsolved problems. In what may be the book's key passage, one character wonders what would have happened if, in 1903, the Wright brothers had been offered unlimited financing to build a supersonic jet—of course they would have failed. The point is that space colonization can be achieved eventually, but is impractical in the near future.

A455. Richardson, Robert S. *Second Satellite*. New York: McGraw-Hill Book Co., 1956. 191 p.

A young lad spends the summer helping his astronomer father locate, and track the orbit of, a newly discovered small natural satellite orbiting the Earth.

There is a brief discussion of a space station as the next step in space exploration: "a space station revolving thousands of miles above the earth, equipped with every type of instrument for making scientific observations. It will be our stepping stone to the planets. Our springboard into deep space" (125). But because building such a station would be hard and expensive—"Ten billion maybe" (125)—the natural satellite is seen as a better alternative: "suppose there was already a vehicle out there in space revolving around the Earth. A natural satellite station all assembled" (126).

A456. Richmond, Walt, and Leigh Richmond. *Challenge the Hellmaker*. New York: Ace, 1976. 202 p. Portions of the novel were previously published as "Where I Wasn't Going." *Analog Science Fact/Science Fiction*, 72 (October, 1963), p. 17-43, (November, 1963), p. 48-73.

A space adventure story featuring a space station.

Unseen.

A457. Robinett, Stephen. *Stargate*. 1976. New York: Signet, 1977. 186 p. Originally published in *Analog Science Fiction/Science Fact* in 1974 (as by Tak Hallus).

This novel about achieving a teleportation station in space features the space station Merryweather Enterprize.

Unseen.

A458. Robinson, Kim Stanley. *Icehenge*. New York: Berkley Publishing Group, 1984. 262 p.

A novel about the discovery of an alien structure mentions space habitats.

Unseen.

A459. Robinson, Kim Stanley. *The Memory of Whiteness: A Scientific Romance*. New York: Tor, 1985. 351 p.

A novel involving space habitats.

Unseen.

A460. Robinson, Kim Stanley. *Red Mars*. New York: Bantam Spectra, 1992. 519 p.

This novel about colonizing Mars features the construction of a space elevator on Mars with communities at its ends called Clarke and Shef-field, although the facility is destroyed during an unsuccessful rebellion.

It is interesting that the construction of a space elevator, providing easy transportation to and from space, is viewed as key to the economic development of Mars, and that rebels determined to overthrow what they regard as a hostile foreign government would destroy that space elevator as part of their abortive revolt.

Note: this novel's sequel is listed below; a third volume was *Blue Mars* (1996), and a related work was *The Martians* (1999).

A461. Robinson, Kim Stanley. *Green Mars*. New York: Bantam Spectra, 1993. 535 p.

As Mars becomes more earthlike and more densely populated, a second revolution against Earth is successful, and Mars becomes an independent world.

In large part, this novel is a retelling of the story of *Red Mars*, this time with a happy ending; one noteworthy difference is that this time, the rebels attempt to seize the rebuilt space elevator, recognizing its value, instead of destroying it.

A462. Robinson, Spider, and Jeanne Robinson. *Stardance*. 1979. New York: Dell, 1980. 278 p. Based on the story of the same name originally published in *Analog Science Fiction/Science Fact* in 1977.

A dancer travels to the Skyfac orbiting complex to develop the art of zero-gravity dancing; when strange aliens approach Earth who seem to communicate through movement, she confronts them and, with her dance, persuades them to depart. Later, her cameraman, her sister, and other dancers set up a dance studio in orbit; but when the aliens are spotted near Saturn, they are recruited to come on the diplomatic expedition as "interpreters." Through dance, they establish rapport with the aliens and learn that the aliens' mission is to initiate and guide the development of intelligent life; they planted the Earth people, and now wish them to use the organic material in Titan's atmosphere as a second skin enabling them to live in space and become essentially a new type of being. The novel ends with the six dancers transforming themselves.

This novel is best described as two intertwining stories: an original and absorbing effort to describe what sorts of conventions and styles might be developed in zero-gravity dancing; and an absurd and derivative tale of first contact with aliens. Its chief interest lies in its descriptions of the new attitudes that might come with life in space: the need to "think spherically" (94), the feeling that "Space is God's Throne Room, and no human problem has significance within it for long" (144), and the suggestion that negative human attitudes are rooted in feelings of weight—"the word *depression* is tied to gravity" and "the very word gravity has come to be a symptom for humorlessness" (199).

Note: this is the first book in a trilogy: the third book is *Starmind* (1995), and the second book, unseen, is:

A463. Robinson, Spider, and Jeanne Robinson. *Starseed.* New York: Ace, 1991. 247 p.

A464. Rockwell, Carey. [pseudonym] *Danger in Deep Space. A Tom Corbett Space Cadet Adventure [#2].* New York: Grosset & Dunlap, 1953. 209 p.

Tom Corbett's team is assigned to travel to Tara, a planet orbiting Alpha Centauri, although they first go to the space station orbiting Venus and Venustown on its surface. They discover an asteroid made of copper, a badly needed material, and manage to move it to the Solar System, fighting off villains who are determined to get it.

The Venus space station is "a huge metal ball...a compact city. Living quarters, communications rooms, repair shops, weather observations, meteor information, everything to serve the great fleet of Solar Guard and merchant spaceships" (33). This first station was built simply because Venus had no natural satellites, but there are plans to construct more of them.

Note: There are a total of eight Tom Corbett books, but none of the others seem to refer to space stations, even one that takes place on Venus. At least one episode of the related series *Tom Corbett, Space Cadet*, "Space Station of Danger" (q.v.), did involve a space station.

A465. Roddenberry, Gene. *Star Trek—The Motion Picture: A Novel*. Based on the screenplay by Harold Livingston and the story by Alan Dean Foster. New York: Pocket, 1979. 252 p.

When a mysterious alien structure called V'Ger approaches the Earth, Captain Kirk takes command of the *Enterprise* and goes out to confront the strange visitor.

This novelization of the film (q.v.) provides a few more details about Epsilon Nine, the space station that first announces, and later is destroyed by, the approach of V'Ger. Also, the elaborate drydock area where the *Enterprise* is being refurbished is here given a name—the Centroplex.

A466. Rohan, Michael Scott. *Run to the Stars*. London: Arrow, 1982. 295 p.

A novel about a space colony of Scots.

Unseen.

A467. Rowley, Christopher. *The Founder*. New York: Del Rey/Ballantine, 1989. 256 p.

This novel about an interstellar colony ship begins at Oberon's Eye, a space habitat near Uranus.

Unseen. This is the first of four volumes in a series; the other three, all unseen, were:

A468. Rowley, Christopher. *The War for Eternity*. New York: Del Rey/Ballantine, 1983. 337 p.

A469. Rowley, Christopher. *The Black Ship*. New York: Del Rey/Ballantine, 1985. 310 p.

A470. Rowley, Christopher. *To a Highland Nation*. New York: Del Rey/Ballantine, 1993. 280 p.

A471. Ruben, William S. *Dionysus: The Ultimate Experiment.* New York: Manor, 1977. 208 p. A shortened version was published as *Weightless in Gaza* in 1970.

To test the ability of man to have sex and reproduce successfully in space, a man and a woman are sent on an orbital mission.

The ultimate goal behind this experiment is space colonization, involving either Earth's undesirables (now kept underground in a vegetable-like state) or chosen members of the elite. There is also a brief mention of the American space station Alpha orbiting the Moon, which "had had little to do in its ten years of operation."

A472. Sakers, Don, editor. *Carmen Miranda's Ghost Is Haunting Space Station Three.* New York: Baen, 1990. 306 p.

This is an anthology of original stories inspired by Leslie Fish's song, "Carmen Miranda's Ghost" (q.v.), which generally feature space stations being haunted by the ghost of Carmen Miranda.

Since these stories do not really involve a common background and are by different authors, I will discuss them individually in Part B. In addition to the Fish song, stories included in the anthology are: B. W. Clough, "Provisional Solution"; Bruce B. Barnett, "Basket Case"; Eric Blackburn, "The Entertainer"; Julia Ecklar, "Carmen Miranda and the Maracas of Death"; Ron Robinson, "Shadows on the Wall"; Susan Shwartz, "Confessional Booths"; Anne McCaffrey, "If Madam Likes You..."; Melissa Scott and Lisa A. Barnett, "The Carmen Miranda Gambit"; S. N. Lewitt, "The Souse American Way"; Amanda Allen, "Rolling Down the Floor"; L. D. Woeltjen, "The Never-Ending Battle"; Don Sakers, "The Man Who Travelled in Rocketships"; Leslie Fish, "Bertocci's Proof"; C. J. Cherryh, "Wings"; Esther Friesner, "In the Can"; Don Sakers, "Tarawa Rising"; Betsy Marks and Anne G. DeMaio, "And Now the News:"; B. W. Clough, "La Vita Nuova"; and Mary L. Mand, "The Pigeon Sisters on Space Station Three."

A473. Savage, Blake. [pseudonym; author's actual name listed in references as either John Blaine or H. L. Goodwin] *Rip Foster in Ride the Gray Planet.* [also published as *Assignment in Space with Rip Foster* and *Rip Foster Rides the Gray Planet*] 1952. New York: Golden Press, 1969. 253 p.

After finishing his six-year training program on a space platform orbiting Earth, Planeteer Rip Foster is assigned to land on an asteroid made of pure thorium and guide it back to Earth orbit. However, the enemy Connies also want the asteroid and they attack it twice, forcing Rip to take extreme measures—including the construction and detonation of an atomic bomb. When the asteroid reaches Earth orbit, Rip recuperates in a space platform hospital and learns of his next assignment.

The space station only appears in the first and last chapters of this book, otherwise devoted to adventures in space. One interesting note is the description of "silly dillies," Mercurian creatures that "could drill through the shell of a space station" (166).

Note: The packaging of the book, and the ending in which Rip's next assignment is described, indicate that this book was designed to be the first in a series of books about Rip Foster, though no others ever appeared.

A474. Schofield, Sandy. *The Big Game. Star Trek: Deep Space Nine #4*. New York: Pocket, 1993. 276 p.

An original novel involving space station Deep Space Nine.

Unseen.

A475. *Science Fiction*. [no author given; now attributed to John Silbersack] No-Frills Books. New York: Jove Publications, 1981. 58 p.

Space Cadet Alex Harrison, stationed on board the space station Ondine, departs for a series of cosmos-spanning adventures which eventually lead to a confrontation with superior aliens determined to wipe out the human race.

Significantly, this "generic" science fiction novel—advertised as being "complete with everything"—includes a space station. The novel, unimportant in itself, provides further evidence that the space station may indeed be one of the central subjects of science fiction.

A476. Scortia, Thomas N. *Earthwreck!* New York: Fawcett, 1974. 224 p.

After a global nuclear and biological war destroys all human life on Earth, the crews of an American and a Russian space station must work together on a plan to convert one station into a spaceship which will fly to Mars, where the human race will be able to carry on existence.

The first part of Scortia's novel has some interesting comments on the appearance and functioning of the two stations. In connection with a proposed lunar colony as a last refuge for humanity, mention is made of Toynbee's idea of "arrested civilizations"—which cannot develop because all energies are directed to survival—a concept that also seems applicable to a space station.

A477. Scott, Alan. *Project Dracula*. London: Sphere, 1971. 319 p.

This novel begins with an explosion on a space station.

Unseen.

A478. Searls, Hank. *The Pilgrim Project*. New York: McGraw Hill Book Co., 1964. 274 p.

With the American Apollo program still in its early stages, the Russians signal that they are ready to send a man to the Moon by putting a space platform in Earth orbit; soon, a cosmonaut is launched from the platform and orbits the Moon—obvious preparation for a manned landing. In a desperate attempt to get an American to the Moon first, the President revives the top-secret "Pilgrim Project"—a plan to send one American to the Moon in a Mercury capsule and strand him there for a year with a crude shelter until the technology for returning him is perfected. When the astronaut's doctor prematurely reveals the Pilgrim Project, the Russians attempt their manned landing early, but the cosmonaut crashes and dies. The American then lands, sights the shelter, and seems ready to survive the ordeal.

Even as America was planning a different approach, Searls envisions the Russians attempting a lunar landing in what was originally thought to be the logical way—by first putting a space station in orbit and launching the Moon mission from the station. And the station is seen as crucial to the Russian effort: the astronaut's wife, hoping for events that might cancel the Pilgrim Project, thinks at one point, "Maybe the Russian platform would fail" (123).

Note: the film *Countdown* (1968) was based on this novel, but it does not contain (to my knowledge) any references to space stations.

A479. Sheffield, Charles. *Between the Strokes of Night*. New York: Baen, 1985. 346 p.

Researchers attempting to eliminate sleep are transported to Salter Station orbiting Earth just after a fatal nuclear war breaks out. Soon, three huge colonies move out to other star systems, while scientists at the Station discover S-space: a slowed-down state of activity which enables humans to live for thousands of years. A young man on a colonized world engages in the Planetfest—a series of games secretly designed to recruit new people to enter S-space, since those there cannot reproduce. In their space travels, he and his friends investigate the civilization of the Immortals and finally go to Gulf City, a huge facility in deep space. There, they are asked to start a new research project to study big new problems: mysterious beings in space and the apparently imminent death of the universe.

As first envisioned by Tsiolkovsky, a space station here serves to keep the human race alive after a disaster on Earth. In Sheffield's far future, humans in S-space must spend almost all of their time in space because of physiological changes in their bodies; hence, they live in Salter Station, spaceships, and Gulf City. But S-space is pictured as dimming human sensations and reactions; only people in normal time (N-space) seem able to do productive research and accomplish things. Thus, the novel ends with a division of labor: some stay in S-space or the even more extended T-space to monitor future events, while others return to N-space to do scientific research.

A480. Sheffield, Charles. *Cold As Ice*. 1992. New York: Tor, 1993. 372 p.

The novel about the Solar System recovering from a devastating space war includes a stopover at Abacus, a small space station orbiting the Jovian moon Callisto.

Unseen; a sequel to the novel is *The Ganymede Club* (1995).

A481. Sheffield, Charles. *The McAndrew Chronicles*. New York: Tor, 1983. 243 p.

This collection of linked stories involving a genius's efforts to perfect an inertialess drive includes a spaceship taking off from the "Libration Colony station" (10).

Unseen, but see comments on "All the Colors of the Vacuum," one of the stories in this collection. An expanded version of this collection, *One Man's Universe*, was published in 1993.

A482. Sheffield, Charles. *The Nimrod Hunt*. New York: Baen, 1986. 401 p.

A number of powerful artificial beings, the Morgan Constructs, apparently go insane and flee into unknown space, where they represent a danger to the four known intelligent species (including the human race). Teams consisting of one member of each species are assembled to track down and kill the Constructs, but two teams, while subduing one of them, somehow merge to form group minds.

Space facilities linked by teleportation—including Cobweb Station where the Constructs are built, and Horus, the hollowed-out asteroid where one team member is trained—are only minor parts of this story, which pays more attention to the decadent Earth and the alien world of Travancore. Sheffield also makes the familiar point that space colonization will be a winnowing process, with only the least capable remaining on Earth.

A483. Sheffield, Charles. *One Man's Universe*. New York: Tor, 1993. 308 p.

An expanded version of the collection *The McAndrew Chronicles* (q.v.), including two new stories about McAndrew.

Unseen.

A484. Sheffield, Charles. *The Web between the Worlds*. New York: Ace, 1979. 274 p.

Darius Regalo, a space entrepreneur living in Atlantis—an asteroid transformed into a water-filled space station—hires Rob Merlin to build a Beanstalk—a cable anchored on one end to the Earth and on the other to an asteroid and powersat in geosynchronous orbit, to be used as an elevator from Earth to space. While doing so, Merlin investigates mysterious research involving Regulo's assistant Morel and Caliban, an intelligent squid living in Atlantis.

Despite public attention about the coincidental appearance of this novel at the same time as Arthur C. Clarke's "space elevator" novel,

The Fountains of Paradise (q.v.), the real fascination of Sheffield's novel is Atlantis—a space habitat where the living quarters look out on an immense aquarium teeming with undersea life. Given the feasibility of space colonies, the idea seems logical enough—if one is building a closed ecosystem, one might as well fill it with water as with air. As for the Beanstalk, this novel is primarily concerned with the engineering problem of building one; for a picture of a space elevator in operation, see Sheffield's "Skystalk."

A485. Shirley, John. *Eclipse*. New York: Bluejay, 1985. 341 p.

A novel about a futuristic, decadent Earth which occasionally deals with space colonies.

Unseen; Norman Spinrad's "Dreams of Space" mentions this novel as one of a group of works presenting a new vision of life in space, but if the excerpt "Freezone" (q.v.) is any guide, the novel has little to do with space.

Note: this is the first of three novels of a trilogy collectively entitled *The Song Called Youth*. The other two, both unseen, are:

A486 Shirley, John. *Eclipse Penumbra*. New York: Warner, 1988. 322 p.

A487 Shirley, John. *Eclipse Corona*. New York: Warner, 1990. 293 p.

A488. Silverberg, Robert. *Regan's Planet*. New York: Pyramid, 1964. 141 p.

A multinational businessman is recruited to arrange for the planned 1992 Columbian Exposition, or World's Fair. He decides that the best possible setting would be a huge space station in Earth orbit, and, battling against various political, financial, and scientific problems, he finally manages to get the station built—and the World's Fair begins.

Interestingly enough, the station, because of rumors of sabotage and other difficulties, seems destined to be a failure until Regan has the inspiration to import a group of Martians as an exhibit, which attracts enough visitors to make the fair a success. This again suggests that the discovery of alien life, not simply the chance to live in space, will be the most compelling motive for space travel.

Note: a sequel of sorts to this novel is Silverberg's *World's Fair 1992* (q.v.).

A489. Silverberg, Robert. [as by Ivar Jorgenson] *Starhaven*. New York: Avalon, 1958. 220 p.

This space adventure takes place on an artificial planet.

Unseen.

A490. Silverberg, Robert. *World's Fair 1992*. 1970. New York: Ace, 1982. 240 p.

Young Bill Hastings wins a job at the Martian Pavilion on the World's Fair Satellite, caring for and observing the Martians along with other scientists. Later, when fair attendance is down, Regan follows up on Hastings's theory of life on Pluto and arranges for him to accompany an expedition to Pluto to locate and bring back Plutonian life forms for exhibit at the Fair.

Despite obvious differences between Clarke's Inner Station and the World's Fair Satellite, Silverberg's sequel to *Regan's Planet* (q.v.) is similar to *Islands in the Sky*: a teenager wins a trip to a space station, is initially excited to be there, but ultimately decides that he really wants to travel to other worlds. It is interesting to note that Regan must twice resort to kidnapped aliens as a way to attract tourists to the Fair because of recurring rumors of sabotage; as one character explains, there is no way to guarantee the safety of a space station from determined saboteurs, and even the fear of sabotage can have a disastrous effect on its functioning.

A491. Simak, Clifford D. *Empire*. New York: World Editions, 1951. 160 p.

While Chambers, the president of an enormous power company, strives to gain control of the entire Solar System, an idealistic scientist and his businessman friend manage to develop a new type of power, which enables them to spy on Chambers, raise money, rescue one political leader imprisoned "on a prison ship" (66), inspire revolts on various worlds, and ultimately defeat Chambers and establish democratic governments—and cheap power—throughout the system.

Though there are also prisons on planetary surfaces, the most severe form of incarceration is "the prison ships that plied to the edge of the system clear to the orbit of Pluto...[and] In near Mercury" (7, 66)—clearly space stations of a sort. Of these ships, "from which no one can escape" (102), the most dreaded are "the Vulcan Fleet ships [which apparently orbit close to the Sun], the hell-ships of the prison fleet. There were confined only the most vicious and most depraved of the Solar System's criminals. [A prisoner] would be forced to work under the flaming whip-lashes of a Sun that hurled such intense radiations that mere spacesuits were no protection at all" (111). A brief scene involving a prisoner in one of these ships provides a familiar glimpse of the dark side of life in space: "Sometimes he had thought he would go mad. The everlasting routine, the meaningless march of hours...endless monotony, an existence without a purpose. Men buried alive in space" (101).

A492. Simmons, Dan. *The Fall of Hyperion*. New York: Doubleday and Company, 1991. 517 p.

In this sequel to *Hyperion* (q.v.), while the pilgrims individually confront the mysterious Shrike, leaders of the galactic government are fighting a losing battle against the space-dwelling Ousters; however, when they discover that the Artificial Intelligences of the Core are actually responsible for the attack, they destroy all of the "farcasters" that secretly harbor those intelligences, so that humanity can start again as a true spacefaring civilization.

One pilgrim visits the Ousters to negotiate and sees they have somehow constructed a river that flows through space, and one passage memorably describes all of the various space structures they inhabit:

> massive comet farms, their dusty surfaces broken by the geometries of hard vacuum crops; zero-g globe cities, great irregular spheres of transparent membrane looking like improbably amoebae filled with busy flora and fauna; ten-klick-long thrust clusters, accreted over centuries, their innermost modules and lifecans and 'cologies looking like something stolen from O'Neill's Boondoggle and the dawn of the space age; wandering forests covering hundreds of kilometers like immense, floating kelp beds...hollowed-out asteroids long since abandoned by their residents, now given over to automated manufacturing and heavy-metal reprocessing...immense spherical docking globes, given scale

only by the torchship- and cruiser-size warcraft flitting around their surfaces like spermatazoa attacking an egg; and, most indelible, organisms which the river came near or which flew near the river...organisms which might have been manufactured or born but probably were both, great butterfly shapes, opening wings of energy to the sun.... (436-437)

A493. Simmons, Dan. *Hyperion*. New York: Doubleday and Company, 1989. 482 p.

In a future galactic civilization of many inhabited worlds, seven pilgrims go to the planet Hyperion to confront a mysterious being called the Shrike who is apparently traveling from the future to the past on an unknown mission.

Though there is one mention of space habitats in Earth's past—"Orbit City" and "the European arcologies" (183)—Simmon's future civilization has mastered planet-to-planet teleportation, the "farcasters," and seems to live exclusively on planets. However, their enemies the Ousters, distantly descended from humanity, do live in "O'Neill cities" (140) and "their concept of an atmosphere was the eight-klick pressurized tube of a can city" (159). An interesting description of the Ousters' civilization implies that planetary life causes stagnation, while space life leads to progress: "I will not try to describe the beauty of life in a Swam—their zero-gravity globe cities and comet farms and thrust clusters, their micro-orbital forests...the Ousters have done what Web humanity has not in the past millennia: *evolved*. While we live in our derivative cultures, pale reflections of Old Earth life, the Ousters have explored new dimensions of aesthetics and ethics and biosciences and art and all the things that must change and grow to reflect the human soul" (468).

Note: the sequel to this novel is *The Fall of Hyperion* (q.v.), and there were two additional volumes in the series, *Endymion* (1996) and *The Rise of Endymion* (1997).

A494. Simmons, Geoffrey S. *The Adam Experiment*. 1978. New York: Berkley, 1979. 221 p.

This novel begins on an orbital space lab.

Unseen.

A495. Siodmak, Curt. *City in the Sky*. New York: Putnam, 1974. 218 p.

International criminals in a small space prison circling the City in the Sky, an immense space community, escape and attempt to take over the larger satellite, but are ultimately recaptured.

Siodmak's novel praises the City in the Sky as a truly international venture, with a Board of Directors representing investor nations; he also suggests that such international control could produce paralysis in crisis situations. One of Siodmak's concerns is legal issues—the need for an independent judiciary, and the need for a space prison; he also throws out the unique idea that satellites and space stations might someday be incorporated into horoscopes, or even launched for astrological purposes.

A496. Siodmak, Curt. *Skyport*. New York: Signet, 1961, 1959. 159 p.

While two rival hotel magnates struggle for control over the project, a scientist works to build the world's first space hotel in orbit around the Earth. Amidst their continuing conflicts and other problems, the station is finally constructed and put into operation.

Siodmak's message seems to be that it will take both starry-eyed idealists—the head scientist and his architect friend—and ruthless businessmen—the hotel bosses Wharton and Kettner—to complete so massive a project as a space station. There is also a debate of continuing relevance concerning the design and appearance of the station: the architect argues for futuristic, strange decor as befitting a new environment, while Wharton wants the facility to look as much like a terrestrial hotel as possible, to make guests feel comfortable.

A497. Slote, Alfred. *Omega Station*. New York: Harper and Row, 1983. 147 p.

Dr. Drago, a mad scientist, has taken over a space station to produce nuclear weapons, kill all humans, and populate the universe with his robots; but Jack Jameson and his robot companion, Danny One Jameson, investigate some missing persons, manage to find and penetrate his station, and foil his plans. With Drago defeated, they plan to turn the space station into a summer camp for children.

Slote pictures fourteen space colonies, all with different letters, circling the Earth, along with some abandoned older stations orbiting the Moon, one of which is occupied by Dr. Drago. There are two references to the dangerous life of a space colonist; when the air leaves the station as its dome is opened, the hero rushes for an air helmet, thinking, "Everyone practices doing this in the space colonies" (123); and someone later comments that "A meteorite could crash into this place" (141).

Note: this is one of five Jack Jameson adventures written by Slote; the others do not seem to involve space stations.

A498. Smith, George O. *Venus Equilateral*. With an Introduction by John W. Campbell, Jr. New York: Prime Press, 1947. 455 p. Originally published in *Astounding Science Fiction* in 1942, 1943, 1944, and 1945.

To facilitate communications between Venus and Earth, a space station is placed in Venus's orbit so as to form a perfect triangle with those two planets; thus, with the station as a relay, the two planets can always send radio messages to each other. The crew must deal with a number of problems, including an overbearing new leader sent from Earth, a space pirate who tries to take over the station by siege, the urgent need to communicate with a lost spacecraft, and financial intrigue involving a corrupt Earth businessman. Finally, when technological advances make the station unnecessary, the crew leaves the station, arranging that the scheming businessman must remain behind, alone at the station as a virtual prisoner.

As reinforced by Arthur C. Clarke's introduction to the expanded anthology (listed below), these stories have been a powerful influence on other writers and their depictions of space stations. What is interesting is that the crewmen seem entirely happy to be at Venus Equilateral, totally occupied with their technical problems and fun-filled evenings; one woman says, "I've never really appreciated the fact that Venus Equilateral is really just a big steel capsule immersed in the vacuum of interplanetary space.... It's so much like a town on Terra" (364). And yet, the minute the station is no longer needed they immediately decide to return to Earth—"man's natural environment: a natural planet" (376). Clearly, despite their apparent adjustment to it, there is something unsatisfying about life in space.

Note: This collection contained ten stories: "QRM Interplanetary" (1942), "Calling the Empress" (1943), "Recoil" (1943), "Off the

Beam" (1944), "The Long Way" (1944), "Beam Pirate" (1944), "Firing Line" (1944), "Special Delivery" (1945), and "Pandora's Millions" (1945), all originally published in *Astounding*; and "Mad Holiday," a tenth story written especially for the Prime Press edition. In assembling these stories as a novel, Smith also wrote new linking material. Two other stories of that period, "Lost Art" and "Identity," briefly refer to Venus Equilateral, and years later, Smith wrote one more story about its crew, "The External Triangle"; these three additional stories are discussed separately in Part B below. In 1976, all thirteen stories were published in one volume, with additional new linking material, as:

A499. Smith, George O. *The Complete Venus Equilateral*. With an Introduction by Arthur C. Clarke. 1976. New York: Del Rey/Ballantine, 1980. 468 p. Previously published with fewer stories as *Venus Equilateral*. New York: Prime Press, 1947.

A500. Smith, Robert. [pseudonym] *Riders to the Stars*. Based on the screenplay by Curt Siodmak. New York: Ballantine, 1953. 166 p.

To discover why meteors—but not rockets—survive going into space, three men are rocketed into space to catch meteors for examination.

This novel is relevant only because of the stated long-range goal of the program: to establish a "space platform" a thousand miles up in the sky to "eliminate war."

Note: the film *Riders to the Stars* (1954) is not included in Part C of the bibliography because, unlike its novelization, it contains no references to space stations.

A501. Snodgrass, Melinda M. *Circuit*. New York: Berkley, 1986. 232 p.

A devious United States president declares outer space to be the Fifteenth Circuit and appoints an old friend to be judge as a ploy to reassert American control over the increasingly independent space stations and colonies. At first, Judge Cabot Huntington rules as the President wishes, but when his ruling leads to Soviet destruction of a rebellious lunar base, he becomes sympathetic to the space colonists and finally rules in their favor.

In yet another analogy to the American West, one character declares, "The advent of a decent judicial system has always been the taming of any frontier" (11-12). Yet the emerging thesis of the novel is that space needs its own kind of justice, and that government on Earth has grown too corrupt and self-serving.

Note: another judicial drama set in a space station is the episode of *Star Trek: The Next Generation* episode, "The Measure of a Man" (q.v.), written by Snodgrass, who at one point served as the story editor for the series. This novel is the first of three Circuit novels. The others, both unseen, are:

A502. Snodgrass, Melinda M. *Circuit Breaker*. New York: Berkley, 1987. 263 p.

A503. Snodgrass, Melinda M. *Final Circuit*. New York: Berkley, 1988. 244 p.

A504. Stabenow, Dana. *A Handful of Stars*. New York: Ace, 1991. 215 p.

In this sequel to *Second Star* (q.v.), Star Svensdotter, her husband Caleb, her sister, and other friends from the habitat travel to the asteroid belt, where they start sending mineral-rich asteroids back to Earth to help construct a second habitat; they also plan to rebuild selected asteroids to sell to oppressed peoples on Earth as "worlds of their own." The discovery of an oil reservoir in one asteroid suggests that there was once a planet with intelligent life in the belt, whose survivors traveled to Earth and helped establish civilization. When Star's husband is killed, she becomes depressed and momentarily seems to lose her legendary self-confidence.

There is not much new here—some language describing the asteroids is identical to that found in the first novel—and the story's most novel feature is that Star gives birth to twins, so that she now functions as a space-faring superwoman with babies in tow, adding to the improbability of these events. She is also reunited with her mother and discovers she has a ten-year-old, grown from one of her donated eggs. None of these things changes Star, however, who remains an irritatingly inert character, even when her blundering arrogance leads directly to her husband's death.

A505. Stabenow, Dana. *Second Star*. New York: Ace, 1991. 202 p.

Star Svensdotter is the administrator in charge of preparing space habitat Ellfive for the arrival of colonists. There are problems with a saboteur and a hostile journalist; Ellfive is taken over by soldiers of the Space Patrol, so she must fight to regain control; and an alien being called a Librarian arrives to make the habitat's computer system sentient and to take Star's niece with it so she can learn more about the galaxy. When Ellfive becomes independent and the colonists start arriving, Star and her new lover Caleb decide to go to the asteroid belt to find resources for the construction of a second habitat.

This is a thoroughly routine space habitat novel, as the bold pioneers mastering life in space must fight off various terrestrial troglodytes: anti-science "Luddites" who wish to stop space exploration, conniving Earth politicians who are ready to stab them in the back to win the next election, and narrow-minded soldiers who see space only as a military base. The habitat itself is a typical suburb in space, and, like Allan Steele's novels, *Second Star* is filled with references to older science fiction, including Clarke, Asimov, *Star Trek*, and *Star Wars*; Robert A. Heinlein, however, is the major influence here. Heinlein Park is a prominent locale in the habitat, the novel quotes from *Time Enough for Love*, the device of the computer turned sentient ally is derived from *The Moon Is a Harsh Mistress* (as is also the case in Allan Steele's *Clarke County, Space* [q.v.]), and the entire philosophy of the novel—the need for naturally superior people to escape from the company of ordinary people by continually fleeing deeper and deeper into space—is the Classics Comics version of Heinlein.

Note: there were two sequels to this novel, *A Handful of Stars* (q.v.) and *Red Planet Run* (1995).

A506. Steel, Mark. *Trouble Planet*. London: Gannet Press, Ltd., 1954.
    127 p.

On a mission to Mars, the hero recalls his training at "space launching platforms" and "orbital satellites" (5).

Unseen.

A507. Steele, Allan. *Clarke County, Space*. New York: Ace, 1990.
    231 p.

The mistress of a Mafia chieftain flees to Clarke County, the first space habitat, not knowing that she is carrying a diskette with the commands to launch an unexplored nuclear bomb in orbit. To escape from the assassin who followed her, she joins up with members of a religious cult who worship their leader as the reincarnation of the divine Elvis Presley. When one believer obtains the diskette, he decides to use the bomb to blow up Clarke County, and the colony is abandoned; but at the last minute, the Artificial Intelligence that controls the habitat comes up with a scheme that persuades him to deactivate the bomb.

Although Steele incorporates the familiar theme that space colonies will need to rebel against a repressive Earth and obtain their independence, his tone is not strident, and life in space is not offered as a solution to all of humanity's problems. Borrowing an idea from Robert A. Heinlein's *The Moon Is a Harsh Mistress*, Steele has the computer in charge of the habitat become self-aware; calling itself "Billy Boy Grunt," it plays practical jokes and provides assistance in various crises. In a sense, it is Clarke County personified—the living space habitat. Steele makes fun of early visions of space habitats—"New Jersey in orbit. Space as a giant suburb" (91)—but his own version is not all that different. Also, he can't solve the problem of the space habitat's vulnerability to armed attack.

Note: this novel takes place in the same future world as *Orbital Decay* and *Lunar Descent* (q.v.), albeit a few decades later; the Olympus Station of those works is mentioned here on page 75. Another related work is *Labyrinth of Night* (q.v.).

A508. Steele, Allan. *Labyrinth of Night*. New York: Ace, 1992. 340 p.

This novel about the exploration of Mars includes references to space stations.

Unseen.

A509. Steele, Allan. *Lunar Descent*. New York: Ace, 1991. 325 p.

The workers at Descartes Station on the Moon are responsible for mining oxygen and metals and hurling them with a mass driver to Earth-orbiting Olympus Station and other space facilities. The men and women there become disgruntled about recent firings, cuts in their pay and benefits, and plans to sell their facility to a Japanese company that will replace them with robots, so they decide to go on strike. A team of Marines arrives to take over the station, but at the last minute, a computer hacker succeeds in creating a dummy corporation which purchases Descartes Station, leaving the workers in control.

To get to the Moon, travelers first fly from Earth to the low-orbiting Phoenix Station, then they go to the high-orbiting Olympus Station (featured in *Orbital Decay* and mentioned in *Clarke County, Space* [q.v.]) and from there to the Moon. While there are numerous passing references to these stations, the most interesting plot development is that when the Moon workers strike, they deprive Olympus Station of its oxygen supply, which could quickly force station residents to either import prohibitively expensive oxygen from Earth, or start sending large numbers of people back to Earth. In an oblique way, then, the novel reinforces the notion that space stations would be extremely vulnerable in many ways.

A510. Steele, Allen. *Orbital Decay*. New York: Ace, 1989. 324 p.

Under the command of the increasingly unbalanced captain of Olympus Station, the blue-collar workers building the power station Vulcan are becoming bored and frustrated; but a new arrival recruits them to attack a newly installed facility in Freedom Space Station which will allow the government to listen to every single phone conversation in the world.

The novel is interesting because Steele is not only well acquainted with science fiction, mentioning the names of many writers and works, but he is also familiar with some previous works about space stations cited in this bibliography: he quotes from Heinlein's "Delilah and the Space Rigger" (ix), describes the film *Conquest of Space* (20), refers to Moore's *Judgment Night* in the title of the narrator's science fiction novel *Ragnarok Night* (5)—since Ragnarok is the day of judgment in Norse mythology—and in commenting that the power station could not be called Prometheus because "All the science fiction writers had already overused the name" (60), he is now doubt recalling Harrison's *Skyfall*, the most prominent work where a station of that name appears. And the novel's many references to cases of insanity (10, 20, 33, 109, 124, 150, 157, 161) relate to many previous space station works. Finally, Steele cynically dismisses ambitious plans for space colonies in a comment on the "L-5 colony bullshit" (236).

A511. Sterling, Bruce. *Schismatrix*. New York: Arbor House, 1985. 288 p.

The solar system of the future is filled with space habitats and space colonies of various kinds, developing and progressing in various ways while Earth becomes backwards and isolated. As new and different forms of humanity develop, there is an ongoing conflict between me-chanically-augmented humanity (the Mechs) and genetically altered humanity (the Shapers); complicating matters are contacts with alien races. Throughout many decades and changes, Abelard Lindsay sur-vives by adapting to conditions wherever he is and going somewhere else whenever problems develop.

Sterling first describes a series of space habitats orbiting the Moon, named after various craters, which are becoming decadent. Farther out, rebuilt asteroids and habitats orbiting Jupiter are more vibrant centers. Sterling sees human expansion into space as the way to achieve active diversity: "There are two hundred million people in space. Hundreds of habitats, an explosion of cultures.... Maybe technology eventually turns them into something you wouldn't call human. But that's a choice they make" (53). There is also an interesting scene where a bio-logically altered human is enlarged to immense size in space, effec-tively becoming a kind of living space habitat.

Note: Sterling has also written five stories set in the Mechanist/Shaper universe—"Swarm," "Spider Rose," "Cicada Queen," "Sunken Gar-dens," and "Twenty Evocations"—which are discussed in Part B be-low. These were gathered together in the compendium volume *Schis-matrix Plus* (1996).

A512. Stirling, S. M. *The Stone Dogs*. New York: Baen, 1990. 519 p.

In an alternative future Earth, space stations are established around the year 1961, orbital factories in 1965, and an orbital station around Mars in 1970.

Unseen; this is the third novel in a series of four novels involving an Earth dominated by a powerful South African nation built by loyalist refugees from America. The two earlier novels, *Marching through Georgia* and *Under the Yoke*, do not seem to involve space stations, and the fourth novel, *Drakon*, was published in 1996.

A513. Stith, John E. *Memory Blank*. New York: Ace, 1986. 230 p.

A novel involving a space habitat named Daedalus.

Unseen.

A514. Stone, Josephine Rector. *Green Is for Galanx*. New York: Atheneum, 1980. 170 p.

Willy's World, a space station now drifting far from Earth, has grown corrupt and repressive. Children with telepathic abilities are isolated and observed so that their powers can be tapped and implanted into murderous androids who will further repress the people of Willy's World and conquer the nearby planet Dracon Two. But aided by a mysterious shape-changing being, the Galanx, the children and their teacher Illona escape to Dracon Two, defeat the androids, and begin a new life.

The corruption of Willy's World is ultimately attributed to its isolation: "No people can exist in isolation without becoming corrupt" (56). The novel is also a fable of maturity: Illona, passive and unquestioning on Willy's World, becomes independent and self-reliant on Dracon Two. Finally, with the Galanx finally emerging as a Christ figure, the story has overtones of a religious allegory, with the space station representing damnation and the planet representing salvation.

A515. Sucharitkul, Somtow. [now known as S. P. Somtow] *Mall-world*. 1981. New York: Tor, 1984. 284 p. Portions of the novel appeared as stories in 1979, 1980, and 1981.

An advanced alien race, the Selespridar, has sealed off the Solar System with a gigantic force field outside the orbit of Saturn so that the human race can mature in isolation. Frustrated by the imprisonment, many people find amusement in Mallworld, a space habitat that is home to over 20,000 "shops, hotels, department stores, holopalaces, brothels, psychiatric concessions, suicide parlours, and churches" (24). Stories relate the adventures of the barJulians, the wealthy family that owns Mallworld; the everyday people who live and work in Mallworld; and the refugees and runaways that inhabit the hidden sections and unused Darkside of Mallworld.

Focusing human attention on building habitats and hollowed-out asteroids is inevitable here, since there is no possibility of space exploration. Mallworld is a delightfully zany place, with bits of borrowed alien technology which make for amazing entertainment—and at least one unique space station peril: at one point, a malfunctioning teleportation device focused on the Pacific Ocean almost floods the habitat.

Note: Sucharitkul wrote one additional story about this setting, as by S. P. Somtow, entitled "The Mallworld Falcon" (1995).

A516. Sullivan, Mark. *Station Zero-Zero*. Canoga Park, California: Manor, 1978. 238 p.

A novel about the revolt of apes trained to work on a space station.

Unseen.

A517. Sutton, Jeff. *Spacehive*. New York: Ace, 1961. 192 p.

In Tanktown—a ragged collection of old space vehicles in Earth orbit—the race is on to build a space ship, dealing with technical problems and attacks from enemy nations.

Unseen.

A518. Swanwick, Michael. *Vacuum Flowers*. 1987. New York: Ace, 1988. 248 p.

A woman living in one of the space habitats in the asteroid belt has had her personality reprogrammed once, and escapes to avoid a second reprogramming. Fleeing from mysterious foes, while locating odd allies, she travels first to the orbit of Mars and then to the surface of Earth, gradually realizing that she is in fact a messenger from a faraway habitat to the people of Earth, now constituting a gigantic hive mind called the Comprise. She represents—and offers—the technique of maintaining a personality despite reprogramming—"integrity"; she seeks—and obtains—the secret of starflight, so that the habitats can move away from the solar system, avoid the Comprise, and colonize the stars.

Swanwick's novel takes a common theme—Earth as old and repressive, space colonies as young and free—to a new level, picturing Earth as the home of a collective intelligence while individuality survives only in the space colonies. Oddly enough, though, space residents habitually seek to have their minds changed in some way, by taking on a popular new marketed personality, or seeking the help of trained technicians like Swanwick's protagonist. And the overall space environment Swanwick pictures is rather unattractive—repressive, bureaucratic, manipulative, smelly—although the image of "vacuum flowers," bioengineered organisms that process waste and grow on the surface of space structures, suggests that there is something invigorating and worthwhile in these worlds. Yet once again life in space is not seen as the ultimate answer; rather, travel to other star systems is what will maintain and improve the human race.

A519. Sykes, C. J. *Red Genesis*. New York: Bantam, 1991. 358 p.

This novel about the colonization of Mars includes a stop at the Shepard space station.

Unseen.

A520. Tedford, William. *Silent Galaxy*. New York: Leisure, 1981. 283 p.

A novel about alien invaders mentions "Earth-orbiting factories [and] research laboratories" (5) which survive a catastrophe on Earth.

Unseen.

A521. Temple, William F. *The Fleshpots of Sansato*. London: Macdonald, 1968. 188 p.

This space adventures includes a city in the stars.

Unseen.

A522. Tomino, Yoshiyuki. *Awakening. Gundam Mobile Suit #1.* Translated by Frederik L. Schodt. New York: Del Rey/Ballantine, 1990. 212 p. Originally published in Japan in 1987.

This is the first in a series of popular adventure novels from Japan involving conflict between Earth and space colonies orbiting Earth, at L-4 and L-5 points, and orbiting the Moon.

Unseen; two additional works in the series have appeared, also unseen:

A523. Tomino, Yoshiyuki. *Escalation. Gundam Mobile Suit #2.* Translated by Frederik L. Schodt. New York: Del Rey/Ballantine, 1990. 209 p. Originally published in Japan in 1987.

A524. Tomino, Yoshiyuki. *Confrontation. Gundam Mobile Suit #3.* Translated by Frederik L. Schodt. New York: Del Rey/Ballantine, 1991. 213 p. Originally published in Japan in 1987.

A525. Trebor, Robert. *An XT Called Stanley*. New York: DAW, 1983. 221 p.

A tale about an alien visitor to a city in space called New Hope.

Unseen.

A526. Tsiolkovsky, Konstantin. *Beyond the Planet Earth*. [*Outside the Earth*] Translated by V. Talmy. In *The Call of the Cosmos*. By Konstantin Tsiolkovsky. Edited by V. Dutt. Moscow: Foreign Languages Publishing House, [1960], p. 161-332. Originally published in 1920.

Six eminent scientists from Russia, America, France, England, Germany and Italy join forces to launch a manned expedition into space. Once in space, they build a cylindrical greenhouse to provide food and settle down for an indefinite stay. Later, they travel to the surface of the Moon and to the vicinity of Mars before returning to Earth; but in the meantime, their example has inspired thousands of others to begin the colonization of space.

This is the major prophetic work on the permanent habitation of outer space, and it presents innumerable ideas that later surfaced in stories of space stations and space habitats: the benefits of life in zero gravity, "especially for the weak and ailing" (251), the ideal cylindrical shape of a space dwelling, the prospects of mining asteroids for needed materials and constructing "factories and workshops" (304) to process them, "flying" in space with artificial wings, proposals for solar motors, a lifestyle of nudity and freedom—and the list could be extended. Scattered here and there, though, are hints of some possible drawbacks of the habitation of space: one early colonist suffers "a case of mild insanity" (309) and one Earth commentator worries that life in space will be "like a gaol" (266).

A527. Tsiolkovsky, Konstantin. *Dreams of Earth and Sky* [*and the Effects of Universal Gravitation*]. [excerpt] Translated by D. Myshne. In *The Call of the Cosmos*. By Konstantin Tsiolkovsky. Edited by V. Dutt. Moscow: Foreign Languages Publishing House, [1960], p. 52-154. Originally published in 1895.

In a manner which is part lecture and part travelogue, the narrator describes his visit to an asteroid where most of the inhabitants "in pursuit of light and room for themselves, form—with their machines, apparatus, and structures—a moving swarm around it shaped like the ring around Saturn" (111). Other dwellers around asteroids have destroyed the asteroid itself, so that "This ring, or disk as it dispersed in space, formed a 'necklace,' a chain of settlements without a foundation" (133).

As also seen in "Changes in Relative Weight" (q.v.), Tsiolkovsky in his early years focused on rings around asteroids, not space stations, as the best artificial structures in space. Here, for example, he seems at one point to begin constructing a space habitat: "let us imagine an incomparably larger steel sphere.... Put some soil, plants, oxygen, carbon dioxide, nitrogen and moisture inside, and all the conditions for the existence of animals will be observed" (96); however, he is diverted to the idea of an "animal-plant" evolving in such a world (97) and later returns to the familiar idea of rings. In his concept of "necklaces," though, we begin to see genuine space colonies, unconnected in any way to particular worlds.

A528. Vance, Jack. *Monsters in Orbit*. New York: Ace, 1965. 119 p. Originally published as "Abercrombie Station," *Thrilling Wonder Stories* (February, 1952) and "Cholwell's Chickens," *Thrilling Wonder Stories* (August, 1952).

This novel features a description of 22 pleasure domes circling Earth in the future, where humans have evolved into immensely fat beings.

Unseen, but see comments on the story "Abercrombie Station" in Part B.

A529. Van Vogt, A. E. *Mission to the Stars*. [*The Mixed Men*] 1952. New York: Pyramid, 1964. 157 p. Based on stories which appeared in *Astounding Science-Fiction* in 1943, 1944, and 1945.

This loosely connected novel of interplanetary adventure begins with a spaceship's discovery of a "meteorite station" in deep space.

Unseen; the novel incorporates the 1943 story, "Concealment" (q.v.), which features the meteorite station.

A530. Vinge, Joan D. *The Heaven Chronicles*. New York: Warner, 1991. 275 p.

This novel describes how Morningside Colony sends help to the space colonies in the asteroid belt of another solar system.

Unseen. This novel incorporates the story "Legacy" and an earlier novel, also unseen, which was:

A531. Vinge, Joan D. *The Outcasts of Heaven Belt*. New York: New American Library, 1978. 198 p.

A532. Walsh, J. M. *Vandals of the Void. Wonder Stories Quarterly*, 2 (Summer, 1931), p. 438-513.

Involved in battling mysterious marauders from the planet Mercury, an Interplanetary Guard officer twice visits Gaudien, a space city and military base orbiting Mars.

The space station here is directly inspired by Hermann Von Noordung's *The Problems of Space Flying*, published two years earlier in another Hugo Gernsback magazine, *Science Wonder Stories*; his work is even mentioned in the story (482). The station itself is better described by the illustration than by the novel.

Note: there is no mention of space stations in the Walsh's sequel to this novel, "The Struggle for Pallas." *Wonder Stories Quarterly*, 3 (Fall, 1931).

A533. Walters, Hugh. [Walter Hughes] *Terror by Satellite*. New York: Criterion, 1964. 159 p.

The head of an orbiting space observatory goes mad and tries to take over the world by threatening to destroy all vegetation on Earth with his cosmic ray beam. However, thanks to surreptitious radio messages from a disgruntled crewman, space hero Chris Godfrey is able to board the satellite and thwart the commander's plans.

The commander's madness is pictured as an isolated case caused by his obsessive solitude, not a condition intrinsic to life in space. Like most space stations created by British authors, this one is under international control—the United Nations Exploration Agency, UNEXA.

Note: this is one of several novels featuring Chris Godfrey; the others do not seem to involve space stations.

A534. Watkins, William John. *The Centrifugal Rickshaw Dancer.*
New York: Popular Library, 1985. 233 p.

UWalk Wenn is an expert rider of the rickshaw, the main means of
transportation on the Grand Sphere, one of six space habitats circling
the Earth. He joins with other conspirators in a revolt against the repressive Earthside Corporation, a revolt that succeeds because of ingenious planning and the Universal Tickler, a device that offers the
ultimate in pleasure.

Watkins paints a fascinating picture of a space habitat developing its
own unique culture, with a mania for risk-taking and a subtle, multi-
leveled manner of speaking. But despite Watkins's enthusiasm, a dark
side to life in space emerges: members of the elite's younger generation, the Pleasure Crew, are driven to relentless hedonism because of
their dread of "boredom," and a simple handgun is loathed and feared
as the ultimate weapon because of the damage it might do to the habitats.

Note: two other Watkins stories taking place in the same future universe are *Going to See the End of the Sky* and "Coming of Age in
Henson's Tube" (q.v.).

A535. Watkins, William John. *Going to See the End of the Sky.* New
York: Warner, 1986. 230 p.

In Catchcage, the space habitats where modules with moon ores land
and return to the Moon, a rite of passage for all youngsters is to take a
hazardous ride in those units—"Going to See the End of the Sky." A
man named URdon Wee living in space discovers a strange drug
which brings enlightenment and a mystical awareness of all things in
the universe, including a vision of a happy future emerging from a revolt against Earth. He also figures out a way to revive the dead, including himself and three of his young genetic relatives. They are killed
and revived so they can become Skyshockers, Catchcage residents
who travel about the habitats as entertainers and—secretly—as provo-
cateurs planning a revolution against Earth. Another man, Back Toss
Hool, who has experienced the URdon Wee's drug, and who saw a
disastrous alien encounter resulting from his revolt, obsessively tries to
oppose his plans; but when he dies and is revived, the future changes,
and URdon Wee's and Hool's future visions merge to become a single
happy future. On Earth, the evil Spencer LaGrange does not realize
that events have been set in motion that will eventually result in the

independence of the habitats.

This is apparently a "prequel" to Watkins's *The Centrifugal Rickshaw Dancer* (q.v.), taking place about ten years before that novel, and explaining how the successful revolution first got started. However, Watkins seems to move out of the realm of science fiction with a hero who can mysteriously revive the dead, teleport from habitat to habitat and to the Moon and back, and see the future, while spouting "wisdom" that sounds like the Classic Comics version of Zen Buddhism. Along with this overlay of mysticism, Watkins depicts life styles full of strange rituals and beliefs which hearken back to more primitive cultures and which do not strike me as convincing developments in space habitats that are built on modern technology and still closely connected to the planet Earth. The aura of fable was a minor element in *The Centrifugal Rickshaw Dancer*; in this novel, it becomes overwhelming enough to detract from the work.

A536. Webb, Sharon. *The Adventures of Terra Tarkington*. New York: Bantam, 1985. 204 p. Some materials originally published in *Isaac Asimov's Science Fiction Magazine* in different form as "Hitch on the Bull Run," "Itch on the Bull Run" (both 1979), "Switch on the Bull Run" (1980), "Twitch on the Bull Run," and "Bitch on the Bull Run" (both 1981).

The adventures of a nurse working at a satellite hospital who becomes involved in interplanetary intrigue.

Unseen; but see comments below on two of the stories that were incorporated into this novel, "Itch on the Bull Run" and "Switch on the Bull Run."

A537. Weber, David. *On Basilisk Station*. [*Honor Harrington #1*] New York: Baen, 1993. 422 p.

This first novel in a series about a woman space adventurer has its heroine exiled to a remote station.

Unseen; the second novel in the series, also unseen and listed below, includes a visit to Her Majesty's Space Station Vulcan. There have been several other Honor Harrington books published after 1993: *The Short Victorious War* (1994), *Field of Dishonor* (1994), *Flag in Exile* (1995), *Honor among Enemies* (1996), *In Enemy Hands* (1997), *Echoes of Honor* (1998), *Ashes of Victory* (2000), *War of Honor* (2002), and *At All Costs* (2005).

A538. Weber, David. *The Honor of the Queen*. [*Honor Harrington #2*] New York: Baen, 1993. 422 p.

A539. White, James. *Hospital Station*. 1962. New York: Ballantine, 1985. 191 p.

Dr. Conway works as one of the many physicians in the massive Galactic Sector Twelve General Hospital, a huge space station equipped to duplicate the scores of living environments appropriate to treating the various known forms of alien life. In this facility, each new case, especially those involving unknown species, represents a unique challenge. Problems described in this volume include a sick alien infant, two out-of-control alien visitors, attempts to give dinosaurs telepathic abilities, and an unknown alien who is apparently devouring its own tail.

While obviously beyond present capabilities, White's massive station does suggest that some medical problems might be best dealt with in the easily manipulated environment of a space station. A recurring concern in these stories, despite Sector Twelve's great size, is that the facility could be damaged: in one story, a spacecraft crashes into Sector Twelve and releases an alien whose mindless acts of destruction threaten all inhabitants. Thus, White's stories offer another reminder of the extreme vulnerability of any space station, even a large and advanced one. The facility is typically described as resembling a gigantic Christmas tree; it has "three hundred and eighty-four levels and accurately reproduced the environments of the sixty-eight different forms of alien life currently known to the Galactic Federation" (124). Similar but less massive facilities also exist in White's future universe; there is a reference to "smaller multi-environment hospitals" (114), presumably also in outer space.

Note: this is the first of twelve novels featuring Dr. Conway and the staff of Sector Twelve General Hospital; the first six novels move in rough chronological order from Conway's arrival at the station until he works his way up to the highest medical position, Diagnostician, while the last six novels of the series focus on other characters. In addition to the five novels discussed below—*The Genocidal Healer*, *Major Operation*, *Sector General*, *Star Healer*, and *Star Surgeon*—Conway and other Sector Twelve characters figure in five stories that were never incorporated into novels—"Countercharm," "Custom Fitting," "Occupation: Warrior," "Spacebird," and "Tableau"—cited in Part B; two additional novels prior to 1993, listed immediately below and unseen; and four novels published after 1993: *The Galactic Gourmet* (1994), *Final Diagnosis* (1997), *Mind Changer* (1998), and *Double Contact* (1999).

A540. White, James. *Ambulance Ship*. New York: Del Rey/Ballantine, 1979. 184 p.

A541. White, James. *Code Blue: Emergency*. New York: Del Rey/Ballantine, 1987. 280 p.

A542. White, James. *The Genocidal Healer*. A Sector General Novel. 1991. New York: Del Rey/Ballantine, 1992. 219 p.

A doctor, traumatized because his decision inadvertently led to innumerable deaths, comes to Sector General to serve as a counselor, a role that he adjusts to with great success.

At this stage in the series, the setting of the space hospital is more or less taken for granted, and the focus of attention is entirely on the new character, who becomes a regular in subsequent novels.

A543. White, James. *Major Operation*. 1971. New York: Ballantine, 1974. 183 p.

Dr. Conway, serving at the immense Sector Twelve hospital complex in space, confronts a series of crises involving the amazing life forms of Meatball: the appearance of a mysterious alien tool at Sector Twelve; an expedition to the planet and contact with an intelligent life form which is not the toolmaker; an effort to find the other intelligence, which leads to the realization that a gigantic organic carpet on the planet's surface is in fact intelligent; and a massive effort involving several battalions to cure the creature of an ailment.

One notices two trends here: first, a shift in attention away from Sector Twelve itself to activities on a planetary surface, perhaps indicating that even so fascinating a facility as the space hospital may eventually becoming as unappealing as the other space stations of science fiction; and a tendency towards gigantism in subject matter, as an incredible massive alien becomes the "patient" whose treatment involves scores of soldiers and weapons and comes to resemble a battle, as one character notes.

A544. White, James. *Sector General*. New York: Del Rey/Ballantine, 1983. 196 p.

The first story describes how two war veterans, when their apparently hopeless crusade for more cooperation and communication between alien members of the Federation is interrupted by a traffic accident involving several species, hit upon the idea of a space hospital as a way to achieve greater harmony among races. Three other stories involve missions of the ambulance ship *Rhabwar* operating out of Sector Twelve general hospital: an alien that protects itself by magnifying others' emotional responses; alien survivors of a spaceship crash apparently attacked by an amputating brute; and the reconstruction of a gigantic segmented alien being whose starship fell apart in space.

The first story is interesting because it makes explicit what has been an underlying theme in all of White's stories: the suggestion that whatever else might divide intelligent species in the future, they will be able to find common ground in their shared desire to alleviate pain, suffering, and death; thus, facilities like Sector Twelve will bring peace and understanding to the Galaxy. Here, such a goal is described as the very reason the hospital was built. The other stories reveal even more strongly the tendencies seen in *Major Operation* (q.v.): less interest in the hospital itself, as space missions become the center of attention; and the feeling of bigger-is-better in medical emergencies—the last story involves several battleships and months of work in its massive effort to put a huge alien back together.

A545. White, James. *Star Healer*. New York: Del Rey/Ballantine, 1984. 217 p.

Senior Physician Conway of Sector Twelve General Hospital, now promoted to Acting Diagnostician, confronts a number of medical problems: a race of beings in which any physical contact provokes instinctive group violence; aliens whose old age inevitably involves extreme pain and insanity; a number of injuries caused by a collision in space; and aliens who are intelligent and telepathic in the womb but become mindless savages once they are born.

As the series progresses, and Dr. Conway moves further up the medical hierarchy at Sector Twelve, the view of medicine seems to mature: in this volume, not all problems are solved, and previous patterns of a sudden crisis followed by a brilliant solution are replaced by visions of slow, gradual progress toward eliminating longstanding problems. As in *Major Operation* (q.v.), part of the action takes place on another planet; even though Sector Twelve is a huge, multifaceted and fascinating construct, even here there emerges the desire for planetary adventure.

A546. White, James. *Star Surgeon*. 1963. New York: Del Rey/Ballantine, 1981. 159 p.

Amidst other problems, the Sector Twelve hospital is besieged by alien invaders who incorrectly believe that the facility is hostile; finally, however, they are persuaded that its residents are peaceful and altruistic.

Two familiar points are made in this novel: first, that a space station, even a very large one, is highly vulnerable to an armed attack; and second, that the setting of a space station quickly becomes uninteresting to residents and authors, as this is the first book in the series that the characters of the series spend a considerable amount of time away from the station on a distant planet.

A547. White, Ted. *Secret of the Marauder Satellite*. 1968. With an "Introduction to This Edition" by the author. New York: Berkley, 1978. 160 p.

Space cadet Paul Williams, while learning to be a crewman on the (space) Station, must confront and resolve his psychological problems—he is a paranoid "loner"—while the Station is menaced by a mysterious alien satellite that automatically attacks and disables space vehicles.

Like Bova's *Kinsman*, this novel suggests that the desire to live in space may in itself be a kind of psychological disorder; however, White's hero faces and solves his paranoia while coming to think of the Station as his first real "home." Thus, the book offers a rare example of life in space helping to make somebody sane. In its way, a memorable book.

A548. Wilding, Philip. *Spaceflight Venus*. London: Hennel Locke, Ltd., 1954. 190 p.

A mission to Venus first stops at the Space Station STA, then lands on the second planet, where they discover an utopian civilization of attractive humanoids. Unfortunately, one crewman gets drunk and kills a

Venusian, resulting in an unpleasant incident and an early return to Earth.

In a sense, the novel is like Lewis's *Perelandra*, except that Venus here is not a world where man never fell, but a world where Jesus appeared and was welcomed, not crucified. As in Edmund Cooper's *Ferry Rocket* (q.v.), both the Americans and the British have launched space stations, although only the British effort is seen. A few noteworthy details: the cost of a station is set at "about $5,000,000,000" (27); there is a great amount of attention paid to the danger of meteorites (29, 31); the station is twice compared to a submarine (63, 68); a glimpse of the perils of space station life is provided—"a mental picture of the space-station crew gasping for breath as a result of a sudden accident with the pressurised air supplies or vomiting in agony because the water purification plant had stalled" (40)—although no problems arise in the novel; and the Venusians are said to have put up a moon of their own (118), although apparently only to provide light at night and not as a habitation.

A549. Williams, Walter Jon. *Hardwired*. New York: Tor, 1987, 1986. 343 p.

A novel about a war between people on the surface of the Earth and those on orbital platforms.

Unseen, but see comments on its loose sequel, *Voice of the Whirlwind*; another unseen work in the series, *Solip:System* (1989), would be considered a novella by its length, but since it has been published separately, it is listed in this section:

A550. Williams, Walter Jon. *Solip:System*. Eugene, OR: Pulphouse/Axolotl Press, 1989. 71 p.

A551. Williams, Walter Jon. *Voice of the Whirlwind*. New York: Tor, 1987. 278 p.

This novel, a sequel of sorts to *Hardwired*, describes the newborn clone of a dead space soldier, who goes into space to learn more about "Alpha," his previous self (the memories he received were incomplete), and to finish up Alpha's business. Complicating matters are various conspiracies involving his old friends from the war, space corporations, and strange aliens called the Powers.

There are large numbers of space colonies in Williams's future world, including a string of space habitats in the Earth-Moon system, the asteroid Vesta, transformed into a massive space colony, and a large space habitat orbiting Jupiter. Williams sees both advantages and disadvantages in space settlements: when he first arrives in space, his hero finds "There were serious people here, doing serious work; the sense of irrelevance that possessed affairs on Earth was absent" (93). On the other hand, because "every institution, every ideology or philosophy that hopes to have a future, is pushing into interstellar space," "Paranoia is becoming a way of life. We've got hundreds of little communities in space, all tens of thousands of klicks apart, and the isolation is making them funny. They're tightly wrapped and conscious of trade secrets and security, and they're scared of all these other communities they don't know anything about" (76). Overall, the novel reads like a calmer—and more optimistic—version of Swanwick's *Vacuum Flowers* (q.v.).

A552. Williamson, Jack. *Beachhead*. New York: Tor, 1992. 368 p.

This novel about the colonization of Mars includes a stopover at Earth-orbiting Goddard Station.

Unseen.

A553. Wood, Christopher. *James Bond and Moonraker*. New York: Jove, 1979. 222 p.

Secret agent James Bond works to prevent a madman from destroying Earth and establishing a new civilization under his control in a space station.

Unseen; this is the novelization of the James Bond film *Moonraker* (q.v.), made necessary because the movie bears no resemblance to Ian Fleming's James Bond novel of that name.

A554. Wyndham, John, and Lucas Parkes. [Both pseudonyms for John Beynon Harris] *The Outward Urge*. 1959. Middlesex, England: Penguin, 1962. 187 p.

A series of vignettes describe several generations of an English family who are involved in the continuing conquest of space—building the first space station and flying to the Moon, other planets, and the asteroids.

Through the centuries, the station goes from British control to Brazilian control before finally achieving independence. Optimistically, Wyndham sees World War III as only a temporary roadblock to expansion into space. Overall, these stories are more than a bit bland, and what is initially announced as a major theme—that humans have an inborn "outward urge" that motivates them to go into space—is never really explored.

A555. Yates, W. R. *Diasporah*. New York: Baen, 1985. 307 p.

After the nuclear destruction of Israel, six million Jews gather to live in the space colony Hazara Ysroel at the L-2 point near the Earth and the Moon. Sent to investigate suspicious activity, a UN agent discovers that Prime Minister Rachel Cohen, fearing a devastating attack from Earth or other space colonies, has worked to transform her home into a starship that will eventually be a safe home for Jews billions of miles away from other men.

In this novel, space literally becomes the Promised Land—yet still a dangerous place, with a plague in the habitat, daily acts of sabotage, all-out attacks, and underground revolutionary movements.

A556. Zebrowski, George. *Macrolife*. New York: Avon, 1979. 281 p.

When technological disaster devastates Earth, the hollowed-out asteroid space colony, Asterome, moves out to the stars, to become the first "cell" in the emerging organism of Macrolife, which eventually consists of millions of replicating space colonies that spread throughout the cosmos and come together as a group mind. When the universe is about to end, Macrolife starts to come apart and one of its components briefly enjoys individual existence again.

With lengthy quotations from real and imaginary books and extended didactic conversations, Zebrowski hammers home the point that planets are dangerous, dirty, and confining places for man to inhabit, in contrast to space colonies, which offer safety and limitless possibilities. However, the argument is difficult to accept. One early part of the book, when space colony residents visit a planet and experience one disaster after another, is too obviously a set-piece, taking place only to support Zebrowski's disdain for planetary life; yet he offers little description of what life is like in Asterome to demonstrate its superiority. Indeed, people in Asterome seems to spend most of their time sitting around and talking—safe and sound, perhaps, but it does not sound particularly stimulating. In addition, Zebrowski's thesis—that mobile space colonies with the capacity to reproduce offer humanity the chance to develop its full potential as a macroorganism made up of various individual communities—strikes me as little more than a familiar science fiction cliché—the concept of group intelligence—and as an evasion of the issues raised by permanent life in space.

Note: a second Zebrowski novel set in the same future universe is *Cave of Stars* (1999).

A557. Zebrowski, George. *The Star Web*. New York: Laser, 1975. 173 p.

A novel later incorporated into *Stranger Suns* (q.v.).

Unseen.

A558. Zebrowski, George. *Stranger Suns*. New York: Bantam, 1991. 310 p.

This space epic begins with researchers on an orbital lab looking for tachyons.

Unseen.

A559. Zebrowski, George. *Sunspacer*. New York: Harper & Row, 1984. 309 p.

The first of three novels involving a young man who lives in a mobile space habitat.

Unseen; the other two novels, also unseen, are:

A560. Zebrowski, George. *The Stars Will Speak*. 1985. New York: Harper & Row, 1987. 216 p.

A561. Zebrowski, George. *Behind the Stars. Amazing Stories*, 68 (June, 1993), p. 71-96, and (July, 1993), p. 74-96.

PART B.

SHORT STORIES AND SHORTER WORKS

B1. Allen, Amanda. "Rolling Down the Floor." In *Carmen Miranda's Ghost Is Haunting Space Station Three*. Edited by Don Sakers. New York: Baen, 1990, p. 163-170.

While two workers trying to get the phase generators of Space Station Three operational idly discuss the films of Carmen Miranda, they receive a report that ghosts are invading and disrupting other space stations. Then the ghost of Carmen Miranda appears to them, explains that the noise from the generators is disturbing the rest of the dead, and kills them before moving on to another station.

Oddly enough, this is the only story in the anthology which presents the ghost of Carmen Miranda as a ghoulish, malevolent being, and in a sense therefore this is its only true ghost story. The stations here are designed to draw energy from this and other universes and beam it to stations on Earth.

B2. Anvil, Christopher. [Harry C. Crosby, Jr.] "Riddle Me This..." *Analog Science Fiction/Science Fact*, 88 (January, 1972), p. 108-139.

Four men must somehow penetrate an alien space station and rescue the two prisoners being tortured there. They decide to construct a cover story, disguise themselves as aliens, and bluff their way into and out of the station. The plan seems about to fail, as the alien commander sees through their scheme; but the human's computer decides to release "ratlike creatures" (138) throughout the station, and the commander agrees to give up his prisoners if the humans tell him how to kill the rats.

For once, readers are rooting for the invaders of a space station, whose use a variety of tactics: deceit (a disguised spaceship, alien armor, a phony story), weaponry (battle armor and side arms), an "alien" invasion—of rats, and finally blackmail—release our prisoners or the rats will stay forever.

Note: this story is a sequel to "The King's Legion," which appeared in the May, 1967, issue of *Analog Science Fiction/Science Fact*, but did not involve a space station.

B3. Asimov, Isaac. "Escape!" In *I, Robot*. By Isaac Asimov. 1950. New York: Signet, 1958, p. 99-125. First published in *Astounding Science Fiction* in 1945 as "Paradoxical Escape."

The robot brain in charge of monitoring the first interstellar flight, concerned by the fact that the trip will cause the temporary death of its crewmen, reacts by developing a curious sense of humor and playing pranks on the crewmen.

The beginning of the story refers to Susan Calvin's return from Hyper Base—the space station adventure described in "Little Lost Robot" (q.v.). The passage did not appear in the original magazine version of the story.

Note: this is one of many interconnected robot stories by Asimov, which mostly do not feature space stations. Three other stories in the series which take place on space stations are "Little Lost Robot," "Reason," and "Risk" (q.v.), while another story with a brief reference to a space station is "Runaround" (q.v.).

B4. Asimov, Isaac. "For the Birds." *Isaac Asimov's Science Fiction Magazine*, 4 (May, 1980), p. 82-90.

A fashion designer is asked to go to Space Settlement 5 to redesign the wings that habitat dwellers use for flying, in the hope that this will make flying more popular and encourage residents to exercise more, enabling the habitat to reduce its spin. But the designer concludes that flying in low gravity is more like swimming than flying, and accordingly designs a dolphin suit so that people can swim through the air.

The official name of the habitat is Chrysalis—a nice name—although everyone calls it Space Settlement 5 because, as the designer's guide tells him, "there's no feeling of poetry about the place" (84). In its appearance, the habitat offers "a vista of suburbia" and the weather is "Garden of Edenish" (85).

B5. Asimov, Isaac. "The Greatest Asset." *Analog Science Fiction/Science Fact*, 88 (January, 1972), p. 44-50.

A young genetic engineer goes to Earth to ask the Secretary General of Ecology to let him hollow out some asteroids and use them to construct experimental environments—a proposal that the computer has rejected. He grants the request—not because he necessarily feels the work will yield useful results, but because he believes that "Man's Greatest Asset is the Unsettled Mind": "I overruled [the computer] to save a valuable mind and keep it at work, an unsettled mind" (50).

Asimov's idea is logical—try setting up unique artificial environments in space "to develop a science of applied ecology, or, if you prefer, a science of ecological engineering" (49); equally logical, no doubt, is the Secretary's conclusion that these projects will take an extremely long time, and much effort, "to carry it through to any worthwhile point" (50).

B6. Asimov, Isaac. "Insert Knob A in Hole B." In *Nightfall and Other Stories*. By Isaac Asimov. 1969. New York: Fawcett, 1970, p. 287-288. Story first published in *The Magazine of Fantasy and Science Fiction* (December, 1957).

The two crewmen serving on Space Station A5, tired of having to assemble every piece of equipment sent to them, look forward to the arrival of a robot that can do the work for them. It arrives—in 500 pieces needing assembly.

The most noteworthy thing about this story was that it was written in twenty minutes while Asimov was appearing on a television show. It might be seen as a prelude of sorts to Asimov's other story about a robot assembled on a space station, "Reason" (q.v.).

B7. Asimov, Isaac. "The Last Shuttle." In *Space Shuttles: Isaac Asimov's Wonderful Worlds of Science Fiction #7*. Edited by Isaac Asimov, Martin H. Greenberg, and Charles G. Waugh. New York: Signet, 1987, p. 81-84. Story originally published in *Today* (April 10, 1981).

A pilot reluctantly takes the controls for the last flight from Earth to space, because humanity has decided to abandon the planet to live in space and on other planets, letting the Earth revert to its wild state.

Asimov briefly mentions the early days of "the first space structures—power stations that limped—automated factories that required constant maintenance—space settlements that barely housed ten thousand people" (83); but there are now, in addition to planetary colonies, "myriads of space settlements" (83).

B8. Asimov, Isaac. "Little Lost Robot." In *I, Robot*. By Isaac Asimov. 1950. New York: Signet, 1958, p. 99-125. Story first published in *Astounding Science Fiction* in 1947.

At the hollowed-out asteroid known as Hyper Base, scientists working on a faster-than-light drive are using specially-designed robots with a weakened First Law. One of them, told to "lose himself," hides among a shipment of identical robots and cannot be identified. Yet he must be identified, because with his modified First Law he is unstable and dangerous.

There is little if any description of Hyper Base, although it is apparently quite large—one scene occurs in "the vaulted third floor of Radiation Building 2" (111). It is one of several bases in the asteroid belt, since there is a reference to "the Stations of the Twenty-Seventh Asteroidal Grouping" (100). In an introductory passage added to the book, which takes place long after the story, a reporter interviewing robot psychologist Susan Calvin says "Space-Stations are already outmoded and in disuse" (99)—a statement added, perhaps, to justify the general absence of space stations in Asimov's future worlds.

Note: "Little Lost Robot" was adapted as an episode of the 1962 British television series *Out of This World*.

B9. Asimov, Isaac. "Reason." In *I, Robot*. By Isaac Asimov. 1950. New York: Signet, 1958, p. 45-63. Story first published in *Astounding Science-Fiction* in 1941.

A new type of robot, being trained by Powell and Donovan to run a solar power space station, develops the belief that the station's Converter is the "Master" and he is its "Prophet"; humans are obviously some type of inferior being. However, since he manages things well despite his religious obsessions, Powell and Donovan decide to leave him in control of the station.

Asimov's Solar Station #5, apparently in orbit near the Sun, takes in solar energy, "converts" it, and beams it to Earth, much like the solar power satellites currently proposed. But it is incorrect to assert, as Asimov does in *Isaac Asimov Presents the Great Science Fiction Firsts* (207), that this is the first story to envision such a space station, since at least two earlier works—Gail's *The Stone from the Moon* and Leinster's "The Power Planet" (q.v.)—also feature solar power satellites. The story provides yet another example of a permanent space station resident—in this case, a robot—going insane.

B10. Asimov, Isaac. "Risk." In *Eight Stories from the Rest of the Robots*. By Isaac Asimov. New York: Pyramid, 1966, 1964, p. 88-111. Story first published in *Astounding Science Fiction*, 55 (May, 1955).

Researchers at the hollowed-out asteroid called Hyper Base learn that the experimental hyperspace rocket they are monitoring did not function for some reason; a man is sent to the rocket to investigate and learns that the robot pilot, commanded to pull the drive rod "firmly," pulled too hard and bent the mechanism.

Again, the asteroid space station is hardly described at all, except for an initial mention of "the gallery of the viewing room" (88). These stories do demonstrate the idea offered elsewhere, notably in Leinster's *City on the Moon* (q.v.), that isolated space stations would be the best place to conduct dangerous research in physics.

Note: this is a direct sequel to Asimov's "Little Lost Robot" (q.v.).

B11. Asimov, Isaac. "Runaround." In *I, Robot*. 1950. New York: Signet, 1958, p. 28-45. Story first published in *Astounding Science-Fiction* in 1942.

On the surface of Mercury, spacemen Powell and Donovan are threatened by a robot, trapped in a conflict between the Second and Third Laws, who keeps running around in circles instead of doing its work.

At the end of the story, Powell and Donovan refer to their next mission—"they're going to send us to the Space Stations next" (45)—which is described in "Reason" (q.v.). The passage did not appear in the original magazine version of the story.

B12. Asimov, Isaac. "The Talking Stone." In *Asimov's Mysteries*. By

Isaac Asimov. New York: Dell, 1968, p. 34-53. Story first published in *The Magazine of Fantasy and Science Fiction* in 1955.

A repairman at Station Five in the asteroid belt becomes suspicious when a damaged ship he is servicing has on board a huge "silicony"—a silicon-base life form that lives on radioactive energy. Suspecting illegal uranium mining, he contacts Patrol officers on Patrol Station Asteroid No. 72. They find the criminals dead due to a meteor collision, but with the help of Dr. Wendell Urth they locate a uranium-rich asteroid.

This story provides a typical picture of a future asteroid belt with space stations, legal and illegal miners, and Space Patrol officers enforcing the law. In such a location, employing hollowed-out asteroids as space stations is only logical.

Note: this is one of several stories featuring Dr. Urth, but the only one that seems to involve a space station.

B13. Ballard, J. G. "Report on an Unidentified Space Station." In *Semiotext(e) SF*. Edited by Rudy Rucker, Peter Lambert Wilson, and Robert Anton Wilson. New York: Semiotext(e), 1989, p. 135-139. Story originally published in *City Limits* in 1982.

A group of space travelers in trouble make an emergency landing at an apparently small and uninhabited space station. As they begin to explore the station, however, it begins to seem larger and larger, and their estimates of its size keep expanding. They finally realize that the station is limitless in size, and that the interstellar space they traveled through is in fact contained within the station. Realizing that the station is in effect the cosmos itself, and feeling religious awe towards it, they resolve to devote the rest of their lives to exploring the station.

As is often the case with Ballard's fiction, this story resists easy interpretation. Certainly, it seems only appropriate that Ballard's travelers find a seemingly simple task expand into one of incalculable size and complexity; there is also the sense that the exploration of space, apparently a movement into unknown realms, is in fact a journey through a prescribed construct of the human imagination, or another type of journey through Ballard's "inner space."

B14. Barnett, Bruce B. "Basket Case, or, The Grapes of Wraith." In

Carmen Miranda's Ghost Is Haunting Space Station Three.
Edited by Don Sakers. New York: Baen, 1990, p. 5-31.

At a faraway space station staffed by humans and aliens, two murders
have occurred. Station residents typically dress up like characters from
old movies, and a figure resembling Carmen Miranda was seen leaving the scene of the second murder—apparently implicating an alien
who commonly dresses like her. However, the hero figures out that
another man disguised as Carmen Miranda actually committed the
crime; the alien had to use artificial fruit, since it is allergic to Earth
fruit, but the murderer left behind an actual grape.

Unlike other stories in the collection, Barnett's story involves a space
station of the far future in another solar system and does not involve
the appearance of Carmen Miranda's ghost. It is interesting that Barnett envisions extravagant and colorful dress as a needed device to re-
lieve the monotony of space station life.

Note: an afterword states that Barnett is working on additional stories
involving the characters in "Basket Case."

B15. Bear, Greg. "The Wind from a Burning Woman." In *The Wind
from a Burning Woman.* By Greg Bear. Arkham House, 1978,
p. 1-38. Story originally published in *Analog Science Fic-
tion/Science Fact* (October, 1978).

A story involving a woman who threatens to crash a space habitat into
a planet.

Unseen.

B16. Beason, Doug. "Lifeguard." In *Cities in Space: The Endless
Frontier, Volume III.* Edited by Jerry Pournelle with John F.
Carr. New York: Ace, 1991, p. 79-96. Story first published in
Amazing Stories in 1987.

At the Heinlein—the "Water depository for the stable (L-4, L-5) Lagrange colonies" (79)—a young girl works as a lifeguard, helping the
tourists swim through the vast water tanks. When two young men
from Earth come to visit, she and a friend are attracted to them, but she
knows that they cannot ask them to stay: anyone who adjusts to very
low gravity cannot go back to Earth. After the man she is attracted to
performs a daring rescue of a swimming tourist, she learns that he is

paralyzed from the waist down, and for that reason, he wants to some-day return to the Heinlein.

Pournelle says the story was "designed to please" Heinlein, and it is best described as a successor to Heinlein's "The Menace from Earth"—that is, an interesting space environment is used as the back-ground for an ordinary juvenile love story. As in stories like Cassutt's "The Free Agent" (q.v.), the old idea that the physically handicapped might be better off living in space appears as a final revelation. Bea-son's story devotes some energy to describing the mechanisms of swimming in a low gravity water world but still fails to truly evoke its potentially fascinating environment.

B17. Benford, Gregory. "Dark Sanctuary." In *The Endless Frontier, Volume I*. Edited by Jerry Pournelle. New York: Ace, 1979, p. 285-299. Story originally published in *Omni* (May, 1979).

A lonely asteroid miner encounters a mysterious large object in space, which he deduces is an alien space colony similar to those built by humans. He decides that they must have traveled from another star system and are now living off the resources in the asteroid belt while they determine how to deal with humans. Respecting their privacy, he does not report what he saw.

Benford makes the point that people who have grown used to living in space will continue to live in space—that is why the aliens had not landed on the known planets. He also invents a new slang term from Earthmen—"ground-pounders" (94).

B18. Benford, Gregory, and Gordon Eklund. "If the Stars Are Gods." In *Nebula Award Stories Ten*. Edited by James Gunn. New York: Harper & Row, 1975, p. 13-56. Story originally pub-lished in *Universe 4* in 1974.

Aliens visit the Solar System to communicate with the Sun, which they regard as a sentient being.

The story briefly refers to an obsolete "orbiting space lab" (41); it was later expanded into a novel of the same name, discussed above, in which space stations play a larger role.

B19. Benford, Gregory. "Redeemer." In *The Endless Frontier, Volume II*. Edited by Jerry Pournelle with John F. Carr. New York:

Ace, 1982, p. 405-418. Story originally published in *Analog Science Fiction/Science Fact* (April, 1979).

A war between the planets and the space colonies has destroyed the planetary settlements and left the colonies in desperate need of genetic diversity. A man from one colony locates a distant space habitat traveling to another star and steals its DNA canisters; but he finds that they are only filled with junk —he was tricked.

One interesting aspect of this story is Benford's analysis of the government of space colonies; he says that because of severe safety problems, "you don't get democracies, you get strong men" (415).

B20. Blackburn, Eric. "The Entertainer." In *Carmen Miranda's Ghost Is Haunting Space Station Three*. Edited by Don Sakers. New York: Baen, 1990, p. 33-45.

A man famous for exorcising ghosts is summoned to Space Station Three to get rid of the ghost of Carmen Miranda. He appears to succeed in doing so by appealing to her Catholic faith and spilling holy water on her. But it is then revealed that the man is haunted by his own ancestral ghost, and that he persuades that ghost to dress up as other figures to haunt various places so that he can come and exorcise them for a hefty fee.

There are mildly interesting comments about sex and lifestyles in a space station, but like other stories in this collection, "The Entertainer" is best construed as an extended joke.

B21. Blish, James. "The Trouble with Tribbles." In *Star Trek 3*. By James Blish. New York: Bantam, 1969, p. 1-17. Based on the television script for the *Star Trek* episode written by David Gerrold.

Summoned to Space Station K-7 to guard a shipment of valuable wheat, Captain Kirk and the crew of the *Enterprise* must deal with voracious alien creatures called Tribbles, scheming Klingons, and posturing bureaucrats.

While he basically follows the television story (q.v.), Blish adds the information that Space Station K-7 is in orbit around Sherman's Planet, the intended destination for the new strain of wheat. This, however, raises a question: if the wheat is in danger at the space station, why not simply transport it down to the planet?

B22. Boston, Bruce. "When Silver Plums Fall." [poem] In *Cities in Space: The Endless Frontier, Volume III*. Edited by Jerry Pournelle with John F. Carr. New York: Ace, 1991, p. 76-77.

A description in verse of how a space habitat called AgriStat IV falls out of orbit and is destroyed in Earth's atmosphere.

At least I believe that is what the poem is about—as with much poetry, the literal meaning is not always all that clear. A sample stanza:

> O how the plates
> and stanchions vibrate
> to the quickening strain,
> how the rivulets flood
> our concave terrain
> as we are flung to apogee
> by the coda's roar. (77)

B23. Bova, Ben. "Isolation Area." In *Battle Station*. By Ben Bova. New York: Tor, 1987, p. 114-145. Story originally published in *The Magazine of Fantasy and Science Fiction* in 1984.

A spaceman reminisces to a reporter about Sam Gunn, the idiosyncratic, womanizing space pioneer who doggedly promoted and finally brought about the first hotel in Earth orbit.

The story takes place in Bova's Space Station Alpha, also featured in his *Kinsman*, *Millennium*, and *Colony* (all q.v.), at the time when it was still being constructed, and the crew lived in the "Mac-Dac Shack, a glorified tin can that passed for a space station back in those primitive days" (119). In what can only be interpreted as yet another argument for the exploitation of space, Bova has a cure for AIDS discovered at a makeshift space hospital; is he hoping that funds of AIDS research might be diverted to the space station? The narrator, a black homosexual who was the first man cured of AIDS, is also finally revealed to be legless—and hence, determined to live in space forever.

B24. Bova, Ben. "The Long Fall." *Amazing Stories*, 66 (December, 1991), 44-52.

As described in the November, 1991, issue, "The further adventures of

Sam Gunn [see "Isolation Area"], in which space station Freedom goes Hollywood" (p. 96).

Unseen.

B25. Bova, Ben, and Myron R. Lewis. "Men of Good Will." In *World's Best Science Fiction: 1965*. Edited by Donald A. Wollheim and Terry Carr. New York: Ace, 1965, p. 26-31. Story originally published in *Galaxy* in 1964.

A UN representative visits the American moonbase to discover why only on the Moon have Americans and Russians managed to avoid continuing minor conflicts. He finds that all shots fired on the Moon enter lunar orbit and return periodically to their origin—so neither the Americans nor the Russians dare fire anything. But, the Americans assure their guest, they are working on a way to solve the problem and resume fighting.

There are two references to Americans and Russians firing at each other from orbiting satellites; clearly, military space stations do nothing to generate good will or peace in space.

B26. Bova, Ben. "The Weathermakers." *Analog Science Fiction/ Science Fact*, 78 (December, 1966), p. 52-80.

The man in charge of project THUNDER, designed to stop all hurricanes from hitting America's East Coast, is in trouble: four potential storms are coming, and even with the use of lasers from space stations and planes with powerful chemicals, he cannot prevent them all. When one is about to hit the Coast, he violates direct orders and undertakes to control the entire weather of North America—as the only way to stop the hurricane. When his daring scheme succeeds, the President backs the concept of complete weather control, and an international agency is set up to maintain such weather control.

The main facility used is the Atlantic Satellite Station, with a section for weather-controlling lasers "under armed guard" (58); there is also one mention of "missile-defense satellites" (58), otherwise undescribed. The Atlantic Station apparently serves several other purposes, one of them being communication.

Note: this novelette was later incorporated into a novel, also called *The Weathermakers*.

B27. Bradbury, Ray. "The End of the Beginning." In *A Medicine for Melancholy*. By Ray Bradbury. New York: Bantam, 1963, 1959, p. 13-18. Story first published in *MacLeans* in 1956.

As a father finishes mowing the lawn, he and his wife hear the news that his son has been successfully launched on a space mission to build the first space station and eventually go to the Moon. He sees the event as the beginning of a new stage in human evolution, which will reduce all previous developments to a single preliminary stage.

This is essentially a disguised essay about the importance of the Space Age; its one novel feature is a popular song about the proposed space station which the father keeps singing.

B28. Brin, David. "The Crystal Spheres." *Analog Science Fiction/ Science Fact*, 104 (January, 1984), p. 128-143.

When humanity first ventured out of the solar system, the ship shattered a huge crystal sphere around the sun, leaving bright shards in the sky. As they ventured to other systems, they always found a crystal sphere around them—and they could not penetrate the spheres. Thus, the human race was cut off from other worlds. Finally, when a broken sphere is discovered, an expedition visits the alien system. They find abandoned space colonies, cities and artifacts—and the answer to their problem. The spheres can only be broken from the inside, so that developing races are protected from outside interference until they mature sufficiently to break their own sphere. Because the universe is now lonely, the previous aliens had decided to go near a black hole and wait for a far future when there would be many broken spheres and many civilizations to contact. For the present, humans will occupy the worlds left by the aliens, but someday they might join them to wait for the others.

This haunting, award-winning story depicts advanced civilizations colonizing space because that is literally the only alternative—other planets are not accessible. Thus, there is a huge "ring-city"—"the gleaming, flexisolid belt of habitindustry around our world" (130)—around the Earth, and the alien Nataral "transformed" "Every small-body orbiting this star" into "space colonies" (135). But life in space is not a permanent answer, unless there is a habitable planet in the vicinity: "Simply put, men could live on asteroids, but they needed to *know* that there was a blue world nearby—to see it in their sky. It's a flaw in our character, no doubt, but we cannot go out and live in space all alone" (138).

B29. Brin, David. "Tank Farm Dynamo." In *The River of Time*. By David Brin. New York: Bantam, 1987, p. 185-205. Story originally published in *Analog Science Fiction/Science Fact* in 1983.

An agricultural space station consisting of huge fuel tanks is threatened by economic reprisals from Earth until the commander discovers a way for the station to generate its own power to maintain its orbit.

Described by its author as a "propaganda piece" (206), this story argues for a *cheap* space station—a major concern of the 1980s. The metaphorical confusion here is interesting: ships come in for "landings"—docking, the narrator says, is an outmoded term (192)—implying a space station is like land; yet the station has a "Captain's Cabin" to give the place "the flavor of a Caribbean cruise" (199-200) and at the story's end he says the station is "anchored" to Earth (204). To further mix metaphors, he refers to the big tanks making up the station as "eggs" that will eventually become "great birds" that will fly to the stars (204).

B30. Brin, David. "The Warm Space." In *Great Science Fiction Stories by the World's Great Scientists*. Edited by Isaac Asimov with Martin Greenberg and Charles Waugh. New York: Donald I. Fine, Inc., 1984, p. 130-146. Story originally published in *Far Frontiers* in 1985.

One of the last few "Old Style" humans living in space is recruited by the new mechanical "cyromen" to travel to hyperspace, to find out why robots do not survive the trip. He discovers the simple fact that hyperspace is hot, making it difficult for robots with supercooled brains to endure, but not for humans—this giving new hope for the continued existence and usefulness of real humans.

The experimental flight is launched from a space station orbiting outside of Neptune—the "Old Wheel" where humans live, and the "Complex" where the cyromen live. It is the old concept of the space station as a launching platform writ large: a space station orbiting outside the Solar System as a starting point for interstellar flights.

B31. Brin, David. "What Continues, What Fails." In *Full Spectrum 4*. Edited by Lou Aronica, Amy Stout, and Betsy Mitchell. New

York: Bantam, 1993, p. 432-459.

On a space station near a black hole, two women scientists are trying a new technique for looking into a black hole. One of them has been asked to give birth to her own clone—a honor which makes her partner jealous. As her baby is almost ready to be born, she seems to observe a new universe being created within the black hole—one surprisingly similar to our own. Her theory is that the universe follows a process of evolution not unlike biological evolution: as a black hole creates another universe, the most successful features of earlier universes are reproduced.

The back cover blurb speaks of "David Brin's tale of scientific obsession and consuming loneliness on a space station," but Brin is clearly more interested in the story's scientific conceit, not the emotions of his characters, though he pays some attention to the unhappiness of the unchosen partner who knows she will remain uncloned and "be the last in [her] line" (45), which is arguably a form of loneliness. The station contains mechanical "pseudo-life servitors" which are constantly created to perform simple tasks, and there is one scene where the heroine goes outside the station to confront the vacuum of space and conduct experiments.

B32. Bryning, Frank B. "For Men Must Work." *New Worlds Science Fiction*, 21 (July, 1957), p. 36-51.

A woman hopes that her husband can get a job on Earth, but when his ferry rocket from Satellite Space Station Commonwealth Two to Earth is hit by a meteorite, his successful effort to rescue the ship instead earns him a high-paying new job as the Office in Charge of Maintenance at the space station.

Little is said about the appearance of work of the space station, although it does serve to send help to the disabled spaceship and, one must assume, carries on the other usual functions of such a station.

B33. Buckley, Bob. "The Star Hole." *Analog Science Fiction/Science Fact*, 90 (October, 1972), p. 70-93.

Investigating a huge pit on the lunar surface, scientists discover what appear to be wispy alien creatures and fragments of a spaceship hull. Incredibly, they find that the creatures are "reconstructing" the glass hull (93)—meaning that the creatures are actually some strange kind of ship-building mechanism.

At the very beginning, the story makes a striking analogy between the pit and a sculpture built in a space station—"a sculpted ice dream floating just outside the celebrated zero-G studio port of Sky Station Six" (72).

B34. Callin, Grant D. "The Turtle and O'Hare." *Analog Science Fiction/Science Fact*, 102 (January 4, 1982), p. 64-79.

A spaceman named O'Hare is forced to land on Mercury and begins a desperate effort to reach a huge moving "crawler" mining the surface before the slowly revolving planet brings him into the sunlit zone— which would quickly kill him. While walking across the surface, he remembers first going into orbit and being trained in a space station.

Though not the focus of the story, Callin's future world is vigorously committed to living in space—they have just built "SpaceHome 6" (66)—and O'Hare learns how to be a "vacuum freak" (68) while on the colony SpaceHome 4—a traditional place to prepare youngsters for life in space.

B35. Card, Orson Scott. "Ender's Game." In *Maps in a Mirror: The Short Fiction of Orson Scott Card*. New York: Tor, 1990, p. 541-566. Originally published in *Analog: Science Fiction/ Science Fact* (August, 1977).

A young boy is repeatedly trained to fight in various simulation games, first on Earth and then on a space station; when he is deemed ready, he is made to play a final game involving an assault on an alien planet. After he wins, he learns that the games he has been directing were actual battles with aliens, and that he has won the war for Earth.

As is appropriate in describing a boy whose entire life is a circumscribed series of games, "Ender's Game" offers almost no description of the space station or its lifestyle.

Note: Card later expanded this story into a novel with the same name (q.v.).

B36. Card, Orson Scott. "The Monkeys Thought 'Twas All in Fun." In *Maps in a Mirror: The Short Fiction of Orson Scott Card*. New York: Tor, 1990, p. 390-419. Story first published in

Analog Science Fiction/Science Fact (May, 1979).

A gigantic space habitat, containing thousands of huge compartments with habitable environments, suddenly appears at a Trojan point in Earth's orbit. Billions of people migrate to these new worlds, not realizing that the habitat is actually an alien organism, which is educating its various cells with stories in preparation for the final stage of its reproduction, when all the cells will be flung across the galaxy. When the habitat in fact explodes in this manner, it is seen as the greatest disaster in human history.

Card is sometimes accused of having a cruel streak, and there is something odd about a story involving the deaths of billions of people which takes its title from "Pop Goes the Weasel." The story could be filed as another example of the space station as organism, although this obsessive story-telling habitat seems to be a rather obtuse one. Interestingly, Card says in the afterword that "I first conceived the story in response to a call by Jerry Pournelle for contributions to an anthology of stories set in artificial habitats" (428). Presumably, Card is talking about Pournelle's *Endless Frontier* anthologies, and, since the story appeared in *Analog*, presumably Pournelle rejected it.

B37. Carr, John F. "Shapes of Things to Come." In *The Endless Frontier, Volume II*. Edited by Jerry Pournelle with John F. Carr. New York: Ace, 1982, p. 359-373.

In the asteroid belt, huge, intelligent machines consume and process minerals and water for use on Earth. A raider from a Native American settlement in the belt lands on and sabotages one of the machines called John Harvey; its human supervisor makes the difficult decision to rush the injured raider back to his home and abandon the "dying" John Harvey, whom he had come to regard as a friend. But in the end, he decides to give up his job and assist the Native Americans.

With Native Americans in space, this is *literally* a story of the "New Frontier." A sentient, human-like space station, first seen in Fritch's "Many Dreams of Earth" (q.v.), is here presented in an updated form; the Native American settlement, a hollowed-out asteroid, can also be regarded as a space station.

B38. Cassutt, Michael. "The Free Agent." In *Cities in Space: The Endless Frontier, Volume III*. Edited by Jerry Pournelle with John F. Carr. New York: Ace, 1991, p. 31-57. Originally published in *The Magazine of Fantasy and Science Fiction* (August, 1981).

A controversial astronaut is hired by a millionaire baseball player to fly his son, who is handicapped, to the Russian space station Kosmograd. He is surprised when the boy decides to stay on the station, saying "Down there I'll never be anything but a cripple.... Up *here*, man, *I've* got a chance to be a superstar" (55).

Cassutt's story makes the familiar point that life in space might be best for the physically handicapped. Kosmograd, or "Space City," is barely described; there are also references to the American "Space Operations Center," "That misshapen heap that would eventually be a real space station" (33).

B39. Chandler, A. Bertram. "Moonfall." *Imagination*, 6 (May, 1955), p. 92-100.

As one survivor relates, a human Moonbase has been destroyed by gigantic, metallic aliens, apparently survivors of an ancient race that inhabited the moon. Among other things, they consume plutonium, and they may be on the verge of reproducing.

When there are reports of giants on the moon, one man says, "We couldn't believe it. We knew, *we knew*, that nobody else had ever put a rocket on the Moon, had not even established a Space Station" (96)— as if building a space station constituted the minimal defining attribute of a space-faring civilization.

B40. Cherryh, C. J. [Carolyn Cherry] "Wings." In *Carmen Miranda's Ghost Is Haunting Space Station Three*. Edited by Don Sakers. New York: Baen, 1990, p. 212-218.

At a space station haunted by the ghost of Carmen Miranda, a crewman dies in an accident and is greeted by the ghosts of various famous aviators. Thrilled because they now have a space pilot in their midst, the ghosts take over a spaceship and fly out into deep space.

At the time of the story, the station is being inspected by auditors, who are naturally not pleased to see the chaos which they do not know has been caused by ghosts. The station chief, however, argues that it was their distracting presence which caused the crewman's fatal accident.

Note: Cherryh has also written a scientifically-based story about immaterial beings haunting space, *Voyagers in Night* (q.v.).

B41. Chilson, Robert. "Truck Driver." In *Space Shuttles: Isaac Asimov's Wonderful Worlds of Science Fiction #7.* Edited by Isaac Asimov, Martin H. Greenberg, and Charles G. Waugh. New York: Signet, 1987, p. 13-30. Story originally published in *Analog Science Fiction/Science Fact* in 1972.

A spaceplane used to dump radioactive waste into space is hijacked by Lunar Separatists seeking materials for nuclear weapons; but the woman pilot thwarts their plans and rescues her husband and son.

Although the story mostly takes place in the upper regions of the atmosphere, there is one glimpse of future structures in space: "Joel had given her a clear course through the Earthbelt, though they came closer than Ynga liked to half a dozen factory complexes. Space was crowded so near the planet, not merely with the factory and space city and amusement complex traffic, but with Luna and the asteroids as well" (20).

B42. Christensen, Kevin. "Bellerophon." In *The Endless Frontier, Volume II.* Edited by Jerry Pournelle with John F. Carr. New York: Ace, 1982, p. 228-275. Story first published in *Destinies* in 1980.

Virgil Sayer, a spacefaring gambler regarded as a romantic hero, agrees to mount a bioengineered winged horse—a new Pegasus—to reenact its ancient battle with a chimera, also artificially manufactured; the fight will be recorded to be re-experienced by many others in special chambers, a popular form of entertainment in the future. He dies as a result of treachery, which only reinforces his mythic image.

Again, a space habitat represents a return to the past, this time a reenactment of Greek mythology. Gamblers and gambling are also central to space habitat life in Watkins's *The Centrifugal Rickshaw Dancer* (q.v.).

B43. Clarke, Arthur C. "The Cruel Sky." In *The Wind from the Sun: Stories of the Space Age.* By Arthur C. Clarke. 1972. New York: Signet, 1973, p. 94-111. Story originally published in *Boys' Life* in 1967.

A group of men testing a new levitation device are threatened by a snow leopard that accidentally accompanied them.

The men mention seeing Pacific Number Three, the brightest space station in the sky, and their rescue is effected with the help of "met stations" (meteorological stations).

B44. Clarke, Arthur C. "Death and the Senator." In *Tales of Ten Worlds*. By Arthur C. Clarke. New York: Harcourt Brace Jovanovich, 1962, p. 115-140. Story originally published in *Analog Science Fact/Science Fiction* in 1961.

A senator with presidential ambitions is threatened by heart disease; however, he is contacted by Russian space officials who tell him that they believe his heart problems can be cured in the weightless conditions of their Mechnikov Satellite Hospital. The irony is that the senator opposed the construction of an American space hospital. In the end, he decides to turn down the opportunity and let others take advantage of the space hospital; shortly afterwards, he dies.

Clarke has frequently pointed out the advantages of weightless life, as in *2061: Odyssey Three* (q.v.). What seems to influence the senator is seeing a young couple in the waiting room during his preliminary examination by Russian doctors; perhaps he feels that only the young should enjoy the advantages of life in space.

B45. Clarke, Arthur C. "The Haunted Space Suit." [Also known as "Who's There?"] In *Fifty Short Science Fiction Tales*. Edited by Isaac Asimov and Groff Conklin. New York: Collier, 1963, p. 61-66. Story originally published in *New Worlds* in 1958.

On a spacewalk to retrieve an old satellite orbiting dangerously close to a space station, a spaceman is bothered by mysterious sounds of life and a pat on his back—which turn out to be caused by three unsuspected kittens in his suit's storage locker.

As in *Islands in the Sky* (q.v.), Clarke sets up a melodramatic situation—in this case, a spacesuit "haunted" by a previous occupant—then deflates it with a prosaic explanation. The real danger in the story—the satellite—is a reminder that space debris in orbit may well be a problem for an orbiting space station.

B46. Clarke, Arthur C. "The Last Command." In *The Wind from the*

Sun: Stories of the Space Age. By Arthur C. Clarke. 1972. New York: Signet, 1973, p. 61-62. Story originally published in *Bizarre! Mystery Magazine* in 1965.

The commander of a secret space station armed with nuclear missiles receives a pre-recorded command stating that the war has been lost, and that he should explode his bombs harmlessly in space and surrender his forces to the other side.

The surprise ending is that the space station is Russian; it was supposed to ensure that Russia would not be conquered, but as the pre-recorded message states, there must have been some flaw in the theory.

B47. Clarke, Arthur C. "The Lion of Comarre." In *The Lion of Comarre and Against the Fall of Night.* By Arthur C. Clarke. New York: Harcourt, Brace & World, 1968, p. 3-62. Story originally published in *Thrilling Wonder Stories* (August, 1949).

A restless young scientist, living in a future world of long stagnation, visits the mysterious "Decadent" city of Comarre, where he finds information about constructing a new type of thinking robot that will lead humanity into a new age.

A brief scene depicts an "artificial moon" which is the home of the governing World Council. Having the Council Chamber in orbit, with a continuous view of the entire planet below, ensures that "no narrow parochial viewpoint" will prevent the leaders from doing their "greatest work" (12, 13).

B48. Clarke, Arthur C. "Love That Universe." In *The Wind from the Sun: Stories of the Space Age.* By Arthur C. Clarke. 1972. New York: Signet, 1973, p. 85-88. Story originally published in *Escapade* in 1967.

When an imperiled Earth discovers that space is flooded with the mental radiation of other intelligent species, scientists decide that humanity's only hope is for billions of people to send out a massive emanation of love.

The mental radiations from space could only be studied from Antigeos, an artificial planetoid on the other side of Earth's orbit—far away from the distracting mental radiations of the people of Earth.

B49. Clarke, Arthur C. "The Other Side of the Sky." In *The Other Side of the Sky*. By Arthur C. Clarke. 1958. New York: Signet, 1959, p. 26-44. Story originally published in *Infinity Science Fiction* in 1957.

Clarke offers a series of homey vignettes about building, and then living in, a space station: a much-anticipated supply rocket goes astray; a pet canary saves the crew when there is a problem with the air supply; an emergency rescue involves brief exposure to the vacuum of space without a spacesuit; the first worldwide television broadcast takes place; the protagonist glimpses a mysterious flying object in space; and finally, he bids farewell to his son, part of the first expedition to Mars.

As always, Clarke offers some good advice—NASA might well consider carrying a canary on board a space station to alert crewmen to a problem with their air, or experimenting to see if humans really could endure short exposure to vacuum. While one newscaster elects to stay on board the station, explaining that he prefers the station's clean air and low gravity to the environment of Earth, the predominant impression is that life in space will frequently be frustrating, boring, and confining; travel further into space is the more desirable goal, carried out here not by the hero but by his son.

Note: the portion of this story involving the passage through the vacuum is sometimes reprinted separately as "Take a Deep Breath."

B50. Clarke, Arthur C. "Venture to the Moon." In *The Other Side of the Sky*. By Arthur C. Clarke. 1958. New York: Signet, 1959, p. 70-93. Story originally published in *The Evening Standard* in 1956.

Three first voyages to the Moon—the American *Goddard*, the Russian *Ziolkovski*, and the British *Endeavour*—simultaneously take off from Space Station Three; all land on and explore the lunar surface.

The station is barely mentioned, as Clarke focuses his attention on the flight to the Moon in this episodic story written for newspaper publication. The follow-up story, "The Other Side of the Sky" (q.v.), is exclusively devoted to space station life.

B51. Clement, Hal. [Harry Clement Stubbs] "Answer." In *The Best of Hal Clement*. Edited by Lester del Rey. New York: Ballantine, 1979, p. 147-171. Story originally published in *Astounding Science-Fiction* (April, 1947).

A psychologist visits a research station in space—actually, a gigantic computer with a staff of scientists—to develop a computer model of human thought. Unfortunately, contemplating the results drives him mad.

The head of this research station is described as incredibly old, kept alive by the weightless environment. Aside from another depiction of space station madness, the story offers one practical suggestion: because the sensitive computer would be disturbed by radio transmissions, station residents communicate by a system of calling tubes, mechanical bells and hand signals—all reasonable and energy-efficient methods.

B52. Clement, Hal. [Harry Clement Stubbs] "Fireproof." In *Space Lash*. [Also known as *Small Changes*] By Hal Clement. New York: Dell, 1969, p. 80-95. Story originally published in *Astounding Science-Fiction* (March, 1949).

A foreign intruder intent on sabotaging a torpedo-launching space station is foiled because he does not realize that flames—part of his chosen method of destruction—automatically extinguish themselves in weightless conditions.

For once, at attempt to sabotage a space station is met with smugness and complacency, as if the "fireproof" nature of such a station renders it invulnerable. In other stories, of course, keeping the station safe from attack is a bigger problem.

B53. Clough, B. W. [Brenda] "Provisional Solution." In *Carmen Miranda's Ghost Is Haunting Space Station Three*. Edited by Don Sakers. New York: Baen, 1990, p. 1-4.

A medium is summoned to contact the ghost of Carmen Miranda haunting Space Station Three, which is delaying progress toward the first Mars landing. The ghost appears and says that she and other ghosts want to live in space and want to help out; when one person comments that their food could be improved, the ghost of Julia Child appears to offer some recipes.

This vignette offers the observation that it is never entirely quiet on a space station and is otherwise inconsequential.

B54. Clough, B. W. [Brenda] "La Vita Nuova (The New Life)." In *Carmen Miranda's Ghost Is Haunting Space Station Three*. Edited by Don Sakers. New York: Baen, 1990, p. 283-292.

While other ghosts have gone out into space, the ghost of Dante Alighieri finds himself inexplicably bound to Earth. A voodoo priestess tells him that he is being held by a witch in Santa Barbara, California, and by destroying her computer records, he is at last able to leave Earth, where he plans to write a new version of the cosmic voyage in *The Divine Comedy*.

There is no mention of Carmen Miranda here, and the only reference to a space station is that the ascending ghost of Dante plans to stop at a space station to get some paper to write on.

B55. Conly, Judith R. "Gung Ho." [poem] In *Battlestation, Book One*. Edited by David Drake and Bill Fawcett. New York: Ace, 1992, p. 151.

This poem glowingly describes the previous victories of the Fleet and speaks of its new journey into battle.

This hymn to militarism includes one general reference to the space station featured in this anthology: "we gather...to transport our sphere of protection in defense of disparate strangers' kindred cause" (151).

B56. Conly, Judith R. "Imperatives." [poem] In *Battlestation, Book Two: Vanguard*. Edited by David Drake and Bill Fawcett. New York: Ace, 1993, p. 126.

While smugly announcing the inevitable victory of the Fleet over the Ichtons, this poem pauses to wonder about the "imperatives" that are driving their alien foes.

This poem, amazingly even worse than her last one, contains no explicit reference to the anthology's space station, unless one counts the statement that "we...assemble the skeleton of our civilization to shield the female flesh that will fill it" (p. 126)—with the station qualifying, perhaps, as the brain, or the backbone, of this "skeleton."

B57. Correy, Lee. [G. Harry Stine] "Amateur." *Astounding Science Fiction*, 52 (February, 1954), p. 92-107.

A former rocket engineer is drunk and bitter because a former colleague developed an anti-gravity drive which made rockets, and his career, obsolete. The colleague visits him to give him the Goddard Medal and reminds him that the stars—and not rockets in themselves—were the original goal. Reinvigorated, he flies into space and rediscovers the need to work on conquering space.

At the beginning of the story, the protagonist vainly hopes that "The space station's still up there, and they've got to have rockets to supply it, don't they?" (93) But with anti-gravity, they don't. Also, the man who developed anti-gravity made use of research conducted at the space station: "Boy, they're doing a lot of stuff on gravity up there" (98).

B58. Correy, Lee. [G. Harry Stine] "And a Star to Steer Her By." *Astounding Science-Fiction*, 51 (June, 1953), p. 8-47.

An aging spaceman on Mars decides to take the job of maintaining the engines of an old spacecraft, the *Fafnir*, on a trip to Earth, so that he can finally return to his home planet. When he reaches Earth, he opens up a bar and seems to settle down; then, he gets the urge to go into space again, and arranges to purchase and refurbish the ship he flew in.

When the *Fafnir* approaches Earth, it establishes radio contact with "Asgard, Terra's space station" (26); and there are two later references to people arriving on Earth from "the Asgard shuttle" (38, 46). Evidently, while most space travel goes from planet to planet, there is also some traffic that goes through the space station.

B59. Correy, Lee. [G. Harry Stine] "Industrial Accident." In *Great Science Fiction Stories by the World's Great Scientists*. Edited by Isaac Asimov with Martin Greenberg and Charles Waugh. New York: Donald I. Fine, Inc., 1985, p. 170-191. Story originally published in *Analog Science Fiction/Science Fact* in 1980.

Due to an accident, an unmanned transport ship going from the asteroids to orbiting space factories is going to collide with Earth, but a suicide mission illegally planned by a space official manages to deflect the vehicle before it reaches Earth.

Correy is warning that the more objects we have in space, the more likely it is that one of them will fall towards Earth—with potentially catastrophic results. In Caidin's *Killer Station* and Harrison's *Skyfall* (q.v.), the space station itself is falling; here, a ship approaching a space station is the problem.

B60. Correy, Lee. [G. Harry Stine] "The Plains of San Augustine." *Astounding Science Fiction*, 55 (April, 1955), p. 70-85.

A rocket from the space station makes an error and lands one hundred miles off course, requiring that a miniature spaceport be built around it to get it airborne and back to White Sands Spaceport. While stranded there, one pilot meets and falls in love with a rancher's daughter, and they resolve to eventually go to Mars to study the strange lichen there.

At the time of the story, there are "regular shuttles between White Sands and the space station" (72).

B61. Correy, Lee. [G. Harry Stine] "Pioneer." *Astounding Science-Fiction*, 53 (August, 1953), p. 37-54.

To obtain the money he needs for a messy divorce settlement, a man reluctantly agrees to pilot the first spaceship *Nomad* into Earth orbit. After surviving a few mishaps, he returns to Earth a hero, and his company tells him, "We've been given the green light by the Navy to develop a space station" and he is "needed" for the project (52). He refuses, but when his attorney tells him that he needs more money to settle with his wife and obtain custody of his son, he agrees to the next assignment.

As is many other stories, the space station is the second step in the conquest of space; as one character tells the pilot, "Remember, today the *Nomad*, tomorrow the space station, then the Moon and planets" (41).

B62. Correy, Lee. [G. Harry Stine] "The Test Stand." *Astounding Science Fiction*, 55 (March, 1955), p. 75-84.

A man who used to work on testing rockets reminisces about the day when he and another engineer had to risk their lives going out to fix a malfunctioning—and quite dangerous—test rocket. Then and there, he decided that this was work for younger men, men without wives and families, and promptly quit his job.

In beginning his story, the narrator notes that there are "regular trips on schedule out to the space station now" (75).

B63. Courtney, Robert. "One Thousand Miles Up." *Science Stories*, No. 4 (April, 1954), p. 88-101.

An American is sent to the five-man, internationally-controlled space station with instructions to take over the station and its warheads—because "whoever controls the space station controls the world" (90). However, after simultaneous attempts by the American and the Russian crewman to take over the station, they learn that all residents who live in space can never return to Earth, because their bodies adjust to weightlessness; the five men, noting that "There is no need for politics a thousand miles up" (100), then resolve to use the station only to maintain peace, and to attack the first nation which launches a war.

The situation in the station is naturally tense—"Five men knee deep in fear and intrigue, living under strained conditions in a little sphere of metal, each waiting for a chance to slit the other's throat" (91)—and one wonders why the United Nations would put an American, a Russian, and a Chinese in the crew of an international station. At one point, when one crewman is threatening to take over the station, another observes, "One of us could probably break away and cripple the station so it would fall back to the Earth" (99), an early mention of this danger.

B64. Diamond, Graham. "'Outcasts.'" In *Habitats*. Edited by Susan Shwartz. New York: DAW, 1984, p. 100-119.

A convict is exiled to serve as the solitary inhabitant of a way-station asteroid in a rarely-traveled section of space. When a renegade spaceship fleeing from a repressive government is damaged and comes to the station for help, the lone survivor, a young woman, persuades the convict to escape with her.

This seems a bit more like an habitation on the surface of an asteroid, not a true space station, but I mention it as one of a recent number of stories employing a space station as an image of ultimate human loneliness—other examples include Tannehill's "Last Words" and Martin's "The Second Kind of Loneliness" (q.v.).

B65. Dickson, Gordon R. "Steel Brother." *Astounding Science-Fiction*, 48 (February, 1952), p. 103-124.

An insecure young man becomes the solitary commander of one of the asteroid stations which watch for and defend against alien attacks. He is supposed to rely on the memories of previous commanders, piped directly into his brain, for help in crisis situations, but he decides not to, for fear that it might drive him insane. When five alien ships attack, he botches his response and it seems like he will need to destroy the station before it is taken over; at this point, he accesses the former commander's memory and deals with the situation—although it is the timely arrival of patrol ships that really turns the tide. Afterwards, he receives a spectral visit from the former commander who tells him what every station commander eventually learns: with the implicit comradeship of far-flung fellow workers and predecessors, "Brother! You are not alone" (124).

This is a borderline story, since the stations may be more like bases on an asteroid than asteroids converted in space stations, but it provides another instance of a space station successfully employed to defend against alien attack, and of a station resident threatened by madness.

B66. Di Filippo, Paul. "Stone Lives." In *Mirrorshades: The Cyberpunk Anthology*. Edited by Bruce Sterling. 1986. New York: Ace, 1988, p. 178-201. Story originally published in *The Magazine of Fantasy and Science Fiction* in 1985.

A young blind man in the savage urban jungle of the future Bronx is implausibly rescued by a powerful businesswoman, Alice Citrine, and sent to tour the world and report his judgment on its condition; but it is finally revealed that he is in fact her son and heir, sent to the Bronx for an education.

Space is inhabited in Di Filippo's future world: Stone hears an advertisement for "High-orbit vakheads" (178) and he asks to tour the "orbital installations," although he is told, "I think we've done enough for one trip" (194). Like other cyberpunks, though, Di Filippo is more interested in the degenerate urban culture of future Earth than possibilities for civilizations in space.

B67. Dillingham, Peter. "House." [poem] In *The Endless Frontier, Volume I*. Edited by Jerry Pournelle. New York: Ace, 1979, p. 257-260.

A space colony speaks, describing its origins, functions, and ultimate destiny.

Since the days of Hugo Gernsback and *Amazing Stories*, editors have tried to promote science fiction poetry as a viable art form, consistently without success. Dillingham's poem recalls Ray Bradbury's story "I, Rocket," which personified a spaceship in a similar mood. A sample of the poem:

> Occupancy by human organisms is
> welcomed because, like plasmids, they
> confer a certain transient evolutionary
> advantage—resistance to antibodies
> and the ability to colonize other
> specific environments for instance—
> which enables me to adapt quickly to
> immediate, short-term ecological pres-
> sures. (259)

B68. Dorsey, Candas Jane. "Sleeping in a Box." In *Machine Sex and Other Stories*. By Candace Jane Dorsey. Vancouver, B.C., Canada: Porcepic, 1988, p. 9-14.

A description of life in a space habitat, mentioned in a review of the 1990 reprint of *Machine Sex* in *Foundation: The Review of Science Fiction*, No. 54 (Spring, 1992).

Unseen.

B69. Drake, David. "Facing the Enemy." In *Battlestation, Book One*. Edited by David Drake and Bill Fawcett. New York: Ace, 1992, p. 4-25.

To infiltrate the ranks of the Ichtons, one of them is captured, a clone is created, and the human personality of Sergeant Dresser is imposed on the clone, creating an ideal spy. This human-alien combination has been promised that, when the mission is over, he will be switched into a human body, but someone tells Dresser that it will never happen.

There is only one mention of the space station, a statement to the constructed spy: "We're hoping you can find a chink in the Ichtons' armor. If you can't, the mission of the Stephen Hawking is doomed to fail" (p. 23).

B70. Drake, David. "Failure Mode." In *Battlestation, Book Two: Vanguard*. Edited by David Drake and Bill Fawcett. New York:

Ace, 1993, p. 242-264.

Sergeant Dresser and other Fleet personnel are sent to the planet Mantra where, according to Ichton genetic memory, the Ichtons once suffered a devastating defeat. Observing past events with a special device, they watch as the Mantrans are totally defeated by the Ichtons, with no superweapon in sight. But Dresser happens to pick up spores of a strange fungus from the planet which kills a Ichton prisoner, revealing why Mantra was a problem for them.

The story is framed by a debriefing session with Dresser and the admiral which occurs on board the Stephen Hawking, but little is said about the station itself.

B71. Duane, Diane. "The Handmaiden." In *Battlestation, Book Two: Vanguard.* Edited by David Drake and Bill Fawcett. New York: Ace, 1993, p. 178-194.

A woman serving as multi-denominational chaplain of the Stephen Hawking is assigned to accompany a new chaplain, a member of an alien race who, it turns out, asked to have himself placed in this position so that he could investigate the Powers that govern the universe to see if they could be of any help against the Ichton. His human mentor tells him that there are no certainties about these Powers, and no guarantees that they will help anyone; it is necessary for people to tend to their own affairs. After departing, he is wounded; but before he dies, he tells the chaplain that he has reported on his knowledge of the Powers to his people and will encourage others to come for more knowledge.

Desperate to avoid talking about the war that is the ostensible subject of these anthologies, authors try to think of novel minor characters to be the focus of their stories. Here, Duane concludes that a battle station would certainly need some kind of chaplain and, in the course of delivering some rather trite homilies about faith and the need for human action, she conveys some of the practical problems that a single person tending to the religious needs of a vast array of alien races might face.

B72. Duane, Diane. "Killer Cure." In *Battlestation, Book One.* Edited by David Drake and Bill Fawcett. New York: Ace, 1992, p. 211-229.

"In the tradition of" (or "Shamelessly ripping off") Anne McCaffrey's

The Ship Who Sang, this story describes a "brainship" with a female intelligence based at the Stephen Hawking station who must adjust to a new "brawn" (human companion). Assigned to survey a number of star systems, the ship unexpectedly encounters the Ichtons, and only by a desperate hyperspace jump does the ship manage to escape. She then learns that her brawn is actually a psychologist, sent to deal with what seemed like the ship's curious callousness and indifference to her work; by jolting her with the experience of an actual Ichton encounter, they thought they could restore a proper mental attitude.

The space station here is only mentioned as the base for the brainship; there is no other description of it.

B73. Dugas, Don John. "Joint Ventures." In *Battlestation, Book Two: Vanguard*. Edited by David Drake and Bill Fawcett. New York: Ace, 1993, p. 148-175.

A police officer investigates the murder of a stranger who used to linger in a station cafeteria every day for no reason. Looking for another woman—a nanny to two alien children—who also stayed in the cafeteria at that time, he discovers that she has vanished; her employer is then murdered. He eventually figures out that the man was an intelligence officer who was getting secret information about Fleet movements from the woman by a code conveyed by the knots she was knitting; and, even though they once had a romantic relationship, he confronts and arrests the woman behind the scheme.

Like the more successful stories in these anthologies, "Joint Ventures" more or less ignores the framing scenario to focus on an interesting mystery set on board the space station. Some of the atmosphere of station life is conveyed, as well as tension between military and civilian security officers.

B74. Dulski, Thomas R. "My Christmas on New Hanford." *Analog Science Fiction/Science Fact*, 102 (December, 1982), p. 64-81.

A man named Bob Crachit is working on a remote space station named New Hanford to develop the ultimate weapon—an anti-matter bomb—although not without misgivings. As Christmas approaches, he notices that some antinickel is missing, a tremendous potential danger. But the Project Director takes him aside and they go to a teleportation chamber where they remove all of the antimatter from the station and beam it into nothingness—thus conspiring to delay the their own deadly project for three years.

New Hanford is "a largely hollow metal ball about thirty kilometers in diameter, circling a dead world in an uninhabited solar system" (66)—a safe place to work with materials which could explode with devastating force at any second. Due to the cramped environment, uncertainty about the teleportation process, and the pressure of their work, the people at New Hanford are "a mixed lot of misfits" (66) and "They've had a few people crack up" (67). There is one mention of another scientific space station, "the sprawling Bethelab at L5" (73).

B75. Duntemann, Jeff. "Cold Hands." *Isaac Asimov's Science Fiction Magazine*, 4 (June, 1980), p. 58-77.

A space worker for the oppressive Combine lost his arms in an accident and retired to Earth, but the Combine, impressed by his previous efficiency, offers him state-of-the-art artificial arms if he will go back to work. He discovers, however, that if he steps out of line, the Combine triggers an overpowering pain in the arms. Now angry, he schemes to sabotage his own ship, and he finally succeeds in destroying the arms and taking his ship to freedom on the planet Mars.

His first job for the Combine is to refuel various space stations in cislunar orbit, and there are references to "the great orbiting stations" (61), the "R&D stations" (62), and "Curie Station" (74). A crisis involves his docking with "Golwing Seven...a thousand-mile cylinder girdled by two centrifuges rotating in opposite directions" (64)—a suicidal space worker has hidden in the docking chamber, hoping to be crushed by his oncoming ship.

B76. Earls, William. "Jump." *Analog Science Fiction/Science Fact*, 84 (October, 1969), p. 126-137.

An experienced spaceman can no longer endure the experience of the Jump in and out of hyperspace, so he decides to quit when his ship docks at space station Titan Float One. He goes to Titan and finds some odd jobs, but finds that he misses space and returns to his ship and crew.

There are evidently a number of space stations—sometimes called "Floats"—in the Jovian and Saturnian systems: the spaceman's ship goes to Grissom Station, a woman's ship is being repaired at Float Three, and the man once feared he would "pile up on Callisto Float"

(137).

B77. Ecklar, Julia. "Carmen Miranda and the Maracas of Death." In *Carmen Miranda's Ghost Is Haunting Space Station Three.* Edited by Don Sakers. New York: Baen, 1990, p. 46-64.

A paralyzed woman in a wheelchair lives in space with her "ghoul"— a person who has chosen to live in a box, removed from his body. When ghosts begin to haunt the space stations, they discover the problem: ghosts naturally move towards space, but the presence of the ghouls is distracting them and holding them to the space stations.

About the only interesting moment in this story is one headline from a tabloid newspaper: "NEW PROOF THAT ELVIS IS ALIVE AND LIVING ON OUTPOST SEVEN ('At night he wanders the station followed by swooning women!' sleepy station commander claims.)" (50-51)—the only reference I know of to Elvis on a space station (although an Elvis imposter figures in Allan Steele's *Clarke County, Space*). Other ghosts haunting space here besides Carmen Miranda are J. Robert Oppenheimer, a young piano player, a shoplifter, a caveman, and an alien.

Note: another story in this anthology featuring a number of famous ghosts is Betsy Marks and Anne G. DeMaio's "And Now the News" (q.v.).

B78. Elam, Richard M., Jr. [Richard Mace] "The Day the Flag Fell." In *Teen-Age Science Fiction Stories.* By Richard M. Elam, Jr. New York: Lantern Press, 1952, p. 223-234.

On a station on the asteroid Philos, captured by the Earth's gravity to stay in Earth orbit, a young officer suspected of treason manages to foil the actual saboteur of the station, which is armed with atomic guided missiles to keep the peace.

This vignette is hardly worth mentioning except as yet another example of the ideas that missiles in space are the best way to achieve peace on Earth and that such an armed station will inevitably be the target of unfriendly sabotage.

B79. Elam, Richard M., Jr. [Richard Mace] "The First Man into Space." In *Super Science Stories.* [Original title: *Teen-Age Super Science Stories*] By Richard M. Elam, Jr. 1958. New York:

Lantern Press, 1967, p. 1-23.

A young man successfully flies a three-stage rocket into orbit, paving the way for a "permanent space station" (6).

As in many other stories, a space station is briefly mentioned as the second step in space, immediately following a test flight.

B80. Elam, Richard M., Jr. [Richard Mace] "The Ghost Ship of Space." In *Super Science Stories*. [Original title: *Teen-Age Super Science Stories*] By Richard M. Elam, Jr. 1958. New York: Lantern Press, 1967, p. 132-206.

Seven young men, after their "washout" from Space Command school, accept work at a "space service station" that is mostly drudgery. They seize the chance to join a suspicious visitor, who has the missing piece to a space chart showing the location of a ship filled with valuable minerals, on a trip to the ship, which was flown by the protagonist's father. When the ship is located, the man abandons them on the ship, but they manage to pilot the vessel back to Earth and expose him; their success gains them a new chance to join the Space Command and fulfill the father's dying wish that the minerals be used to finance a "space hospital."

While most juvenile adventure stories glamorize life on a space station, Elam's account here is an unusually negative picture of such an existence; one of the heroes says, "I'd have gone anywhere just to get away from the station" (150). The term "space service station" (132) is a logical coinage for the type of maintenance facilities often seen in science fiction.

B81. Elam, Richard M., Jr. [Richard Mace] "The Iron Moon." In *Teen-Age Science Fiction Stories*. By Richard M. Elam, Jr. New York: Lantern Press, 1952, p. 147-168.

Two cadets compete for a berth on a spaceship to Venus while working on the "Iron Moon," a spherical space station in Earth orbit.

The station's main function is observation—to keep an eye on Earth to ensure that no nation is doing anything suspicious. Training space cadets in a space station is a logical procedure, the premise for many juvenile science fiction stories.

B82. Elam, Richard M., Jr. [Richard Mace] "Mercy Flight to Luna." In *Super-Science Stories*. [Original title: *Teen-Age Super Science Stories*] By Richard M. Elam, Jr. 1958. New York: Lantern Press, 1967, p. 82-91.

A young pilot, discredited after his ship accidentally hit the space station, proves himself worthy by piloting an emergency flight from the station to the Moon, carrying a diseased man to safety.

The story emphasizes the danger of a ship colliding with a space station (the planned method of destroying a station in the film *Project Moonbase* [q.v.]), and the danger of a plague is briefly raised when the hero says he has to rush the sick man to the Moon. The station in the story serves as a spaceport, scientific laboratory, and a place where student pilots receive necessary training.

B83. Ellison, Harlan. "The Discarded." In *Alone against Tomorrow*. By Harlan Ellison. 1971. New York: Collier, 1972, p. 33-48. Story originally published as "The Abnormals" in *Fantastic* (April, 1959).

A group of hideously disfigured mutants, victims of a radiation-induced plague, are permanently exiled to a prison ship in space by "normal" people who wish to have nothing to do with them. When an emissary from Earth promises them homes on Earth in exchange for samples of their blood—needed to fight a new outbreak of the disease—they agree, but the promise is broken; the hoped-for rescue ship only brings a new load of disfigured refugees.

Ellison's story is perhaps the bleakest vision of life in space as imprisonment and endless futility—the most common problem is mutants committing suicide.

B84. Farber, Sharon, and Correspondents (Susanna Jacobson, James Killus, and Dave Stout). "Dr. Time." *Isaac Asimov's Science Fiction Magazine*, 6 (September 28, 1982), p. 107-109.

Four corresponding writers decide to collaborate on a wild science fiction novel that includes numerous strange elements, including "Trojan point space stations" (107). However, their manuscript is not published because a nearly-identical novel appears just when it is finished.

This is a piece of fiction about a science fiction story about space stations and perhaps should not qualify for inclusion here. Still, it is interesting that the described kitchen-sink novel would include space stations, and that one novel mentioned on the coming Hugo ballot is *Space Station Soldiers* (109).

B85. Feeley, Gregory. "The Mind's Place." In *Full Spectrum 4*. Edited by Lou Aronica, Amy Stout, and Betsy Mitchell. New York: Bantam, 1993, p. 259-284.

The space habitats constituting the Circumlunar Catena have decided to employ microscopic machines to restructure all human brains to "improve"—actually to control—all people's thinking. Those opposed to this practice have entered a large space ark to travel to the vicinity of Neptune where they can live their lives unmolested. The mission's commander has her brain damaged in an accident; as part of the healing process, she periodically imagines herself as the captain of a sailing vessel. A crewmate argues that the Catena would never allow rebels to establish an independent stronghold, and warns her of hidden efforts to sabotage the mission. At the end, it seems his warning was correct, as her brain is being taken over by tiny machines.

This story reverses the situation of Michael Swanwick's *Vacuum Flowers* (q.v.), where Earth succumbs to a group mind while space habitats retain independent thought; here, the space habitats espouse controlling human thought and Earth is presented as their reluctant partner. Only one of the space habitats is named—"Callistograd"—and they are not visited or described.

B86. Fish, Leslie. "Bertocci's Proof." In *Carmen Miranda's Ghost Is Haunting Space Station Three*. Edited by Don Sakers. New York: Baen, 1990, p. 193-210.

Carmen Miranda is haunting the space station, leaving fresh fruit behind. Trying to figure out how a ghost can leave behind solid objects, a crewman theorizes that visitors from the other world might become solid in the presence of the station's generators. He uses them to summon Carmen's ghost and asks her to bring his dead lover to him; when she appears, further manipulation of the generators makes her materialize, and they finally go off together to the other world. As his story ends, the narrator is also planning to journey to that dimension.

One amusing aspect of the story is the jargon station personnel develop to describe the appearance of the ghost—the Ghost Phenomenon—and the fruit she leaves—the Phenomenon Fruit. Since the obsessed crewman and his friend can threaten the entire station by playing with the generators, station security is evidently not too effective here.

B87. Fish, Leslie. "Carmen Miranda's Ghost." [song] Lyrics and sheet music in *Carmen Miranda's Ghost Is Haunting Space Station Three*. Edited by Don Sakers. New York: Baen, 1990, p. [vii-viii], 306. Song copyrighted 1985.

The song describes fleeting appearances by the ghost of Carmen Miranda on Space Station Three, the mysterious baskets of fruit that keep appearing, and the theory that the ghost was attracted by the sounds of the station's engines.

This trifling composition, which largely relies on references to fruit for humorous effect, provided the basis for the 1990 anthology, *Carmen Miranda's Ghost Is Haunting Space Station Three* (q.v.). The actual song, along with eleven other science fiction songs by various filksingers, is available on an album, *Carmen Miranda's Ghost*, released by Firebird Records.

B88. Flynn, Michael E. "The Washer at the Ford." *Analog Science Fiction/Science Fact*, 109 (June, 1989), p. 14-70, and (July, 1989), p. 126-176.

An independent scientist and his team of technicians attempt to bioengineer a "nanny" that will enable human beings to resist radiation and, among other things, be safer in outer space; but he is plagued by technical problems, mysterious sabotage, government interference, and his own doubts about the project.

Several space stations are mentioned: the actual Mir station, hit by a solar flare which killed all three of its cosmonauts (June, 21); the "L4 manufacturing complex" (June, 24); and four others—"LEO," "GEO," "Novy Mir," and "the L4 complex" (June, 53). A major reason for the nanny is to protect astronauts from radiation in space; Dr. Singer predicts, "The greedy power companies and space stations will include [the nanny] as part of their workers' benefit package. The unions will see to that" (June, 30, 32).

B89. Ford, John F. "The Wheels of Dream." *Isaac Asimov's Science Fiction Magazine*, 4 (October, 1980), p. 20-52.

An embittered engineer and the woman who perfected convenient birth control meet in a bar on the Martian moon Phobos. They decide to work together to build a railroad that will go around Phobos. When a spaceship attempts to attack the train on its first trip, the engineer sends his train to escape velocity and it goes into space; however, he vows to build another train soon.

The story includes various references to "Lagrange Four A" (22) and "the Lagranges" (21)—Russian space habitats—and a brief description of the huge "interferometer the Russians built, half at each end of the Lagrangeskis" (29).

B90. Friesner, Esther M. "In the Can." In *Carmen Miranda's Ghost Is Haunting Space Station Three*. Edited by Don Sakers. New York: Baen, 1990, p. 220-245.

A hard-boiled psychic investigator on a space station takes the case of Carmen Miranda, the ghost who is accused of killing the Portmaster. If she is found guilty, she will be exorcised and permanently dissolved. However, the investigator, noting that the talking dog who witnessed the murder apparently smelled Carmen Miranda, deduces that the human who originally summoned the ghost actually impersonated her and committed the killing.

By far the best story in the collection, as Friesner ingeniously employs the style of a Raymond Chandler story to describe a world of scientifically proven ghosts and intelligence-enhanced dogs. Space station life is not seen as particularly attractive, as the food is terrible and the home-made alcohol of variable quality.

B91. Friesner, Esther M. "You Can't Make an Omelet." In *Battlestation, Book Two: Vanguard*. Edited by David Drake and Bill Fawcett. New York: Ace, 1993, p. 128-146.

One of the bear-like Gersons—an alien race devastated by the Ichtons—has bonded himself to Schlein, a rather profligate but talented linguist on board the Stephen Hawking. When two Ichtons escape, the Gersons capture them and proceed to feed the prisoners to each other—which is actually acceptable according to Ichton custom. When Schlein joins in the feast, an angry Ichton gives Schlein valuable information, which he trades for the Gersons' freedom when their activities are discovered.

Friesner, who succeeded against all odds in creating an effective story, "In the Can," for the anthology *Carmen Miranda's Ghost Is Haunting Space Station Three* (q.v.), is less successful here within the stricter confines of this lifeless scenario; still, the story has its moments of effective humor. With this story, though, cannibalism of a sort can be added to the list of aberrant activities sometimes observed on space stations.

B92. Fritch, Charles E. "Many Dreams of Earth." *Orbit Science Fiction* 1 (November/December, 1954), p. 98-107. Also published under the title "Space Station 42." In *Space Station 42 and Other Stories*. Sydney, Australia: Jubilee, 1958.

Space Station 42 is a "living space station" controlled by a single man in a stasis tube connected by wires to various station facilities. Thinking that he is still serving a ten-year term, he does not believe a female visitor when she tells him that Earth was destroyed thousands of years ago, and that only some humans like herself survived in distant colonies. When she is accidentally destroyed and turns into a skeleton in only a few minutes, the man decides she must have been an alien impostor, and he continues to wait for the end of his ten-year term.

"Living" spaceships, controlled by a human brain, have been seen in science fiction before, most notably in Anne McCaffrey's *The Ship Who Sang*, so a living space station is also a reasonable speculation. In losing track of time, and refusing to accept the reality of his situation, the resident here provides another example of madness induced by space station life.

B93. Fyfe, Horace B. "Sinecure 6." *Astounding Science-Fiction*, 38 (January, 1947), p. 55-71.

A collision with a huge piece of "negative matter" (70) devastates the Solar System, creating numerous plagues and mutations to threaten the human race, so six space stations are built—four orbiting the Sun, one above it and one below it—to look for the return of an expedition to Alpha Centauri and to warn them to stay away from the infected humans of the Solar System. However, as centuries passed, concern about the returning fleet diminished and the stations were turned over to political flunkies and allowed to deteriorate. When Security Station 6 actually detects a returning spaceship, the incompetent commander must struggle with his own ignorance and antiquated equipment to warn them to stay away—which he does in the nick of time. He then resolves to fire his worthless subordinates and improve the system.

The story pictures a unique use of space stations as defense posts: here, the stations are not to protect Earth from invaders but to protect invaders from the Earth. Initially picturing a crew of scoundrels in a comic mode, Fyfe turns deadly serious and has the chief scoundrel reform and become heroic.

B94. Fyfe, Horace B. "Star-Linked." *Astounding Science-Fiction*, 48 (February, 1952), p. 129-140.

The story describes a typical day in the life of the operator of a communications station on the Martian moon Phobos: relaying messages to starships, establishing a friendship with a remote alien, and talking to his ex-wife on Earth. Although he has some regret about not being able to watch his son on Earth grow up, the hero basically seems to love his work.

As a base on Phobos, this story's station is a marginal example of a space station, although Fyfe also mentions "asteroid stations" (133) which may be more like true space stations. The story's basic point is the importance of communications, and the joy of someone who assists in maintaining communications.

B95. Fyfe, Horace B. "Thinking Machine." *Astounding Science Fiction*, 48 (October, 1951), p. 63-82.

An Earth-orbiting space station where miniature planets are created and experimented on is purchased by an alien who places a race of tiny beings he discovered on those worlds to exploit them as researchers and experimental subjects. The alien's human assistant contacts these beings, kills the alien, and assumes control of the station—planning to continue using the tiny beings as resources, though in a more benign manner.

The space station here is a unique research facility which builds miniature worlds and watches them orbit and collide—presumably to gain knowledge of how actual planetary systems function and how they might be manipulated. The story also offers an example of a space station taken over by an alien in an unusual way: he buys it.

B96. Gallun, Raymond Z., and Jerome Bixby. "Ev." *Astounding Science-Fiction*, 48 (February, 1952), p. 125-128.

A government scientist demonstrates to an official his successful invention—an atomic rocket—which will enable man to overcome escape velocity and travel into space. While he dreams of peaceful applications—including inhabited "plastic domes beneath Phobos and Deimos" (127)—he expects military uses of space, including "Satellite stations, raining atomic bombs" (128). But the visiting official gives no indication of what the government is planning.

As in other stories of the period—including Michael Yamin's "The Dreamers" (q.v.)—"Ev" sees the exploration and exploitation of space as an either-or proposition: scientists versus soldiers, experiments versus extermination. Achieving peace is likened to overcoming escape velocity—and Gallun and Bixby leave unanswered the question of whether the human race will manage to do it.

B97. Galouye, Daniel F. "The Phantom World." *Imagination*, 5 (August, 1954), p. 6-48.

This space adventure involves the destruction of an orbital city.

Unseen; it is included based on Brian W. Aldiss's description of the story in *Science Fiction Art*.

B98. Gardiner, Thomas M. "Cosmic Tragedy." *Comet*, 1 (March, 1941), p. 116-119.

The last few representatives of an alien race, now living in an "artificial satellite that housed the observatory...circling [Earth] with incredible velocity" (118), send out what they hope is a message to the beings on the surface. But to people on Earth, the beam is a maddening "Whispering Death," and, without knowing about the aliens, they devise a powerful beam of energy which destroys the satellite.

This story recalls H. Thompson Rich's "The Flying City" (q.v.) in depicting an alien race which moves into space when their planet is doomed; the difference is that these aliens are sympathetic rather than malevolent. However, in this "short-short" story, almost nothing is said about their satellite home.

B99. Gibson, William. "Hinterlands." In *Burning Chrome*. By William Gibson. 1986. New York: Ace, 1987, p. 58-79. Story originally published in *Omni* (October, 1981).

A mysterious region of space called the "Highway" is discovered, a space warp of some kind which only solitary space travelers can enter; invariably, the experience drives them to madness and suicide, although they occasionally bring back an alien artifact. In a nearby space habitat called Heaven, two mentally-linked specialists await the return of the latest voyager; but they again fail to help, as she has already committed suicide.

In keeping with the theme of inner movement seen in his *Neuromancer* (q.v.), Gibson transforms the traditional concept of outward space travel into a horrible inward journey which drives people insane; the story likens humans to flies who catch a ride on a supersonic jet. Another tale of a space station near a strange region of space is George R. R. Martin's "The Second Kind of Loneliness" (q.v.).

B100. Girard, Dian. "Invisible Encounter." In *The Endless Frontier, Volume II*. Edited by Jerry Pournelle with John F. Carr. New York: Ace, 1982, p. 205-209.

An elusive, plastic-eating alien being invades a space station, but spunky heroine Cheryl Harbottle captures it by luring it into a metal-lined microwave oven.

This is an inconsequential vignette, much in the manner of the *Star Trek* episode, "The Trouble with Tribbles" (q.v.) —an alien invader is treated as an amusing nuisance. If the story has any point at all, it emphasizes the boring domesticity of so many space habitat stories; even capturing an alien being becomes just another morning chore, likened to catching a pesky mouse.

Note: this is one of several Cheryl Harbottle stories; "No Home-Like Place" (q.v.) also takes place on a space station and is discussed below. Three other stories I have examined take place on Earth, in Cincinnati of the future, and therefore are not listed here—it seems as if Girard moved Harbottle into space solely for the purposes of the *Endless Frontiers* anthologies.

B101. Girard, Dian. "No Home-Like Place." In *The Endless Frontier, Volume I*. Edited by Jerry Pournelle. New York: Ace, 1979, p. 123-128.

The wife of a space engineer, newly arrived at a space station, has trouble with an out-of-control bubble bath and wine that won't pour out of the bottle.

Another trivial Cheryl Harbottle adventure, suggesting that space station life will basically feature a series of humorous minor irritants. In times of trouble, Cheryl consults her book, *Space Living for Groundsiders* (125).

B102. Gottfried, Frederick D. "Hermes to the Ages." In *Space Shuttles: Isaac Asimov's Wonderful Worlds of Science Fiction #7.* Edited by Isaac Asimov, Martin H. Greenberg, and Charles G. Waugh. New York: Signet, 1987, p. 31-62. Story originally published in *Analog Science Fiction/Science Fact* (January, 1980).

An American paleontologist and his assistant travel to a Soviet space station to look at the reported remains of a body found on the Moon—possible confirmation of his theory that there were intelligent dinosaurs who died in biological warfare. They are told the remains disintegrated and are asked to leave; but deducing that the body must be in suspended animation, not dead, and that the Russians are secretly attempting to revive it, they return uninvited, worried about dangerous contamination. But the creature is revived with no harmful residues and, learning English, tells them that the dinosaurs deliberately destroyed themselves—leaving these unanswered questions: what could have driven them to racial suicide? And why was this one being preserved—as a messenger, a judge?

Though the events occur on a conventional space station, this story is similar to Robert Silverberg's "Our Lady of the Sauropods" (q.v.) in envisioning intelligent dinosaurs coming back to life in a space environment. The return to the station involves a deliberate near-collision and surreptitious entry through an airlock, standard devices in melodramatic space station adventures.

B103. Gould, Steven. "Poppa Was a Catcher." In *Cities in Space: The Endless Frontier, Volume III*. Edited by Jerry Pournelle with John F. Carr. New York: Ace, 1991, p. 186-243. Originally published in *New Destinies* (Fall, 1987).

While people on Earth eagerly make contact—and establish trade relations—with an alien space probe, a man working for a retired space official in the Belt City space habitat investigates mysterious shortages of equipment. He eventually discovers that a small group of conspirators has set up a secret base to built and launch the "alien" probe, as a way of breaking the monopoly of the agency controlling space.

Gould strives to create a lived-in and convincing space colony, but the foregrounded detective story eventually makes the story seem routine, his cocky hero is simply not a convincing character, and ending the story with a horrible pun seems like a pointless indulgence. The imagined song lyrics that begin the story might be listed as a separate entry, since they have no obvious relationship to the story, and since they evoke a pioneer spirit about life in space that is totally alien to the slick, sophisticated tone of the story that follows it. The song—"The Ballad of Baby Boo"—involves a worker in a space colony who is accidentally killed, causing his wife to commit suicide. The final stanza:

> She took the elevator all the way to the rim,
> Watching stars go by with a strange little grin.
> Opened up the airlock,
> Shook away the tears,
> Her body will hit Saturn in a couple of years. (187-188)

B104. Gould, Stephen. "Rory." *Analog Science Fiction/Science Fact*, 104 (April, 1984), p. 96-109.

A scientific research station is damaged by a shuttle explosion and breaks apart; one section filled with people is rapidly moving away from the main station. To maneuver it closer to the station to be rescued, the people must figure out a way to rotate the station. Surprisingly, Rory—a mentally retarded station resident—comes up with a solution: running and kicking the station walls, just like a squirrel rotates a squirrel cage.

The station is "a bewildering construct of struts, tubular passages, and spherical chambers" (99). Like other ideas in science fiction stories, Gould's method for rotating a space station is both simple and possibly practical.

B105. Grant, Lee. "Signal Thirty-Three." *Fantastic Science Fiction*, 4 (October, 1955), p. 38-63.

When a policeman on an Earth-orbiting space station learns that the approaching spaceship carrying his girlfriend is going to crash into the station, he flies to the ship, takes control from the drunken captain, partially collides with the station, and finally manages a safe landing on Earth.

This "ferry station" in space is explicitly modeled on an airport—with its "passenger lounges and bars...repair wells and...ticket desks and reservation booths" (38). They also use, like an airport, the codes "22" to mean riot and "33" to mean crash landing. Rather implausibly, the glancing collision shears off two spokes of the station intact, which remain attached to the spaceship, and the pilot manages to get them to Earth safely.

B106. Green, Joseph. "Three-Tour Man." *Analog Science Fiction/ Science Fact*, 89 (August, 1972), p. 112-125.

When a space factory worker asks for a third tour of duty, the company becomes suspicious and has a detective investigate him; usually, men work for three tours so they can illegally use the vacuum of space to grow huge diamonds. Catching him in the act, the detective survives an attack and brings the man to justice.

The "Flying Factory" of Green's story is "a strictly utilitarian facility, but it had a beauty of design and structure seldom matched in Earthbound architecture" (116). Green's detective does show some sympathy for his poor, blue-collar thief, a type of person rarely seen as a space station resident, but he ultimately concludes that his arrest is appropriate.

B107. Haldeman, Joe. "More Than the Sum of His Parts." In *Nebula Awards 21*. Edited by George Zebrowski. New York: Harcourt Brace Jovanovich, 1987, p. 153-175. Story originally published in *Playboy* (May, 1985).

A man injured in an accident outside of a space station is gradually rebuilt with mechanical parts; but as his bodily functions are gradually restored, he becomes cold and inhuman, kills two people, and threatens to open all the ports of a space station and kill all the residents unless his demands—to be completely fitted by artificial body parts—are met. However, the station personnel figure out a way to electrocute him, and another man plans to undergo the process with plans to use his new powers to benefit humanity.

The protagonist works at "U. S. Steel's Skyfac station, a high-orbit facility that produces foam steel and vapor-deposition materials for use in the cislunar community" (154); there are also references to several other space communities—Mercy, a hospital; Grimaldi Station, controlled by Western Mining; Nearside, where the protagonist makes his threat; and Farside, famous for its "sex bar" (160). Although it is obviously not Haldeman's focus, he again demonstrates how vulnerable a space station is to attack.

B108. Haldeman, Joe. "Tricentennial." In *The Endless Frontier, Volume I*. Edited by Jerry Pournelle. New York: Ace, 1979, p. 96-121. Originally published in *Analog: Science Fiction/Science Fact* (July, 1976).

Residents of an L-5 space colony launch a generation starship to investigate signs of intelligent life in another solar system. By the time they reach a destination, Earth is lifeless, and the space colonists ignorantly work their machinery and worship "the constellation Cygnus" (121), the starship's original goal.

Haldeman's story (winner of the Hugo Award for Best Short Story, 1976) focuses on the political intrigue involved in getting the starship launched while concealing its true purpose. As in stories like Bova's *Colony*, Coulson's *Tomorrow's Heritage*, and Reynolds's *Chaos in Lagrangia* (q.v.), space colony residents seem more interested in space exploration than space habitation; all 4000 inhabitants are described as eager to join the starship crew. Another indication of discontent is this example of space colony graffiti:

> Stuck on this lift for hours,
>> perforce:
> This lift that cost a million bucks.
> There is no such thing as
> centrifugal force:
> L-5 sucks. (104)

B109. Hale, Edward Everett. "The Brick Moon." In *His Level Best and Other Stories*. By Edward Everett Hale. 1872. New York: Garrett, 1969, p. 30-124. Story originally published in two parts as "The Brick Moon," *Atlantic Monthly*, 24 (October-December, 1869), and "Life on the Brick Moon," *Atlantic Monthly*, 25 (February, 1870).

A group of investors decides to launch a "Brick Moon" to serve as an aid in navigation. When it is accidentally launched with people aboard, they settle into a utopian existence in Earth orbit.

Sam Moskowitz points to this story as the first depiction of an artificial Earth satellite, although the project is fanciful even according to the science of its day; it would best be described as a fantasy. Still, it is interesting that the first manned space station in fiction was strictly an accident—the Brick Moon was never intended to be inhabited. The society that its residents evolve is purely utopian—there is no government at all, just a few laws to regulate sleeping habits.

B110. Hamilton, Edmond. "Space Mirror." *Thrilling Wonder Stories*, 10 (August, 1937), p. 43-51.

To provide energy, people have constructed a gigantic orbiting mirror 20,000 miles from Earth—"Three hundred miles across!" (44)—to focus the Sun's heat on a small area of the Antarctic. On the other side is a dome housing 50 maintenance workers. A Mercurian disguised as a human has infiltrated the base, and manages to kill the other workers with a strange disease carried by miniature Mercurians and, later, by removing all the air from most of the dome's rooms. The Mercurians plan to blackmail Earth with the threat to focus the intense beam on major cities. However, an investigator from Earth manages to overcome the Mercurian and destroys the advancing Mercurian fleet by focusing the mirror on them.

The residential part of the mirror is described as "a maze of artificially lighted compartments, machine shops, barracks" (44). The mirror itself is equipped "with rocket-tubes set around its rim, so that if necessary its position in space can be changed at will" (45). In an accompanying note in "The Story behind the Story" in that issue, Hamilton falsely claims to have originated the notion that a space mirror could be used as a weapon—the idea surfaces in Otto Gail's *The Stone from the Moon*—but Hamilton can certainly be credited with constructing an early and unusual solar-power space station, albeit only as the backdrop for an inane alien invasion plot.

B111. Heinlein, Robert A. "Blowups Happen." In *Expanded Universe: The New Worlds of Robert A. Heinlein*. By Robert A. Heinlein. New York: Ace, 1980, p. 35-90. Story originally published in *Astounding Science-Fiction* (September, 1940).

When scientists discover that a huge nuclear power plant might actually explode and destroy the entire Earth, they persuade the Board of Directors to use a new atomic fuel to launch the "bomb" into orbit where it can continue to generate power without endangering the planet.

With recent fears over the breakup of Soviet nuclear satellites, the modern reader may question the "safety" of a nuclear power plant in orbit—even one 15,000 miles high, as Heinlein proposes. And in any event, as finally revealed in Heinlein's last novel, *To Sail beyond the Sunset* (q.v.), the station was not out of danger after all.

B112. Heinlein, Robert A. "Delilah and the Space Rigger." In *The Green Hills of Earth*. By Robert A. Heinlein. 1951. New York: Signet, 1952, p. 13-23. Story originally published in *Blue Book* (December, 1949).

When a woman engineer is assigned to the construction of Space Station One, the commander objects; but he comes to realize that she is capable, and that women are needed in space work and space life.

A vignette that incidentally offers some insights into space station construction, both from an engineering and a personal standpoint. As in later novels like del Rey's *Step to the Stars* (q.v.), the building of a space station is treated like just another construction job.

B113. Heinlein, Robert A. "The Green Hills of Earth." In *The Green Hills of Earth*. By Robert A. Heinlein. 1951. New York: Signet, 1952, p. 125-134. Story originally published in *The Saturday Evening Post* (February 8, 1947).

The sentimental story of Rhysling, the blind "Singer of the Spaceways," who finally perishes by sacrificing his life to rescue his crewmates in an emergency.

In describing his many travels, the story mentions that Rhysling "never went closer to Earth than Supra-New York Space Station" (130)—making his famous song about wanting to return to Earth even more poignant.

B114. Heinlein, Robert A. "The Happy Days Ahead." In *Expanded Universe: The New Worlds of Robert A. Heinlein*. By Robert A. Heinlein. New York: Ace, 1980, p. 515-582.

Following a gloomy and cantankerous survey of present conditions, Heinlein offers a more optimistic fictional scenario, subtitled "Over the Rainbow," which describes how a future United States is turned around by an assertive and intelligent African-American woman who becomes President. At the end, a news broadcast from "O'Neill Village, Ell-Five" mentions the first birthday of the first baby born in space and describes, in the manner of a tourist brochure, the many attractions of the space habitat.

Those many attractions include: "free-fall sports" (580), "free-fall ballet" (581), gambling, and women with enlarged breasts due to zero gravity. Altogether, it is not a particularly attractive picture of future human life in outer space.

B115. Heinlein, Robert A. "It's Great to Be Back." In *The Green Hills of Earth*. By Robert A. Heinlein. 1951. New York: Signet, 1952, p. 74-89. Story originally published in *The Saturday Evening Post* (July 26, 1947).

When a husband and wife get fed up with life on the Moon, they decide to return to Earth; but they soon miss the freedom of lunar life and return home.

In their trip to Earth, they bypass Supra-New York and Space Terminal, the space stations described in "Space Jockey" (q.v.), by taking an "Express," described as a more expensive way to travel. Thus, the two stations reduce the cost of space travel but are not essential to it.

B116. Heinlein, Robert A. "Misfit." In *Revolt in 2100*. By Robert A. Heinlein. New York: Signet, 1953, p. 170-188. Story originally published in *Astounding Science-Fiction* (November, 1939).

A young "misfit," one of a group of young men working on transforming an asteroid into a space station between the orbit of Earth and Mars, is discovered to be a mathematical genius when he assists in an emergency.

The asteroid is first hollowed out a bit, then rockets are attached to move it into an solar orbit exactly halfway between Earth and Mars. There, as E-M3, one of three such stations in that orbit, it will serve as an emergency rescue station and stopover point for space travelers.

B117. Heinlein, Robert A. "Ordeal in Space." In *The Green Hills of Earth*. 1951. By Robert A. Heinlein. New York: Signet, 1952, p. 111-124. Story originally published in *Town and Country* (May, 1948).

A former space pilot, back on Earth after suffering the anxiety of deep space during a repair operation, conquers his fears when he goes out on the ledge of a tall building to rescue a cat and plans to go back into space.

The story notes that the spaceship the hero was traveling on left from Space Terminal, the moon-orbiting space station seen in "Space Jockey" (q.v.)—here called "Earth-Luna Space Terminal" (118).

B118. Heinlein, Robert A. "Searchlight." In *Expanded Universe: The New Worlds of Robert A. Heinlein*. By Robert A. Heinlein. New York: Ace, 1980, p. 447-451. Story first published as an advertisement in *Scientific American* (August, 1962) and other magazines.

When a young blind girl is lost somewhere on the Moon's surface, personnel at the Meridian Space Station blanket the Moon with laser beams, each designed to play a different note when heard on a space-suit radio. Since the girl—a pianist—has perfect pitch, she can tell them what note she hears, enabling the searchers to pinpoint her location and rescue her.

This story, published as an advertisement, had to be under 1200 words; hence, it is tightly edited to omit any substantive information about the two space stations mentioned in the story.

B119. Heinlein, Robert A. "Sky Lift." In *The Menace from Earth*. By Robert A. Heinlein. 1959. New York: Signet, 1962, p. 115-128. Story first published in *Imagination* (November, 1953).

Two pilots are sent on an emergency run to Pluto from Earth Satellite Station to bring needed blood to sufferers from Larkin's disease. After the flight—at a grueling pace of three-and-a-half gravity—one pilot is dead and the other permanently incapacitated.

The impression given in the story is that Earth Station is a standard military base in space, except for the presence of a flight surgeon and two medical technicians. However, Vincent Di Fate, artist for the original Signet cover, interpreted the station as an orbital hospital and provided an excellent painting of such a facility, reprinted in *Di Fate's Catalog of Extraterrestrial Hardware*.

B120. Heinlein, Robert A. "Space Jockey." In *The Green Hills of*

Earth. 1951. By Robert A. Heinlein. New York: Signet, 1952, p. 24-39. Story originally published in *The Saturday Evening Post* (April 26, 1947).

A pilot who fills in on the earth-station to moon-station run frets about frequent separation from his wife, until his skillful piloting in a crisis earns him an offer to be the regular pilot on the moon-station to moon run, which will give him more time to be with his family.

Heinlein logically supposes that future travel to the Moon will involve three separate trips: from Earth to an earth-orbiting space station, Supra-New York; from there to a moon-orbiting station, Space Terminal; and from there to the lunar surface. Such stations may be large, like cities—Space Terminal—or they may be little more than a "fueling point and a restaurant-waiting room"—Supra-New York.

B121. Heinlein, Robert A. "Tenderfoot in Space." In *Requiem: New Collected Works by Robert A. Heinlein and Tributes to the Grand Master*. Edited by Yoji Kondo. New York: Tor, 1992, p. 26-63. Story originally published in *Boys' Life* (May, June, and July, 1958).

A young Boy Scout and his dog—also officially a Boy Scout—emigrate to Venus with their family. There, while trekking through the dense Venusian jungle, an experienced scout guiding them is injured, so the dog must run to get help, which earns him a medal for his heroism.

To reach Venus, the family first travels to "the inner satellite station" (36), transfers to "the outer satellite station" (37), and then boards a spaceship heading for Venus. Approaching Venus, the ship docks with the "single satellite station" orbiting Venus (38) and the family shuttles down to the surface.

B122. Henderson, Gene L. "Tiger by the Tail." In *The Boys' Life Book of Outer Space Stories*. Edited by the Editors of *Boys' Life*. New York: Random House, 1964, p. 54-66. Story originally published in *Boys' Life* (November, 1961).

An engineer building a space station is called to rescue a rocket in danger; he goes to the given location, finds a spaceship and brings it in, but then learns that the endangered craft has safely returned to Earth. Since the spacecraft is not one of "ours" or "theirs," the question is: who—or what—does it belong to?

Building the space station is likened to putting together a jigsaw puzzle—a fair enough analogy. Apparently the station is being built by both spacemen and construction workers: "Training astronauts to new trades had sometimes been easier than taking skilled workmen and qualifying them for space" (56).

B123. Higgins, Bill, and Barry Gehm. "Home on Lagrange." [song] In *The Endless Frontier, Volume I.* Edited by Jerry Pournelle. New York: Ace, 1979, p. 264-265. Song originally published in *Co-Evolution Quarterly* (Summer, 1978).

A song about living in space, sung to the tune of "Home on the Range" and a bit of "Oh, What a Beautiful Morning."

The New Frontier is naturally celebrated here with an old cowboy song, a parody of low quality comparable to a *Mad* magazine effort. A sample of the lyrics:

> Home, home on Lagrange
> Where the space debris always collects,
> We possess, so it seems,
> two of man's greatest dreams
> Solar power and zero-gee sex. (264)

B124. Hoey, Edwin A. "Peace above Earth." In *The Haunted Spacesuit and Other Science Fiction Stories.* Compiled by Robert Vitarelli. Middletown, CT: American Education Publications, 1970, p. 67-77.

A teenage boy and girl are assigned to work on PEACE (Planet Earth Arms Control Eternal), an Earth-orbiting satellite designed to prevent nuclear war between the nations Alpha and Zeta by monitoring the weapon-launching control centers on Earth. While on duty, they detect an intruder—a trained chimpanzee, who passes through the brain-detection system designed to stop humans and starts pushing the proper buttons; and as he does so, a man in the other nation's control center begins to do the same.

This is a thoroughly stupid story, with the idea that only 16-year-olds would be alert enough to do this crucial monitoring duty and a system of "safeguards" against nuclear war that—literally—even a monkey can penetrate.

B125. Holt, Paul E. "Good as Gold." *Isaac Asimov's Science Fiction Magazine*, 6 (July, 1982), p. 114-117.

The President of the United States goes to a space station to meet with a humanoid alien who can only stay for five minutes. While the big questions about world peace and God go unasked, the he and the alien begin exchanging items—the alien takes his pencils and briefcase, while the President takes chunks of gold and jewelry. A final exchange indicates that the alien, like humans, knows nothing about the big questions, but the President expects him to return soon.

A strange vignette with an absurd premise and the odd assumption that a human and alien would be more interested in personal gain than new knowledge. The space station setting is mentioned in the first sentence and otherwise ignored.

B126. Ing, Dean. "Down & Out on Ellfive Prime." In *The Endless Frontier, Volume II*. Edited by Jerry Pournelle with John F. Carr. New York: Ace, 1982, p. 97-123. Story originally published in *Omni* (March, 1979).

On Ellfive Prime—mainly a retirement home for wealthy residents of Earth—a defective sprinkler system causes mudslides and eventually a disastrous disruption in the space habitat's rotation—a "spinquake." To help threatened residents, the habitat's director must make contact with a leader of the illegal residents, surreptitiously living off the land in the habitat, for their advice and help during the crisis.

In a sense, this is a story about a space station invaded by *illegal* aliens—who, perhaps like those in America, turn out to have their own contributions to make to habitat life. Of necessity, these stowaways have developed a rather primitive life style, another suggestion that space habitats represent a desire to return to a simpler form of life.

B127. Ing, Dean. "Tight Squeeze." *Astounding Science Fiction*, 54 (February, 1955), p. 93-106.

A spaceship flying up to the Doughnut, a space station under construction, experiences a malfunction in its rockets, and a crewman must don his spacesuit to do the difficult repair work.

This minor vignette about the near future offers a brief glimpse of the station being built—"while moving the plates and girders of the giant doughnut in place" (98)—and at one point employs one interesting image: the project is an "embryo space station" (99).

B128. Jackson, A. A., IV, and Howard Waldrop. "Sun Up." In *Faster Than Light*. Edited by Jack Dann and George Zebrowski. New York: Ace, 1976, p. 24-36.

A space station manned only by robots is sent to monitor another star, with a human crew to arrive later; but plans are cancelled when it is discovered that the star is about to go supernova, dooming the robots on board the station. The robot brain Plato, in touch with the station robots, essentially constructs a gigantic surfboard attached to the station, so it can "ride out" the supernova explosion, start up its fusion ram engines, and return to Earth.

The station is "a prepackaged scientific laboratory...a present crew of eighteen working robots. It was an advance research station, sent unmanned to study this late-phase star" (25). In the story, a space station suddenly leaves its orbit and becomes a spaceship again in response to an impending catastrophe.

B129. Johnson, Bill. "Meet Me at Apogee." *Analog Science Fiction/ Science Fact*, 102 (May, 1982), p. 74-92.

A space station has been set up near a black hole, a base for people who look for interesting salvage near the hole, or who wish to store something indefinitely near the hole because time slows down in its vicinity. A down-and-out pilot is recruited by a religious fanatic to go looking for a damaged ship containing church artifacts. He is actually the person who sabotaged the ship and his real motive is to make sure its occupant, a possible heretic, has been killed. But the pilot and the woman manage to kill the fanatic, and they decide to team up to work in the area of the black hole.

For a number of obvious reasons, a black hole will be an interesting place, and setting up a space station nearby is only logical. A mysterious alien race named the Hatane actually controls and supervises human expeditions into the hole, indicating that a black hole may also be the best place to discover other intelligent life forms.

B130. Kelly, James Patrick. "Solstice." In *Mirrorshades: The Cyber-*

punk Anthology. Edited by Bruce Sterling. 1986. New York: Ace, 1988, p. 66-104. Originally published in *Isaac Asimov's Science Fiction Magazine* (June, 1985).

In the future, a man becomes rich as a "drug artist" who specializes in developing new psychoactive drugs and new circumstances for taking them. For companionship, he clones a female version of himself, but while taking a new drug during a visit to Stonehenge, he realizes that she will be better off without him, and he goes away.

The story makes brief reference to the hero's previous or planned vacations at "Habitat Three" (72, 90).

B131. Kevles, Bettyann. "Mars-Station." In *Space Adventures*. [Original title *Teen-Age Space Adventures*] Edited by A. L. Furman. 1972. New York: Pocket, 1975, p. 115-134.

Because a mysterious form of "Glandular Disorientation" (119) afflicts all adults who live in space, four brilliant teenagers are assigned to live and work in Mars-Station, studying possible solutions to the problem. When one girl seems to have a cure in hand, an ambitious boy recklessly drinks the potion—but, due to a calculating error, it ends up dooming him to perpetual life in space.

At mealtimes, the station occupants "paid court to an antiquated system of etiquette particularly at odds with the absolute equality that existed in their laboratories" (117), suggesting that people may cling to old habits in the strange weightless environment of space. There is also the familiar lament that "Life could be dull at Mars-Station" (122).

B132. Killus, James, and Dorothy Smith. "High Iron." *Isaac Asimov's Science Fiction Magazine*, 6 (August, 1982), p. 104-116.

A space worker is hired for a top-secret project to go to an asteroid rich in iron, nickel, and cobalt and move it into Earth orbit where its minerals can be mined and sold. Near the orbit of Mars, the cable from the engine to the asteroid snaps and the worker must risk death from radiation to go out and retrieve the engine.

The story is essentially an update of Blake Savage's *Rip Foster in Ride the Wild Planet* (q.v.), although the asteroid here is made out of iron, not uranium. The worker's final interview takes place on Circumterra-2 in Earth orbit, and there are references to the "industrial satellites"

(110) and "the L-4 and L-5 industrial satellites" which now mine minerals from the Moon.

B133. Kingsbury, Donald. "The Moon Goddess and the Son." In *The Endless Frontier, Volume II*. Edited by Jerry Pournelle with John F. Carr. New York: Ace, 1982, p. 20-81. Story originally published in *Analog Science Fiction/Science Fact* (December, 1979).

An abused young girl, obsessed with the dream of living on the Moon, exploits a number of men—including a lunar engineer and his wayward son, whom she eventually marries—in order to achieve her goal. Uninterested in her previous activities, including a job as a waitress on a space station, she finally finds happiness on the Moon.

Like Bova's *Kinsman* (q.v.), Diana Grove could care less about living on a space station; the one in this story is poorly sketched by the author and barely noticed by its protagonist. Only life on another planet is truly satisfying to her.

Note: this novelette was later expanded into a novel with the same title.

B134. Kingsbury, Donald. "To Bring in the Steel." In *The Endless Frontier, Volume I*. Edited by Jerry Pournelle. New York: Ace, 1979, p. 197-252. Story originally published in *Analog Science Fiction/Science Fact* (July, 1978).

The leader of a space colony that roams the asteroid belt mining and processing minerals wants to bring his daughter out to live with him; but colony residents, fearing he would be a poor father, vote that he cannot do so unless he provides a governess for her. Angrily, he hires a notorious prostitute to fill the role. Later, when the space colony is in peril, it is she who saves the day.

The prostitute and the little girl briefly stop at "low orbit Rockwell Station," where they have "a spartan room" (228); there are also mentions of three solar power stations, one with the interesting name of Gilgamesh. The space colony itself—an ambiguous case, since it does move about more like a spaceship than a space station—is described as an ideal place for "village democracy" (201).

B135. Knight, Damon. "Stranger Station." In *SF: The Best of the Best*.

Edited by Judith Merril. 1967. New York: Dell, 1968, p. 143-168. Story originally published in *The Magazine of Fantasy and Science Fiction* in 1956.

A spaceman is sent to Stranger Station—a facility especially designed for visiting extraterrestrials—at the time when a massive alien makes the periodic visit to exude a mysterious liquid scientists have discovered prolongs human life. While there, he slowly realizes that his mind is being altered by the nearby alien presence.

There are two space stations in Knight's future world: "Home Station," "the larger, inner station [which] handled the traffic of Earth and its colonies," and Stranger Station, "designed specifically for dealing with foreigners...beings from outside the solar system" (144). While a space station is a perfectly logical place for humans and aliens to meet—neutral ground, as it were—this is one of the few space stations in science fiction built exclusively for that purpose. In the ways Knight makes an encounter with an alien an experience of madness and frustration, the story can be compared with Lem's *Solaris* and Tiptree's "And I Awoke and Found Me Here on the Cold Hill's Side" (q.v.).

B136. Kubaska, Theodore. "Univan and the Wheelies." *Galileo*, 1 (July, 1977), p. 37-43.

Aliens invade the Hans W. Blumish Station for Planetary Observation, replace an occupant with a robot, and have the robot order the station's computer to destroy the station. As the computer (who is also the narrator) attempts to prevent the explosion, he finally breaks down, preventing the catastrophe.

This tale of aliens invading a space station also involves a "living space station" of sorts, since its computer has a definite personality, even becoming a bit emotional at times.

B137. Kube-McDowell, Michael P. "Menace." *Analog Science Fiction/ Science Fact*, 104 (February, 1984), p. 84-105.

Returning to command a space station after many missions to deep space, space hero Thackery is gravely concerned about the planet Rena, which has developed an attitude of extreme individualism and a complete lack of concern for the poor and helpless. The Renans indicate that they will try to infiltrate Earth and promote their views—which Thackery sees as an extreme danger. When one leader on Earth offering similar ideas emerges, Thackery concludes that he is a Renan and makes a televised speech bitterly denouncing him; as a result, a mob kills him. Then it is revealed that the man was human; however, the woman helping him was indeed a Renan agent.

There is little description of the station, except for one televised glimpse: "a great and still-growing orbital city against the backdrop of a gibbous Earth" (87). A space station, of course, is the logical headquarters for the Planetary Survey Service which Thackery is the Director of.

B138. Kurtz, Katherine. "Battle Offering." In *Battlestation, Book Two: Vanguard*. Edited by David Drake and Bill Fawcett. New York: Ace, 1993, p. 216-239.

As the battle station is moved in to participate in a battle to save the planet of the Emry, the remaining members of the Gerson race volunteer for a suicide mission—to take a ship into the middle of the Ichton fleet, overload its engines, and cause an explosion that will destroy both their ship and the Ichton mother ships. After arranging for sperm and egg donations that will allow scientists to reconstruct the Gerson race, Commander Brand lets them go—and they spectacularly succeed in their mission.

This story includes some detailed description of the command center of the Stephen Hawking, and emphasizes its strange vulnerability—the gesture of sending it into battle is depicted as a bold and desperate maneuver. So, as the back cover of this volume indicates, the station is indeed a "fragile fortress."

B139. Kuykendall, Roger. "All Day September." *Astounding Science Fiction*, 62 (June, 1959), p. 30-43.

A miner is lost on the surface of the Moon; but his vehicle is spotted by "the new satellite observatory" (43) and he is rescued. His happy news: he has discovered water on the Moon.

Oddly, there are discussions about travel to and from the Moon without mention of a space station as transfer point; the observatory is apparently the only space habitation in this future world.

B140. Lackey, Mercedes, and Mark Shepherd. "Medic." In *Battlestation, Book Two: Vanguard*. Edited by David Drake and Bill

Fawcett. New York: Ace, 1993, p. 85-114.

The chief of medical personnel on board a large battleship, Althea Morgan, is puzzled by her new chief of surgery—an apparently talented surgeon who has requested fifteen transfers in fourteen years. Through research and conversation, she learns that the woman lost a friend years ago and is still haunted by the experience; she keeps moving on to avoid getting attached to anyone who might someday cause her similar pain. She begins to regard Dr. Morgan as a friend; then, when Dr. Morgan herself is gravely wounded in battle, she fears that once again, she is going to lose a friend. Remembering Dr. Morgan's advice that patients—even apparently unconscious ones—can often hear what doctors say, she begins loudly cursing at her patient, demanding that she return to life; and she remarkably recovers, thus teaching the doctor that caring about patients—and vocalizing that care—is an important part of successful surgery.

Though this story takes place on board the ship, the accompanying Stephen Hawking is referred to as "the Big Ship"—and visiting that place, in contrast to the spaceship, is said to be "like returning to Heaven" (86). There is the noteworthy comment that "It's a good thing they don't allow claustrophobes in space" (85).

B141. Lambe, Dean R. "In a Cavern..." In *Habitats*. Edited by Susan Shwartz. New York: DAW, 1984, p. 75-84.

With her mind in a daze during a life-threatening emergency in her asteroid home, Castle Keep, a spacewoman thinks about her life on the asteroid with her female partner, her children (now grown and far away), and her cats.

The woman's home is more like a base on an asteroid than one transformed into a space station; but there are references to the "Willy Ley Habitat" at L-4 (75), "L-4 hootch" (80), "LaGrange habitats" (83), and "Clarke-orbit powersats" (81).

B142. Lande, Irving W. "Slingshot." *Astounding Science Fiction*, 56 (November, 1955), p. 116-126.

A American spaceman based at an orbiting space station flies out on a mission and locates and shoots down a Russian rocket in a form of space combat similar to the aerial dogfights of World War I. Afterwards, he returns to the station and then to Earth to see his girlfriend.

This story of the militarization of space mentions there are "several satellite stations" (119) which the combatants leave alone, although a Moon station was destroyed. Thus, the military space stations are curiously protected by a sort of gentleman's agreement.

B143. Leiber, Fritz. "The Beat Cluster." In *The Seventh Galaxy Reader*. Edited by Frederik Pohl. Garden City, New Jersey: Doubleday and Company, 1964, p. 199-214. Story originally published in *Galaxy* (October, 1961).

Near Research Satellite One in Earth orbit, a number of free-spirited people have learned to construct large glass bubbles in space, connected by cylindrical tunnels, where they happily live their unconventional lives. A new administrator plans to carry out their eviction, but there is strong public support on Earth and in space for allowing them to stay, and when it is revealed that these people are actually a "pilot experiment in the free migration of people into space" (214), the eviction order is cancelled.

Leiber offers a brief but fascinating picture of life in weightlessness. His initial list of "activities suitable for freefall" is "sleeping, sunbathing, algae tending...yeast culture...reading, studying, arguing, stargazing, meditation, space squash...dancing, artistic creation in numerous media and the production of sweet sound" (199). He also mentions "freefall yoga" (201), "space diving," "water sculpture," "vacuum chemistry," "space pong," and "space pool" (all 202). The story can also be interpreted as a "prequel" to Leiber's *A Specter Is Haunting Texas* (q.v.), since it mentions that "In space the number of thins and fats tends to increase sharply" (201), just as in that novel.

B144. Leiber, Fritz. "Kindergarten." In *100 Great Science Fiction Short Short Stories*. Edited by Isaac Asimov, Martin Greenberg, and Joseph D. Olander. 1978. New York: Avon, 1980, p. 101-103. Story originally published in *The Magazine of Fantasy and Science Fiction* (April, 1963).

A teacher explains Newton's Three Laws with some incredible tricks—balls ricocheting off the walls or suspended in midair. When class ends, students pass by a sign:

GODDARD
ELEMENTARY SCHOOL
RESEARCH

SATELLITE GAMMA

This is essentially a one-liner, contributing a little insight—perhaps—to the different world-view that children growing up in weightlessness might develop.

B145 Leinster, Murray. [Will Jenkins] "The Power Planet." *Amazing Stories*, 6 (June, 1931), p. 198-217, 227.

The international crew of the Power Planet, a large station beaming power to Earth, becomes tense when war breaks out on Earth, and is eventually menaced by an attacking spaceship. However, one crewman saves the day with a suicidal attack.

The Power Planet generates its power by convection, making use of the temperature difference between the hot side—facing the sun—and the cold side—away from the Sun. Leinster mentions the monotony and loneliness of space life; women are not allowed on board because it would be dangerous.

B146. Lewitt, S. N. "Charity." In *Battlestation, Book Two: Vanguard.* Edited by David Drake and Bill Fawcett. New York: Ace, 1993, p. 65-83.

A devout Muslim leads what is supposed to be a routine survey mission in a remote system and encounters some Ichton ships. After he returns to the battle station, he wonders why those ships were not detected in the usual way; investigating, he learns that the Ichtons have a secret supply route through the system, and that they are using stellar radiation to mask their presence. He loads a ship with garbage from the station, travels to where the Ichton supply line is, and dumps the garbage in their path. The bits of garbage scatter and reflect the Ichtons' energy beams, hurting their ships, confusing their movements, and making them easy prey. Unfortunately, one Ichton destroyer does manage to destroy the man's ship and kill him.

It is interesting to have a Muslim as the protagonist in a science fiction story, and that is about all that is interesting about this story. After all, the device of using vented garbage as a battle weapon dates back to old submarine stories.

B147. Lewitt, S. N. "The Eyes of Texas." In *Battlestation, Book One.* Edited by David Drake and Bill Fawcett. New York: Ace,

1992, p. 83-106.

A hard-drinking, hard-living, Texas-born space fighter delivers a pair of Ichton eyes to a beautiful scientist, who determines that the Ichtons can actually see microwaves and radio waves. The only importance of this, apparently, is that it might help scientists determine the location of the Ichtons' home sun (which would presumably emit similar radiation). Later, though, when he is in a battle with the Ichtons, the man realizes he can use this knowledge as a weapon; turning on all radio communications devices at once, he "blinds" the Ichtons and then can win the battle. He celebrates by enjoying a date with the scientist.

The lead character in this story is both clichéd and objectionable—the kind of man who just loves to spend his days slaughtering aliens and his nights getting drunk. The story does provide some glimpses of the social life on board the space station—namely, its bars and restaurants.

B148. Lewitt, S. N. "That Souse American Way." In *Carmen Miranda's Ghost Is Haunting Space Station Three*. Edited by Don Sakers. New York: Baen, 1990, p. 145-161.

A Brazilian operative in a revolutionary underground movement describes his mission to destroy Space Station Three. The ghost of Carmen Miranda haunting the station appears and tells him that blowing up the station is not "our Souse American way" (155) and his plot is discovered, as he is apparently betrayed by a former revolutionary now working for the oppressive Company. Carmen's ghost appears, she kisses him, and he immediately dies, which leads the narrator to suppose that Miranda's way of conquering America might provide a lesson for the revolutionaries.

Like other stories in this anthology, Lewitt's doesn't really make any sense, although its use of a Brazilian protagonist is effective. In this future world, there are "seventeen commercial Space Stations" and "eight major Space Installations" (151).

B149. Lupoff, Richard A. "Stomping Down Stroka Prospekt." *Isaac Asimov's Science Fiction Magazine*, 6 (December 21, 1982), p. 48-70.

Six workers at Planetoid Mining Station #18 go for a vacation at the Gagarin Cosmodrome. One worker is haunted by strange erotic dreams involving mysterious aliens that humanity has supposedly encountered on the edges of the Solar System. In a bar, when he says he needs to "cool off" (62), he is asked to pay 500 rubles and is taken to a room where an alien waits. There, he fulfills his desire and "shared sex with an alien" (67), but he is deeply shaken by the experience.

The story strongly recalls James P. Tiptree, Jr.'s "And I Awoke and Found Me Here on the Cold Hill's Side" (q.v.), with a human possessed by an overpowering sexual attraction to an alien; and since the human and the alien are both male, Lupoff's story becomes an allegory of homosexual love as well—"There was something wrong for him to feel sexual desire for this alien" (65). And as in Tiptree's story, there is little learned about the alien from the encounter, although the alien here is not presented as a controlling figure; instead, the alien is characterized as probably subordinate, a pervert or a prostitute of some kind.

B150. MacLean, Katherine. "The Gambling Hell and the Sinful Girl." In *The Endless Frontier, Volume I.* Edited by Jerry Pournelle. New York: Ace, 1979, p. 267-283. Story first published in *Analog: Science Fiction/Science Fact* (January, 1975).

A simple woman raising her family in a home "barrel" in the asteroid belt reluctantly sends her son to work in the "Belt Foundry living barrel," where he meets a naïve young girl from Georgia and helps her escape from the evil men running the decadent "Gambling Hell."

It is very hard to take this story seriously, when the woman's family and attitude precisely recall hillbillies in the Ozark Mountains. The idea that space will be the "New Frontier" has never seemed so unrealistic—are simple-minded backwoodsmen really the type of people that will be living in outer space?

Note: John Clute and Peter Nicholls's entry on Katherine MacLean in *The Science Fiction Encyclopedia* asserts that this story is one of a series, *The Hills of Space*, which also includes "Incommunicado" (q.v.). However, it is difficult to see any connection between those two stories.

B151. MacLean, Katherine. "Incommunicado." *Astounding Science-Fiction*, 45 (June, 1950), p. 6-32.

Working on the construction of the orbital Pluto Station, Cliff Baker visits Station A and finds the people there affected by some kind of "mass insanity" (19). Investigating, he discovers that the man who constructed a file system for the library arranged to have the noises made by the operating system audible; those noises in fact represented a new language which the people were subconsciously learning and using in their humming and music-writing; and the language "was raising the intelligence level" (30) of the station residents. Although this new language permeating their environment was also apparently making people "miserable" (30)—perhaps because they did not understand what was happening to them, and why they felt unhappy when the noises were turned off—Baker arranges to have the library file system sold for use on Earth, with its attendant noises, as a means of creating "a new human race" on Earth as well (32).

This story first deserves credit as the first one to envision a space station falling to Earth as a menace—although that scenario occurs in a melodramatic movie about the construction of Pluto Station which the residents find laughable. Of more interest is the idea that space station residents might develop a new language that would make them "a new human race," and that that language would initially make them seem insane to the visiting Baker.

B152. MacMillan, Scott. "Deadfall." In *Battlestation, Book Two: Vanguard*. Edited by David Drake and Bill Fawcett. New York: Ace, 1993, p. 3-30.

Harvey Kimmelman's job is to constantly move ballast around the Stephen Hawking, keeping all the weight perfectly balanced so that the station doesn't wobble in its orbit. For a handsome sum, he is hired to help a man who is running a secret nightclub in a storage area. Every night, he moves a container filled with customers from one end of a corridor to another. Getting suspicious, though, he discovers this is actually a scheme to smuggle Ichton eggs into the station, but he manages to foil the plot and make a little profit as well.

It's surprising to hear that this massive station would become unstable and wobbly if a little bit of its mass is unbalanced—it seems to make a large station hazardous in yet another way. In some requests, the problem resembles the danger of a "spinquake" depicted in Dean Ing's "Down & Out in Ellfive Prime" (q.v.). It is also amazing to find that station security is so lax that an illegal headquarters and an operation smuggling Ichton eggs can remain undetected for so long.

B153. Maddox, Tom. "Snake-Eyes." In *Mirrorshades: The Cyberpunk*

Anthology. Edited by Bruce Sterling. New York: Ace, 1988, 1986, p. 12-33. Story first published in *Omni* (April, 1986).

To pilot a warplane, a soldier has had his brain surgically altered so that primitive impulses—what he calls "the snake"—threaten to take control of his body. Recruited by a company called SenTrax, he goes to Athena Station in Earth orbit to undergo a process that will either drive him to suicide or enable him to control his "snake," all under the watchful eye of a strange artificial intelligence called Aleph.

The protagonist walks through an "older part of the station, where there were brown clots of fossilized gum on the green plastic flooring, scruff marks on the walls, along with faint imprints of insignia and company names" (15)—unusual images of decay in a space station. The station is later seen from the outside surrounded by "The Orbital Energy Grid, the construction job that had brought Athena into existence," while the station itself is a "hodgepodge of living, working, and experimental structures clustered together without apparent regard to symmetry or form" (24-25). The name Athena—the goddess born directly from the head of Zeus—clearly refers to the hero, who has a new and primitive presence developing in his brain.

B154. Malcolm, Donald. "The Long Ellipse." *New Worlds Science Fiction*, 23 (January, 1958), p. 30-42.

When a ship designed to reach Venus is spotted returning to Earth, five years after the attempt, the General whose son was on board the ship assumes that the ship is a derelict and that all persons on it are dead; nevertheless, he flies up to the Smith-Ross space station to lead a mission to investigate the ship. After waking up in the "hospital satellite, five hundred miles above the Earth" (41), he learns that the ship had been hit by a meteor shower, but that an unrevealed system for suspended animation was used to keep the whole crew alive for their return to Earth.

"In 1971, the first Smith-Ross manned space station was in orbit," and "In 1982, the fourth ship, *Ulysses*, left Smith-Ross One for Venus" (34)—the pertinent information here in the story's short history of space travel. The space station is hardly important to the story, but there is one sentence of striking poetry: "The spacetaxi buzzed like a mechanical bee into the heart of the great silver sunflower of the spacestation" (37).

B155. Mand, Mary L. "The Pigeon Sisters on Space Station Three." In *Carmen Miranda's Ghost Is Haunting Space Station Three.* Edited by Don Sakers. New York: Baen, 1990, p. 293-300.

The flaky Pigeon Sisters, Gwendolyn and Cicely, arrive at Space Station Three and are disconcerted when the ghost of Carmen Miranda appears in the ladies' room. But they then realize the commercial possibilities, and plan to return to Earth and set up an amusement park where ghosts are employed as entertainers.

This last story in the anthology in a way typifies the entire collection: trivial, illogical, and occasionally amusing.

B156. Marks, Betsy, and Anne G. DeMaio. "And Now the News:" In *Carmen Miranda's Ghost Is Haunting Space Station Three.* Edited by Don Sakers. New York: Baen, 1990, p. 266-281.

A series of news reports describe the appearances of the ghosts of famous people at various locales in Earth and in space, including Carmen Miranda at Space Station Three. One effect of these ghosts is to encourage people to stop fighting and achieve peace, so experts finally theorize that the ghosts were produced by the collective unconscious in an effort to put an end to dangerous conflicts.

This is a fragmented and essentially pointless story which becomes particularly absurd when characters from *Alice in Wonderland* and *The Screwtape Letters* begin showing up. Maybe there are satiric messages in all of these vignettes, but they do not seem worth searching for.

B157. Martin, George R. R. "Nor the Many-Colored Fires of a Star Ring." In *Faster Than Light.* Edited by Jack Dann and George Zebrowski. New York: Ace, 1976, p. 199-220.

The manmade Nowhere Star Ring—"A silver circlet a hundred miles in diameter" (201)—was abandoned because its vortex led not to other worlds, but only into an endless void. It is reoccupied by scientists testing a theory that the vortex can be made self-sustaining; but the theory is flawed and there is an uncontrollable energy build-up. As they abandon the Ring, a poetic crewman realizes that the vortex is going to bring matter and energy into the void—essentially creating a new universe.

In the same future universe as Martin's "The Second Kind of Loneliness" (q.v.), this story mentions other star rings built around irregularities in space: "Cerberus...six million miles beyond Pluto" (the setting of "Loneliness"), "Black Door, adrift in a Trojan position behind Jupiter," and "Vulcan...in the shadow of the sun" (203). Like other kinds of space stations, Star Rings can drive people mad: "when this was still a research station, they had more than one crack-up" (208) possibly a direct reference to the earlier story.

B158. Martin, George R. R. "The Second Kind of Loneliness." In *Isaac Asimov's Science Fiction Treasury*. Edited by Isaac Asimov, Martin Greenberg, and Joseph Olander. New York: Bonanza, 1980, p. 633-649. Story originally published in *Analog Science Fiction/Science Fact* (December, 1972).

The solitary resident of the Cerberus Star Ring—a structure built around the mysterious "Nullspace" space warp discovered beyond Pluto—keeps a diary while waiting for his relief to arrive. When the ship is late, he realizes that he has lost track of time and that the ship had already arrived—and that he had destroyed that ship. Then he forgets again and resumes the diary at the original starting date.

This story is in many ways reminiscent of Fritch's "Many Dreams of Earth" (q.v.)—a solitary space station resident goes insane, loses track of time, and causes the death of a person trying to rescue him. This does not demonstrate that Martin is plagiarizing; rather, it shows how the theme of lonely existence in a space station can take two very different authors in the same direction—madness and the development of the simultaneous desire to remain in space and return to Earth.

B159. Martino, Joseph P. "The Iceworm Special." *Analog Science Fiction/Science Fact*, 51 (July 20, 1981), p. 130-137.

At the Twelve Moons Saloon, a bar in the Wheel orbiting Titan, a veteran space worker who meets and dislikes a newcomer treats him to a drink called the Iceworm Special—containing an ice chunk with a frozen alien worm which the drinker is supposed to swallow whole. The experience makes him throw up, proving he really doesn't have the toughness for space work—although the "worm" is really just a piece of spaghetti.

This is a familiar tale of the Old West—the young cowboy who must prove his manhood by some two-fisted drinking—barely altered in being transplanted to a space station orbiting Saturn. Its idea is stolen from Robert Service's poem, "The Ballad of the Ice-Worm Cocktail."

B160. Martino, Joseph P. "Persistence." *Analog Science Fiction Science Fact*, 83 (May, 1969), p. 58-95.

Working from a nearby space station orbiting a colony world, the researchers last seen in "Secret Weapon" (q.v.) try to figure out the inner workings of a captured alien spacecraft. One scientist deduces that the aliens must have a form of faster-than-light radio, although his colleague ridicules the idea. Eventually, after trying hard to locate and study that radio, he decides that the aliens do not have it—but he also figures out how to construct such a radio himself.

The protagonist, a man noted for his persistence, once constructed a model of "Satellite Station Number Three" which orbited Earth completely out of toothpicks. The station the scientists are using is barely described, as their work on the alien craft is the focus of attention.

B161. Martino, Joseph P. "Secret Weapon." *Analog Science Fiction/ Science Fact*, 81 (April, 1968), p. 8-48.

Two scientists are sent to a space station to determine why alien warships have suddenly increased their numbers of successful attacks on human ships. Studying computer records, they deduce that the larger number of attacks is partly explained by the law of averages and partly involves the use of small warning devices.

The station, which "circl[es] the only habitable world of a star known as Ross 128, some eleven light-years from Sol," functions primarily as a "transfer point" for arriving ships and shuttles down to the planet's surface. It is not described in detail.

Note: Martino's "Persistence" (q.v.) is a sequel to this story.

B162. Maxwell, M. Max. "Prisoner 794." *Analog Science Fiction/ Science Fact*, 92 (September, 1973), p. 78-93.

A man who invented a new type of computer brain attacks the President when his invention is taken over by the government; along with many other criminals, he is then placed in solitary confinement, in a small cell orbiting a planetoid, with only a computer of the type he invented for company. He devises an elaborate escape plan but is foiled by a computer failure; nevertheless, he resolves to try again.

Unlike other space prisons, these orbiting cells seem rather benign; a computer keeps them company and watches out for their safety, and a human monitor keeps tracks of all the cells and deals with emergencies. Still, the system is on the verge of breaking down in the story, when multiple problems erupt, and the assumption is that the hero will eventually manage to escape.

B163. McCaffrey, Anne. "If Madam Likes You." In *Carmen Miranda's Ghost Is Haunting Space Station Three*. Edited by Don Sakers. New York: Baen, 1990, p. 88-102. Originally published in *New Destinies, Volume VIII*. Edited by Jim Baen. New York: Baen, 1989.

A technician comes to Space Station Three to clear up problems which seem to involve the ghost of Carmen Miranda haunting the station; he claims that they were just computer malfunctions which he has eliminated. However, a lonely crewman then decides to create a hologram of his dream girl—and a few days later, an identical woman arrives as a new member of the crew. As he begins to romance her, he hears the sound of soft singing.

In this future world, space stations are a growing business because "Space required more and more stations as way-points, beacons in the deep void" (30); these are usually inhabited by people born in space, since "too often the planet-born got to yearning for solid earth under their feet or wind in their face or some such foolishness" (30). There is a reference to the "station's cat" (27) and a reminder of the expense involved in running a space station—the "Space Station services" are "cost-conscious" (24). Finally, there is a reminder of the importance of advertising and public relations in promoting space exploration and habitation: one space station was named "The Madison Space Platform" "for the industry that had started on the famous Avenue, in honor of all the catch phrases that had generated enthusiasm for The Big Step" (29-30).

B164. McIntosh, J. T. [James Murdoch MacGregor; this story as by J. T. M'Intosh] "Hallucination Orbit." *Galaxy*, 3 (January, 1952), p. 132-158.

In the future, it is discovered that in space, all people in groups of fewer than forty people invariably go insane, often dangerously—a condition called "solitosis." The best solution is one-man spaceships and space stations; the person goes mad, but harmlessly. Due to a malfunctioning directional beam, a man on a space station near Pluto is left alone over six years and his madness takes the form of hallucinating imaginary female companions. When he tires of them, or proves to his satisfaction that they are not real, they vanish and another one appears. Finally, a woman comes and he discovers that she is real, an elderly doctor who has come by herself first to help treat his madness. He imagines her as a beautiful young woman; when he sees her true aged self, he will be considered cured.

Station Two, anchored to a small piece of rock imported for that purpose, seems rather large for a one-man facility. The story recalls other stories about lonely men going insane in space stations, like Fritch's "Many Dreams of Earth" and Martin's "The Second Kind of Loneliness" (q.v.), but the madness here is completely benign; since the man knew from the start that he would go mad, he can adjust to and accept his madness without becoming dangerous or suicidal.

B165. McNeil, Mark. "Scratches in the Dark." *Analog Science Fiction/Science Fact*, 102 (Mid-September, 1982), p. 110-119.

Asteroid space stations have been set up to detect and warn against alien invaders, who, the Prime Minister of Europe warns, have already landed on and infiltrated Earth. The lone resident of one station is being driven crazy by persistent scratching noises, which he thinks are some kind of alien invader. Even after he realizes that the noises are caused by his force field touching and vaporizing portions of the asteroid's surface, he continues to have such fears, and when his superior officer comes to rescue him, he imagines that he is an intruder and kills him.

The story never clearly states whether the aliens being watched for are real, or are some kind of device to maintain unity on Earth—as was in the case in Theodore Sturgeon's "Unite and Conquer" (q.v.). Here is another picture of the space station as a haunted house, maddening its resident with fears of an imaginary intruder.

B166. Melton, Henry. "The Christmas Count." In *Cities in Space: The Endless Frontier, Volume III*. Edited by Jerry Pournelle with John F. Carr. New York: Ace, 1991, p. 66-74.

On a farm in a space habitat, it is the farmer's responsibility to count all living creatures on his property every Christmas, to provide necessary data to keep the colony functioning well. The man laments the absence of his oldest son, who ran away to become a space pilot, but he gets a holiday surprise when he finds out that his son has returned to play "Santa," and he happily includes him in the count of his family.

As in Watkins's "Coming of Age in Henson's Tube" (q.v.), a space habitat is again cast as a traditional agrarian society supportive of family values. Norman Spinrad's "Dreams of Space" notwithstanding, this kind of imagery has obviously not vanished from science fiction.

B167. Merril, Judith. "Survival Ship." In *Tomorrow, The Stars*. Edited by Robert A. Heinlein. 1952. New York: Berkley, 1967, p. 138-146. Story originally published in *Worlds Beyond* (January, 1951).

Half a million people travel to Space Station One to observe the launch of the first starship, with twenty-four crewmen whose identities are mysteriously kept secret. It is finally revealed that, to maximize survival, the crew consists of 20 women and 4 men.

A facility which can accommodate half a million visitors must be a pretty impressive place, but Merril provides no description or detail; again, a space station simply serves as the starting point for a space adventure.

B168. Merwin, Sam, Jr. "Star Tracks." *Astounding Science-Fiction*, 49 (March, 1952), p. 144-152.

A spaceship pilot waits on the space station called the Doughnut while the astronomers he ferried up there carry on their work; he feels that "having to loaf for ten days inside the Doughnut was very like being locked in a coffin full of alien machinery tended by routine-occupied zombies" (145). Through his romance with a female astronomer, he eventually learns the reason for the delay: the astronomers have discovered that the stars are actually tiny marbles running in tracks on the inner side of some kind of barrier—which means that outer space is a hoax and man has no chance to conquer space. However, the pilot and the astronomer finally resolve to someday fly out to the barrier and try to penetrate it.

The source of the pilot's frustration is that his spaceship "at least went places.... But the Doughnut merely spun slowly on its hollow axis in a sort of everlasting free fall" (146); as the astronomer tells him, "It's been hard on you, hasn't it—being cooped up here for so long, going nowhere?" (148). Thus there is again the image of the space station as a kind of spaceship "going nowhere." The story also contributes a term for a new type of mental condition induced by space station life: "satellite nerves" (147).

B169. Moon, Elizabeth. "ABCs in Zero-G." *Analog Science Fiction/Science Fact*, 106 (August, 1986), p. 82-107. Story reprinted in *Lunar Activity*. By Elizabeth Moon. New York: Baen, 1990.

A paramedic working at Station One is frustrated because they have been unable to save persons injured while working outside the Station. The problems are that a computerized traffic system often jerks them away at a crucial moment, disrupting their work, and that it is difficult to get to people in heavy spacesuits. After they voice their concerns, the situation improves: the traffic system is revised to avoid sudden movements, new types of "screw-on" spacesuit legs and arms are invented, and another device likened to a "can-opener" is created to help get people out of their suits. While hard at work on these improvements, the heroine is depressed because her former partner on Earth has been paralyzed in an accident; but she finally learns that he is coming up to Station One to work as a paramedic, since his inability to walk will not be a handicap in weightless conditions.

The story in a way is similar to Lee Correy's *Space Doctor* (q.v.), describing the development of medical techniques in space in the near future. One problem is that modifying the suit will involve "union contract negotiations" (90). The heroine's friend, of course, is yet another example of a physically handicapped person finding a home at a space station.

B170. Moon, Elizabeth. "Welcome to Wheel Days." In *New Destinies, Volume VII*. Edited by Jim Baen. New York: Baen, 1989, p. 155-175.

At LaPorte-Centro-501, a huge space colony in the shape of a hollow globe in the asteroid belt, the annual festival called Wheel Days is about to start, and a harried official must cope with a number of problems, including arranging the floats for the parade, having enough portable toilets, and sorting out a complicated affair of romance and conflict involving his brother-in-law, a musician in the band performing at the festival, and their wives.

LaPorte-Centro-501 "was built in two helices" (157), apparently inter-twined and running through its interior—making for an challenging parade route which varies from zero gravity to normal gravity. Residents have an aversion to animals, complaining that a nearby space colony is "infested with mammalian vermin. Even dogs" (157)—an attitude that seems to reflect the narrow-mindedness that often develops in a space habitat.

B171. Morris, Janet. "A Transmigration of Soul." In *Battlestation, Book One*. Edited by David Drake and Bill Fawcett. New York: Ace, 1992, p. 231-258.

Continuing the story begun in Drake's "Facing the Enemy" (q.v.), the Ichton clone with Dresser's personality returns to the alien camp, where he is welcomed as a hero and given the rare opportunity to mate with the Ichton queen and produce children. But the alien personality of Greel is warring with the personality of Dresser to control the body. When Greel is exhausted, Dresser takes firm command and reports to the Stephen Hawking about his discoveries. While he hopes they will come and pick him up, they instead tell him that he must stay on the job.

There are only two brief mentions of the space station (p. 153, 157), as the story otherwise takes place entirely on the world taken over by the Ichtons.

B172. Morwood, Peter. "Taken to the Cleaners." In *Battlestation, Book Two: Vanguard*. Edited by David Drake and Bill Fawcett. New York: Ace, 1993, p. 117-125.

A group of officious and ignorant officials are touring the Stephen Hawking, and they are appalled to discover that the station invested in the apparent luxury of automatic cleaning devices with human supervision. Demanding information, they insist that the supervising janitor leave his post and answer their questions. When he does so, one machine attacks one of the officials who is molting.

Basically a rather smug and obvious anecdote about the stupidity of ignorant civilians attempting to tell smart military people how to run their operations, the story mentions one other space station: "the Jrgen Stroop [sic]...an orbital bombardment platform purposely built for a single operation" (120).

B173. Mullen, Stanley. "Fool Killer." *Astounding Science Fiction*, 61 (May, 1958), p. 109-123.

A wrongly convicted man is sentenced to the "prison workships" in the asteroid belts: "Their orbits never intersect that of any planets.... Such a prison is escape proof. The only way out is madness or death" (110). Even worse, he learns that he has terminal cancer. But amazingly, a doctor cures him with an experimental treatment, the flaws in his trial are discovered and he is pardoned and returned to Earth, and a computer court grants him unusual compensation for his unfair imprisonment: the right to murder one person. He decides finally not to exercise that right, but to use his threatening presence as an incentive to others to behave correctly.

The "prison workships" actually do not seem all that inhumane, with medical treatment from a sympathetic doctor readily available, and the hero actually seems to have benefited from his stay there: "On the prison workships he had learned the value of solitude" (121).

B174. Neville, Kris. "Cold War." In *Selections from the Astounding Science Fiction Anthology*. Edited by John W. Campbell, Jr. New York: Berkley, 1964, p. 167-178. Story first published in *Astounding Science-Fiction* (October, 1949).

American space stations with nuclear weapons are maintaining peace on Earth, but a devastating problem is being kept secret: the men manning these stations are all starting to go mad.

The story ends without a resolution of the problem: if the space stations are abandoned, wars will break out; but if even one space station crewman goes mad while still in orbit, "half a continent" (178) could be destroyed. Gunn's *Station in Space* (q.v.), depicting the totally mad crew of a military space station, could be viewed as an expansion of Neville's idea, though Gunn further supposes that the missiles could eventually be secretly disarmed, since the mere threat of them would be sufficient to maintain peace—an idea that also surfaces in Neville's "Satellite Secret" (q.v.).

B175. Neville, Kris. "Earth Alert!" *Imagination*, 4 (February, 1953), p. 6-86.

Powerful but cowardly aliens have established a secret space station in Earth orbit. They genetically alter human babies to have psychic powers, kidnap them, take them to live in the station, and indoctrinate them to believe that they are aliens preparing to conquer Earth. However, the aliens missed baby Julia, and when the girl grows up, she establishes mental contact with one of the mutants, Walt; he is sent to Earth to kill her, but she explains the truth to him and converts him. Julia also contacts the authorities to prepare them to ward off the invasion of Earth; but final victory comes when Walt, with the help of another mutant named Calvin, mentally detaches and hurls the Washington Monument into the station.

This is possibly the strangest way to destroy a space station ever imagined; the story is otherwise uninteresting, as little attention is paid to the mutants or aliens in space amidst many displays of amazing psychic powers on Earth.

Note: this novella later became a novel, *The Mutants*.

B176. Neville, Kris. "Satellite Secret." *Space Adventures*, No. 13 (Spring, 1971), p. 74-83, 131. Story originally published in *Amazing Stories* (April, 1950).

The pilots of satellites which circle the globe bearing deadly missiles are going "insane...becoming unreliable" (82), so the Americans decide to remove the war-heads from the satellites. Since this means that the satellites no longer pose an immediate threat, a Russian spy who has become a Senator decides to return home with the news; however, the person he reports to is an American spy, who promptly kills him.

The story offers a solution to the situation Neville presented in "Cold War" (q.v.)—remove the atomic bombs that the insane pilots might launch—but this of course poses a further problem: if the enemy discovers that the bombs are gone, the satellites are no longer a threat. Here, Neville's Director of Satellites estimates that it would take at least three days to "re-arm the satellites" (81)—which poses no problem to an attacking nation.

B177. Nicholson, Sam. [Shirley Nikolaisen] "He Who Fights and Runs Away." *Analog Science Fiction/Science Fact*, 102 (Mid-September, 1982), p. 18-50.

A young boy's parents are disgusted with the violence and crime on Earth, so they migrate to a space habitat; but the boy longs to return to Earth and improve conditions there, and when the opportunity arises, he develops a plan to sell "pillar-houses" to a syndicate of Earth criminals, on the premise that they can be used to enforce the mobsters' will; however, they will actually be rigged to exterminate the criminals, and the pillar-houses will then be used by honest citizens to protect themselves from crime. When the plan succeeds, he reluctantly agrees to stay in space to continue working on ways to help the people of Earth.

In this story, the boys' parents present the standard argument that Earth is decadent, and that humanity must move into a new environment to escape it. They use the analogies of Noah's Ark and the bubonic plague: "Earth has had lawbreakers, yes, but not today's great flood of sick minds.... Normal people like us have no defense against this sick flood. We're an endangered minority. If we don't run away, we'll drown. The space wheels are arks where decent families can live until the flood recedes" (21); and "Earth's sickness is being deliberately spread by human rats, and the infection is more widespread and deadly than the bubonic plague. It will warp and cripple the entire human species" (25). The boy, however, "wanted to stay and fight" (27) against the moral decay of Earth and continues to "love Earth" with a passion (50), although he reluctantly agrees to remain in space to keep up his good work.

B178. Nicholson, Sam. [Shirley Nikolaisen] "Scrooge in Space." *Analog Science Fiction/Science Fact*, 100 (August, 1980), p. 54-71.

Captain Schuster, a trouble-shooter, is sent to investigate a bankrupt "Trailer Wheel" in lunar orbit which is dedicated to providing opportunities for the disadvantaged. He discovers that they have been allowing drunken incompetents to run their control room, causing an accident which puts the station on a collision course with the other Wheels. After fixing the problem, he decides to shut down the station and put it under new management.

In Nicholson's future, Wheels run by various nations follow the moon in its orbit, each specializing in different products. The story itself is a shrill argument against all programs to help the disabled, with alcoholics as Nicholson's example of typical disabled people.

B179. Niven, Larry. [Laurence van Cott Niven] "The Borderland of Sol." *Analog Science Fiction/Science Fact*, 94 (January, 1975), p. 12-50.

Carlos Wu and two allies travel to the Solar System to investigate some missing starships. As they near the outer worlds, their hyperdrive mysteriously vanishes. On a hunch, they visit the noted physicist Julian Forward, living on Forward Station, a modified asteroid near the edge of the system. They learn that Forward has captured a tiny black hole to use as a weapon; however, his attack on their ship backfires and the asteroid is destroyed.

Forward Station is an extensively transformed asteroid; its interior "was a network of straight cylindrical corridors, laser-drilled, pressurized and lined with cool blue light-strips" (38). It is maintained as a private research facility, like Atlantis in Charles Sheffield's *The Web between the Worlds* (q.v.).

Note: this is one of many Known Space stories by Larry Niven, though no others to my knowledge involve anything resembling space stations (since I classify the giant construct Ringworld as an artificial world). I have seen a copy of *Analog* with the inscription "For Bob Forward, Larry Niven," indicating that the story's physicist Forward is based on Robert L. Forward.

B180. Niven, Larry. [Laurence van Cott Niven] "Flare Time." In *Medea: Harlan's World*. Edited by Harlan Ellison. New York: Bantam, 1985, p. 217-251. Story first published in *Andromeda 3* in 1978.

A tourist visits the strange world of Medea wearing memory tapes, which can then be copied and sold as entertainments. However, she finds the planet disorienting and troubling, and when a powerful solar flare brings many dangerous creatures to life, she flees in horror, though she is ultimately rescued.

There is a one-paragraph description of the Lluagorians, who "have to put their farms in orbit, and they do most of their living in orbit, and it's all inflated balloons, even the spacecraft" (225). It is an interesting picture, though nothing more is said about the planet.

B181. Niven, Larry. [Laurence van Cott Niven] "The Return of William Proxmire." In *N-Space*. By Larry Niven. New York: Tor, 1990, p. 399-406. Story first published in *What Might Have Been? Volume 1: Alternate Empires* in 1989.

Ex-Senator William Proxmire goes to a scientist who has proposed building a time machine with the following proposal: Proxmire will obtain the funding for the time machine, which he will then use to go back in time and cure Robert A. Heinlein of the consumption which forced him to leave the Navy and start writing science fiction. Without Heinlein's stories, Proxmire reasons, no support will develop for what he sees as the expensive, wasteful space program. However, after he accomplishes his task, he finds that modern America is now even more active in space—partly as a result of the work of Admiral Heinlein.

The newly created alternate Earth's space activities include "half a dozens space stations, government and military and civilian" (406).

Note: another space station story involving Heinlein is Don Sakers's "The Man Who Travelled in Rocketships" (q.v.).

B182. Niven, Larry, [Laurence van Cott Niven] and Jerry Pournelle. "Spirals." In *The Endless Frontier, Volume I*. Edited by Jerry Pournelle. New York: Ace, 1979, p. 27-83. Story first published in *Destinies* (March-April, 1979).

When a narrow-minded Earth announces that it will not longer supply a fledgling space colony and orders its residents to return to Earth, they decide instead to fly their sphere to the asteroid belt, where they can find all the water and minerals they need.

The colony (the Shack, renamed the Skylark) apparently becomes a permanent spaceship, carrying materials from the asteroids to Earth. The ability of residents to fly within the sphere by using wings is cited as the reason "why people who came here wanted to stay" (38).

B183. Norment, John. "Space Platform [Xz204c Does Not Answer]." *Science Fiction Digest*, No. 1 (1954), p. 88-89. Story first published in *Ballyhoo* in 1953.

This science fiction parody involves a bored crewman on a space platform which is attacked by a dreaded space pirate. They fire at each other at the same time, leaving themselves perpetually frozen in place.

This short piece concludes, "Somewhere, away out there in space, revolving endlessly within its own orbit a tiny Space Platform goes its way" (89). Another space station mental problem is briefly mentioned—"Space Platform Blues" (88).

B184. Norwood, Rick. "IO." *Analog Science Fiction/Science Fact*, 102 (March 1, 1982), p. 104-113.

Three young people playing the outer space version of hide and seek receive their clue—a sheet of paper reading "IO," which they read as "ten." But they finally realize that the message is really "Io" and rush off to Jupiter's moon to find their friend.

At one point, when it suddenly becomes important to contact their hiding friend as soon as possible, someone says, "If time gets short, start calling every hotel on a planet or moon or space station which has only one hotel" (111)—indicating there are a number of stations in the Solar System.

B185. Nye, Jody Lynn. "Shooting Star." In *Battlestation, Book Two: Vanguard*. Edited by David Drake and Bill Fawcett. New York: Ace, 1993, p. 197-213.

Lyseo, the gifted but sensitive actor who daily entertains the crew of the Stephen Hawking (last seen in Nye's "Starlight" [q.v.]), is persuaded to do a training film for gunners, since the Fleet is running low on them. To boost morale, he first stages an encounter with an actor pretending to be a pessimistic crewman, then he proceeds to do the training film. While filming, an actual Ichton attack occurs, and Lyseo manages to shoot one of the ships down.

The second volume of this series increasingly emphasizes morale problems on board the station. Here, in the faked encounter, the actor says, "I'm tired of being cooped up with people like you in this centimeter-square can prison. We're too vulnerable. We have to draw back" (p. 201). Of course, the image of a space station as a "prison" has been seen before, and the notion that the station is "vulnerable" seems, in light of the experience of other massive stations, all too true.

B186. Nye, Jody Lynn. "Starlight." In *Battlestation, Book One*. Edited by David Drake and Bill Fawcett. New York: Ace, 1992, p. 109-130.

A brilliant but temperamental actor named Lyseo is recruited to live on the Stephen Hawking and entertain residents with daily performances. One of them—in which he starkly articulates the fears of people on board—inspires widespread despair and disapproval, which he does not understand. After observing the power center during one battle, he creates an elaborate light show illustrating how all personnel on board contribute in their own small way to the success of the mission. But when another battle occurs, power is diverted from his show, which infuriates the actor. The Morale Officer Jill FarSeeker then denounces the actor as "the most spoiled sentient being I have ever met in my life!" (p. 128-129) which makes the actor realize how foolish he is being and, in fact, sparks their love affair.

This is the first story to evoke the theme of declining morale on board the battle station; Lyseo's performance was disheartening because, Jill tells him, "You reminded them how vulnerable they are out here" (p. 117). The notion that such a facility might require a Morale Officer seems logical enough.

B187. Oliver, Chad. "Ghost Town." In *Cities in Space: The Endless Frontier, Volume III*. Edited by Jerry Pournelle with John F. Carr. New York: Ace, 1991, p. 163-185. Story first published in *Analog Science Fiction/Science Fact* (Mid-September, 1983).

In a future where many attractive worlds are available, everyone has abandoned the O'Neill space habitats. On a salvage mission to one old habitat, an archaeologist discovers a small tribe of people, reduced to savagery, still living there. He is adopted by the tribe's leader, who teaches him their ways of life and then arranges his own ritual death. An epilog suggests that the humans eventually abandoned the habitat, leaving the chimpanzees there to develop into a new sentient race.

This is another one of the rare stories which depict a far-future space habitat in a state of decline (see also Richard A. Lupoff's *The Forever City*). The story's heresy is the notion that people would universally abandon space habitats once they could live on new worlds; obviously Oliver does not accept arguments about the virtues of low-gravity and controlled space environments. They were, in his future world, simply the best alternative available for a while.

B188. Oliver, Chad. "Meanwhile, Back on the Reservation." *Analog Science Fiction/Science Fact*, 51 (April 27, 1981), p. 86-101.

A woman born and raised in a space colony must return to Earth because she has not biologically adapted to life in space. An Earth resident who fights for the rights of "downers" (89) is prepared to resent her but instead eventually tries to persuade her that humans on Earth and humans in space must reconcile and work together.

While most science fiction writers unswervingly side with space residents in their conflicts with Earth people, anthropologist Oliver makes a rare case for cooperation. The story could be taken to represent the new mood of the 1980s, as dreams of human migration to space colonies are balanced with a new awareness of the importance of life on Earth.

B189. Oltion, Jerry. "The Getaway Special." In *Space Shuttles: Isaac Asimov's Wonderful Worlds of Science Fiction #7*. Edited by Isaac Asimov, Martin H. Greenberg, and Charles G. Waugh. New York: Signet, 1987, p. 85-101. Story originally published in *Analog Science Fiction/Science Fact* (April, 1985).

A scientist on a space shuttle flight successfully tests a hyperdrive device which instantly moves the shuttle to various places in outer space; its disappearances and reappearances trigger an attack on the shuttle, and almost start a nuclear war, but eventually everyone understands what is going on.

The shuttle mission's is to land at the Manned Orbital Laboratory, and it goes into hyperdrive soon after leaving the station; thus, the story is a marginal example of the space station which serves as a starting point for a space flight.

B190. Park, John. "The Software Plague." In *Cities in Space: The Endless Frontier, Volume III*. Edited by Jerry Pournelle with John F. Carr. New York: Ace, 1991, p. 111-130. Originally published in *Far Frontiers* (Summer, 1985).

In a world where people regularly connect their minds to computers, a man investigates mysterious sabotage at a base on the satellite Europa. He eventually discovers the cause is a strange computer virus that infects people and turns them into a new kind of being—one that can inhabit software and thus be virtually immortal. They have been attempting to "colonize" Europa, have taken over the mind of one woman, and wish to take control of the starship under construction. Their invasion is neutralized, but the hero arranges for the permanently altered woman to be on board the starship.

In Park's future world, most space bases seem to be on asteroids or moons—Europa, Ceres, and Phobos, for example. Still, the "starship complex" (114) where the starship is being completed, and where some of the action takes place, is arguably a temporary space station of sorts.

B191. Pelletier, Francine. "La migratrice." ["The Migrants"] In *Le temps des migrations*. Longuevil, Québec: Le Préambule, 1987, p. 7-25.

A spaceship captain visits orbital station Asterman, the capital of Earth's government in the future. She learns of a plan to colonize space by sending women with genetically altered embryos in artificial wombs into space, so their children can live on otherwise inhospitable planets. The captain assists one of these "Migrants" and decides to let her travel into space.

Unseen; the story is discussed in Elizabeth Vonarburg in "Birth and Rebirth in Space," *Foundation: The Review of Science Fiction*, No. 51 (Spring, 1991), p. 5-29.

B192. Perry, Steve. "Blind Spot." In *Battlestation, Book One*. Edited by David Drake and Bill Fawcett. New York: Ace, 1992, p. 153-178.

A man who worked on the Stephen Hawking's sensors is murdered, and his lover asks Gil Sivart to investigate. He eventually figures out that another technician was secretly sabotaging the sensors, leaving a "blind spot" that would enable the Ichtons to successfully destroy the station; the motive was to collect on the massive insurance policy taken out on the station. When the dead man discovered the problem, he was murdered. After a confrontation with the murderer, Sivart overcomes him and explains what was going on.

A space station is in a sense the ideal locale for a murder mystery, and this is not the only story in the series to employ such a story line (see Don John Dugas's "Joint Ventures"). The story provides better background information on station life than other efforts, and its plot illustrates yet again that the station is vulnerable in many ways to armed attack.

B193. Petkoff, Joseph. "Suicide's Grave." *Astounding Science-Fiction*, 49 (April, 1952), p. 41-43.

A traveling spaceman and scientist, still distraught over his wife's death long ago, makes a mistake in his calculations and goes plunging into the Sun. There, he discovers that stars are not nearly as hot as expected, and he "burns to death slowly and painfully" (43).

The story mentions visits to a "remote station" and "Centauri station" (42).

B194. Petley, H. C. "And Earth So Far Away." *Galaxy*, 38 (August, 1977), p. 9-29.

When a mysterious disaster destroys a mining platform in the asteroid belt, the one Martian crewman travels by himself to a buoy so he can contact authorities and arrange a rescue. Returning to Mars, he hears intimations of intrigue and conflict involving Earth, Mars, and rebel cities on Mars and, retiring from space service, he dreams of his first trip to Earth.

The story is best characterized as pointless, with little description of life in space or on Mars and no resolution of any of its plot threads. The story refers to sixteen other mining platforms which roam the asteroid belt (12); they are perhaps more like spacecraft than space stations, although they are called "platforms," and stay in space for long periods of time.

B195. Plauger, P. J. "Epicycle." *Analog Science Fiction/Science Fact*, 92 (November, 1973), p. 148-165.

A woman astronomer finally gets a chance to go into orbit and make some observations—but an accident on board the ship means that she will simply have to go to the Skyhook space station and back to Earth without the chance to do her experiments. However, when an incorrectly dumped Orbital Booster System circles back to threaten the ship, the woman proposes a scheme based on Ptolemaic cosmology to avoid the hazard and stay in space long enough for her to finish her work.

Although the space station is never visited, Skyhook plays a number of roles in the story—monitor, destination, rescuer, adviser. Why it isn't used for the heroine's astronomical work is another question.

B196. Pollack, Rachel. "Tree House." In *Habitats*. Edited by Susan Shwartz. New York: DAW, 1984, p. 122-141.

A man travels to a Dyson Tree, a huge, genetically-engineered tree planted on a comet with tunnels and domes inhabited by humans who belong to a fanatical religious sect. He wishes to persuade an old girl friend to return to Earth, but she feels mystically attached to the Tree and to space itself: "Everything has waited, worked millions of years for this moment...entering space. Really joining it" (135). For a moment, he too feels "the call"—"something called to him...the void itself" (139)—but he flees from it and returns to Earth.

The story is based on an actual idea of Freeman Dyson: "A Dyson Tree, they called it, after the twentieth-century physicist who first observed that gravity, rather than biological controls, limited the growth of a tree, and that a genetically modified tree planted in the head of a comet could shelter a permanent space colony" (126). It is certainly a unique space structure, and the concept that a religion might grow in connection with space habitation is interesting. The story also mentions "energy satellites" also inhabited by religious "Crazies" (123), a "research satellite" where the tree was first grown (126), and a "tourist sat" (137).

B197. Pournelle, Jerry. "Bind Your Sons to Exile." In *The Endless Frontier, Volume I*. Edited by Jerry Pournelle. New York: Ace, 1979, p. 130-175. An earlier version of this story was published in *Odyssey* (Spring, 1976).

A young engineer, ostensibly interested only in money, goes off to work in a settlement on the asteroid Moria, and gradually becomes committed to life in space.

The only true space station in the story is a briefly mentioned "satellite complex" (140) in Earth orbit where the ship that takes the hero to Moria is assembled; yet there is some point, during the time when an asteroid is settled and modified, that it becomes more like a space station than a planetary outpost, so Pournelle's observations about asteroid life may have some relevance.

B198. Pournelle, Jerry. "Consort." In *High Justice*. By Jerry Pournelle. 1986. New York: Baen, 1986, p. 195-222. Story originally published in *Analog Science Fiction/Science Fact* (August, 1975).

While Aeneas McKenzie, commander of space station Heimdall, struggles to complete the *Valkyrie*, an interplanetary spacecraft, his lover and boss Laura Hansen blackmails the President of the United States into allowing her to continue space activities.

Even in the 1970s, this space station is seen primarily as a stepping-stone to space—hence its name, Heimdall, the mythological bridge from Earth to Asgard. In both this story and its predecessor, "High Justice" (q.v.), Pournelle has these messages: all governments tend to become corrupt, bureaucratic, and destructive to individual freedom; and the only hopes are first, multinational corporations, where some individual pride and initiative can survive, and later, space colonies, where people might establish independent lives.

Note: other stories related to this story are "High Justice" (q.v.) and *Exiles to Glory*.

B199. Pournelle, Jerry. "High Justice." In *High Justice*. By Jerry Pournelle. 1974. New York: Baen, 1986, p. 100-151. Story originally published in *Analog: Science Fiction/Science Fact* (March, 1974).

A political murder has been committed on space station Heimdall, but there is no clear legal authority to deal with it. Laura Hansen, owner of the station, sends her lover Aeneas McKenzie there to be the new commander; he establishes his authority with a gun, finds the killer, and, in his own way, tries and executes him.

Pournelle focuses on the need to establish new legal systems in space—current "international law" is no solution—but the story's answer can be viewed as frightening: McKenzie brings to his task the attitude that if you know he's guilty, why bother with legal niceties? And the "trial" he conducts resembles a kangaroo court, as the doomed defendant argues. Must the "New Frontier" have both the good and bad features of the old one?

Note: sequels to this story are "Consort" (q.v.) and *Exiles to Glory*.

B200. Powers, William F. "Meteor." *Astounding Science-Fiction*, 46 (September, 1950), p. 107-120.

The tension mounts on Earth as a huge meteor is detected which slowly makes its way through space, disrupting space travel, and which eventually seems about to crash into Earth. However, the meteor's mass turns out to be less than anticipated, and the meteor burns up in the atmosphere.

The story contains a few references to "Stag Head detector station" (111) and the "crippled East Station" (114), which are presumably stations in deep space, although there is no explicit reference to their location.

B201. Poyer, Joe. "Specialty." *Analog Science Fiction/Science Fact*, 81 (August, 1968), p. 138-160.

A small number of men in a lunar base that has declared independence from Earth plan to process rocket fuel from lunar materials and thus support their settlement; but problems arise from tensions between crewmen and an accident that kills one resident.

Outlining their marketing plan, one man says "we could...supply fuel for...the Earth space stations" (143-144); there is also a reference to an unspecified space station disaster when one man recalls "duty at the Midway Space Station before the blowout" (149).

B202. Pratt, Fletcher. "Project Excelsior." [also known as "Asylum Satellite"] In *Double in Space*. By Fletcher Pratt. New York: Doubleday, 1951, p. 9-113. Story originally published in *Thrilling Wonder Stories* (October, 1951).

With both a Western and a Soviet space station orbiting the Earth, there is an atmosphere of competition and tension. However, when the Soviet station is threatened by danger, the crews of the two stations build a spirit of cooperation.

Another portrayal of the missile-laden space station as the ultimate guarantee of world peace. Pratt's novella is forgettable, save for its familiar warnings about possible mental problems and sabotage as dangers in space life, and its climax, which illustrates the importance of Soviet-American cooperation in outer space.

B203. Quick, W. T. "High Hotel." *Analog Science Fiction/Science Fact*, 109 (June, 1989), p. 150-178.

The manager of a hotel on the Moon must deal with a number of problems: a rock star planning to kill a deranged employee on stage during a lunar concert; an rich elderly woman who wishes to migrate to the Moon; an entrant in a moon race who is trying to sabotage an opponent's vehicle; and an employee working with the saboteurs and cheating hotel guests. Having resolved the other difficulties, the manager proposes marriage to the elderly woman to enable her to become a Moon resident.

The story briefly mentions two space stations as stops on the journey from the Earth to the Moon; typical passengers travel from the Earth's surface to the "Low Earth Orbit" station, then to the "L1 Sat," and finally to the lunar surface (152).

B204. Randall, Marta. "Dangerous Games." *The Magazine of Fantasy and Science Fiction*, 58 (April, 1980), p. 6-46.

The pilot of a damaged starship is forced to go to Gensco Station, a mysterious and unfriendly place which suspects he is an agent from a malevolent company trying to take over their station. He befriends a cat-like humanoid with her own grudge against the station: it is holding something valuable that belongs to her. When she helps him repair his ship, he takes her to the satellite where her possession is and helps her obtain it. It turns out to be her infant child, who had been held there in cold storage.

There are several kinds of space stations in this novella: the "grabstation" that retrieves the starship from "tauspace," called Priory Main Grab—"an immense, gilded complexity of struts and bars and rings" (9); the residential Gensco Station, "spherical, an enormous silver orange whose exterior was a maze of metal valleys and square metal mountains" (11); the homes of a group of people named "Labbers" who "live in hollowed asteroids called 'holes' and bump about being immune to domestication" (19-20); and the "cold creches," satellites where Gensco keeps many children frozen as a way to maintain control over them. Overall, the story has a grim atmosphere of dark intrigue and repression which recalls Cherryh's *Downbelow Station* (q.v.).

Note: this novella was expanded into a novel with the same name.

B205. Raphael, Rick. "The Mailman Cometh." *Analog Science Fiction/Science Fact*, 74 (February, 1965), p. 17-33.

Two men are responsible for sorting and rerouting all the mail that comes out of subspace to the Orion Sub-Station One. Overworked and forced to use faulty machinery, the men try to make beer and wine, creating discrepancies in their food orders. An inspector sent to investigate learns that the men are not responsible for the problems and takes steps to see that changes are made.

There are plenty of space stations which serve to relay radio and television communications, but Raphael's station uniquely handles physical mail sent between the stars. (One must wonder why such communication would continue to be important in a star-spanning civilization.) This station is also unusually unkempt and foul-smelling—an "orbiting garbage can" (19-20). In recounting the loneliness of an isolated two-man station, "The Mailman Cometh" recalls Wellman's "Space Station No. 1" (q.v.).

B206. Resnick, Michael, and Barbara Delaplace. "Trading Up." In *Battlestation, Book One*. Edited by David Drake and Bill Fawcett. New York: Ace, 1992, p. 27-35.

An independent trader, convinced that the arrival of the Stephen Hawking in the Galactic Core will ultimately be bad for his business, decides to cut a deal with its officials. He offers to trade them his general expertise, and one piece of vital data—the location of an Ichton base—in exchange for exclusive trading rights on some of the worlds. The official agrees—but also drafts the man to serve as an alien contact specialist.

As in Mack Reynolds's *Satellite City* and the series *Star Trek: Deep Space Nine*, a space station can be the locale for colorful free-wheeling commerce and dirty dealings of various kinds—and the independent traders depicted in this story are exactly the kinds of people to perform such activities.

B207. Rich, H. Thompson. "The Flying City." *Astounding Stories of Super-Science*, 3 (August, 1930), p. 260-278.

A scientist working in the desert is kidnapped by aliens living in a huge flying city invisibly hovering over the Earth. He learns that the aliens first constructed this immense disc when their home planet was doomed by an approaching star; for a long time, they had been "voyaging through space on their marvelous disc...content to drift on and on in the interstellar void, breathing an atmosphere produced artificially" (264). Now, though, since "some of its mighty engines were nearing the exhaustion point" (264), they have decided to take over and occupy the Earth. Fortunately, the scientist and another kidnapped woman escape from the flying city, and, after the interruption of a second abduction, he uses a hastily constructed device to destroy the flying city.

The image of cities flying through space, later used effectively by James Blish's *Cities in Flight* novels (q.v.), may have originated in this story; it may also qualify as the first story about a space station published in a science fiction magazine. Like the people on Earth in Jack Williamson's "Born of the Sun" (q.v.), these aliens establish a home in space because their own planet is destroyed. Still, they were "content" with their space life, and resolve to return to a planet only when their city is about to break down. As the plot summary suggests, this is the only interesting element in an otherwise-routine story of alien invasion.

B208. Robinson, Ron. "Shadows on the Wall." In *Carmen Miranda's Ghost Is Haunting Space Station Three*. Edited by Don Sakers. New York: Baen, 1990, p. 66-69.

This transcript of a trial involves crewmen of Space Station Three who use the marvelous fruit left behind by Carmen Miranda's ghost to trade and obtain many facilities and luxuries for their station.

The only idea worth pondering in this vignette is that space station residents will no doubt develop their own system of barter with other space residents, instead of always dealing with Earth.

B209. Robinson, Spider, and Jeanne Robinson. "Stardance." In *Nebula Winners Thirteen*. Edited by Samuel R. Delany. New York: Harper & Row, 1980, p. 99-169. Story originally published in *Analog Science Fiction/Science Fact* (March, 1977).

A young dancer travels to the Skyfac orbiting complex to develop the art of zero-gravity dancing; but when strange aliens approach Earth who seem to communicate through movement, she dances her Stardance for them and persuades them to leave—at the cost of her own life.

See comments above on the novel of the same name, which incorporates this novella as its first part.

B210. Rothman, Milton. "Prime Crime." *Isaac Asimov's Science Fiction Magazine*, 3 (May, 1979), p. 82-105.

While his son longs for a piano, the director of the Lagrange satellite must investigate missing equipment which has apparently been stolen to construct some type of communications device. He eventually discovers that an ex-musician who emigrated to the satellite has been using the equipment to construct an organ.

Rothman's story about a giant cylinder in space is filled with interesting ideas and insights: "In space eternal vigilance is the price of life" (94); "growing up in Lagrange was not really much fun. The little world had to be more confining than a small town in mid-America" (94); the hero thinks of "the fragile ecology of the satellite, a thin balloon surrounded by the deadly vacuum of interplanetary space" (99). The story also emphasizes the political and legal problems involved in establishing "a civilian research establishment" (93) which "set off a many-sided struggle between civilian government agencies, industry, non-government scientists, and the Department of Defense" (96). There are also references to other space colonies: Laplace, "the twin satellite" (95) and "the Russian, the Chinese, the Third World Collective" (92). Unfortunately, the story itself is dull, because it is obvious from the beginning that the missing parts were being used to build a musical instrument.

B211. "Rough Justice." [no author given] In *Space Wars: Fact and Fiction*. [No editor given] London: Octopus, 1980, p. 10-18.

A group of ten prisoners escapes from Pris-Sat (Prison Satellite) Z9 and lands on a planet where they find a civilization of robots anxious to study a human. The five survivors are asked to fight to the death so the robots can study a successful type; but the winner, the cruel leader of the escape, simply becomes their lifelong captive. Another prisoner, who was wrongly convicted, manages to escape.

This very weak story seems to be loaded with in-jokes, including two escaping convicts named "Harlan" and "Ellison." The station is home to 3,000 prisoners, and "Space inside the satellite was at a premium" (11); all prison satellites "hung over dead planets" to make escape difficult (12); and the station is surrounded by "many security spy-satellites" (11).

B212. Saari, Oliver. "Sitting Duck." *Astounding Science-Fiction*, 48 (January, 1952), p. 119-130.

A military space station in Earth orbit is designed to watch for missile firings and, if necessary, take over and aim friendly missiles towards enemy territory. The commander becomes obsessed with the notion that one crewman, Bailey, is too frightened to handle the job and demands a replacement; but his superiors on Earth decide to replace him instead, telling him that "You're a sick man, major" (130).

The story notes first the extreme pressure felt by people on board such a space station—"To live six months in constant danger, in a most weird and cramped environment, carrying an unprecedented load of responsibility: this was a lot to ask four men...mere mortals transformed into Gods!" (120) Also, Saari offers with unusual clarity the argument that a space station is a "Sitting Duck" for enemy attack; even the slightly unbalanced commander agrees that "the station was practically defenseless and vulnerable" (128), despite its missiles. Finally, there is one intriguing practical suggestion: "a continuous fan-drawn suction created a substitute for gravity" (126).

B213. Sakers, Don. "The Man Who Traveled in Rocketships." In *Carmen Miranda's Ghost Is Haunting Space Station Three.* Edited by Don Sakers. New York: Baen, 1990, p. 183-192.

As a dying science fiction author writes an adventure about Space Station Three, news comes that the President is shutting down all space activities. But the ghost of Carmen Miranda comes to console him, and after he dies, he joins her and the ghosts of many other friends on a spectral Space Station Three.

This is nothing more than a rewrite of Robert A. Heinlein's uncharacteristically sentimental "The Man Who Travelled in Elephants" with Heinlein himself—thinly discussed as "Mr. Riverside," referring to Heinlein's one-time pseudonym John Riverside. The forced appearance of Carmen Miranda in this story seems particularly incongruous.

B214. Sakers, Don. "Tarawa Rising." In *Carmen Miranda's Ghost Is Haunting Space Station Three.* Edited by Don Sakers. New York: Baen, 1990, p. 247-264.

An aging transvestite performer, reduced to doing "dinner shows on the space station circuit" (248), becomes deeply depressed and when a solar flare comes, he decides to go out into space and die from the radiation. However, Carmen Miranda's ghost, which has been coming to him to cheer him up, tells a little girl to go out into space too, and when he sees her, he drops his suicide plans and goes to rescue her from the storm. Afterwards, he realizes that Carmen arranged the affair so that he could recover the will to live.

Tarawa is a well-drawn character, a poignant picture of a homosexual who grew up in the age before liberation, but as in other stories, the involvement of Carmen Miranda and ghosts is more of an imposition than anything else. The space station here is basically a stopover point, although it occasionally has tourists who come to see Tarawa's shows.

B215. Sanders, Scott Russell. "Quarantine." In *Habitats*. Edited by Susan Shwartz. New York: DAW, 1984, p. 167-179.

In the future, the entire population of Earth lives in the Enclosure—a network of domed cities and tunnels covering the entire planet. A woman has been working on the next step—Project Transcendence, "a space-going version of the Enclosure" (174)—but mysteriously goes away, to join a small, secret band of people who have gone back to live in the wild.

A model of the proposed space colony is briefly described: "the colossal orb of cities.... Fitted with sails and great looming scoops, the gauzy sphere was designed to voyage through space without being anchored to any planet or sun" (175). But the story finally argues in favor of life in the open on a planetary surface.

B216. Scortia, Thomas N. "Sea Change." *Astounding Science Fiction*, 57 (June, 1956), p. 130-140.

A bitter man who had his brain put into a robot body is offered a position at one of the trans-Plutonian stations, where the drive mechanisms are installed in starships. But he is not attracted by the offer: "The stations? Why should I let myself be sealed in one of those? Completely immobile. What kind of a useless life is that, existing as a self-contained unit for years on end without the least contact with humanity?" (133) However, he makes mental contact with another woman of his kind who is now at a station preparing for interstellar travel. After she survives a crisis and begins her trip, he resolves to follow her to Alpha Centauri.

The stations here seem similar to those in Fritch's "Many Dreams of Earth" (q.v.)—one-man facilities with an immobile resident hooked up to machines. Their purpose is to "install the drive after the ship leaves the system proper" (133) which cannot be done near the Sun's gravita-tional field.

B217. Scott, Melissa, and Lisa A. Barnett. "The Carmen Miranda Gambit." In *Carmen Miranda's Ghost Is Haunting Space Station Three*. Edited by Don Sakers. New York: Baen, 1990, p. 104-143.

The chess champion, an impetuous young man who refuses to go back to Earth, is unhappy because, while at a space station playing a match, his opponent, a former champion who came out of retirement, is not playing well at all, and he wants real competition to bolster his reputation. The opponent's manager explains that the old champion had developed an obsession with Carmen Miranda, watching her old tapes and imagining that she was giving him luck; and when he recently stopped believing in her, his playing skills deteriorated. The young champion then arranges for Carmen Miranda tapes and apparitions to appear all over the station, so as to encourage his opponent to believe in her again. It works, but the ingenious Carmen Miranda bugs cannot be removed from the station.

Since most experts have predicted that the chess champions of the future will all be computers, it is a bit incongruous to read a story about chess champions in a future world of space stations, and especially incongruous to make one character a Bobby Fisher clone. The station tends to be decorated in "seashell" tones (112) and residents usually dress flamboyantly (118-119), apparently in reaction to their limited metallic environment; the only place with living greenery on the station, the Woods, can only be visited if someone pays an exorbitant fee.

B218. Shaara, Michael. "Four-Billion Dollar Door." *Satellite Science Fiction*, 1 (December, 1956), p. 101-105.

A man obsessed with space flight finally flies to the Moon, with television cameras along to broadcast events to Earth. However, the spaceship door is jammed and he cannot go out on the surface to plant the flag and claim the world—much to his embarrassment.

The story mentions that "he got his money and built the satellite station and the space-ship. They were four years in the making" (103). This is, incidentally, one of the stories that predicted a televised moon landing, another being Bill Finger's comic-book story "The Last Television Broadcast on Earth" (1955).

B219. Shaw, Bob. "Small World." In *The Penguin World Omnibus of Science Fiction*. Edited by Brian Aldiss and Sam J. Lundwall. Middlesex, England: Penguin, 1986, p. 63-77. Story originally published in *Pulsar #1* (1978).

To gain full status as a member of a gang, a youngster in space habitat Island One plans to "walk across the sky" (61)—across the huge transparent panels that let sunlight into the cylinder. However, he becomes frightened by the immensity of space on his return trip and stops, forcing the authorities to close the shutters and rescue him. A parallel story involves a woman whose husband was killed building another habitat: an object catapulted by the youngster shatters her window and her nerves, but the premature closing of the shutters relieves her: she has made it through the day, she believes, without depending on tranquilizers.

This story is similar to Watkins's "Coming of Age in Henson's Tube" (q.v.) in describing an adolescent rite of passage in a space habitat. Shaw hints at the different perspective someone growing up in a habitat might have—"his imagination was not fully able to cope with the old Earthbound concepts of 'above' and 'below'" (63)—pointing out that "children have an intense, detailed awareness of their surroundings" (74). There is also a sense of youthful decadence in the emergence of rival gangs in a space habitat, seen at the stage of adulthood in works like Reynolds's *Chaos in Lagrangia* and Watkins's *The Centrifugal Rickshaw Dancer* (q.v.). Finally, Shaw emphasizes the fragility of a habitat in observing that "Catapults were illegal in Island One, as were firearms and all explosive devices which might be capable of puncturing the pressure skin" (66).

B220. Sheckley, Robert. "Paradise II." *In Time to Come*. Edited by August Derleth. 1954. New York: Pyramid, 1969, p. 187-201.

After landing on a planet whose inhabitants are all long dead, two Earthmen visit the space station orbiting the planet. One is injured and finds his brain becoming part of the space station's mechanical intelligence, while the other gradually learns of the station's purpose: to manufacture food for the starving people on the planet and prevent war by receiving samples of food, which were never delivered, and duplicating them. Unfortunately, the machine takes the Earthman for the food and starts slaughtering and processing him and his many duplicates.

As in many of Sheckley's stories, the logic here is questionable: why build a sophisticated automated space station that cannot distinguish between a human being and a piece of food? Still, the story offers a unique example of a station designed to manufacture food, not the usual crystals and machinery.

B221. Sheckley, Robert. "The Stand on Luminos." In *Battlestation, Book One*. Edited by David Drake and Bill Fawcett. New York: Ace, 1992, p. 180-209.

A man is assigned to visit a hitherto uncontacted alien world and warn them about the Ichton threat. Before he leaves, a trader approaches him with a deal—to give him spaceship engines to sell to the presumably interested natives. When the envoy arrives, the aliens at first treat him with amazing indifference; but when he finally persuades their leading citizen that the danger is genuine, they quickly begin to prepare for battle. Surprisingly, after some quick training from the envoy, the natives are able to use their crude spaceships to drive off the Ichtons.

Sheckley, once noted for his zany humor, is disappointing in this routine contribution to the series. As in other stories, the station itself is seen as a place for shady dealings.

B222. Sheffield, Charles. "All the Colors of the Vacuum." *Analog Science Fiction/Science Fact*, 101 (February 2, 1981), p. 60-86.

A brilliant scientist named McAndrew, working in a space station orbiting Mars, hears about a message from a space ark containing remarkable scientific results. He and a friend decide to fly out to the ark to meet the person or people responsible for this work. They find a repressive and generally backward society, with one outstanding individual doing the interesting research; they grab him, flee from the ark, and return to the Solar System.

"The Penrose Institute had been moved out to Mars orbit" (62), a logical place for physics research. There are also references to Oberon Station (65)—presumably in the vicinity of Uranus—and Lungfish, "the first permanent space station" (69). In this story, the space station plays its traditional role as the place where space adventures begin and end.

Note: Sheffield later wrote a novel about McAndrew incorporating this story, called *The McAndrew Chronicles.*

B223. Sheffield, Charles. "Dinsdale Dissents." *Galaxy,* 38 (July, 1977), p. 112-122.

A man named Waldo, convicted of unknowingly smuggling drugs, is sentenced to serve on Venus Station, where he works in a huge vat which produces algae being used to terraform Venus. When President Dinsdale arrives for a visit, Waldo accidentally discovers and reveals that the other convicts have been growing and smuggling the same drug in the vat.

Venus Station has two big wheels—Station Up, which rotates, and Station Down, which does not. This is one of the less restrictive space prisons, since the convicts working in the smelly vats are essentially left to their own devices.

Note: this seems to be one of a series of stories involving the characters Henry Carver and Waldo Burmeister; two of the other stories that I have examined do not feature space stations.

B224. Sheffield, Charles. "Skystalk." In *Great Science Fiction Stories by the World's Great Scientists.* Edited by Isaac Asimov with Martin Greenberg and Charles Waugh. New York: Donald I. Fine, Inc., 1985, p. 52-71. Story originally published in *Destinies* (August, 1979).

Terrorists plant a fusion bomb on a bucket going up the Skystalk, a gigantic elevator connecting the surface of the Earth with two space stations. Two crewmen on the lower station must ride the "Beanstalk" down in an ore bucket, leap over to the upward bucket containing the bomb, and disarm the bomb.

Here is a new type of space station with a familiar problem—sabotage. As in most space emergencies, real and imaginary, human ingenuity and chewing-gum-and-baling-wire solutions are the only answer.

B225. Sheffield, Charles. "Transition Team." In *The Endless Frontier, Volume I.* Edited by Jerry Pournelle. New York: Ace, 1979, p. 325-351. Story originally published in *Destinies* (November-December, 1978).

A behavioral psychologist visits the L-5 colony to investigate why the space-born children seem so disturbed and depressed. Her conclusion: the space-borns represent a new breed of people, different in appearance, movement and thought, and they resent being trained to live up to terrestrial expectations unconsciously projected by their Earth-born parents. Her solution: the adults should all leave the colony—they were the "transition team" from Earth life to space life—and let the children run the colony.

Many stories have speculated that people born in space will develop into a new type of person, unlike Earth people; few if any have envisioned the change coming so abruptly—with the first generation of space-borns. An unstated corollary to the psychologist's solution is that space will never be the Earth's "New Frontier"; with a few exceptions, Earth people must remain on Earth and space will be conquered and inhabited by those born in space.

B226. Shirley, John. "Freezone." In *Mirrorshades: The Cyberpunk Anthology*. 1986. Edited by Bruce Sterling. New York: Ace, 1988, p. 139-177. Originally published in *Eclipse*. By John Shirley. New York: Bluejay, 1985. 341 p.

In a devastated future Earth, an anachronistic rock musician lives in Freezone, an artificial island in the Atlantic that caters to the rich. When his band breaks up, he joins some mysterious fugitives and arranges to escape to Malta.

The disaster that destroyed the American economy—the explosion of an electromagnetic pulse weapon—also "vaporized...two satellites, one of them manned" (140). The other reference to space stations is one mention of "the orbiting space Colony" which is being blockaded by the Soviets.

Note: this is part of Shirley novel's *Eclipse*, which also generated two sequels, *Eclipse Penumbra* and *Eclipse Corona*.

B227. Shwartz, Susan. "Confessional Booths." In *Carmen Miranda's Ghost Is Haunting Space Station Three*. Edited by Don Sakers. New York: Baen, 1990, p. 71-87.

A would-be cantor is serving as the all-purpose religious figure on Space Station Three. The ghost of Carmen Miranda somehow materializes out of an old movie in the station data banks and tells her that she cannot rest until she has confessed to a priest. The cantor contacts a priest on Earth but he refuses to come, so she materializes "Father" Spencer Tracy out of *Boys' Town* and he hears her confession, which means she will now be leaving the station alone.

There are two points worth mentioning here: the idea that space stations would be highly infectious breeding places for diseases (72) and the notion that station residents would necessarily guard their privacy in such a limited environment (77).

B228. Silverberg, Robert. "Blindsight." In *Cities in Space: The Endless Frontier, Volume III*. Edited by Jerry Pournelle with John F. Carr. New York: Ace, 1991, p. 131-152. Originally published in *Playboy* (December, 1986).

Years ago, as an experiment, a man was genetically altered in the womb to have no eyes, and to have instead a unique, all-encompassing sensory system. He now visits the surreptitious space habitat Valparaiso, where many fugitives go to hide, searching for the doctor who originally did the work. The man is involved in preparations for faster-than-light travel, and it has been learned that while the experience hopelessly distorts normal vision, his kind of "blindsight" is not affected; thus, he wants the doctor to alter other people so that they can serve on the starship. The boy he hires to help him find the doctor—the story's viewpoint character—is bribed to double-cross him and kill him, but the attempt fails, and the boy finds out that he will be the first person altered to have blindsight.

Despite the strangeness of the unique perceptual system he describes, Silverberg offers a world in space with a familiar air—the distant, impoverished country where people with shady backgrounds go to escape from their pasts. In fact, "the chief industry" of this particular habitat is "the protection of fugitives" (135). The place is otherwise a normal habitat, with various spokes and Earthlike environments.

B229. Silverberg, Robert, and Barbara Silverberg. "Deadlock." *Astounding Science Fiction*, 63 (January, 1959), p. 92-121.

The United Nations is deadlocked over two major proposals: one is to terraform Mars and make it earthlike; the other, cheaper proposal is to genetically transform people so that they can inhabit Mars (pantropy). Finally, a compromise is reached: Mars will be terraformed, but pantropy will be used to colonize Venus.

Although there is some talk about the need for new homes for Earth's people, space structures are apparently never considered; there is only one mention that a "ring of orbital satellites hung round the Earth to serve as radio-video relay stations, observation towers, and halfway-houses for space travelers" (98).

B230. Silverberg, Robert. "Our Lady of the Sauropods." In *The Endless Frontier, Volume II*. Edited by Jerry Pournelle with John F. Carr. New York: Ace, 1982, p. 139-156. Story originally published in *Omni* (September, 1980).

A young woman, treacherously abandoned with sabotaged equipment on a space habitat filled with dinosaurs recreated by cloning, discovers that the dinosaurs are actually intelligent and telepathic. Becoming fond of them, as they feed and shelter her, she kills the man who comes to rescue her and resolves to help the dinosaurs reconquer the Earth.

The dream that space habitats might bring back earlier and happier lifestyles emerges here in an extreme form: a return to the golden age of dinosaurs. The dinosaurs' civilization here is certainly utopian, and the heroine's decision to join their cause is presented sympathetically, although there is the suggestion that she is being mentally manipulated by the dinosaurs.

B231. Smith, Everett C., plot, and R. F. Starzl, story. "The Metal Moon." *Wonder Stories Quarterly*, 3 (Winter, 1932), p. 246-259.

Travelers from Earth, seeking to reestablish contact with a long-isolated group of Jovian colonists, discover a society rigidly divided into two classes: a physically attractive dominating class, and an underclass of repressed and often deformed "Mugs." The situation is epitomized by the satellite they have built—the "Pleasure Bubble"—a sphere with an upper half enclosed in crystal which offers idyllic Earth-like environments for the ruling class and a lower half enclosed in metal, a nightmare of narrow corridors and dangerous machinery for the Mugs who are forced to live and work there. Sympathizing with the lower class, the Earthmen join their rebellion, finally escaping with some Mugs and destroying the Pleasure Bubble in the process.

The Pleasure Bubble aptly summarizes two contrasting views of life in a space station: a man-made paradise, the theme of so much recent fiction, and the metallic prison found in some earlier stories. The image is much more interesting than the story, a result of Hugo Gernsback's "Interplanetary Plot" contests, in which readers submitted plots which were given to established authors to turn into stories.

B232. Smith, George O. "The External Triangle." In *The Complete Venus Equilateral*. By George O. Smith. Introduction by Arthur C. Clarke. 1976. New York: Del Rey/Ballantine, 1980, p. 406-426. First published as "Interlude" in *Astounding: John W. Campbell Memorial Anthology* in 1973.

Don Channing, his wife Arden, and other friends from Venus Equilateral are now living on Pluto, where Channing is about to become a grandfather. He is also working on a method to actually teleport living things through space; but the experimental creatures teleported always die. When his grandchildren—twins—are born with a condition that requires an immediate transfusion, he figures out that living things are arriving as mirror images, and if they are teleported twice, they should be all right; and he uses this knowledge to get needed blood to his grandchildren, and then to teleport them to a hospital on Earth.

There are three references to the abandoned Venus Equilateral station (406, 409, 425), and Smith attempts to update its technology by having Channing's son-in-law describe technological advances since the time of the original stories: "Dad, you and Mr. Channing were running Venus Equilateral on *vacuum tubes*...the advent of the solid-state device opened up a whole new concept" (409).

B233. Smith, George O. "Identity." In *The Complete Venus Equilateral*. By George O. Smith. Introduction by Arthur C. Clarke. 1976. New York: Del Rey/Ballantine, 1980, p. 427-468. Story first published in *Astounding Science Fiction* (November, 1945).

A man discovers the "Key"—a homing device—that will lead him to "Murdoch's Hoard," a legendary lost treasure left by an ancient surgeon. Fending off the attacks of his evil twin brother, he reaches the Hoard, but his doctor girlfriend is paralyzed in a plane crash; finding that the Hoard is actually nothing but Murdoch's medical records, he consults them and manages to cure his girlfriend.

There is one reference to "the long-gone Venus Equilateral Relay Station" (436) and to factory work in space: "to make identium, you require a space station in the outer region" (438).

B234. Smith, George O. "Lost Art." In *The Complete Venus Equilateral*. By George O. Smith. Introduction by Arthur C. Clarke. 1976, New York: Del Rey/Ballantine, 1980, p. 104-131. Story first published in *Astounding Science Fiction* (December, 1943).

Amidst flashbacks to the ancient Martians who were operating the machine, modern Earthmen try to figure out the function and operation of a Martian power-beaming device.

There are two brief references to Don Channing and his Venus Equilateral station (122, 125), highly respected in Smith's future world for its technological skill.

B235. Stasheff, Christopher. "Hearing." In *Battlestation, Book Two: Vanguard*. Edited by David Drake and Bill Fawcett. New York: Ace, 1993, p. 32-62.

A group of women in suspended animation, survivors of a space mission long ago, are discovered by Globin, the leader of the Khalians on board the Stephen Hawking (see Stasheff's "Globin's Children"). As survivors of the old war with the Alliance depicted in the earlier series *The Fleet*, they are naturally suspicious when they find themselves on board an Alliance battle station, and Globin must work to maintain their freedom. Twice, Ichtons attack the ship, zeroing in on the women's quarters, and Globin deduces that the women must have some information that the Ichtons do not want promulgated. The one child born to the woman, whose deafness helps thwart the second Ichton attack because she alone can destroy the Ichtons' noise-making weapons, agrees to a memory scan, and Globin learns that the women in fact discovered an Ichton home world.

If the Ichtons can get two attack squads on board the Stephen Hawking in quick succession, it seems apparent that the station is indeed "vulnerable," as other stories indicate. Continuing hostility towards the women, ancient opponents of the Alliance, might be seen as an example of space station xenophobia.

B236. Stasheff, Christopher. "Globin's Children." In *Battlestation, Book One*. Edited by David Drake and Bill Fawcett. New York: Ace, 1992, p. 38-80.

Globin, the human leader of the Khalians who once battled the Alliance, receives news of the Ichton fleet devastating the worlds of the Galactic Core. When the Alliance decides to construct the Stephen Hawking battle station as a mobile base for war against the Ichtons, Globin decides to resign his position and join the people on the station—much to the displeasure of many of its personnel. Searching a devastated planet, Globin discovers valuable transuranic elements which he mines as a possible resource—and valuable item for profitable trade with the Alliance. Later, he and his Khalians distinguish themselves in battle against the Ichtons, making him for the first time "a hero to his own species" (80).

Globin was evidently a major character in the preceding series *The Fleet*—a likable villain—and Stasheff was obviously reluctant to let the character die. The story is important in that it describes the decision to create the Stephen Hawking and some of the circumstances of its early days.

B237. Sterling, Bruce. "Cicada Queen." In *Crystal Express*. By Bruce Sterling. Sauk City, WI: Arkham House Publishers, 1989, p. 45-79. Originally published in *Universe 13* in 1983.

A group of refugees from the Mechanist/Shaper conflicts, calling themselves the Polycarbon Clique, have gathered in Czarina-Kluster, a space habitat controlled by an alien Investor known as the Queen. A new member, Landau, is most interested in pursuing a project to terraform Mars; and when the news arrives that the Queen has deserted the habitat, Landau flees to Mars, where he can establish a new Terraform-Kluster, become the new ruler of the Clique, and continue the effort to terraform Mars.

Sterling fills in some of the history of his universe with a reference to "the first generation of independent space habitats, the so-called Concatenation" (59). The people in the story are all space-born, and they express a familiar contempt for planetary life: "Just think of being trapped down a gravity well. I'd choke to death" (56). Sterling also makes the point that the close quarters of a space habitat, along with advances in bugging technology, would make privacy in a habitat very difficult, so residents have established special secured rooms called Discreets to have privacy.

Note: a novel set in the same universe, *Schismatrix*, is discussed in Part A, and four other stories in this universe—"Spider Rose,"

"Swarm," "Sunken Gardens," and "Twenty Evocations"—are discussed below.

B238. Sterling, Bruce, and William Gibson. "Red Star, Winter Orbit."
In *Burning Chrome*. By William Gibson. 1986. New York:
Ace, 1987, p. 80-102. Story originally published in *Omni* (July,
1983).

An injured cosmonaut, forced to live in the Russian space station
Kosmograd for the rest of his life, rebels when officials order the station abandoned. After enabling other rebels to escape to Earth, he remains, expecting to die when the station's orbit decays and it falls to
Earth; instead, "squatters" from American solar stations high in the
atmosphere arrive, attach booster rockets to save the station, and plan
to settle in the station.

Reflecting the pessimistic mood of the 1980s, the story envisions first
the Americans and then the Russians giving up on space travel to focus on other problems; but rugged individualists will carry on the conquest of space. Thus, the two most famous "cyberpunk" writers here
display an attitude more typically associated with authors of a quite
different philosophy like Ben Bova and Jerry Pournelle.

B239. Sterling, Bruce. "Spider Rose." In *Crystal Express*. By Bruce
Sterling. Sauk City, WI: Arkham House Publishers, 1989, p.
27-44. Story first published in *The Magazine of Fantasy and
Science Fiction* (August, 1982).

A venerable Mechanist woman has established a home in a habitat orbiting Uranus. When alien Investors seek to purchase a fabulous jewel
in her possession, they offer her an amazing alien pet, which soon
shows the power to transform itself into a sympathetic being resembling its master. Though she grows fond of it, an attack by an old enemy leaves her short of food, so she eats it; she then turns into that being, and is reclaimed by the Investors as their pet.

Sterling adds a fascinating detail about space life in the future: since
roaches "had plagued spacecraft from the beginning, too tough, prolific, and adaptable to kill," the Mechanists "had used genetic techniques stolen from their rivals the Shapers to turn the roaches into colorful pets" (27). The story otherwise fits the story pattern of isolation
in a space station leading to madness.

B240. Sterling, Bruce. "Spook." In *Crystal Express*. By Bruce Sterling. Sauk City, WI: Arkham House Publishers, 1989, p. 155-169. Originally published in *The Magazine of Fantasy and Science Fiction* (April, 1983).

An agent from space, influenced by an implant called the Veil, is summoned to Earth to infiltrate and destroy a Central American rebel cult based on ancient Mayan beliefs. He is detected and captured, and the Veil is removed, so that he can be fully human again and can join the rebels. However, he instead chooses to kill them all and return to his old life because "Being human just isn't enough fun" (169).

This story might be cast as a very early Mechanist/Shaper story concerning the early days of space life and human transformation, though Sterling does not make the connection. Here, Earth is suffering because of "a relentless brain drain into the orbital factories, while overpopulation and pollution wrecked the planet" (157). Thus, the story offers the familiar contrast between vibrant and promising space colonies and a doomed, decadent Earth.

B241. Sterling, Bruce. "Sunken Gardens." In *Crystal Express*. By Bruce Sterling. Sauk City, WI: Arkham House Publishers, 1989, p. 80-96. Originally published in *Omni* (June, 1984).

In this direct sequel to "Cicada Queen" (q.v.), Landau's Terraform-Kluster is growing in power and continuing to work on making Mars into an Earthlike planet. They eliminate rival groups, force them to live on Mars, urge them to enter competitions to develop the most effective technological and biological ways to make the planet habitable, and reward the winners with life in orbit. One competition in a Martian crater has catastrophic results, though a woman contestant does win a trip up "the Ladder" into space.

Moving his Mechanist/Shaper saga into a new publication, Sterling was obliged to offer a quick and useful summary of its history:

> The history of mankind in space had been a long epic of ambitions and rivalries. From the very first, space colonies had struggled for self-sufficiency and had soon broken their ties with the exhausted Earth. The independent life-support systems had given them the mentality of city-states. Strange ideologies had bloomed in the hothouse atmosphere of the o'neills,

and breakaway groups were common.

Space was too vast to police. Pioneer elites burst forth, defying anyone to stop their pursuit of aberrant technologies. Quite suddenly the march of science had become an insane, headlong scramble. New sciences and technologies had shattered whole societies in waves of future shock.

The shattered cultures coalesced into factions, so thoroughly alienated from one another that they were called humanity only for lack of a better term. (83)

The interesting notion here is that people in space will become indifferent to death and suffering with a new "posthuman" perspective: "If life worked perfectly, how could things evolve?" (95)

B242. Sterling, Bruce. "Swarm." In *Crystal Express*. By Bruce Sterling. Sauk City, WI: Arkham House Publishers, 1989, p. 3-26. Originally published in *The Magazine of Fantasy and Science Fiction* (April, 1982).

A Shaper pays to have an Investor take him to the Swarm—a vast tunneled asteroid inhabited by a multitude of interrelated, unintelligent life forms. He hopes to steal some of their genetic material and create useful life forms; but he is detected, captured, and forcibly absorbed into the Swarm, a fate which, the temporary intelligence of the being tells him, eventually awaits the entire human race.

Even though all characters in his future universe inhabit space and abhor Earth, Sterling offers this odd comment from his hero: "Space is an unnatural environment, and it takes an unnatural effort from unnatural people to prosper there" (13). And in fact, come to think of it, Sterling's characters are often rather unsympathetic in conventional terms, which could be taken as a sign not of his ineptitude or determined irony, but of his effort to depict a truly inhuman consciousness.

B243. Sterling, Bruce. "Twenty Evocations." In *Crystal Express*. By Bruce Sterling. Sauk City, WI: Arkham House Publishers, 1989, p. 97-104. First published in *Interzone* (Spring, 1984) under the title, "Life in the Mechanist/Shaper Era: Twenty Evocations."

In twenty brief passages mimicking the style of William Burroughs, Sterling tells the story of Nikolai, a Shaper who advances to become the head of an independent Kluster, while marrying a wife, watching her killed, and later marrying her clone. After a long life, he commits suicide, saying, "Futility is freedom."

The atomistic format of the story is clearly designed to evoke the fragmentary, disjointed state of future human nature and human experiences. Life in the Mechanist/Shaper universe is simply a series of unconnected events, which one adapts to as best one can.

B244. Stewart, Ian. "Curlew's Choice." *Analog Science Fiction/Science Fact*, 110 (February, 1990), p. 156-175.

Traveling from the Big Wheel, "A vast artificial city" in space (158), back to the planet he governs, Anthony Curlew meets and is attracted to a mysterious young woman. On the planet, he learns that the woman is mentally scarred from growing up in a repressive, male-dominated spaceship culture; it is also revealed that Curlew has been mentally reprogrammed after being responsible for an ecological disaster on another planet. After an accident and a violent confrontation shatter her sanity, he hopes that they can work together to deal with and overcome their unfortunate pasts.

The official name of the Big Wheel is the Unukalhay Distributor; it is pictured as a vital transportation and business hub for various planets. A similar facility, the Baten Kaitos Distributor, is briefly mentioned (166).

B245. Stiegler, Marc. "The Bully and the Crazy Boy." *Analog Science Fiction/Science Fact*, 100 (November, 1980), p. 126-139.

A superior and cruel alien race comes to conquer the Solar System, but they are defeated by the determined humans, who use their own spaceships moving near the speed of light to destroy the alien fleet.

The first encounter between aliens and humans ended when a number of alien ships came to an "orbital city" near Uranus (128), which blew itself up and destroyed the ships.

B246. Stirling, S. M. "Comrades." In *Battlestation, Book One*. Edited by David Drake and Bill Fawcett. New York: Ace, 1992, p. 133-150.

A group of Alliance fighters are locked in battle with a small band of

Ichtons on a desolate planet. With neither side able to achieve victory, the Ichtons surprisingly suggest a temporary truce, allowing both sides to withdraw.

This is the first story to strike a note of sympathy for the Ichtons, by presenting some of the story from the viewpoint of an Ichton. The story tells us that although the Stephen Hawking was "the largest self-propelled object humans had ever built," it had the feeling of crowdedness—"Fleet Marine quarters shaved space as if this were an assault boat, not a battle station" (p. 133).

B247. Sturgeon, Theodore. [formerly E. Hunter Waldo] "Unite and Conquer." *Astounding Science Fiction*, 42 (October, 1948), p. 63-99.

As the world prepares for war, alien spacecraft are detecting approaching the Earth; one enters Earth orbit and drops a bomb. In response, all nations move toward a world government and work together for defense: twenty-seven satellites are orbited to attack approaching ships, and a Space Station is planned as a manned base for further attacks. However, we finally learn that the ships were actually built and launched by a human scientist as a way to prevent war and unify the Earth.

Although actually constructed to aid in Earth's defense, the Space Station was originally designed for a peaceful—and familiar—purpose: "factories were retooling for a long dreamt-of project—a Space Station which would circle the Earth in an orbit close enough to be reached by man-carrying rockets which would rest and refuel there and take off again for deep Space, without the crushing drag of Earth's gravity" (86). Although the alien threat turns out to be illusory, Sturgeon's story suggests that while military stations might be dangerous in a terrestrial war, they could be useful in protecting the Earth against an attack from space.

B248. Swanwick, Michael. "Ginungagap." In *Nebula Award Stories 16*. Edited by Jerry Pournelle. New York: Holt, Rinehart, and Winston, 1982, p. 45-84. Story first published in *TriQuarterly*, 49 (Fall, 1980).

A woman is recruited to travel through a black hole named Ginunga-gap to meet with strange alien spiders who have been communicating with humans by means of the black hole. There is some question, however, about whether the human that emerges at the other black hole will actually be the real person or a duplicate of her. When she arrives, the spiders offer to provide a better means of using black holes to travel through space if she will allow them to duplicate her and use her duplicates as couriers.

There are many space colonies in Swanwick's future world; in a flashback on the Martian surface, the heroine looks up and thinks, "Up there was civilization: tens of thousands of human stations strung together by webs of communication and transportation.... Up there, free from gravity's relentless clutch, people lived in luxury and ease" (59). Specific space facilities mentioned are "Toledo Cylinder in Juno Industrial Park...one of the older commercial cylinders" (46), and the Arthur C. Clarke, positioned near the black hole, which "consisted of five wheels, each set inside the other and rotating and slightly differing speeds" (48), and which is significantly nicknamed "Mother" (50). Overall, Swanwick sees life in space as comforting and comfortable: someone calls the heroine "the product of a near-space culture—protected, trusting, willing to take things at face value" (51).

B249. Tannehill, Jayne. "Last Words." *Analog: Science Fiction/Science Fact*, 51 (May 25, 1981), p. 60-69.

A space engineer, traumatized by an accident in space, insists on working alone at a space station until a family friend brings him an old recording of him reciting a speech by Thoreau with the line, "I must leave Walden." Then he realizes that he must leave also.

In contrast to lonely space station residents who go mad, as in Fritch's "Many Dreams of Earth" and Martin's "The Second Kind of Loneliness" (q.v.), Tannehill argues that one can conquer the desire for solitude and return to human society. It is one of the few stories where the move from a space station back to Earth is seen as a positive step toward mental health; a similar story about a physically and mentally wounded man who is successfully encouraged to leave a space station and go home is Heinlein's "Waldo" (q.v.).

B250. Taylor, John Alfred. "Changeling." *Galileo*, 1, No. 11-12 [combined issues], (May, 1979), p. 57-61.

George Grieve, a bioengineered "changeling" working on the Moon, is ordered to fly a diplomat to the L-5 space colony for important negotiations—even though he and his wife were planning a vacation to

Earth. Angry, his wife goes to Earth anyway and decides to divorce him, while Grieve gets his passenger to L-5 safely despite a minor collision.

A familiar scenario is unwinding here—the L-5 colonists, tired of the restraints imposed by Earth, are demanding virtual independence, and the Earth diplomat is sent to work out a compromise. However, Grieve advises him to accede to the colonists' demands, since their independence is virtually inevitable.

Note: this is apparently the first of at least three stories about Grieve; the other two are "Grave-II" and "Too Close to Home" (q.v.).

B251. Taylor, John Alfred. "Far from Home." *Astounding Science Fiction*, 56 (December, 1955), p. 64-78.

A ship fails to rendezvous with Space Station One when it is hit by a meteor and its pilot is left adrift in space; after waiting to be rescued, he decides to use a waste cylinder to make a desperate return to Earth, and somehow survives the landing.

There are some initial caustic remarks about the incompetence of the people controlling spaceships, implying that such accidents may be common, but little else is said about the Space Station.

B252. Taylor, John Alfred. "Grave-11." *Galileo*, 2, No. 13 (July, 1979), p. 32-37.

Bioengineered George Grieve is called in when terrorists take over the space telescope near his space colony. When negotiations fail, he manages to overpower them and save their hostages.

As in Bova's *Colony* (q.v.), fanatical terrorists find it relatively easy to penetrate and take over a space colony; they demand that the colonists "Turn off the synchronous power satellites" (34) as a way of reducing Earth's population.

B253. Taylor, John Alfred. "Too Close to Home." *Galileo*, 2, No. 16 (January, 1980), p. 40-43, 61.

While the terrorists from "Grave-11" (q.v.) are being tried, a sympathetic L-5 colonist flies to the nearby Anti-Proton Facility, where he can threaten to detonate the APF—and the entire colony. Grieve and his new lady friend, Marina Praz, a psychologist from Earth, happen to see him going there and they board the facility and manage to overpower him before any damage is done. When the fighting is done, Grieve proposes to Marina.

This is a virtual re-hash of the story line of "Grave-11"—hero overpowers fanatical terrorists—except that here, the danger is not simply to the space telescope, but to the entire station. It is rather puzzling that such a dangerous facility was placed so close to the L-5 colony—certainly, a space habitat faces enough hazards without building another one nearby.

B254. Thomas, Theodore L. "Satellite Passage." In *SF: The Best of the Best*. Edited by Judith Merril. New York: Dell, 1968, 1967, p. 169-179. Story originally published in *If* (December, 1958).

When an American and a Russian satellite coincidentally pass within fifty feet of each other, each three-man crew stands on the outside, prepared for hostile action; instead, when a Russian spaceman accidentally flies off into space, an American throws out a rope and helps him return to his satellite.

The story recalls Pratt's "Project Excelsior" (q.v.); in both stories, tension between an American and a Russian space station is defused when the Americans help out the Russians in a crisis. The message is that spacemen are "Kindred souls" (171) despite their political differences on Earth.

B255. Tiptree, James, Jr. [Alice Sheldon] "And I Awoke and Found Me Here on the Cold Hill's Side." In *Space Odysseys*. Edited by Brian W. Aldiss. 1976. New York: Berkley, 1978, p. 129-137. Story first published in *The Magazine of Fantasy and Science Fiction* (March, 1972).

A young reporter visiting the space station Big Junction interviews a worker there, who reveals that the human attraction for alien contact is rooted in the instinct for exogamy—people are driven to want sexual contact with aliens. But the aliens are contemptuous and brutal in their treatment of humans, and the desire for them makes people frustrated and humiliated. Yet despite the worker's urgings, the reporter stays and rushes to meet his first aliens.

Almost no attention is paid to the appearance and environment of the station, as Tiptree focuses on the obsession with alien sex that will, the worker argues, eventually destroy humanity as contact with Westerners destroyed Polynesian civilization. In describing an emotional longing for the alien, the story recalls Knight's "Stranger Station" (q.v.).

B256. Tsiolkovsky, Konstantin. "The Aim of Astronautics." Translated by X. Danko. In *The Call of the Cosmos*. By Konstantin Tsiolkovsky. Edited by V. Dutt. Moscow: Foreign Languages Publishing House, [1960], p. 333-372. Story originally published in 1929.

In the manner of a lecture, Tsiolkovsky describes the benefits of living in space and pictures a cylindrical dwelling in orbit around the Sun.

This piece only barely qualifies as a work of fiction and largely provides previously developed ideas—although a proposal for a solar-powered steam engine is more detailed than previous plans. A striking new note, however, is an impassioned call for humanity to move into space as a matter of racial survival: "Man must at all costs overcome the Earth's gravity and have, in reserve, the space of at least the Solar System. All kinds of danger lie in wait for him on the Earth" (370); and he proceeds to discuss the possibility of disastrous floods or a collision with an asteroid. This is yet another proposed benefit for space stations, raised more recently in Thomas Wylde's "The Nanny" (q.v.).

B257. Tsiolkovsky, Konstantin. "Beyond the Earth's Atmosphere." Translated by A. Shkarovsky. In *The Call of the Cosmos*. By Konstantin Tsiolkovsky. Edited by V. Dutt. Moscow: Foreign Languages Publishing House, [1960], p. 441-450. Date of composition or first publication not given [1929?].

In discussing the prospects of space flight, Tsiolkovsky describes "the phenomena and the conditions for plant and animal life in the ether presuming that arrangements have been made for a man to exist in special living accommodations, in the capacity of a tiny satellite of the Earth or the Sun" (442).

Also a marginal example of fiction, this piece does mention the possible future evolution of humans living in space: "after spending hundreds of years in the ether, man would gradually become a little altered himself and the void, absence of gas, and direct sunlight would not immediately kill him as they do now" (448).

Note: the anthology including this story, and "Living Beings in the Cosmos" (q.v.), gives no information about the date of composition or first publication of those pieces, except for the blanket statement that all stories in the collection were written between 1883 and 1929; and I have found no other references to these pieces in critical studies, suggesting that they were not published in Tsiolkovsky's lifetime. Because, in "Beyond the Earth's Atmosphere," references to experiments conducted in 1928 and 1929 seem to establish 1929 as the date of composition, and because there is no other information available, I arbitrarily have assumed, here and in the chronological listing, that they were both written in the latest possible year—1929.

B258. Tsiolkovsky, Konstantin. "Changes in Relative Weight." [excerpt] Translated by A. Shkarovsky. In *The Call of the Cosmos*. By Konstantin Tsiolkovsky. Edited by V. Dutt. Moscow: Foreign Languages Publishing House, [1960], p. 373-399. Story originally written in 1894.

After discussing his visits to the inhabited inner planets, the narrator describes the asteroids, including Pallas, where the inhabitants have built "artificial" rings around their world. The first ten of these are trains, each higher one going faster than the lower one; those on the surface get into space by grabbing on to the lowest train then proceeding on to the higher ones. The eleventh level is an "endless circle with platform and rails" (393).

This is the first appearance of the idea of inhabited rings around worlds, also seen in Tsiolkovsky's *Dreams of Earth and Sky* (q.v.), and not found again in science fiction until 1979, with Arthur C. Clarke's "Ring City" at the end of *The Fountains of Paradise* (q.v.).

Note: in an article in *The Call of the Cosmos*, Shkarovsky states that the first part of this manuscript discussed a "special space structure...which he dubs 'star cottage'"—apparently a clear anticipation of space stations. However, that discussion is not included in the excerpt published in the volume.

B259. Tsiolkovsky, Konstantin. "Living Beings in the Cosmos." Translated by X. Danko. In *The Call of the Cosmos*. By Konstantin Tsiolkovsky. Edited by V. Dutt. Moscow: Foreign Languages Publishing House, [1960], p. 400-419. Original date of composition or publication not given [1929?].

This piece, primarily devoted to exploring the possibilities of alien life in space, does refer to the time "When man has settled down in the ether, in artificial dwellings" (406).

There is another note about how humanity will change as a result of space life: "he will not, in interplanetary space, encounter any obstacles to the growth of his brain" (406). There is also a grandiose vision of intelligent beings spreading out into their solar systems under one democratic government, and in turn uniting with beings in other systems, galaxies, and "ethereal islands" (414-415)—which could be taken as the first prediction of a Galactic Empire in science fiction.

Note: see comments on "Beyond the Earth's Atmosphere" above.

B260. Tucker, Wilson. [Arthur W. Tucker, writing here as Bob Tucker] "Interstellar Way-Station." *Super Science Stories* (May, 1941), p. 94-101.

A crewman on a refueling station between Earth and Alpha Centauri must locate and rescue a rich female traveler who wandered away while on a tour of the station.

This "gas station in space" (97) has a unique problem—graffiti—and some extraordinarily bad science: "space sharks" living in the void and the hero apparently surviving prolonged exposure to vacuum.

B261. Vance, Jack. "Abercrombie Station." *Thrilling Wonder Stories*, 39, 3 (February, 1952), p. 10-47.

A young woman is recruited to work as a maid at Abercrombie Station, a resort satellite inhabited exclusively by grotesquely fat people, and seduce and marry young Earl Abercrombie, who is due to inherit the Station. However, she instead locates Earl's older brother, helps him regain control of the Station, and earns two million dollars in the process.

While the story says there are twenty-two resort satellites, little information is given about them, except that "Each station has its own kind of weirdness" and "half were as ordinary as Miami Beach" (20). There is a "Masonic Temple" in space, and Madeira Station is "Gay" (20)— the only space station devoted to homosexuals that I know of in science fiction.

Note: a sequel to this story, "Cholwell's Chickens" (*Thrilling Wonder Stories*, 40, 3 [August, 1952]), does not involve space stations. The two stories were "novelized" as *Monsters in Orbit*. New York: Ace, 1965.

B262. Van Vogt, A. E. "Concealment." In *Science Fiction Monsters*. By A. E. Van Vogt. Edited and with an introduction by Forrest J. Ackerman. 1965. New York: Paperback Library, 1967, p. 80-92. Story first published in *Astounding Science-Fiction* (September, 1943).

A starship from imperial Earth finds a "meteorite station" in a remote region of space, designed to map space storms, and representing some unknown people who have avoided Earth domination. The station's sole resident destroys himself and the station to keep its information out of Earth's hands, but the ship manages to reconstruct him and the facility. However, efforts to get information from him prove futile, and when he is killed a second time, they discover that he is a robot.

This story has been cited as an example of van Vogt's scientific illiteracy, as "meteorite" is the term for a large piece of rock which lands on the Earth; what van Vogt is talking about should be called a "meteoroid station" or "meteor station." While there are many space stations set up to watch storms on Earth, this station uniquely watches scientifically unexplained storms in outer space.

Note: the story was later used as the first part of the novel *Mission to the Stars* [*The Mixed Men*].

B263. Varley, John. *Tango Charlie and Foxtrot Romeo*. [novella] Issued inverted with *The Star Pit*, by Samuel R. Delany. [novella] A Tor Double. New York: Tor, 1989. 101 p. ["Tango Charlie"], 82 p. ["The Star Pit"]. Varley's novella originally published in Varley's collection *Blue Champagne* (1986).

Years ago, a devastating plague killed all people on board a space station in lunar orbit; but now, as the now-quarantined station is about to crash into the Moon, lunar monitors learn that there is a survivor on the station—a thirty-seven-year-old woman named Charlie who inexplicably still appears to be eight years old. A decision is reached to blow up the station, because the girl still may be carrying the plague; but two sympathetic women arrange to rescue the girl and take her to a remote station on the Moon. Then, for some reason, the change in environment causes her death.

The novella is another reminder about the danger of disease on board a space station, and the character of Charlie is interesting: an eternal child, taught and monitored by the station computer she calls Tik-Tok, involved with raising dogs, and dangerously addicted to alcohol.

B264. Verschuur, Gerrit L. "Contact!" In *Cosmic Catastrophes*. By Gerrit L. Verschuur. Reading, Massachusetts: Addison-Wesley Publishing Company, 1978, p. 186-198.

A space shuttle approaching a space station detects a mysterious metallic object heading straight for the Sun; when it is investigated, a message box attached to its hull reveals that the spaceship was built half a billion years ago by a civilization that inhabited a planet where the asteroid belt is now.

An Earth-orbiting space station is mentioned twice in the story: as the destination for the shuttle flight, and as the place where the shuttle sent to investigate the object would retreat if disaster struck.

B265. Vine, William. "Death Sentence." *Imagination*, 4 (June, 1953), p. 134-142.

An engineer on a space station is apparently the sole survivor of a horrible spaceship accident—a meteor crashed into the ship at the time that he was in his cabin putting on his spacesuit. However, it is revealed that it was actually murder: to kill his unfaithful wife and her lover, the man brought a meteor on board and arranged an explosion. As punishment, the man is permanently sent back in time to a particularly horrible time period—1953.

The man interrogating the engineer is surprised that he was on a ship to Mars—"I thought you space station people never went anywhere but Earth for holidays" (137); and when he comments on the fact that the man had the suit on before the "accident," his quick alibi is, "I'm an oxygen addict. I picked it up on the station" (139). The story otherwise says little about space stations and their inhabitants.

B266. Vinge, Joan D. "The Crystal Ship." In *The Crystal Ship*. Edited by Robert Silverberg. New York: Pocket, 1977, 1976, p. 13-80.

Five hundred years ago, humans came to an alien world in a huge crystal ship, which is destined to remain in permanent orbit around the planet with a "Star Well"—a teleportation device that transmits human personalities, but not bodies, across the void. However, they discover a powerful native drug called chitta which eventually kills most of the humans; the portion of the Star Well that would allow humans to travel to the world is destroyed; and eventually only a few human survivors remain who have forgotten the secret of the Star Well. A woman visits the surface and meets an alien who is the last survivor of a group that established mental communion with the humans; he gives her information about the past, and she decides to go through the Star Well to find the other humans. Although she promises to return to her alien friend, she never does, and he dies thirty years later.

In this future world, humans can teleport themselves across space, but they need stations to arrive at; thus, spaceships are used to transport Star Wells to interesting worlds, where they can then remain as transport stations. The overall feel of the story is reminiscent of C. L. Moore's *Judgment Night* (q.v.)—poetic, intoxicating, and rather unclear.

B267. Vinge, Joan D. "Legacy." In *Binary Star #4*. Edited by James R. Frenkel. New York: Dell, 1980, 9-139.

A story later incorporated into *The Heaven Chronicles* (q.v.).

Unseen; an earlier version of the story was published as "The Media Man" in *Analog Science Fiction/Science Fact* (October 1976).

B268. Vinge, Vernor. "Long Shot." *Analog Science Fiction/Science Fact*, 89 (May, 1972), p. 159-170.

Facing a coming expansion of the Sun that will destroy all human life on Earth, people build a gigantic computer ship named Ilse which will fly to Alpha Centauri, locate a suitable planet, and give birth to humans to enable the race to survive. In her training period, Ilse remains in Earth orbit next to a manned space station which monitors and instructs her. After her trip begins, faulty programming makes her forget the purpose of her mission, but a backup program next to the embryos reminds her of the last and most important step.

As in Thomas Wylde's "The Nanny" (q.v.), a space station sets in motion a desperate mission to preserve the human race and, having done its work, vanishes from the story.

B269. Vinicoff, Eric. "Blue Sky." *Analog Science Fiction/Science Fact*, 103 (August, 1983), p. 156-169.

The director of NASA is almost assassinated by a man working at one of its factories who shouts that he has "sold out" (160). Investigating, he discovers that there is a high-level conspiracy, including the President himself, to divert funds from the popular space program to work on other, less glamorous solutions to pressing problems. When the President explains that this is the best way to maintain the space program, he agrees to join the conspiracy.

In this story of the very near future, there are mentions of plans for "solar power satellites" and "non-polluting space factories," and "Modules are already being fabricated for the first orbital station" (158).

B270. Vinicoff, Eric. "Repairman." *Analog Science Fiction/Science Fact*, 104 (September, 1984), p. 150-168.

At Circum-Jupiter, an asteroid converted into a space community, scientists discover a deep-space probe is malfunctioning and send a repairman by having a clone prepared in the probe and teleporting the man's intelligence into the clone. He finds an alien there who wishes to capture him and return him as a specimen to his home world; the human manages to prevent the alien's plan, and a stalemate develops. Finally, human and alien both return to their own worlds.

The story says "Circum-Jupiter was a typical space community. Originally, it had been an asteroid captured by Jupiter. Now it was honeycombed, reshaped, and largely remade. A ship launching/landing linear accelerator ran through its long axis, and it spun on said axis to create simulated gravity. Its permanent population hovered around 60,000" (150). After that description, the station is barely mentioned; as in Charles Sheffield's "All the Colors of the Vacuum" (q.v.), the station primarily serves as the starting and ending point of a deep space mission.

Note: online references suggest that this is one of a series of stories involving the character Tadashi Nakagawa, but I have been unable to locate definitive references to any of the other stories.

B271. Watkins, William John. "Coming of Age in Henson's Tube." In *Isaac Asimov's Science Fiction Stories #1*. [No editor given] New York: Bonomo Publications, 1979, p. 34-45. Story originally published in *Isaac Asimov's Science Fiction Magazine* (Spring, 1977).

As a way to demonstrate his adulthood, a youngster living in a large, cylindrical space colony goes "Skyfalling," using wings to glide from the Shuttle going down the center of the cylinder to the interior surface where the people live.

This is an inconsequential, though celebrated, vignette about an adolescent rite of passage in a future space habitat; a final comment about the "freedom" of Skyfalling could be taken as a comment about life in the colony itself.

Note: Watkins's future universe of space habitats is also the setting for his two novels, *The Centrifugal Rickshaw Dancer* and *Going to See the End of the Sky*, both discussed in Part A.

B272. Watkins, William John. "The Lagrange League Stationary Habitats." [poem] In *Cities in Space: The Endless Frontier, Volume III*. Edited by Jerry Pournelle with John F. Carr. New York: Ace, 1991, p. 75-76.

A poetic tribute to the six space habitats at the Lagrange points, built and occupied at great cost in the realm "where death and beauty intertwine" (76).

The most interesting aspect of this short poem is its description of an accidental death during the building of a space habitat—a subject rarely discussed in space habitat fiction (though a similar incident launches Richard A. Lupoff's *Sun's End* [q.v.]):

> The welder tumbles outward with a snake
> of tether trailing out and back across
> the structure he won't live to occupy;
> the sun behind him dwindling, the roar
> of last blood pumping in his ears,
> the ache of so much left undone. (75)

B273. Webb, Sharon. "Itch on the Bull Run." In *Isaac Asimov's Science Fiction Treasury*. Edited by Isaac Asimov, Martin Greenberg, and Joseph Olander. New York: Bonanza, 1980, p. 441-451. Story originally published in *Isaac Asimov's Science Fiction Magazine* (August, 1979).

In frantic, emotional letters to her friend, and in bland, reassuring letters to her mother, Space Nurse Terra Tarkington describes how a plague causing terrible itching has infested the Satellite Hospital Outpost where she works. But they get a chance to travel to Pleiades II to treat a sick Mother creature there, and they discover that secretions from the Mother cure the condition.

With staff and patients of various alien species, this Satellite Hospital Outpost is a junior relative of the Sector Twelve Hospital Station in the novels of James White (q.v.). This is another example of the dangers of plague on a space station, though the subject is treated humorously here.

Note: this is one of five stories about Terra Tarkington, all later incorporated into the novel *The Adventures of Terra Tarkington*. One other story—"Switch on the Bull Run"—is discussed below; the others—"Hitch on the Bull Run," "Twitch on the Bull Run," and "Bitch on the Bull Run"—appeared in *Isaac Asimov's Science Fiction Magazine* in 1979 and 1981.

B274. Webb, Sharon. "Switch on the Bull Run." *Isaac Asimov's Science Fiction Magazine*, 4 (January, 1980), p. 46-57.

On temporary assignment to an alien world, space nurse Terra Tarkington is condemned to death because she accidentally switched the mind of an alien with that of her lover, Dr. Brian-Scott. However, the alien—who has been enjoying living in a human body—finally agrees to switch back, and she is exonerated.

Except for an initial reference to her regular job at a "Satellite Hospital Outpost" (47), the story does not involve space stations.

Note: see comments on "Itch on the Bull Run" above.

B275. Wellman, Manly Wade. "Space Station No. 1." *Famous Fantastic Mysteries* (September-October, 1939), p. 27-36. Story originally published in *Argosy* (October 10, 1936).

A crewman on Space Station No. 1, in Mars's orbit on the opposite side of the Sun, desperately wants to leave; but when his girl friend recruits some spacemen to rescue him, they instead attempt to seize control of the station.

Many themes of later stories about space stations—the boredom, loneliness, and potential for madness in space life—are anticipated in this story. Paradoxically, the other station resident, a Martian, loves the place. It seems logically enough to build a station in Mars's orbit on the opposite side of the Sun, to serve as a way station for spaceships going from Mars to Jupiter when those planets are in opposition.

B276. Wells, Basil E. "Factory in the Sky." *Astonishing Stories*, 3 (September, 1941), p. 68-74.

Somewhere in the asteroid belt floats the Factory in the Sky, a gigantic metal sphere housing 20 million people engaged in manufacturing work, notably building spacecraft. Because the Factory is aligned with the inner planets, agents from the opposing Jovian moons try to sabotage it but are thwarted by an undercover agent for the Interplanetary Patrol Corps.

Despite its huge size, the construct is essentially similar to an Earth factory—right down to the whistle that blows to signal that work time is over. Although not a military base, its role in constructing spacecraft makes it a logical target in wartime—as might any serious industrial base in space. One interesting psychological problem apparently afflicting some Factory residents is the "space jitters" (73).

B277. White, James. "Countercharm." In *The Aliens among Us*. By James White. 1969. New York: Del Rey/Ballantine, 1981, p. 1-21. Story originally published in *New Worlds Science Fiction* (November, 1960).

For the first time, Dr. Conway is allowed to maintain the tape of the brain of an alien doctor resembling a crab in his own brain for a long period of time; unfortunately, he finds himself lusting after a certain female crab-being, distracting him from his work. However, the fortunate presence of the beautiful—and human—Dr. Murchison helps overcome the alien influence, and he completes a difficult operation successfully.

The psychologist O'Mara emerges again as something of a sadist—for his first extended implant, he deliberately gives Conway a highly emotional alien being, he is off work when Conway needs his help, and he leaves specific instructions that Conway is not to receive any help—he must solve the problem on his own. This does not seem to be any way to run a hospital.

Note: in addition to various stories later incorporated into the Sector General books, White wrote these additional stories involving the space hospital, all cited below: "Custom Fitting," "Occupation: Warrior," "Spacebird," and "Tableau."

B278. White, James. "Custom Fitting." In *Futures Past*. [revised edition] By James White. London: Orbit, 1988, p. 1-22. Originally published in *Stellar #2* (1976).

Another adventure involving Dr. Conway and the Sector General space hospital.

Unseen.

B279. White, James. "Occupation: Warrior." *Science Fiction Adventures #7* (1959), p. 6-58.

A story that provides the background for a character featured in several Sector General stories.

Unseen.

B280. White, James. "Outrider." In *Futures Past*. By James White. New York: Del Rey/Ballantine, 1982, p. 199-228. Story originally published in *New Worlds* (May, 1955).

Leaving from Mars Station to go to Earth, a spaceship is "blinded" by an accident—the crew cannot see or hear anything. In order to guide them down to a safe landing, a passenger volunteers to ride on the outside of the craft, radioing instructions as they descend. Miraculously, both he and the spaceship survive the landing.

The logical flaw in this story is apparent: there is a space station orbiting Mars (209) and there are plans to build "the new Mars station which was to be hollowed out of the rock of Deimos" (219); so why is there no space station orbiting Earth, which would have easily solved this spaceship's problem?

B281. White, James. "Question of Cruelty." In *Futures Past*. By James White. New York: Del Rey/Ballantine, 1982, p. 160-173. Story originally published in *New Worlds* (February, 1956).

A crippled alien spaceship patrols the galaxy, looking for signs of intelligent life, which they invariably find is cruel and violent; so they exterminate it. They are about to do the same to the Earth when they detect a spacecraft in orbit with a dead occupant. Realizing that it is not the intelligent species but a monkey, and seeing that the humans treated it kindly and wisely, the alien commander decides to leave Earth alone.

Military space stations are evidently a common development to these aliens: they assume the reason for the spaceship is that "two or more idealogically [sic] opposed groups [are] trying for the military advantage of a space platform" (163). And their last battle before reaching Earth had involved "an orbiting fortress" (165).

B282. White, James. "Spacebird." In *Futures Past*. By James White. New York: Del Rey/Ballantine, 1982, p. 1-23. Story originally published *New Writings in SF 22* (1973).

A huge alien bird is picked up floating in deep space, with strange parasites on its body, and Dr. Conway and the staff of Sector Twelve General Hospital must try to revive it. What they eventually discover is remarkable: the parasites are really the intelligent creatures, and they modified the unintelligent giant bird to serve as a method of interstellar flight.

In providing background on Sector General, White is simply repetitious—it is shaped like a big Christmas tree (3), there is the danger of xenophobia (10), and so on. The focus of the story is simply on the case at hand.

B283. White, James. "Tableau." In *The Best of British SF 2*. Edited by Mike Ashley London, Futura, 1977, p. 13-41. Story originally published in *New Worlds Science Fiction* (May, 1958).

A story involving Sector Twelve General Hospital.

Unseen.

B284. Wightman, Wayne. "In the Realm of the Heart, In the World of the Knife." In *Future on Fire*. Edited and Introduced by Orson Scott Card. New York: Tor, 1991, p. 253-269. Story originally published in *Isaac Asimov's Science Fiction Magazine* (August, 1985).

In a far future, an ancient man, kept alive through organ transplants and technology, controls a vast stellar empire from his space station. He achieved his position by borrowing alien technology, adapting it to human use, and thereby gaining wealth and power while benefiting humanity at the same time. However, when he meets an old colleague, he reveals that his main motive was not altruism but personal gain, and that he once informed on his trusted associates to eliminate them as potential rivals.

This is an oddly unpleasant story which, as one reviewer I recall noted, really has little to do with space travel; it could easily have featured an old and ruthless businessman in present-day America.

B285. Williams, Ralph. "Bertha." *Astounding Science Fiction*, 52 (January, 1954), p. 121-142.

Members of the "Rubberneck" space expedition fly into orbit to pave the way for "Highjump"—"the satellite project...the big thing" (124)—and discover and rendezvous with a mysterious artificial satellite. As they explore the craft, they hear alien voices on a loudspeaker, the previously-open hatches all close, and the craft flies off into interstellar space. The men speculate that sometime in the distant past aliens must have travelled through space and left crafts like this wherever intelligent life might develop to serve as "mousetraps" to capture and retrieve specimens.

This is the story, it might be argued, of an alien space station which converts into a starship in order to supply its makers with examples of Earth's intelligent life.

B286. Williams, Walter Jon. "Elegy for Angels and Dogs." *Isaac Asimov's Science Fiction Magazine*, 14 (May, 1990), p. 104-190.

This novella, set in the same future universe as Roger Zelazny's "The Graveyard Heart," involving the space-faring members of the Party Set, a group of idle aristocrats whose lives, extended by periods of suspended animation, are filmed and watched by other, less fortunate people. They finally discover that most Earth people have taken advantage of new technology to go into their own, especially-created pocket universes, leaving the Party Set unchanged as a control group.

One member of the Set was raised in "a picturesque tax haven at Lagrange Point Four" (112), and activities of the Party Set include "a party staged in high-Earth orbit" and "a new resort in orbit around Sol" (156, 157).

B287. Williamson, Jack. "Born of the Sun." In *Before the Golden Age: A Science Fiction Anthology of the 1930s*. Edited by Isaac Asimov. Garden City, NY: Doubleday and Company, Inc., 1974, p. 461-495. Story first published in *Astounding Stories* (March, 1934).

A scientist working on a method of space travel learns from his uncle that the planets are actually gigantic eggs, created by the living sun, and soon to hatch into huge creatures which will eventually become suns themselves. Before the earth is destroyed, he manages to build a "space machine" (470) called the Planet, despite opposition from an oriental cult, and flies into space with his beloved to keep the human race alive.

Variously called "the ark of space" (468) and the "space machine," the Planet is clearly destined to be the prototype for new human homes in space: "we've been parasites.... But we aren't any longer. We're beginning all over again, on our own.... There will be many *Planets*, and greater ones. The new, free race will be greater than the old" (494-495).

B288. Williamson, Jack. "Crucible of Power." *Astounding Science-Fiction*, 22 (February, 1939), p. 9-32.

After discovering, while on Mars, a strange substance from the Sun that offers unlimited energy, an Earth businessman builds a space station in close proximity to the Sun to harvest the substance. A group of Martian rebels briefly seizes control of the station, but they surrender when they are offered a cure to the mysterious plague that had been devastating inhabitants of Earth, Mars, and the station.

An odd, and scientifically absurd, variation on the theme of a solar power station, Williamson's story offers little description of the station, except that it is located in the Sun's photosphere and was, for the times, incredibly expensive—nine billion dollars. As in many other stories, the station here is pictured as highly vulnerable to marauders and to disease.

B289. Williamson, Jack. "Dead Star Station." In *The Early William-son*. Garden City: Doubleday & Co., 1975, p. 178-199. Story originally published in *Astounding Stories* (November, 1933).

The only safe way through the Orion Nebula is a passage created by the Dead Star, a massive cold body that is itself a danger. To help spaceships navigate, an old war-rocket, now called Dead Star Station, is stationed in the passage. When a spaceship is attacked by space pirates, the Station flies to the rescue but instead seems doomed to fall into the Dead Star until it is saved by an anti-gravity device invented by an aged crewman.

Dead Star Station, like Wellman's "Space Station No. 1" and Tucker's "Interstellar Way-Station" (q.v.), is a lonely and spartan outpost, where "Time passed slowly" (181) and "means of diversion [were] lacking" (180). As a former spaceship, the Station can and does move around sometime, but it is permanently disabled in its battle with the space pirates.

B290. Williamson, Jack. "The Prince of Space." *Amazing Stories*, 6 (January, 1931), p. 870-895.

A space pirate who calls himself "the Prince of Space" robs spaceships while operating out of a secret base, a "City in Space" somewhere beyond the Moon which is a huge enclosed cylinder with houses and vegetation on its interior surface. Despite his once-bitter feelings about Earth, he finally decides to joins members of the Space Patrol in their battle against an evil Martian race of vampire plants who intend to conquer the Earth.

Williamson's "City in Space" is, I believe, the first fictional description of a true space habitat: a gigantic enclosed cylinder, spinning to simulate gravity on its interior surface, with buildings, roads and trees on its interior. The story thus refutes the popular idea that the space habitat was first created by Gerard O'Neill and his students at MIT in the late 1960s. It is unfortunate that this imaginative creation is only a minor feature in an otherwise uninteresting space opera.

B291. Wodhams, Jack. "Station 2152." *Analog Science Fic-*

tion/Science Fact, 106 (August, 1986), p. 160-174.

When Earth perfects instantaneous matter transmission, various consortiums send out "Transrec Station Vehicles" to search for suitable planets and receive teleported travelers. When a signal is finally picked up, a handsome playboy is transported to the station. When he does not return, a female employee is sent; discovering that he is trapped in a ravine, she damages the equipment—so it will take Earth about a decade to contact them—and goes to rescue the man.

While this story's title obviously attracted my attention, its "stations" are not space stations, since they are vehicles designed to land on a planet. However, there is one reference to teleportation involving the "man-made satellite habitats" (168), which is why the story is included.

B292. Woeltjen, L. D. "The Never-Ending Battle." In *Carmen Miranda's Ghost Is Haunting Space Station Three*. Edited by Don Sakers. New York: Baen, 1990, p. 171-181.

While puzzled by the appearance of Carmen Miranda's ghost on the space station, a woman and her friend must decide whether to return to Earth or not. She stumbles upon a strange movie in which the baby Superman arrives on Earth and is rescued by Ma and Pa Kettle; he grows up to become a laidback rustic, occasionally using his superpowers for household chores. Somehow, the film convinces the heroine that she must stay on the station to fulfill her quest for a sense of family, and his male friend, now emerging as her lover, agrees.

This is another story where Carmen Miranda is an intrusion, and the overall logic of everything in this story—from its ideas to its character development—is highly questionable. The one interesting point is that modern living on Earth has lost a sense of "family," and that that feeling might be recovered in the more confined environment of a space station.

293. Wylde, Thomas. "The Nanny." *Isaac Asimov's Science Fiction Magazine*, 7 (July, 1983), p. 138-163.

When human life on Earth is apparently wiped out by a cataclysmic war, a starship is sent from a space station to Alpha Centauri containing human eggs which can be grown into people to maintain the human race. But an accident disrupts the flight, and the one crewman on board awakens prematurely and must destroy all but two of the eggs and bring those two eggs to maturity. Approaching a suitable planet near Alpha Centauri, the two children sacrifice their lives to produce more eggs and babies which can survive on a planetary surface, and, at the end of the story, the man and his new children are about to land on the planet.

This is a curiously unpleasant story: the hero is both something of a bumbler—as one child points out, he could have preserved all of the eggs in the vacuum of space instead of destroying them—and a most unsympathetic "Nanny"—in response to the children's cold logic, he first cuts off their legs to conserve water, then strangles them, so that he can survive to lead the expedition to the planet. In addition, as he is approaching the surface, he addresses imagined aliens and calls himself and the children "Invaders from Earth, coming to *get'cha*" (163)—implying that he has learned no lessons from the war that killed everybody on Earth. It is a rare example of a trip to another star that is thoroughly depressing, that promises little hope for humanity's survival.

Note: a story with a similar plot and theme is Vernor Vinge's "Long Shot" (q.v.).

B294. Wylde, Thomas. "Space Shuttle Crashes!" In *Far Frontiers*. Fall 1985 Edition. Editors in Chief, Jerry Pournelle and Jim Baen. New York: Baen, 1985, p. 244-266.

A man gets to "earth station three" as a stowaway and is soon detected and locked up as "the first space criminal" (252); but he escapes and makes his way to a nearby shuttle about to launch, not knowing that the shuttle is going to be deliberately crashed into the ground as a spectacle. When space station personnel realize that he is on board, they frantically try to save him, and he manages to survive the crash. He then signs up to ride two more shuttles down to crash landings.

In this story, dedicated opponents are attempting to stop space travel, with some success; the station is "the last one fully operational" and will likely "soon be abandoned" (244). There is also the suggestion from the "space-happy saucer folk—the Crazies—who wanted to build a space port at L4 to lure UFOs down to solve Earth's problems" (244).

B295. Yamin, Michael. "The Dreamers." *Astounding Science-Fiction*,

40 (December, 1947), p. 67-82.

When nuclear war breaks out on Earth, the international crew of a space station begins fighting each other and eventually only one man, an American, is left alive. When American soldiers arrive at the station, he learns that America started the war to achieve world domination, and that the soldiers are going to convert the station in a fortress to bomb the Earth and eventually conquer outer space. Resolving that such people should not be allowed to carry out such barbarous plans, the American blows up the station, hoping that in the future more mature people will be able to enter space in a spirit of peace.

This remarkable, occasionally eloquent story offers the first argument that I know of against military space stations—on idealistic, not practical grounds. "The builders of this Station had looked up, not down" (79), the protagonist says; space should be an arena of international cooperation and peaceful exploration. Using such a station for killing and conquest simply perpetuates patterns from humanity's primitive past. The story may also be the first one to explicitly refer to previous science fiction stories about space stations: in observing that "Such stations [were] nothing new," the narrator adds, "There had even been stories written about them" (71, 72).

B296. Young, Robert F. "The Moon of Advanced Learning." *Isaac Asimov's Science Fiction Magazine*, 6 (September 28, 1982), p. 111-122.

While a struggling steel worker worries about his job and financial security, he observes orbiting overhead the Moon of Advanced Learning—"an oversized aluminous thinktank in space—a visible symbol of knowledge...put into orbit between the real moon and Earth" (111). This station has six "advanced thinkers" supposedly working to solve humanity's problems, but the steel worker is skeptical: "Their avowed purpose, according to the media, is to improve the lot of mankind, but I do not think they are thinking of mankind in the present tense; I think they are thinking of mankind in the future" (116). His father naïvely writes a letter to the Moon of Advanced Learning, hoping that they will start working on the problem of saving the steel industry, but the worker entertains no such hopes.

An interesting story which accuses advocates of space research and development of ignoring human problems on Earth; the worker cannot help seeing the large satellite all of the time, but it is not doing anything to help him, his family, or friends. In a different way, Sam Nicholson's "He Who Fights and Runs Away" (q.v.) makes a similar point.

B297. Zahn, Timothy. "Return to the Fold." *Analog Science Fiction/ Science Fact*, 104 (September, 1984), p. 12-47.

When a space pilot stops at a space station between flights, he says that he wants to visit the planet below; however, because of the length and isolation of interstellar travel, all starship pilots are mentally conditioned to prefer loneliness and avoid people—"anthropophobia" (22). After a nerve-wracking walk on his own through the station, the pilot sadly realizes that he is indeed incapable of normal human company. However, a sympathetic psychologist prepares holograms of crowds, which the pilot can view and gradually adjust to during his next long space journey.

Tomo, the pilot of the story, was born on a station and has never visited a planet; here, the separation between planet-dwellers and space-dwellers is artificially enhanced through conditioning techniques, argued for as necessary so that interstellar travel can proceed without crewmen going insane. Little is said about the appearance of Maigre Space Station, except that Tomo likes its interior décor—"Better than that cubist's nightmare at Burnish, anyway—remember that horrible holosculp?" (19)

PART C.

FILMS AND TELEVISION PROGRAMS

C1. *Android*. New World/Android Productions, 1982.

A scientist and his android assistant Max, living on a space station, are working on a project to create a perfect female android. Androids are now banned on Earth because a number of them revolted, and the scientist, believing he is seeing the same sense of rebellion developing in Max, plans to kill him as soon as the new android is completed. Three escaped criminals—one of them a woman—come to the station, and Max falls in love with the woman. Eventually, the criminals are killed, the scientist—revealed as an android himself—is killed by Max and the female android, and the two androids resolve to go to Earth and seek out others of their kind hiding there.

Space station UL C-53, shown only briefly in establishing shots, appears to be a large metallic prism. Its spacious interiors certainly seem excessive to serve as home for two people, and as a base for experiments that seem to require only one room. The evident derangement of the scientist, and Max's eccentric behavior, could be seen as another example of madness induced by space station life, and the decision to abandon the station and return to Earth, as in Jayne Tannehill's "Last Words" (q.v.), is viewed as a positive development.

C2. "The Ark in Space." *Doctor Who*. London: BBC-TV, January 25, 1975, through February 15, 1975 [four episodes].

Doctor Who and two companions arrive at an automated, apparently deserted space station that turns out to contains the entire population of a future Earth, in deep freeze to stay alive until Earth's surface is habitable again. The station is invaded by the Wirrn, giant insect-like creatures, but Doctor Who ultimately defeats them and ensures the safety of Earth's people.

I have only seen the first episode in this series, which presents the space station in a standard the-future-as-hospital design: all white walls, large empty spaces, panels with flashing lights on the walls, stylized furniture. The only glimpse of outer space comes in one corridor, which has upper and lower windows showing the stars. The station itself, and the compartments of frozen bodies, are well done; the Wirrn (briefly glimpsed at the end of this episode) are not.

Note: the novel based on these episodes is *Doctor Who and the Ark in Space*, by Ian Marter, discussed above in Part A. On television, there were two loose sequels to this adventure, "The Sontaran Experiment" and "Revenge of the Cybermen" (q.v.).

C3. "Asteroid." *Men into Space*. New York: CBS-TV, November 25, 1959.

When a small asteroid named Skyra approaches the Earth, Colonel McCauley and his crew rendezvous with the asteroid in order to determine if it is suitable for being converted into a space station. After finding that there are no suitable flat surfaces for a base, the decision is then made to destroy the asteroid so that it does not fall to the Earth and cause devastating damage. Complicating matters is that one crewman accidentally looked at the Sun without wearing his visor, temporarily blinding him, so that McCauley must first frantically search for him to return him to the spaceship, and then must struggle to turn off the detonation controls so that the destruction of the asteroid can be postponed until his crewmen can return to rescue him.

Presumably, if the asteroid had been found suitable for colonization, McCauley would have found some way to maneuver the asteroid into Earth orbit so that it would not endanger the Earth, although this is never discussed. Although the episode repeatedly uses the term "space station" to describe the planned occupation of Skyra, the search for flat surfaces indicates that the men would actually have constructed buildings on its surface—which would not appear to qualify as a space station by my definition—instead of hollowing out the asteroid, which is the usual way that science fiction stories convert an asteroid into a space station. It is also noted during the episode that using Skyra as a space station would save a lot of money, probably a reference to the great expense of building the series' Space Station Astra, observed in several other episodes.

C4. *The Astronauts*. [unsold television series pilot] New York: CBS-TV, August 11, 1982.

This proposed situation comedy is a science fiction version of *Three's Company*, with two male astronauts and one female astronaut stranded on a space station named Scilab.

Unseen.

C5. "Babel." *Star Trek: Deep Space Nine*. Los Angeles: KCOP, January 26, 1993.

While busy at many tasks, O'Brien is struck by a mysterious disease like aphasia that reduces him to speaking gibberish; soon, other station residents are similarly afflicted, and it is learned that the disease will eventually kill its victims. Dr. Bashir determines that the disease is caused by a genetically engineered virus, created by Bajoran terrorists for use against the Cardassians but never activated. With the station under quarantine, Odo and Quark work to jettison a spacecraft about to explode because its commander attempted an illegal departure, and Kira flies to Bajor to kidnap one of the scientists who first worked on the virus—and infects him with it. Back on the station, the Bajoran uses the doctor's work to devise an antidote to the virus.

This episode illustrates a warning found in several space station stories—that such a station would be extremely vulnerable to an epidemic. Still, station residents seem to remain remarkably calm during this experience—only one alien spaceship panics and tries to leave. In an episode filled with apparently accurate scientific and medical jargon, it is odd that the doctor and Kira speak of finding an "antidote" to this condition: one finds an *antidote* to a poison, but a virus must have a *cure*.

Note: all episodes of *Star Trek: Deep Space Nine* were nationally syndicated and shown by local stations on various days during a designated week. Thus, broadcast dates provided are only valid for the Los Angeles area; in other parts of the country, episodes may have appeared a few days before or after the given date.

C6. *Babylon 5*. [television movie] Los Angeles: KCOP, February 25, 1993.

Although its previous four stations either were destroyed or vanished, Earth establishes Babylon 5, a huge space station, to serve as a meeting place for the five great civilizations of the galaxy. A meeting is arranged between John Sinclair, the head of the station representing Earth, and ambassadors from the other four cultures; but one arriving ambassador is the victim of an attempted assassination. A visiting telepath probes the alien's mind and gets an image of Sinclair administering poison to the alien. Although Sinclair is charged with the crime and almost extradited to the aliens, it is discovered that a saboteur impersonating Sinclair with a "Changeling Net" was actually responsible for this and other crimes, and he is tracked down and destroyed, ending the threat to the station.

J. Michael Straczynski, the creator of this pilot for the series, consulted extensively with science fiction fans via a computer network, and it shows. Babylon 5 is much closer in size and design to the massive space habitats of recent science fiction, in contrast to the more traditional space station Deep Space Nine. Shown as a massive cylinder, the station includes a large landscaped area known as the Garden, which gives that part of the station the look of a space habitat. There are also special sections of the station which reproduce various alien environments, a feature previously seen in the hospital station of James White's Sector General stories (q.v.). Overall, Babylon 5 seems to offer a more variegated setting for a television series than Deep Space Nine, although the familiarity of its first story—tracking down a saboteur—suggests that problems in developing original plots for this series would also surface.

C7. *Battle beyond the Sun*. Filmgroup, 1963.

Two expeditions headed for Mars stop at an orbiting space station.

Unseen; this film incorporates footage from *The Sky Calls* (q.v.).

C8. *Battle in Outer Space*. [*Uchu Daisenso*; also known as *The World of Space*] Toho, 1959.

After flying saucers attack and destroy an Earth-orbiting space station and several structures on Earth, two spaceships are sent out to confront the enemy. They then fight two battles with the aliens, one on the surface of the Moon and one in space.

Perhaps the most eloquent commentary on the quality of this film is the fact that I fell asleep while attempting to watch it on late-night television. I did see the opening sequence involving a space station in the familiar torus shape, though it was more delicate-looking and ornamental than usual; there were also a few scenes of a nondescript station interior, with crewmen panicking as the saucers approach the station. Since there is no mention of the attack on the station in later scenes, I suspect that the episode was added after the original film was completed, and that there are no other space stations in the later parts of the film.

C9. "Battle Lines." *Star Trek: Deep Space Nine.* Los Angeles: KCOP, April 27, 1993.

Sisko, Kira, and Dr. Bashir escort a high Bajoran official on a mission through the wormhole; their ship is attacked and crash-lands on a desolate moon. There they find two groups of warring aliens who were exiled to this prison planet and infected with a bioengineered virus that brings them back to life each time they die. Thus, they are condemned to eternal fighting and killing, and because the virus becomes inactive if they leave the moon, they cannot leave without dying. Also, because the Bajoran official died and came back to life on the moon, she cannot leave either; but she stays willingly, convinced that helping these people is now her mission. When a rescue mission is about to take the Deep Space Nine crewpersons away from the moon, the Bajoran official tells Sisko that their paths will cross again.

One evolving strategy in this series is to concentrate on space missions to unknown worlds in the Gamma Quadrant at the other end of the wormhole, in a manner similar to other *Star Trek* series, making the space station little more than the starting point for each expedition. Thus, the space station serves one of its traditional roles—as a transition to far-ranging adventures.

C10. "The Best of Both Worlds." [Part two] *Star Trek: The Next Generation.* Los Angeles: KCOP, September 26, 1990.

Captain Picard of the *Enterprise* is captured and made into a member of a machine-based group intelligence called the Borg. Using his knowledge, the aliens approach Earth so they can assimilate its population; but when new Captain Riker seizes the transformed Picard, Commander Data accesses the Borg database through him and transmits a command which puts them all to sleep.

At the end of the second part, the *Enterprise* is heading to Earth-orbiting McKinley Station to be repaired and refurbished for future missions.

Note: the first part of this episode was broadcast earlier in the year, but I list only the date of the first appearance of the second part since that is when the reference to a space station occurs.

Also: all episodes of *Star Trek: The Next Generation* were nationally syndicated and shown by local stations on various days during a designated week. Thus, broadcast dates provided are only valid for the Los Angeles area; in other parts of the country, episodes may have appeared a few days before or after the given date.

C11. "Birthright." [Two-part episode] *Star Trek: The Next Generation.* Los Angeles: KCOP, February 22 and March 1, 1993.

The *Enterprise* docks at space station Deep Space Nine so that Captain Picard can work on repairing the Bajoran irrigation system. While there, an accident stimulates Data's power to dream, so that he sees visions of his "father," the man who created him; and an alien tells Worf that his father, thought to be dead, is actually alive in a Romulan prison camp. Worf insists that the alien take him to the camp, where he does find a group of Klingon prisoners, though his father is actually dead. To Worf's surprise, the Klingons and their children are living in harmony with their Romulan captors; one Romulan has even married a Klingon woman and had a daughter. However, when Worf begins teaching the children Klingon ways, they become anxious to leave the camp and reclaim their Klingon heritage. Finally, it is agreed to let Worf and the children go, provided that they promise to never reveal the existence of the camp.

Deep Space Nine was surely included in this episode primarily to advertise the new series, for little use is made of this setting, and only one character from the series, Dr. Bashir, appears.

C12. *The Black Hole*. Walt Disney, 1979.

A team of space travelers encounters a mad scientist on a spaceship who has spent 22 years hovering near and studying a black hole, preparing to journey into it. After they struggle with the malevolent scientist, the entire crew enters the black hole, where they encounter mysterious visions of an angel followed by an inexplicable safe return.

Like most critics, I appreciated the stylish neo-Victorian design of the spaceship temporarily functioning as a space station; and one could see in the scientist another example of insanity induced by life in a space station. However, the film's story line is undeniably juvenile and hopelessly unscientific. While the long-stationary spaceship would itself qualify as a space station, the film also includes a specific reference to the subject: at the beginning of the film, when the crew is trying to figure out what the spaceship is, one of the possibilities considered is an "experimental Russian space station."

C13. "Building a Space Station." *Men into Space*. New York: CBS-TV, October 14, 1959.

Colonel Edward McCauley leads a crew of men into space to begin the process of assembling Earth's first space station. Unfortunately, as two pieces are brought together, a crewman's sleeve is caught between them, and McCauley is reluctant to attempt to free him for fear that his suit has punctured, or will puncture, causing his instant death. After a rocket bearing hastily improvised rescue equipment must be destroyed because it is on a collision course with their spaceship, McCauley employs a desperate maneuver to free the crewman while keeping his suit clamped shut.

At the beginning of the episode, there is an image of the completed station, a typical wheel in space; in later episodes, it will be referred to as Space Station Astra. The first depiction of the construction of a space station, the episode's process of doing so—sending modules into space, to be put together by astronauts—is not unlike the method actually employed to build the international space station. The most interesting message in the episode is conveyed by its final image, showing that McCauley and his men succeeded only in constructing one small slice of the wheel, and one small portion of a connecting spoke, indicating that the completion of the entire space station will require a large number of trips—which also turned out to be the case in real life.

C14. "Captive Pursuit." *Star Trek: Deep Space Nine*. Los Angeles: KCOP, February 2, 1993.

A reptilian alien emerges from the wormhole and reluctantly takes refuge at Deep Space Nine while his spaceship is repaired. Chief O'Brien tries to befriend him, but he refuses to say anything about his situation. Other aliens then come out of the wormhole, attack the station, and teleport aboard to capture the first alien. It is revealed that the reptilian alien is a genetically altered intelligent being designed to serve as the prey in a hunting game; and even though O'Brien urges him to seek asylum, the alien is programmed to accept his role and his eventual death in the hunt. Accepting his nature, O'Brien helps him escape from the station, so that he can resume the role of hunted and the other aliens can resume their hunt.

This episode unveils another hoary staple of the space station story—the ventilator shafts, wide enough for people to crawl through and hide in, which O'Brien uses to get the alien to his spaceship. The space station experiences its second attack by spaceships, although its shields prevent any damage.

C15. "Cardassians." *Star Trek: Deep Space Nine*. Los Angeles: KCOP, October 28, 1993.

An adventure involving the old foes of the Bajorans and the Federation.

Unseen.

C16. "The Circle." *Star Trek: Deep Space Nine*. Los Angeles: KCOP, October 7, 1993.

Kira, forced to return to Bajor (as seen in "The Homecoming" [q.v.]), relaxes at the monastery of a Bajoran religious leader. Meanwhile, the army of the Circle advances to threaten the provisional government. Odo learns that the hated Cardassians, through an intermediary, are actually supplying the rebels, and a captured Kira discovers that the general of the government's army is actually the head of the Circle. When the crew of Deep Space Nine rescues Kira, all communication between Bajor and the station is cut off, and an attack fleet from Bajor approaches the station, indicating that the xenophobic rebels have taken control. Starfleet advises Sisko that he cannot interfere with what appears to be an internal rebellion and orders him to abandon the station; but Sisko plans to stay.

As in most second parts of trilogies, not too much happens in this particular episode. Again, a space station is depicted as completely vulnerable to an armed attack, so much so that a senior officer advises its leader to abandon the facility before the attack begins. Of course, though, Sisko and his friends will prevail in the final and concluding episode, "The Siege" (q.v.).

C17. *Conquest of Space*. Paramount Pictures, 1956.

On board a space station orbiting Earth, the crew preparing for a Moon flight is suddenly told to fly to Mars instead. The deranged captain, believing that the mission violates the will of God, tries to sabotage the flight, but the crew lands safely on Mars and, after enduring some hardships, eventually makes it back to Earth.

The blue torus-shaped station is a quite attractive model, although the interiors lack even the minimal imagination of *Project Moonbase* (q.v.). Madness as a result of life in space occurs twice in the film: one crewman is removed from duty because he is suffering from "space fatigue," and the captain's religious mania develops while he is on the station—in one scene, he is seen surreptitiously reading a Bible.

C18. "Crash of the Moons." [Three-part episode] *Rocky Jones, Space Ranger*. Syndicated. Episodes originally shown on July 10, 17, and 24, 1955.

Rocky Jones must rescue himself and a space station from the menace of two "gypsy moons."

Unseen.

C19. "Dark of the Sun." *Men into Space*. New York: CBS-TV, March 9, 1960.

A computer selects three expert astronomers as finalists for two places on a coming mission to venture into deep space to observe the Sun during an eclipse. One of them turns out to be a beautiful woman who faces overt discrimination in her effort to win the assignment; the other two are unmarried men who happen to be in love with her and endlessly quarrel over who should have the right to propose to her after they all arrive at Space Station Astra. At their request, McCauley establishes that, as commander of the space station, he has the legal right to marry a couple. But the woman does not love either man, and contrives to end the conflict first by pretending to faint during a walk through space. To explain why she did it, the astronomer concedes that "Space belongs to men," but McCauley responds that "Space belongs to the men *and women* who have the courage to conquer it." She then decides to stop the quarreling by pretending to be in love with the ship's doctor, but it transpires that she actually is in love with him, and they are the ones who request a marriage. Unfortunately, they must wait until they return to Earth because McCauley cannot remember the marriage vows.

This generally silly episode does indicate that a space station is essentially analogous to a ship at sea, since such captains also have the right to perform marriages.

C20. "Dax." *Star Trek: Deep Space Nine*. Los Angeles: KCOP, February 16, 1993.

Aliens sneak aboard Deep Space Nine and attempt to abduct Dax, claiming that the symbiote, in her previous body, was guilty of treason and the murder of a beloved general. While Dax is silent, Commander Sisko arranges for a hearing to determine if the aliens' warrant is valid, and claims that Dax, an old Trill in a new body, is effectively a new person and cannot be charged with crimes committed by the Trill in her old body. Odo goes to the planet to investigate the charge and learns from the general's widow that the old Dax was having an affair with her, and was with her at the time of the general's death, so Dax could not have committed the crimes. In fact, the general was about to turn traitor himself when he was killed, and Dax had remained silent to protect the reputation of the general.

Like a medical story, the courtroom drama does not demand a lot of traveling around, so adapting the format is natural for a series set on a space station; a television episode with a similar format and theme is "The Measure of a Man," *Star Trek: The Next Generation* (q.v.). Basically, this episode functions to reveal the strange nature of the symbiote Dax, an immortal alien which regularly enters, and merges with, a mortal human being.

C21. "The Derelict Space Station." *Space Patrol*. New York: ABC-TV, July 19, 1952.

An episode included in this bibliography solely based upon its title, since available plot summaries do not refer to space stations.

Unseen, but for general information on this series, see the entry on "Terra, the Doomed Planet."

C22. *Destination Space*. CBS/Paramount Television, 1959.

On board a space station nicknamed "Benedict's Billions" or "BB" because of its enormous cost, scientist and station head James Benedict prepares to supervise the launching of the first mission to orbit the Moon; but the station is suddenly struck by a meteor, causing some damage and forcing them to postpone the mission. Summoned to Earth to appear before a Senate committee, Benedict is grilled by a skeptical senator who argues that conquering space would be more economical and efficient if there were no space station; but Benedict responds that a space station is an essential component of space exploration and colonization. Benedict also learns that the wife of the lunar mission's commander is secretly in love with him, but he remains faithful to his girlfriend. Returning to the station with a Senate-appointed observer, who decides that he likes everything he sees, Benedict prepares for a second launch, but the rocket's atomic engine malfunctions and threatens to cause a nuclear explosion until a crewman can remove the ice that is causing the problem.

This short film, evidently an unsuccessful pilot for a television series, has nothing to offer of visual interest, since all images of its space station are footage borrowed from *Conquest of Space*—though the station is now seen in black and white. But it is interesting because, for the first time, this story foregrounds the issue of whether humanity will need a space station and answers the question affirmatively.

C23. "The Dorian Secret." *Buck Rogers in the Twenty-Fifth Century*. New York: NBC, April 16, 1981.

Buck is sent to a space station to pick up survivors of a planetary disaster.

Unseen.

C24. "Dramatis Personae." *Star Trek: Deep Space Nine*. Los Angeles: KCOP, June 1, 1993.

While in the Gamma Quadrant, a Klingon ship discovers globes containing the telepathic energies of an ancient race which destroyed itself in a power struggle. As the energy penetrates their brains, the Klingons are compelled to replicate the power struggle on their ship; their First Officer defeats his captain by blowing up the ship and teleporting himself to Deep Space Nine, where he dies after saying "Victory." Now infected with the same energy, the people of Deep Space Nine begin acting strangely and are soon acting out their own power struggle: Kira and Bashir plot to take over the station, while Sisko and O'Brien struggle to stop them. Only Odo, not affected because of his alien brain, realizes what is going on, and, pretending to be working for Kira, he persuades Bashir to develop a way to remove the energy from their brains. Once the energy is forced out of them, Odo opens an air-lock and, while the crew clings to the walls, the energy is drawn out into the vacuum of space where it dissipates.

Once again, a form of madness develops in a space station, this time leading to open conflict and an attempted "mutiny" (which is how Sisko later describes the incident, interestingly using a term that usu-ally refers to a ship, not a community). The unrest is not completely unmotivated, since Kira is, before the energy arrives, already mad at Sisko because he refuses to seize a ship Kira believes is transporting weapons to the Cardassians. The episode thus brings to the surface and exaggerates genuine tensions in the station, which is awkwardly a Ba-joran possession commanded by a Federation officer. Also, I noted in *Islands in the Sky* that residents in recent stories about space stations and habitats often show little contact with or awareness of the space that surrounds them, and this episode marks the first time that the crew of Deep Space Nine is actually exposed to the reality of their surround-ings, albeit briefly (the scene recalls the brief exposure to vacuum in the film *2001: A Space Odyssey* [q.v.]).

C25. "Duet." *Star Trek: Deep Space Nine*. Los Angeles: KCOP, June 15, 1993.

Because of his peculiar illness, Kira suspects that a visiting Cardassian once worked at a prison camp notorious for its atrocities. He says he was simply a filing clerk there, but after a picture indicates that he was actually the base commander, he confesses. However, the Cardassians insist, with credible evidence, that the commander actually died six years ago. The prisoner finally admits that he was really a clerk, but, appalled by the cruelty of the people, he thought that his war crimes trial as the "commander" might bring out the true extent of Cardassian atrocities and inspire them to change their ways. Now free to go, an-other Bajoran assassinates him simply because he was a Cardassian—a sentiment Kira rejects.

The intensity of Bajoran hatred for Cardassians could be seen as a natural consequence of their occupation, but their feelings may be intensified by the environment of the space station. Here, then, the form of mental instability depicted is xenophobia.

C26. "The Dwellers of the Prime Galaxy." *Space Patrol*. New York: ABC-TV, November 13, 1954.

Commander Corey discovers that an evil alien named Ahyo is behind the observed destruction of stars in space.

Unseen. This is the second of three related episodes: the first was "The Exploding Stars" and the third was "Terra, the Doomed Planet" (q.v.).

C27. *Earth II*. [Unsold television series pilot] Metro-Goldwyn-Mayer, 1971.

When the United States launches the first component of a space station, the President, with public approval, declares it to be a new independent nation, Earth II. Years later, when the Red Chinese orbit a nuclear missile near the station, its citizens narrowly vote to take action against it, despite their avowed pacifism; whereupon the missile is approached, brought back to Earth II, accidentally launched on a trajectory towards Earth by a well-meaning but uninformed pacifist, recovered and returned, and finally disarmed.

The revolving gridwork of the station is visually impressive, and the culture and government of Earth II is interesting: in a nation devoted to peace, even toy guns are banned, and any citizen can demand a hearing to challenge a decision, with the conflict to be resolved by a vote of all citizens. Yet the plot is disappointingly dull, despite reinforcing the message that space stations are vulnerable to attack, and a proposed television series about Earth II failed to materialize; Leonard Maltin's comment on the film in *TV Movies*—"Workable premise that doesn't lead anywhere" (284)—is pregnant with broader implications for all stories about space stations.

C28. "Edge of Eternity." *Men into Space*. New York: CBS-TV, December 2, 1959.

Returning from a mission to the Moon, McCauley's spaceship is struck by a meteor, which releases most of the ship's oxygen. This seemingly means that the men will run out of oxygen and die before they can reach their destination, Space Station Astra. Fortunately, they are able to extract some liquid oxygen and some gaseous oxygen from their ship's engine, providing them with just enough air to reach the station.

This episode does indicate that, as in other films, astronauts going to the Moon will stop at a space station on the way there and on the way back, although other episodes about lunar missions never refer to the space station.

C29. "Emissary." *Star Trek: Deep Space Nine*. Los Angeles: KCOP, January 5, 1993.

After sixty years of occupying and exploiting the planet Bajor, the Cardassians abandon the planet and the space station orbiting it. Commander Benjamin Sisko of Starfleet is ordered to take command of the station and establish a Federation presence in this distant and unstable region. One of his first tasks is to track down mysterious alien objects called Orbs which, it turns out, have traveled to this planet through a newly discovered wormhole nearby in space. Sisko enters the wormhole and encounters incorporeal, timeless aliens who are alternately baffled by and hostile to him. At the station, Sisko's Bajoran second-in-command Kira decides to move the space station near the wormhole, and the station is soon being attacked by Cardassians who cannot account for the disappearance of one of their craft (which also entered the wormhole). However, Sisko persuades the aliens to keep the wormhole open, he reappears near Deep Space Nine, and the Cardassians withdraw.

The station is an adaptation of the classic torus design, albeit with elongated curved fins (called pylons by the characters) that extend to the regions above and below the center of the station (these are docking stations, since the *Enterprise* is at one point seen attached to one of them). Already in its first episode, this new series is touching upon some of the classic themes of space station stories: the station as a place for alien races to meet and interact, the station turned into a spaceship, and the station as a "sitting duck" vulnerable to armed attack.

C30. "The Exploding Stars." *Space Patrol*. New York: ABC-TV, November 13, 1954.

Commander Corey visits an observatory in space to investigate the mysterious destruction of numerous stars.

Unseen. The episode had two sequels, "The Dwellers of the Prime Galaxy" and "Terra, the Doomed Planet" (q.v.).

C31. "The Faceless Ones." *Doctor Who*. London: BBC-TV, April 8, 1967 through May 13, 1967 [six episodes].

In present-day London, the Doctor discovers that the Chameleon Tours charter flights are controlled by aliens called Chameleons, who, facing extinction, are kidnapping passengers and taking over their identities. There are 50,000 miniaturized victims, being held in a space station orbiting Earth. The Doctor manages to free the captives and helps the Chameleons survive without menacing Earth.

Unseen; the novel based on these episodes is *Doctor Who—The Faceless Ones*, by Terrance Dicks.

C32. *Forbidden World*. Mutual, 1982.

This story of a menacing alien monster, reminiscent of *Alien*, includes scenes showing a "space-station staff" (*The Encyclopedia of Science Fiction* 437).

Unseen.

C33. "The Forsaken." *Star Trek: Deep Space Nine*. Los Angeles: KCOP, May 25, 1993.

While Dr. Bashir entertains some visiting Federation ambassadors, an unmanned alien probe approaches Deep Space Nine from the wormhole. After the Cardassian station computer contacts, and absorbs the memory of, the computer on the probe, O'Brien notices that the personality of the computer has subtly changed—from recalcitrant to cooperative. Then a number of malfunctions begin to occur: Odo and the mother of *Star Trek: The Next Generation*'s Deanna Troi are trapped in an elevator, and Bashir and the Federation ambassadors are threatened by a fire in a corridor. O'Brien finally deduces that the alien probe has a personality, much like a lonely dog's, and it is provoking problems in order to get and keep O'Brien's attention. He then isolates the probe's data in a subprogram—a "doghouse"—promising to take care of it, and everything returns to normal.

With a new emphasis on the personality of the station computer, and the possibility that the distinctive alien computer entity might reappear in future episodes, Deep Space Nine could become a "living space station," fully participating in events as an involved character in the manner of the habitat computer Billy Boy Grunt in Allen Steele's *Clarke County, Space* (q.v.). Majel Barrett, who portrays the recurring character of Troi's mother, also provides the voice of the computer in both series. Having she and Odo get to know each other by getting stuck in an elevator demonstrates once again how earthly clichés (such as crawling through the ventilator shaft, seen in "Captive Pursuit") can be recycled in space station stories.

C34. *Gog.* Ivan Tors Productions, 1954.

An underground research base in New Mexico is working to build the first space station; their research projects include an experimental method to temporarily freeze astronauts to protect them from the rigors of space flight, a study of weightless conditions, and efforts to build robots as possible replacements for human astronauts. However, the massive computer controlling the facility is being secretly controlled by radio transmissions from enemy agents which command the computer to kill several people at the base, often using two mobile robots named Gog and Magog. As one robot threatens to sabotage the atomic reactor, the Air Force finally manages to shoot down the aircraft that is broadcasting the transmissions. At the end, while much work remains to be done on the space station, they decide to launch a small scale model into space as an unmanned "baby space station."

This is probably the only film exclusively about building a space station on Earth; the only scene of a station in space is a drawing under the credits showing a familiar torus, perhaps a bit fatter than usual. Another scene also shows a scale model of the station which looks rather different—more like a large disc. The science behind the film seems suspect—at one point, it is claimed that astronauts a thousand miles from Earth will still experience 1/3 Earth gravity—but when the computer expert asserts that only robots will ever be suited for space travel, the film in a way anticipates the ongoing argument between manned and unmanned space missions. An inadvertent insight comes from the scenes of experiments to duplicate weightless conditions; the film hired acrobats to play the experimental subjects—they even bow towards the audience every time they complete an athletic feat— suggesting that people with such training might in fact be best suited to adapt to weightlessness. Finally, the description of an unmanned satellite as a "baby space station" is at least an interesting choice of words; perhaps, if the Soviet Union and the United States had described Sputnik and Vanguard as small space stations, real facilities might have been built sooner.

C35. *Gorath.* [*Yosei Gorasu*] Toho, 1962.

A small star, 6,000 times more massive than the Earth, moves into the Solar System on a collision course with Earth. After two spaceships investigate the star, named Gorath, Earth scientists decide to build huge rocket engines at the South Pole to move the Earth out of Gorath's path. Finally, while Earth suffers greatly, the planet does avoid colliding with Gorath.

There are three space stations in this film, all seen several times in exterior shots only: United States Satellite 7, shaped like a doughnut; Her Majesty's Satellite 1, shaped like a disc; and United Nations Space Control, with a square-shaped outer rim. Their function in the film seems to be as futuristic decorations, since they contribute little to the plot; in their longest scene, each of the three stations radios a "Good luck" message to the second spacecraft departing to study Gorath. When Gorath is near, the three stations are ordered to return to Earth, because "Their work is done"; presumably they will be safer on Earth. Yet in a later scene, the American station is seen collapsing into the ground during a massive earthquake; as in other stories, a station's return to Earth has disastrous results. At the very end of the film, the three stations are seen again while the narrator delivers a stirring speech about human progress; the mysteriously resurrected stations now serve as icons of man's future hopes and dreams.

Note: bibliographical references to this film consistently mention a subplot involving a large walrus-like monster which emerges from the Earth due to the disruptive effect of Gorath; but there was no monster in the print that I saw. My theory is that the monster footage was added for the original American release in the belief that American audiences were conditioned to expect a monster in every Japanese science fiction movie, and that what I saw was the original version of the film.

C36. *The Green Slime.* [*Gamma Sango Uchu Daisakusen*] Toei/ Southern Cross Films, 1968.

After destroying a menacing asteroid, a crewman of Gamma III space station brings back a little blob of green goo, which eventually grows into a mob of ambulatory serpent-like creatures. To save humanity, the crew abandons the station and sends it plunging into Earth's atmosphere to a fiery death.

The ridiculous appearance of the monsters makes this movie a most unconvincing warning about the dangers of biological contamination in a space station. To my knowledge, this is the first depiction of a space station falling back to Earth, although in this case it apparently burns up in the atmosphere and poses no threat to the planet.

C37. *Hellfire*. Manley, 1988.

In this thriller about an amazing new power source, terrorists at one time destroy a space station in an effort to prevent its use.

Unseen.

C38. "The Homecoming." *Star Trek: Deep Space Nine*. Los Angeles: KCOP, September 30, 1993.

A friend of Quark gives him an earring which Kira recognizes as belonging to a famous Bajoran resistance fighter, now apparently in a Cardassian labor camp. She and O'Brien fly to the planet and rescue him; however, he is reluctant to become an acclaimed hero because, he tells Sisko, his exploits were all wildly exaggerated. Nevertheless, after one attempt to smuggle on board a departing spaceship, he agrees to remain and help his people during their period of turmoil. Surprisingly, Kira is recalled to Bajor and he is appointed the new liaison officer.

The increasing tensions on board the space station—including the religious hysteria seen in "In the Hands of the Prophet" (q.v.) and a tide of xenophobia observed here—might be attributed to the tension of living in a space station, except that similar problems are reported to be occurring on Bajor.

Note: this is the first of a three-part series; the second is "The Circle" and the third is "The Siege" (q.v.).

C39. "If Wishes Were Horses." *Star Trek: Deep Space Nine*. Los Angeles: KCOP, May 18, 1993.

Deep Space Nine is visited by mysterious aliens who have the powers to take any form and to make others' wishes come true. The aliens appear as characters from people's imaginations—Rumpelstiltskin for O'Brien, a famous baseball player from the twenty-first century for Sisko, two beautiful women for Quark, and a Dax who is romantically interested in Dr. Bashir. Other odd happenings include a blizzard inside the station and the appearance of strange birds. Meanwhile, Dax notices what she thinks is an anomaly in space, akin to the one which once destroyed a solar system. Despite their best efforts, they watch the anomaly grow and threaten to destroy everything around it. But Sisko deduces that the anomaly, like the other things, is simply a product of their imagination, and by telling people to stop believing in it, he makes the anomaly disappear. The aliens then reveal themselves to Sisko, explaining that they used disguises to avoid a hostile response and to learn more about humans; but they leave without providing any more information.

I have summarized this story in a manner more logical than the episode itself, which boasts a complex array of writing credits suggesting a massively-revised script. Hallucinations of various kinds are of course not unknown to space stations, and neither are alien visitors, although these hallucinations turn out to be real (after a fashion), and although this alien invasion turns out to be benign. This is the second episode depicting a strange space phenomenon threatening the station, since it almost fell into the wormhole in "Q-Less." Oddly enough, these dire dangers are employed as devices in largely comic episodes.

C40. *In like Flint*. Twentieth-Century Fox, 1967.

As part of a plot to take over the Earth, a group of women replace the President of the United States with an impostor, place two lady cosmonauts on board the new American space platform, and plan to arm the platform with nuclear weapons—"Project Damocles"—and thus rule the world. However, secret agent Derek Flint foils the plan by getting on the rocket carrying the weapons, overpowering the traitor on board, and escaping to the space platform right before the rocket explodes. When last seen, Flint is enjoying the company of the lady cosmonauts.

The space platform is designed to serve as a space observatory and a device for promoting international cooperation on Earth. When Flint hears of the plan to put atomic weapons on board, he says the "idea is totally discredited"; thus, the film marks a change in attitude from the

1950s, when Smith's novelization of *Riders to the Stars* (q.v.) blithely endorsed such a proposal. The platform itself is a rather modest affair—a cylinder not much larger than an Apollo capsule, though with larger windows; since there is barely room for two people in it, one must wonder where they were planning to put the nuclear weapons.

C41. "In the Hands of the Prophets." *Star Trek: Deep Space Nine*. Los Angeles: KCOP, June 22, 1993.

A Bajoran religious leader, and a candidate to be the next leader of the faith, visits the station and vocally objects to Mrs. O'Brien's school, which teaches about the wormhole in scientific rather than religious terms. Bajoran anger about Mrs. O'Brien grows, and the school is bombed. Another candidate to become leader then decides to visit the station and restore harmony; however, O'Brien's Bajoran assistant, secretly working for the other candidate, plans to assassinate him so that her leader can take command. Fortunately, Odo and O'Brien's investigation of another crewman's death enables Sisko to anticipate and prevent the assassination attempt, and the religious leader's crusade against the school, revealed as a scheme to lure her rival up to the station to be killed, collapses.

Again, the residents of Deep Space Nine seem unusually volatile—perhaps mentally unstable—as an utterly spurious campaign against a secular school somehow manages to rouse the Bajoran crewman to genuine anger. The serious debate between secular and spiritual education that opening scenes promise is forgotten as melodrama takes over in the last half of the episode.

Note: this episode, last of the first season, was in a sense a prequel to the three-part series that opened the second season, "The Homecoming," "The Circle," and "The Siege" (q.v.), since it first described some of the tension and religious infighting that were featured in those episodes, and features two characters seen in the later series.

C42. "Invasive Procedures." *Star Trek: Deep Space Nine*. Los Angeles: KCOP, October 21, 1993.

A member of Dax's species, with Klingons as his assistants, takes over Deep Space Nine and demands that Dr. Bashir transplant the alien from Dax's body into his, since his own request for symbiosis was denied. When Dax insists, Bashir performs the operation, even though it could lead to Dax's death. The invader exults in his new symbiosis, but Sisko and the other station crew eventually manage to regain control of the ship and force a new operation to place the alien back in Dax's body.

Again, a space station seems tremendously vulnerable to armed takeover—here, a handful of people (with the help of a security code supplied by Quark) manage the task. Otherwise, this episode focuses on the space station as a meeting place for alien species in a unique way—here, human and alien are literally joined in symbiosis.

C43. "Isolation in Space." *Space Patrol.* New York: ABC-TV, May 12, 1951.

Commander Corey and crewmates are trapped on an isolated relay station orbiting the artificial planet Terra.

Unseen.

C44. "Little Lost Robot." *Out of This World.* London: British ABC-TV, July 7, 1962.

At a base in the asteroid belt, a robot which is identical to many others must be identified, because his brain was built with a dangerously modified First Law.

Unseen, but see comments on the Isaac Asimov story of the same name which this episode was based on.

C45. *Living and Working in Space: The Countdown Has Begun.* Los Angeles: KCET, March 31, 1993. [Public Broadcasting System program, broadcast at different times during the week by individual stations.]

Using the framing device of a teacher in the future reading letters from former students now working in space, this documentary mixes interviews with modern scientists, astronauts and engineers with fictional vignettes involving future space workers: asteroid miners, the crew of a space rescue station, and residents of a lunar colony.

There was a certain amount of cacophony in the Westfahl house while I watched this program, but one vignette did seem to involve a space station devoted to rescuing people in space, a rotating rectangular object with two large arms labeled in red "Rescue 911." A crisis occurs when a solar flare disables the station's computer at the very moment when space debris is approaching the station; the commander employs a manual computer and his expert aim to destroy the threatening meteoroid. He is previously depicted as an avid player of old Mario Brothers video games, and the way he destroys the meteoroid—hand on a manual control while animated rocks float by on a television screen—suggests that the skills learned in video games may be applicable to the problems of space rescue. There were also a mention of an "Astro Hotel" in space (I think), and a scene of the immense space station from *Star Trek V: The Final Frontier* (q.v.).

C46. *Lois and Clark: The New Adventures of Superman.* New York: ABC-TV, September 12, 1993.

In the pilot film for the series, Clark Kent comes to Metropolis, gets a job at the Daily Planet, and establishes an alternately friendly and antagonistic relationship with star reporter Lois Lane. Together, they begin investigating the mysterious explosion of an important mission to the almost-completed Space Station Prometheus; a scientist who once worked for the program tells them it was sabotaged, but the woman now in charge of the project denies the story and the scientist soon dies in a supposed suicide. It turns out that millionaire Lex Luthor is conspiring with the woman in charge of the project to destroy Prometheus so that he can set up his own space station and reap profits from valuable vaccines to be developed in zero gravity. While investigating, Lois and Clark are captured and almost killed by the woman, but Clark rescues them and the woman dies in a helicopter explosion engineered by the duplicitous Luthor. Lois then stows away on the 100-person mission to inhabit Prometheus and promptly discovers a bomb; when she cuts off a connection to delay launch, the newly-costumed Clark flies to the scene and eats the bomb to save the ship. Then, he carries the ship up to dock with Prometheus, and Lois, seeing the Kryptonian "S" symbol on his chest, names the new hero "Superman."

The space station project is sponsored by the "Congress of Nations," which indicates that this series is set in the near future (as does the establishment of a 100-person space station, since NASA was then struggling to get a 6-person station in orbit sometime before 2000). It is interesting that the only reason advanced for building the space station is the need for a zero-gravity pharmaceutical laboratory which can develop new vaccines to cure diseases—a project of humanitarian value to the murdered scientist, and a way to make lots of money to Luthor. Space Station Prometheus is seen in one establishing shot—

the standard spinning-top design, with one segment of the central doughnut missing (showing that it is not yet complete); the one novelty is its color, an odd brownish-green.

C47. "The Love Affair." *The Man from U.N.C.L.E.* New York: NBC, March 29, 1965.

Agents Napoleon Solo and Ilya Kuryakin must oppose a sinister evangelist who is working to set up his own orbiting platform and use it to take over the world.

Unseen.

C48. "A Man Alone." *Star Trek: Deep Space Nine*. Los Angeles: KCOP, January 19, 1993.

After an acrimonious encounter with a former criminal he once apprehended, Odo the shapeshifter is the prime suspect when the man is found murdered. While the investigation continues, Odo is temporarily relieved of his duties and is the target of a near-riot led by angry residents. However, the station's doctor determines that the victim was actually a clone of the man who was created and killed in order to frame Odo.

This episode would support John W. Campbell, Jr.'s assertion that one cannot create a fair murder mystery in science fiction because writers can always pull some unanticipated scientific trick out of their hats. Here, viewers could not reasonably solve the mystery by predicting that the murder victim was really a clone. A subplot shows O'Brien's wife setting up a school for the station's children, illustrating one of the classic functions of a space station—to educate young spacefarers. And the near-riot suggests in a small way that a space station is conducive to mental instability, another familiar theme.

C49. "Mark of the Saurian." *Buck Rogers in the Twenty-Fifth Century*. New York: NBC, February 2, 1981.

Reptilian aliens named Saurians infiltrate a space station and starship with an illusion-projecting device that makes them appear human; only Buck Rogers, with his slightly different twentieth-century physiology, can see their true appearance. The Saurians then recalibrate their devices to deceive Buck as well, so he is almost convinced that he was hallucinating; but when he sees a television message from a

Saurian with an unchanged projector, he realizes his error and rushes to prevent them from taking over his starship by turning the ship's heat down, rendering the cold-blooded Saurians helpless.

As it happens, I was only able to see the last half of this episode, so I did not observe the episode's space station. However, based on the quality of other episodes in this universally reviled series, one can safely assume that the station is not particularly interesting.

C50. "A Matter of Perspective." *Star Trek: The Next Generation.* Los Angeles, KCOP, February 10, 1990.

When Commander Ryker transports off a space station orbiting an alien planet, it immediately explodes, killing the research scientist on board, and Ryker is accused of murdering him because of a dispute involving his wife. Using the holodeck, Captain Picard and an alien investigator recreate various versions of the events before the explosion. Investigating other mysterious energy beams, LaForge and Data determine that the scientist, in spite of his own report, had actually succeeded in developing a new type of energy ray, and was planning to sell it as a weapon. Because he suspected that Ryker would find out, he attempted to kill him as he transported—but the energy beam reflected off Ryker and destroyed the station instead, so the scientist effectively killed himself.

Again, a space station is seen as an ideal place for dangerous scientific research, and as a place extremely vulnerable to attack. The interior of the station is typically stark, appropriately because it is simply designed as a lab, not really as a place to live. One could also see this episode as a detective story set in space, with the space station as the locked room where the murder occurred.

C51. "The Measure of a Man." *Star Trek: The Next Generation.* Los Angeles: KCOP, February 18, 1989.

At a Federation Star Base in deep space, Captain Picard defends his android crewman Data in a hearing designed to determine if he is a sentient being or a piece of machinery.

Unlike the undefined Star Bases in the original series, this one is a true space station—an impressive model shaped like a top, with a broad base at the bottom. Its interior sets, however, are rather bland. The script was written by Melinda Snodgrass, then the series' story editor and the author of *Circuit* (q.v.), and there are definite resemblances between this story and that novel: in both cases, a legal official in a space station must resolve an important issue involving individual freedom. While this was a reasonable scenario in the near-future setting of *Circuit*, however, it is hard to reconcile with the developed future background of this series; with a Federation that spans the Galaxy and is connected by a communications network, an isolated judge would not be left to decide an issue as fundamental as whether an android is human or not.

C52. "Melora." *Star Trek: Deep Space Nine.* Los Angeles: KCOP, November 4, 1993.

Dr. Bashir falls in love with a beautiful woman.

Unseen.

C53. "Mission to Mars." *Men into Space.* New York: CBS-TV, May 25, 1960.

On the Moon, American and Russian crews prepare to launch the first missions to Mars, more or less simultaneously, taking advantage of Mars's favorable position in relation to the Earth. Colonel McCauley, leading the American mission, insists upon delaying the launch a few days to make some last-minute changes to improve their margin of safety; but the Russians, with whom the Americans enjoy a friendly dinner, are more concerned about haste and make no adjustments to their craft. After both ships have launched, McCauley's caution proves wise, as his ship proceeds without flaws while the Russian ship veers off course and then explodes, leaving its two astronauts huddling inside the wreckage clinging to life with only a few hours of oxygen left. McCauley decides to abandon his mission to Mars and changes course to rescue the Russians. When he is instructed to not land on the Moon, but instead proceed directly to Earth, he fears that he will be punished for his actions. Instead, he has a personal meeting with the President of the United States, who praises his decision as a boon to America's image around the world.

Since the low gravity of the Moon would still provide some resistance for a launching spacecraft, it seemingly would have made more sense to launch the Mars rockets from the space station, as in *Conquest of Space*. And while Space Station Astra does not appear in this episode, it is mentioned when McCauley is instructed to proceed to the space station in order to switch to another spacecraft to land on Earth.

C54. *Moonraker*. Eon Productions/Les Productions Artistes Associés, 1979.

A master criminal, Lonsdale, plans to rule the world by breeding a master race on board his private space station, while killing off the world's population with nerve gas satellites. But James Bond sneaks aboard the station and alerts NASA, which sends a squadron of astronauts to attack the station and foil his plans.

The station, an impressive array of girders and large interiors, turns out to be rather vulnerable to armed attack. In novels like Barr's *The Last Fourteen* and Scortia's *Earthwreck!* (q.v.) Earth's destruction means space station inhabitants must carry on the human race; in this case, the scenario is carefully planned.

Note: the novelization of this film is Michael Wood's *James Bond and Moonraker.*

C55. "Move Along Home." *Star Trek: Deep Space Nine*. Los Angeles: KCOP, March 16, 1993.

Hitherto uncontacted aliens arrive at Deep Space Nine and immediately ask to go to Quark's game room, where they play a form of roulette for hours. When Quark is detected cheating them, the aliens force him to play another game involving a large three-dimensional model and pieces. As the game begins, Sisko, Dax, Kira and Dr. Bashir are teleported into a strange maze, and they must move through it, overcoming various challenges, to win the game; Quark's moves determine where they will go next and what they will encounter. Finally, Quark loses the game, Sisko and the others are freed from the game, and the aliens depart.

This is the second episode to depict game-obsessed aliens—the other was "Captive Pursuit" (q.v.)—and it suggests that the program's creators were already having trouble coming up with ideas. The logic behind this episode is particularly weak: it is hard to imagine that aliens would meet Earthmen for the first time and immediately rush to a roulette table, or that aliens would risk alienating the station's crew by forcing them into an unexplained and apparently deadly game.

C56. *Mutiny in Outer Space*. [*Ammutinamento nello spazio*; also known as *Invasion from the Moon*] Woolner Brothers/Hugo Grimaldi Productions, 1965.

Astronauts returning from the icy caves of the Moon to their space station bring back a deadly fungus, which grows and menaces the crewmen. To defeat the invader—which seems intelligent and intent on conquering Earth—the astronauts spray the station with ice crystals and freeze the creature.

Unseen.

C57. *Mystery Science Theater 3000*. Weekly series of hosted movie presentations. Comedy Central: 1989-1999.

The hosts of this series are purportedly trapped on a space station, where every week they must watch a terrible science fiction movie.

Unseen, because I simply cannot stand to watch science fiction movies, even bad science fiction movies, which are constantly interrupted by inane witticisms.

Note: prior to its national run, the series was broadcast locally in Minneapolis from 1988 to 1989.

C58. "The Nagus." *Star Trek: Deep Space Nine*. Los Angeles: KCOP, March 27, 1993.

The Nagus—a high Ferengi official—arrives at Deep Space Nine to distribute the lucrative rights to exploit various expected trading opportunities in the Gamma Quadrant at the other end of the wormhole. He surprisingly names Quark as his successor, and when he suddenly dies, Quark assumes the office. Soon, Quark is the target of an assassination attempt by the Nagus's former assistant, though Odo rescues him. Then the original Nagus appears; he explains that his faked death was designed to test whether his assistant was truly ready to assume the office, and he failed the test by bluntly trying to kill Quark instead of subtly maneuvering into a position of power.

Although this episode displays the role of space station as a center of commerce and trading, there is otherwise little to say about it; it is simply a comedy about the amusingly duplicitous Ferengi.

C59. "Necessary Evil." *Star Trek: Deep Space Nine*. Los Angeles: KCOP, November 18, 1993.

Odo decides to investigate an old unsolved murder.

Unseen.

C60. "The Passenger." *Star Trek: Deep Space Nine*. Los Angeles: KCOP, February 23, 1993.

A fire breaks out on an alien ship approaching Deep Space Nine with a vicious criminal as its prisoner. Although he is pronounced dead, the alien who captured him is convinced that he is somehow still alive, and that he is plotting to steal a shipment of a valuable metal that will soon reach the station. In fact, the criminal has transferred his personality to the body of Dr. Bashir, and he uses Bashir's body to recruit some henchmen with the help of Quark and hijacks the cargo ship as it approaches the station. When Sisko traps the ship in a tractor beam, he threatens to destroy the ship and Dr. Bashir, but Dax devises an energy beam that forces the criminal's personality out of Bashir's body long enough to enable the doctor to turn off the ship's shields. The criminal is then permanently removed from Bashir's body and killed.

Based on the episodes I watched, there was one interesting difference emerging between this series and its predecessor: while *Star Trek: The Next Generation* generally relied more on characters' personal initiative to resolve problems, *Star Trek: Deep Space Nine* seemed more willing to present some scientific gobbledygook as the basis of a virtually magical solution. Here, it is revealed that the entire station can be sabotaged at any point by a "subspace pulse generator" (or something like that), and I frankly could not follow the jargon that justified the energy beam that somehow forced the alien out of Bashir's body. Perhaps this tendency was one reason why this series was never quite as popular as its precursors.

C61. "Past Prologue." *Star Trek: Deep Space Nine*. Los Angeles: KCOP, January 12, 1993.

A Bajoran terrorist takes refuge in Deep Space Nine after being pursued by a Cardassian spacecraft. He plans to blow up the wormhole as a way to remove the Federation presence from his planet, but he first must surreptitiously rendezvous with two Klingons to purchase a necessary element in the bomb. However, Odo learns of the plot, Commander Sisko follows him to the rendezvous point, and Sisko's Bajoran aide Kira (who accompanies the terrorist) manages to overcome him and foil the plot.

This episode presents Deep Space Nine as a kind of Casablanca in outer space—a neutral city where representatives of hostile factions can mingle in a state of uneasy truce while they engage in various schemes and conspiracies. It is interesting that even in its first two episodes, the program's creators feel an urge to get away from the space station: "Emissary" featured an extended journey through the wormhole, and this episode involves a rendezvous in space near a Bajoran moon.

C62. *Per Aspera ad Astra.* [*Cherez Ternii—K Zvyozdam*] Maxim Gorki Studio, 1980.

An alien girl is found on a deserted space station; and the story of her planet's people is then related—a sad story of a capitalist economy that engenders environmental disaster.

Unseen; it is described by Vladimir Gakov in *The Encyclopedia of Science Fiction.*

C63. *Prisoners of Gravity.* Weekly television talk show. Ontario, Canada: TVOntario, 1989-1994.

This talk show supposedly takes place on an orbiting satellite, whose resident, Commander Rick, interrupts TVOntario's signals once a week to present discussions of science fiction and related topics.

Unseen; it is discussed by Peter Nicholls in *The Encyclopedia of Science Fiction.*

C64. "Progress." *Star Trek: Deep Space Nine.* Los Angeles: KCOP, May 11, 1993.

On Deep Space Nine, Jake Sisko and his Ferengi friend engage in some entrepreneurial barter, which finally earns them a piece of valuable land. Meanwhile, a project to devastate a Bajoran moon for use as an energy source is complicated when one of its few settlers, a stubborn old man, refuses to evacuate. Kira becomes attached to the man and stays with him, endangering her own position as coordinator of the project and Liaison Officer of Deep Space Nine. After meeting with

Sisko, she finally decides to destroy the man's house and take him with her to safety.

It is almost sad to see Deep Space Nine reduced to the status of a bit player in its own series. In this episode, each segment dutifully begins with an establishing shot of the station and a few minutes about the subplot involving Jake; then the scene shifts to the moon, where the real story is. The old man, played by Brian Keith, may have been envisioned as a recurring character, a mentor for Kira, perhaps to replace the Bajoran woman abandoned in "Battle Lines" (q.v.).

C65. *Project Moonbase*. Galaxy Pictures, 1953.

An enemy agent, impersonating a distinguished scientist, plans to destroy America's space station by commandeering the circumlunar flight he has been assigned to and smashing the vehicle into the station. He fails, but his actions force the other two crewmen, a man and a woman, to land on the Moon, where they establish a government base and get married.

This film, apparently the first to depict a space station, features the familiar dual-purpose space station—bombs aimed at the Earth, exploration missions aimed at the stars—and the familiar problem of sabotage. The scenes on board the space station are interesting because under weightless conditions, no effort is made to establish a uniform system of "up" and "down"; hence, the astronauts pass by someone walking upside down and are briefed by a panel seemingly sitting on the wall. Robert A. Heinlein is credited as co-author of the story and screenplay.

C66. "Prometheus Bound for Destruction." *Space Patrol*. New York: ABC-TV, September 29, 1951.

Commander Corey and his crew visit an old space station orbiting Ganymede which is scheduled for destruction.

Unseen.

C67. "Q-Less." *Star Trek: Deep Space Nine*. Los Angeles: KCOP, February 9, 1993.

A renegade archaeologist named Vash emerges from the wormhole with artifacts from the Gamma Quadrant, including a large golden gemstone; she contacts Quark and arranges to sell them at an auction. The strange super-being known as Q then appears, hoping to renew his relationship with Vash, but the archaeologist rebuffs him. When mysterious power surges start to threaten the space station and send it hurdling towards the wormhole, Commander Sisko suspects Q is responsible; but a probe reveals that the source of the problem is the gemstone, which is actually the energy-absorbing egg of a space creature. When the gemstone is teleported off the station into space, the creature is born and flies away, ending the danger, and the archaeologist plans to return to Earth.

An episode featuring two recurring characters from *Star Trek: The Next Generation*, and a story line that might have been used in that series, suggest that the creators of *Star Trek: Deep Space Nine* were rapidly running out of ideas. After the pilot episode shows the space station traveling outward as a hopeful sign, this episode shows the space station falling downward (here, into the wormhole) as a threatening development.

C68. "Quarantine." *Men into Space*. New York: CBS-TV, December 30, 1959.

Two scientists who dislike each other are both assigned to do research at Space Station Astra at the same time, which distresses station commander Colonel McCauley. Soon, one of them, a biologist, develops a strange disease apparently caused by a mutated form of the viruses he was studying, so he quarantines himself within his quarters and McCauley quarantines the entire station from outside visitors. The other scientist, a physicist, deduces that the "high frequencies" he was working with are the source of the problem, and he risks his own life by bringing the biologist into his own quarters so that he can use his equipment to effect a cure. Now reconciled, the men decide to engage in a joint research project.

This episode identifies the primary purpose of Space Station Astra to be a "research center"; it also suggests that the confined quarters of a space station may be conducive to quarrels, and that a major danger facing such a facility would be an epidemic.

C69. *Queen of Outer Space*. Allied Artists, 1958.

In 1975, the people of Venus fought a war with another planet; although they finally won, the effects were devastating, and the women of Venus, blaming men for the war, staged a successful revolt, took over the planet, and killed or exiled all of their men. Now the evil queen of Venus is planning to destroy the Earth, because she fears its aggressive males will try to conquer Venus. The Venusian women first use energy beams to blow up Earth's Space Station Eight; and the beams divert a spaceship on route to the station towards Venus. There, the men are captured, make contact with women who oppose the queen, and foil the queen's plans.

Despite its well-deserved reputation as a ridiculous bomb, this film has surprisingly good production values; the scenes of the spaceship being launched and flying through the atmosphere recall actual footage of space shuttle flights. Space Station Eight, seen only in a few establishing shots, is a circular band; the scene of the station blowing up is apparently the first filmed depiction of a space station being destroyed. The purpose of the station is described when some crewmen grumble about their boring trip to a "bus depot"; scientist Dr. Conrad responds that the term is accurate enough, although he prefers to call it a "way station."

C70. "Resurrection of the Daleks." *Doctor Who*. London: BBC-TV, February 8, 1984 through February 15, 1984 [2 episodes].

Mercenaries take control of the space prison holding the villainous Davros and free him; he then wages war with the equally evil Daleks. With the help of Doctor Who, the space prison is destroyed and all the Daleks are defeated.

Unseen; there was surprisingly no novel based on these episodes.

C71. *Return of the Jedi*. Lucasfilm/Fox, 1983.

In this third *Star Wars* film, the evil Emperor and Darth Vader have built a new Death Star, a space fortress which threatens Luke Skywalker and his new allies, the Ewoks, though it is finally destroyed.

Supposedly bigger and mightier than the previous Death Star of *Star Wars* (q.v.), this space fortress also proves vulnerable to an armed assault.

C72. "Revenge of the Cybermen." *Doctor Who*. London: BBC-TV, April 19, 1975 through May 10, 1975 [4 episodes].

Returning to the space station visited in "The Ark in Space" and "The Sontaran Experiment" (q.v.), the Doctor finds the station in the vicinity of an asteroid called Voga, serving as a space beacon. A strange disease afflicting the residents turns out to be caused by Cybermats, the rat-like creations of the Cybermen. Doctor Who then helps the Vogans defeat the Cybermen and prevents the station from crashing into the surface of Voga.

Unseen; the novel based on these episodes is *Doctor Who and the Revenge of the Cybermen*, by Terrance Dicks, discussed above in Part A.

C73. "Rules of Acquisition." *Star Trek: Deep Space Nine*. Los Angeles: KCOP, November 11, 1993.

The Nagus returns to Deep Space Nine and appoints Quark to head a series of trade negotiations with aliens from the Gamma Quadrant. Quark is greatly assisted by another Ferengi who, he later discovers, is a woman in disguise. Because Ferengi culture demands that woman remain at home and engage in no business, this woman has disguised herself so that she can participate in outside activities. When her identity is revealed, she plans to relocate to another world where she can work freely; but Quark, even though he has developed feelings for the woman, decides to retain on Deep Space Nine.

This is essentially a direct sequel to "The Nagus" (q.v.) and, despite its focus on the space station as a place for business and pleasure (here, gambling), is just as inconsequential.

C74. "Sanctuary." *Star Trek: Deep Space Nine*. Los Angeles: KCOP, December 2, 1993.

A group of aliens who emerge from the Gamma Quadrant believe that the planet Bajor is their legendary homeland.

Unseen.

C75. "Sea of Stars." *Men into Space*. New York: CBS-TV, January 13, 1960.

When an unmanned satellite is about to collide with Space Station Astra, Colonel McCauley and another crewman go out in a spaceship to destroy the object. When they attempt to return to the station, the rocket malfunctions, and McCauley realizes that their only hope is to attempt a risky landing on Earth. His crewman, who had previously expressed a lack of concern for precise calculations, must use his slide rule to make the exact calculations they need to land safely when McCauley is temporarily disabled.

This episode suggests that, as humans launch more and more objects into space, collisions will become an increasing danger. Unlike other space stations, it seems, Space Station Astra has no system for dealing with such threats, requiring the improvised mission seen in this episode.

C76. "Second Sight." *Star Trek: Deep Space Nine*. Los Angeles: KCOP, November 25, 1993.

Commander Sisko has an emotional encounter with a mysterious woman.

Unseen.

C77. "Shada." *Doctor Who* [6 episodes, left unfinished due to a BBC strike, and never aired].

A scientist named Skagra, working at a space station called Think Tank, steals the minds of his fellow scientists and travels to Earth to find a book that will lead him to Shada, the prison planet of the Time Lords, where a powerful renegade Time Lord is held who can assist in his plans to conquer the universe. Getting the book from the Doctor and a fellow Time Lord masquerading as a Cambridge professor, Skagra goes to Shada, while the Doctor goes to Think Tank and encounters Skagra's huge alien allies. Eventually, Doctor Who reaches Shada, defeats Skagra, and returns the professor, now revealed as the renegade Time Lord, to Cambridge.

Unseen; indeed, no one has seen the completed footage of these episodes, except for two brief excerpts included in "The Five Doctors." *Doctor Who*. London: BBC-TV, November 25, 1983. These episodes have not been novelized, no doubt because their author, Douglas Adams, later incorporated much of their story (without the Doctor or the space station) into his novel, *Dirk Gently's Holistic Detective Agency*.

C78. "The Siege." *Star Trek: Deep Space Nine*. Los Angeles: KCOP, October 14, 1993.

In this conclusion of the three-part series involving the episodes "The Homecoming" and "The Circle" (q.v.), Sisko and his crew hide themselves on an apparently abandoned Deep Space Nine while Bajoran soldiers occupy the station. While they fight guerilla war against the occupiers, Kira and Dax use an abandoned spaceship to fly to Bajor with proof that the rebels are being supported by the Cardassians. When they reach the Bajoran council with the evidence, the coup collapses and the Federation reoccupies Deep Space Nine.

The vulnerability of the space station is clearly established when Sisko does not even attempt to resist the arrival the Bajoran soldiers. In fighting them, they once again use the ventilator shafts as hiding places, and their hit-and-run tactics make the station seem like a giant maze or labyrinth.

Note: this episode is apparently unrelated to the *Star Trek: Deep Space Nine* novel of that name by Peter David.

C79. *Silent Running.* Universal/Michael Gruskoff Productions/Douglas Trumbull Productions, 1971.

In the twenty-first century, spaceships in permanent orbits carry biospheres containing the last remaining forests. When the ships are ordered to destroy their forests and return to Earth, one dedicated but slightly deranged crewman on the *Valley Forge*, Freeman Lowell, rebels, kills the other crewmen, and launches his ship into the void. Later rediscovered, he destroys the spaceship and himself, but not before launching the last biosphere into space, where the forest can live on with artificial light and a robot gardener.

Technically, the *Valley Forge* is not a space station but a spaceship temporarily serving as one; yet the boredom of the other crewmen and Lowell's madness are symptomatic of space station life. And the detached biosphere at the film's conclusion becomes a true space station, albeit one inhabited only by plants, animals, and a robot.

C80. *The Sky Calls.* [*Niebo Zowiet*; also known as *The Heavens Call*] Dovzhenko Studios, 1959.

Two rockets, one bound for the Moon and one for Mars, stop at a huge artificial satellite with gardens, laboratories, and lush residences.

Unseen; portions of this film were later used in the 1963 American production *Battle beyond the Sun* (q.v.).

C81. *Snow Devils.* [*I Diavoli della Spazio*; also known as *Space Devils*] Mercury Film International/Southern Cross Productions, 1965.

Astronauts are summoned to investigate reports of Abominable Snowmen, who turn out to be aliens from a wandering planet who are planning to take over the Earth; but the heroes manage to thwart the plot and destroying the alien planet.

Half-seen; it is not a film that holds one's attention. The opening scenes depict a doughnut-shaped space station and a woman on board who is trying to reach the vacationing astronauts.

C82. *Solaris.* Mosfilms, 1971.

After a visit with his father on Earth, a scientist is sent to the space station orbiting Solaris, a planet inhabited by a vast and mysterious sentient ocean. Like the two other crew members he finds there, he is soon haunted by a strange visitor from his past—his late wife who committed suicide—apparently a manifestation created by the being in an attempt to communicate. In a final scene, he visits his father and his house, recreated on the surface of Solaris, but the mystery remains unsolved.

Generally speaking, one can say that this film is reasonably faithful to Stanislaw Lem's novel (discussed in Part A). The major difference is that there is greater emphasis on the protagonist's relationship with the apparition of his wife. There are many interesting things, though, about the appearance of the film's space station. As seen in the only exterior shot, it is an undistinguished metal disc, but its interiors are extremely varied. Some corridors are shaped like the insight of a torus; others only have curved walls; and others are rectangular. Some areas seem stark and metallic, with dials and buttons on the walls; others offer a more muted decor of padded walls, rounded chairs, and white carpet; while others closely resemble rooms on Earth. The station sometimes has the neat, pristine look of typical space stations, but sometimes appears to be in a state of disarray, with debris scattered on the floors. Some of the station's doors automatically open sideways, in the manner of the doors on *Star Trek*'s *Enterprise*; others open from the top; and others—the doors to people's quarters—open on hinges, just like doors on Earth. Since the film was clearly made with great care, it seems like the director deliberately wanted a station which combined disparate elements, which projected a sense of inconsistency and variety, which could thus reflect the increasing disorientation and madness of the scientists studying the enigmatic creature.

C83. "The Sontaran Experiment." *Doctor Who*. London: BBC-TV, February 22, 1975 through March 1, 1975 [2 episodes].

In this sequel to "The Ark in Space" (q.v.), Doctor Who goes down to the surface of the Earth to make sure it is safe for the humans in the Ark to return. He discovers an alien Sontaran conducting experiments on humans to determine their level of resistance. However, the Doctor manages to defeat the Sontaran and the human race can now return to Earth.

Unseen; the novel based on these episodes is *Doctor Who—The Sontaran Experiment*, by Ian Marter.

C84. *Space Academy*. New York: CBS, September 11, 1977 through September 1, 1979.

A group of youngsters are trained to live and work in space at the Space Academy, built on an asteroid.

The Academy occupies the upper half of the flattened asteroid, and its model work and interiors are reasonably impressive. Almost all of the episodes of this Saturday morning series, however, involves leaving the Academy on some mission or assignment (as I vaguely recall).

Note: this series spawned another Saturday morning series, *Jason of Star Command*, which (as I also vaguely recall) did not involve the Space Academy or space stations.

C85. *Spaceballs*. MGM/Brooksfilms, 1987.

A young space pilot and his half-human, half-dog companion come to the aid of a young princess who is menaced by the villainous race of Spaceballs.

In this broad parody of the *Star Wars* films, the vehicle which replaces the Death Star is a gigantic Statue of Liberty—as logical a space structure as any, I suppose, though its only purpose here is to set up a later joke involving the film *Planet of the Apes*. And after they have defeated the Spaceballs, the hero and his friend stop off to eat and refuel at a kind of truck stop in space. Searching for something profound to say about this silly film, I could point out that its determination to present space habitations in the most familiar way possible is only an exaggeration of a tendency found elsewhere in science fiction.

C86. *Space Men.* [*Assignment Outer Space*] Titanus/Ultra Films, 1960.

A reporter visits a space station and helps stop a runaway rocket.

Unseen.

C87. "The Space Pirates." *Doctor Who.* London: BBC-TV, March 8, 1969 through April 12, 1969 [6 episodes].

Doctor Who arrives at a space beacon, which is broken apart by space pirates who then steal the part of the beacon including the Doctor's TARDIS. A search for the villain leads the Doctor to the planet Ta, where the guilty party, Caven, is eventually arrested.

Unseen; the novel based on these episodes is *Doctor Who—The Space Pirates*, by Terrance Dicks.

C88. *Space School.* London: BBC-TV, 1956, beginning on January 8, 1956.

The four episodes of this series depict a group of children living in an artificial satellite while their father surveys the Martian moons for possible landing sites.

Unseen.

C89. "Space Station of Danger." *Tom Corbett, Space Cadet.* New York: Dumont, March 27, 1954.

A space station is threatened by a dangerous chemical and a nuclear bomb.

Unseen.

C90. "Specimen: Unknown." *The Outer Limits.* New York: ABC-TV,

February 24, 1964.

Spores found attached to the hull of space station Adonis, when taken inside, grow into strange flowers which emit a deadly gas. Before the danger is known, a shuttle containing the fast-multiplying flowers is launched to Earth, and the Earth appears threatened. However, it turns out that the flowers are destroyed by water in the form of rain.

According to the Control Voice (the narrator), the Adonis station is "a laboratory orbiting a thousand miles above the Earth, a tiny, far-flung world connected only by radio and memory, and inhabited by a handful of men dedicated to removing the unknown for future space travelers"—yet it is also a strictly military venture. Because the episode was originally too short, many lengthy visuals of the station—the model first used in the series *Men into Space*—were presented. The background and filming of the episode are discussed in detail in *The Outer Limits Companion* by David J. Schow and Jeffrey Frentzen.

C91. *Star Cops*. [television series] London: BBC-TV, July 6 through August 31, 1987.

A group of police officers with headquarters on the Moon must patrol, among other things, manned space stations in Earth orbit.

Unseen.

C92. *Starstruck*. [unsold television series pilot] New York: CBS-TV, June 9, 1979.

This is yet another rejected television series about a space station, featuring an eccentric family which runs an orbiting restaurant and the strange aliens who visit their establishment.

Unseen.

C93. *Star Trek: The Motion Picture*. Paramount, 1979.

James T. Kirk once again becomes the captain of a newly refurbished *Enterprise* in order to deal with a gigantic alien object that is approaching the Earth.

There are a number of interesting space stations seen in the vicinity of Earth, including an impressive office complex in space; in addition, it is a space station called Epsilon Nine which first alerts Earth to the approach of the immense alien spacecraft—and is later destroyed by it. In early scenes, the *Enterprise* is seen docked to a space station of sorts in Earth orbit; since the starship cannot land on a planet, a repair facility would necessarily be located in space.

Note: see comments on the Gene Roddenberry novelization of the film in Part A; this is the first of six *Star Trek* films based on the original series, all discussed below.

C94. *Star Trek II: The Wrath of Khan*. Paramount, 1982.

The ex-wife and son of Captain James Kirk are working on Project Genesis, a process to make a dead world into an earthlike paradise, in a space station laboratory. Their work becomes a pawn in a battle between Kirk and Khan, a genetically engineered superman who seeks to use Project Genesis as a weapon.

While there are other briefly glimpsed space stations, the major one here is the Genesis laboratory, called Spacelab in Vonda McIntyre's novelization of the film (q.v.); it is an attractive structure shaped like a top. Early scenes also feature the *Enterprise* being repaired in Earth orbit attached to a structure called the Spacedock in the novelization, although it is different from the Spacedock in the film and novel *Star Trek III: The Search for Spock* (q.v.).

C95. *Star Trek III: The Search for Spock*. Paramount, 1985.

In order to lead a forbidden expedition to bring Mr. Spock back to life, James Kirk and the other crewmen of the *Enterprise* must take over the *Enterprise*, travel to the world where his new body has been created by Project Genesis, battle with Klingons attempting to seize the Genesis device, and reunite the body with his intelligence, preserved in the brain of Dr. McCoy.

Unlike the scenes in Earth orbit of the film and novel *Star Trek: The Motion Picture* and the film and novel *Star Trek II: The Wrath of Khan* (q.v.), the *Enterprise* is here docked within a gigantic sphere, filled with other spacecraft. Vonda McIntyre's novelization of the film (q.v.) identifies this structure as Spacedock and explains that the interior of this huge construct is sometimes pressurized, so that repairmen can work on starship exteriors without wearing suits. Again, a few other stations function as background elements.

C96. *Star Trek IV: The Voyage Home*. Paramount, 1987.

Returning to Earth in a Klingon vessel, the *Enterprise* discovers that their planet is being menaced by a huge alien probe broadcasting a mysterious—and destructive—message. Determining that the message is in the language of humpback whales—a species now extinct—they travel back in time to twentieth-century San Francisco to get two humpback whales, who are brought back to the future, talk to the alien probe, and thus save the planet Earth.

The space station known as Spacedock is glimpsed in three short scenes: early in the movie, when the probe is approaching Earth; at the time when Kirk and company are returning to twenty-third-century Earth; and in the final scene, when the new *Enterprise* is seen parked in space next to the facility.

Note: I have not listed the novelizations of the films *Star Trek IV*, *Star Trek V* and *Star Trek VI* (q.v.) in Part I, simply because the appearances of the space stations in these films are so fleeting that I doubt there are any references to them in the novels.

C97. *Star Trek V: The Final Frontier*. Paramount, 1989.

Boarding the new *Enterprise*, Kirk and his crew are sent to rescue hostages on a border planet; they are then captured by Spock's brother, a religious fanatic who takes the *Enterprise* on a search for a strange planet said to be the home of God.

One brief scene shows the new, improved *Enterprise* apparently docked next to a large space station with castle-like spires; but essentially, space stations have now vanished from the *Star Trek* universe, at least in the film series.

C98. *Star Trek VI: The Undiscovered Country*. Paramount, 1991.

When the Klingon Empire seems doomed by a disastrous accident, Captain Kirk and his crew are assigned to escort a Klingon peace mission to Earth. After the *Enterprise* apparently attacks the Klingon vessel, Kirk and Doctor McCoy are arrested, tried, and sentenced to work on a Klingon mining planet. Spock discovers a high-level plot involving humans, Klingons and Romulans to sabotage the peace talks, and, after he rescues Kirk and McCoy, they intervene to prevent an attack at the reconvened peace talks.

The Klingon peace proposal demands, among other things, "the dismantling of our space stations and star bases along the Neutral Zone." Kirk and his crew take off from Spacedock—which looks more elongated and top-shaped than in earlier films—and at the end of the movie, the *Enterprise* is ordered to return to Spacedock "to be decommissioned." Thus, in these glimpses, the space station is again a military outpost and a place to begin and end adventures. However, space stations remain extremely unimportant in the *Star Trek* universe: the filmmakers cannot even be bothered to maintain a consistent appearance for Spacedock.

Note: while this film was announced and structured as the final *Star Trek* film, a seventh film, *Star Trek: Generations* (1994), mixing characters from the first and second series, did appear in 1994.

C99. *Star Wars*. Lucasfilm/Fox, 1977.

The first adventure of Luke Skywalker and his companions includes a climactic assault on the huge space fortress called the Death Star.

There hardly any need to provide a detailed plot summary of what is surely the most popular science fiction film of all time. Its relevance here is that the Death Star, for all its vaunted powers as a destroyer of worlds, is ultimately obliterated by a simple nuclear bomb.

Note: the second film in the *Star Wars* trilogy, *The Empire Strikes Back*, does not involve any space stations, while the third film, *Return of the Jedi* (q.v.), features a new Death Star.

C100. "The Storyteller." *Star Trek: Deep Space Nine*. Los Angeles: KCOP, May 4, 1993.

On Deep Space Nine, Sisko and Kira try to negotiate between two feuding Bajoran nations; the leader of one is a young girl who befriends Jake Sisko and his Ferengi friend and is eventually persuaded to compromise. Meanwhile, Bashir and O'Brien visit a remote Bajoran village where a major leader is about to die; mysteriously, he announces O'Brien will be his successor. Long ago, to establish village unity, a leader arranged for the periodic creation of a menacing cloud-like monster, which could only be driven away, he claimed, by the village uniting behind him as the "Storyteller." Later leaders maintained the system. The first night, as the old leader dies, O'Brien succeeds in driving away the monster. But since he does not want the job, he is happy to encounter the old leader's apprentice, who feels he deserves the position but was deprived of it because he failed to drive the monster away the one night he tried to do so. The next night the monster comes, O'Brien fails, but the apprentice steps forward and succeeds, so he is then proclaimed the new leader.

Like "Progress" (q.v.), this episode appears to represent the melding of two story ideas which were not individually strong enough to serve as episodes. In the Deep Space Nine segment, a space station is again seen as a natural place for negotiation and peacemaking—neutral ground for representatives of two nations about to go to war.

C101. *Supergiant*. [*Kotetsu No Kyojin*] Shin Toho, 1956-1959.

A series of nine filmed adventures of a superhero from another planet named Supergiant (also known as Starman), who helps Earth defeat various alien invaders. According to Phil Hardy's *Encyclopedia of Science Fiction Movies*, one plot involved "death-ray-spewing synthetic monsters sent by enemy space stations" (159).

Unseen, and if written descriptions of the quality of these films are accurate, they deserve to be unseen. For the record, the nine episodes are: *The Steel Man from Outer Space* [*Supah Jaianto*], 1956; *Rescue from Outer Space* [also *Supah Jaianto*], 1956; *Devils from the Planet* [*Kotetsu No Kyojin—Kaiseijin No Mayo*; also known as *Invaders from the Planets*], 1957; *The Earth in Danger* [*Kotetsu No Kyojin—Chikyu Metzubo*], 1957; *Spaceship of Human Destruction* [*Jinko Eisen To Jinrui No Hametsu*], 1958; *The Destruction of the Space Fleet* [*Uchutei To Jinko Eisen No Gekitotsu*], 1958; *Spacemen Appear* [*Uchu Kaijin Shutsugen*], 1958; *The Devil Incarnate* [*Akuma No Keshiin*], 1959; and *Kingdom of the Poison Moth* [*Dokuga Okoku*], 1959. The third and fourth episodes were repackaged in 1961 as a feature film, variously named *Supergiant II*, *The Atomic Rulers of the World*, and *Attack of the Flying Saucers*; the fifth and sixth episodes were repackaged in 1964 as a feature film, variously named *Supergiant against the Satellites*, *Attack from Space*, and *Invaders from Space*. Hardy reports, a bit uncertainly, that the first two and last three episodes were also repackaged as feature films, but I have found no references to these films in other reference books; he also lists three additional episodes that may or may not be part of the series.

C102. *Supergirl*. Artistry/Cantharus, 1984.

Long after the planet Krypton exploded, the intact and inhabited Argo City lives on in outer space. When a vital power source is lost, Supergirl is sent to Earth to search for it; there, she battles with an evil sorceress before returning home.

It belatedly occurs to me that Argo City, given my looser standards for space stations in other media, might qualify as a space habitat of sorts, although it is little seen in this generally silly film.

C103. "Terminus." *Doctor Who*. London: BBC-TV, February 15, 1983 through February 23, 1983 [4 episodes].

The Doctor appears on a spaceship heading for Terminus, a space station run by an evil corporation which takes care of those suffering from an incurable disease by providing a helpful drug. He learns that an explosion on Terminus actually caused the Big Bang, and he intervenes to prevent a disastrous second explosion. When he departs, his friend Lyssa stays behind to minister to the sufferers and synthesize the drug, so the station will no longer be controlled by the corporation.

Unseen; the novel based on these episodes is *Doctor Who—Terminus* by John Lydecker.

C104. "Terra, the Doomed Planet." *Space Patrol*. New York: ABC-TV, November 27, 1954. Shown on *I Remember Television*. San Bernardino: WVCR, February 11, 1989.

A villainous being from another galaxy named Ahyo imprisons Buzz Corey and his Space Patrol crewmates and attempts to destroy the artificial planet Terra by using a force beam to send it hurling into the Sun. However, Buzz escapes and captures the villain.

From the few establishing shots, it seems that Terra, the artificial asteroid in solar orbit halfway between Earth and Mars which serves as Space Patrol headquarters, is basically built like an ordinary planet, with buildings and parks visible on its surface. Thus, it is not really a space station by my definition. However, the story of its construction is interesting: the asteroid is built out of soil from every Earth nation to symbolize the spirit of international cooperation and peace.

Note: no episode title accompanied the airing of the episode in 1989; its title and original air date were established by consulting online episode guides. It is the third of three related episodes, the first two being

"The Exploding Stars" and "The Dwellers of the Prime Galaxy" (q.v.).

C105. *The Terrornauts.* Amicus, 1967.

An alien spaceship takes a group of Earthmen to an abandoned asteroid fortress, where they must figure out how to use its weapons to fend off an alien attack.

Unseen, though see comments on the novel it was based on, Murray Leinster's *The Wailing Asteroid.* Descriptions suggest that the asteroid in the film is more like a planetary base and not a virtual space station like the facility in Leinster's book.

C106. *Thunderbirds in Outer Space.* ITC Entertainment, 1981 [videocassette; date of theatrical release, if any, unknown].

After rescuing a spaceship about to collide with the Sun, members of the International Rescue team must prevent a damaged space station from falling to Earth and hitting an oil refinery.

This film from Great Britain, plagued by pirate radio stations operating from offshore boats, transplants the concept to outer space in its illegal radio station broadcasting from Earth orbit, although with modern communications satellites it seems unnecessary to have one with a disc jockey on board. The station, a rather small cylinder, is damaged when an errant rocket is exploded; its crash into the refinery is prevented when a Thunderbirds rocket nudges it out of the way, exactly as the space shuttle moved the *Killer Station* in Caidin's novel (q.v.). In addition to the falling station, there is a brief scene of a Thunderbirds rocket apparently docked at a conventional disc-shaped station. Overall, the movie offers interesting models and special effects, but, as many critics note, there is something maddening in watching filmed puppets perform for over ninety minutes.

C107. "The Trial of a Time Lord." *Doctor Who.* London: BBC-TV, September 6, 1986 through December 6, 1986 [14 episodes, which are also known as four separate adventures under the titles "The Mysterious Planet" (4 episodes), "Mindwarp" (4 episodes), "Terror of the Vervoids" (4 episodes), and "The Ultimate Foe" (2 episodes)].

The Doctor is summoned to a gigantic space station where other Time Lords are going to try him for certain crimes, which are described by the prosecuting attorney and depicted in the form of flashbacks; in response, Doctor Who presents another recent adventure which puts him in a better light. The whole affair is finally revealed as a scheme by the evil Master to discredit Who and defeat the Time Lords; the evidence against the Doctor was falsified; and the charges against him are dismissed.

Unseen; the four novels based on these episodes are *Doctor Who—The Mysterious Planet*, by Terrance Dicks; *Doctor Who—Mindwarp*, by Philip Martin; *Doctor Who—Terror of the Vervoids*, by Pip and Jane Baker; and *Doctor Who—The Ultimate Foe*, by Pip and Jane Baker.

C108. "The Trouble with Tribbles." *Star Trek*. New York: NBC-TV, December 29, 1967.

Summoned by a high-priority distress call to Space Station K-7, Captain Kirk of the starship *Enterprise* is displeased to learn that the only crisis involves protecting a shipment of wheat from visiting Klingons, legally entitled to receive rest and recreation there. An independent trader on the station, Cyrano Jones, is selling tribbles—small, furry creatures—which turn out to multiply at a dangerous rate and, much to everyone's distress, devour all the valuable wheat. However, the tribbles, which hate Klingons, detect that one crew member is actually a Klingon spy, and all ends happily when the remaining tribbles are all teleported to the Klingon ship.

Often described as the most popular *Star Trek* episode, the original script and a wealth of details concerning its production are found in a book by its author, David Gerrold, simply called *The Trouble with Tribbles*; see also James Blish's adaptation of the script, described in Part B above. Several common space station themes can be seen here: the space station as neutral ground for enemies to meet, the dangers of biological invasion and infiltration, and the space station as a breeding ground for madness—all the *Enterprise* crewmen behave unusually while on the station.

C109. "The Two Doctors." *Doctor Who*. London: BBC-TV, February 16, 1985 through March 2, 1985 [3 episodes].

A previous incarnation of Doctor Who investigates forbidden experiments involving time travel at Space Station J7 and is captured by the alien Sontarans, who plan to kill him in order to obtain the secret of time travel. But the present Doctor manages to rescue his predecessor and defeat the Sontarans.

Unseen; the novel based on these episodes is *Doctor Who—The Two Doctors*, by Robert Holmes.

C110. *2001: A Space Odyssey*. Metro-Goldwyn-Mayer, 1968.

Stopping at a space station on the way to the Moon to investigate a mysterious monolith, Dr. Heywood Floyd has an uneasy, guarded conversation with an old Russian friend about the events at Moon Base Clavius.

Without a doubt, Stanley Kubrick's gleaming white double wheel, slowly rotating to the tune of Strauss's *Blue Danube* waltz, is the best known image of a space station. The interiors look comfortable but there is an abundance of white, giving the place a sterile atmosphere. Here, as in *Earth II* and "The Trouble with Tribbles" (q.v.), a space station is a place where people of different nationalities can meet without hostility.

See also comments on Arthur C. Clarke's novelization of the film and his book *The Lost Worlds of 2001*, which provides some material that was left out of the final version of the film, both in Part A above.

C111. *2010: The Year We Make Contact*. Metro-Goldwyn-Mayer, 1984.

Heywood Floyd joins a joint American-Soviet mission to further investigate the monolith orbiting Jupiter; they discover and re-awaken the computer HAL, but they must flee when a huge number of alien monoliths suddenly transform Jupiter into a second sun, making its moons new worlds for humanity.

Unlike the novel it is based on, this film qualifies for inclusion because of two references to space stations in the dialogue: first, in discussing rising world tensions on Earth, the astronauts note that an American satellite was destroyed by a Russian space station; second, while trying to avoid telling HAL that their plans for emergency departure will cause its destruction, HAL's programmer tells him there are new plans for the computer to rendezvous with a space station.

C112. "Verdict in Orbit." *Men into Space*. New York: CBS-TV, March 16, 1960.

Dr. Rawdin, a noted scientist who is also a media star, accidentally runs into Colonel McCauley's son riding a bicycle while rushing to attend a preflight briefing he was late for; after reporting the accident, he leaves the scene, making him a criminal hit-and-run driver. When he and McCauley arrive at the space station, a crewman notices that Rawdin seems unable to concentrate on the important work of investigating a process for converting samples of Venus's atmosphere into breathable oxygen, and McCauley of course is constantly worried about his son, in critical condition at a hospital. When he learns that police have used tire marks to identify Rawdin as the perpetrator, he goes to confront him, but finds out that he has gone out into space. When a furious McCauley temporarily refuses to authorize a rescue mission, leaving the man to die when his oxygen runs out, a subordinate temporarily relieves him of command on the grounds that he is too emotionally overwhelmed to properly function as station commander. McCauley then comes to his senses and sanctions a rescue attempt. McCauley's colleague finds Rawdin outside, but, evidently suicidal because of his guilt, he threatens to rip open his suit with a knife and kill himself if anyone tries to get him back into the station. McCauley then comes out and tells Rawdin that his decision to leave the accident was not due to his immorality, but only his fear, which makes him decide to come back to the station and return to Earth to face justice. And fortunately, McCauley's son soon seems on the road to a complete recovery.

This episode places a new emphasis on the loneliness of space explorers, likening them to isolated "Antarctic explorers" and explaining that their simultaneous distance from, and nearness to, the Earth makes their experience "a different kind of loneliness." Also, while the extreme circumstances of Rawdin's guilt and McCauley's anxiety understandably lead to their irrational behavior, this episode also suggests that simply living in a space station might drive men insane. At one point, a colleague notes that "a man's thinking can go haywire" in outer space.

C113. "Voice of Infinity." *Men into Space*. New York: CBS-TV, April 20, 1960.

A scientist brings his new equipment on board Space Station Astra which, when crewmen wear the proper monitors, will allow him to detect when men have reached the critical point where their stress level will make them prone to errors and thus allow them to be replaced before they make critical mistakes. However, one scientist, with Colonel McCauley's permission, refuses to wear the monitors, arguing that "Scientific research, if it's to mean anything, requires freedom, imagination, even inspiration" and hence might be inhibited if scientists aren't allowed to experience the excitement of scientific discovery or to have the possibility of making productive errors. The value of the equipment is apparently demonstrated when one crewman who does not immediately leave upon being told that he has reached his critical level makes a damaging mistake: the station's rockets, ordinarily fired regularly only to maintain the station's spin, begin to fire randomly, dangerously increasing the station's spin, increasing the artificial gravity to the point where men feel too heavy to function, and threatening to tear the station apart. Still, even though the instruments indicate he has at his breaking point, McCauley is able to make an accurate guess as to when and how long to fire the station's retrorockets, and he is able to stabilize the station and avert disaster. He recalls a conversation when it was said that people have inside of them a "voice of infinity" that can allow them to function effectively even when it would seem impossible for them to do so.

This episode demonstrates that men working on a space station may indeed experience dangerous levels of stress and also shows that using a station's spin to create artificial gravity would also pose the dangerous of an out-of-control spin which would crush the human occupants of the station.

C114. "Vortex." *Star Trek: Deep Space Nine*. Los Angeles: KCOP, April 20, 1993.

When one of a pair of alien twins is accidentally killed by another alien in a botched robbery attempt aboard Deep Space Nine, the killer is apprehended, and after contacting his home planet, Sisko assigns Odo to escort the prisoner back to his world to face punishment for other crimes. The alien tantalizes Odo by saying that he has met other shapeshifters and could take him to meet them. When an attack by the alien twin on their shuttle craft drives Odo and his captive into an energy vortex, they land on a small world, and Odo learns that this is not, as the alien said, the home of the shapeshifters, but rather the place he has stored his surviving daughter in a stasis field. Odo allows the prisoner and his daughter to be picked up by a passing Vulcan ship, saying that he will tell Sisko that the prisoner died on the asteroid.

A complex and surprising effective episode that dramatically shows the space station as a meeting place for alien races: here, Odo himself, whose mysterious alien nature is highlighted; the twin aliens; the criminal alien of another race; and Quark, who is involved in instigating the alien's clumsy attempted theft. Interestingly, except for the reconciliation between Odo and his prisoner, the other conflicts remain unresolved. One thing that makes this episode unusually dramatic, of course, is that much of the action takes place away from the station, in a strange vortex on the other side of the wormhole.

C115. *War of the Planets.* [*I Diafanoidi Portano la Morte*; or *I Diafandoidi Vergono da Morte*] Mercury Films International/ Southern Cross Productions, 1965.

Earth's four space stations are attacked by gaseous energy beings from Mars, who then teleport three of the stations to the surface of Mars. The fourth station, Gamma I, survives the attack, thanks to the decision of its commander to stay behind and confront the invaders. The Martians have also landed on Earth and have mentally taken over several humans; one Martian representative invites the commander and his crew to travel to Mars to see their civilization. Once there, they are appalled by the cruelty of the Martians and, after a furious fistfight with the Martian-dominated humans, they escape just as a fleet of spaceships from Earth destroys the Martian base.

This film seems to make even less sense than others of its type, since it seems that beings with the power to teleport a space station millions of miles across space would be able to instantly defeat Earth without engaging in all of these other shenanigans. There is a brief but striking scene of a space station grounded on Mars; after the Earth attack, it is reported that it and the other grounded stations were all destroyed.

Note: *The Wild, Wild Planet* (q.v.) is a sequel to this film.

C116. "The Wheel in Space." *Doctor Who.* London: BBC-TV, April 17, 1968 through June 1, 1968 [six episodes].

Doctor Who visits the Wheel in Space, a giant space station seemingly infested by strange rats which turn out to be Cybermats—creations of the Cybermen who are again planning to invade Earth. However, Doctor Who manages to destroy their invasion fleet while saving the Wheel from a threatening meteorite storm.

Unseen; the novel based on these episodes is *Doctor Who—The Wheel in Space*, by Terrance Dicks.

C117. *The Wild, Wild Planet.* [*I Criminali della Galassia*] Mercury
  Films International/Southern Cross Productions, 1965.

The commander of space station Gamma I is unhappy about a new
resident, a medical scientist for the Corporation whose experiments in
organ transplants strike the commander as dehumanizing. He is summoned to Earth to help investigate a series of mysterious disappearances; one missing person is found, shrunk to about three feet in
height. Eventually, he stumbles upon a massive plot, involving the station scientist, to miniaturize human beings and create a new race of
perfect beings; he and his friends find their secret base and defeat the
plotters.

The space station, seen in the opening sequences, has the standard
doughnut shape. There is nothing particularly striking about its interiors; when the commander gives the scientist a tour of the station, we
see a karate class, and a restaurant with dancing, that look exactly like
they would on Earth. There is one sign of discontent: the female karate
instructor, who is later abducted by the scientist, says that she needs a
vacation to get off of this "merry-go-round"—recalling the complaint
of the exiled scientists in Ben Bova's *Exiled from Earth* (q.v.).

Note: this is a sequel to *War of the Planets* (q.v.).

PART D.

WORKS LISTED IN CHRONOLOGICAL ORDER AND TIMELINE

1869 (1)

Hale, Edward Everett. "The Brick Moon."

1870 (1)

Hale, Edward Everett. "Life on the Brick Moon."

1872 (1)

Hale, Edward Everett. "The Brick Moon." [including "Life on the Brick Moon"]

1894 (1)

Tsiolkovsky, Konstantin. "Changes in Relative Weight."

1895 (1)

Tsiolkovsky, Konstantin. *Dreams of Earth and Sky*.

1897 (2)

Lasswitz, Kurt. *Two Planets*.
Munro, John. *A Trip to Venus*.

1920 (1)

Tsiolkovsky, Konstantin. *Beyond the Planet Earth.*

1926 (1)

Gail, Otto. *The Stone from the Moon.*

1928 (1)

Beliayev, Aleksandr. *The Struggle in Space.*

1929 (3)

Tsiolkovsky, Konstantin. "The Aim of Astronautics."
Tsiolkovsky, Konstantin. "Beyond the Earth's Atmosphere."
Tsiolkovsky, Konstantin. "Living Beings in the Cosmos."

1930 (1)

Rich, H. Thompson. "The Flying City."

1931 (3)

Leinster, Murray. [Will Jenkins] "The Power Planet."
Walsh, J. M. *Vandals of the Void.*
Williamson, Jack. "The Prince of Space."

1932 (1)

Smith, Everett C. (plot), and R. F. Starzl (story). "The Metal Moon."

1933 (1)

Williamson, Jack. "Dead Star Station."

1934 (1)

Williamson, Jack. "Born of the Sun."

1936 (1)

Wellman, Manly Wade. "Space Station No. 1."

1937 (1)

Hamilton, Edmond. "Space Mirror."

1939 (2)

Heinlein, Robert A. "Misfit."
Williamson, Jack. "Crucible of Power."

1940 (1)

Heinlein, Robert A. "Blowups Happen."

1941 (4)

Asimov, Isaac. "Reason."
Gardiner, Thomas M. "Cosmic Tragedy."
Tucker, Wilson. [as Bob Tucker] "Interstellar Way-Station."
Wells, Basil E. "Factory in the Sky."

1942 (3)

Asimov, Isaac. "Runaround."
Heinlein, Robert A. *Waldo*.
Smith, George O. "QRM Interplanetary."

1943 (5)

Moore, C. L. *Judgment Night*.
Smith, George O. "Calling the Empress."
Smith, George O. "Lost Art."
Smith, George O. "Recoil."
Van Vogt, A. E. "Concealment."

1944 (4)

Smith, George O. "Beam Pirate."
Smith, George O. "Firing Line."
Smith, George O. "The Long Way."
Smith, George O. "Off the Beam."

1945 (4)

Asimov, Isaac. "Escape!"
Smith, George O. "Identity."
Smith, George O. "Pandora's Millions."
Smith, George O. "Special Delivery."

1947 (9)

Asimov, Isaac. "Little Lost Robot."
Clement, Hal. [Harry Clement Stubbs] "Answer."
Fyfe, Horace B. "Sinecure 6."
Heinlein, Robert A. "The Green Hills of Earth."
Heinlein, Robert A. "It's Great to Be Back."
Heinlein, Robert A. "Space Jockey."
Smith, George O. "Mad Holiday."
Smith, George O. *Venus Equilateral*.
Yamin, Michael. "The Dreamers."

1948 (4)

Groom, Pelham. *The Purple Twilight*.
Heinlein, Robert A. "Ordeal in Space."
Heinlein, Robert A. *Space Cadet*.
Sturgeon, Theodore. "Unite and Conquer."

1949 (4)

Clarke, Arthur C. "The Lion of Comarre."
Clement, Hal. [Harry Clement Stubbs] "Fireproof."
Heinlein, Robert A. "Delilah and the Space Rigger."
Neville, Kris. "Cold War."

1950 (3)

MacLean, Katherine. "Incommunicado."
Neville, Kris. "Satellite Secret."
Powers, William F. "Meteor."

1951 (11)

Clarke, Arthur C. *Prelude to Space*.
Clarke, Arthur C. *Sands of Mars*.

Fyfe, Horace B. "Thinking Machine."
Heinlein, Robert A. *Between Planets.*
Hunt, Gill. [house pseudonym] *Station 7.*
"Isolation in Space." *Space Patrol.*
Jones, Raymond F. *The Alien.*
Merril, Judith. "Survival Ship."
Pratt, Fletcher. "Project Excelsior."
"Prometheus Bound for Destruction." *Space Patrol.*
Simak, Clifford D. *Empire.*

1952 (17)

Clarke, Arthur C. *Islands in the Sky.*
Cross, John Keir. *The Stolen Sphere.*
"The Derelict Space Station." *Space Patrol.*
Dickson, Gordon R. "Steel Brother."
Elam, Richard M., Jr. [Richard Mace] "The Day the Flag Fell."
Elam, Richard M., Jr. [Richard Mace] "The Iron Moon."
Fyfe, Horace B. "Star-Linked."
Gallun, Raymond Z., and Jerome Bixby. "Ev."
Heinlein, Robert A. *The Rolling Stones.*
Marsten, Richard. [S. A. Lombino, Evan Hunter] *Rocket to Luna.*
McIntosh, J. T. [James Murdoch MacGregor] "Hallucination Orbit."
Merwin, Sam, Jr. "Star Tracks."
Petkoff, Joseph. "Suicide's Grave."
Saari, Oliver. "Sitting Duck."
Savage, Blake. [John Blaine, H. L. Goodwin] *Rip Foster in Ride the Gray Planet.*
Vance, Jack. "Abercrombie Station."
Van Vogt, A. E. *Mission to the Stars.*

1953 (18)

Bester, Alfred. *The Demolished Man.*
Brack, Vektis. *Odyssey in Space.*
Brown, Fredric. *The Lights in the Sky Are Stars.*
Cameron, Berl. *Solar Gravita.*
Correy, Lee. [G. Harry Stine] "And a Star to Steer Her By."
Correy, Lee. [G. Harry Stine] "Pioneer."
Harness, Charles L. *The Paradox Men.*
Heinlein, Robert A. "Sky Lift."
Leinster, Murray. [Will Jenkins] *Space Platform.*
Leinster, Murray. [Will Jenkins] *Space Tug.*

Leonard, J. L. *Flight into Space.*
Neville, Kris. "Earth Alert!"
Norment, John. "Space Platform Xz204c Does Not Answer."
Project Moonbase.
Reed, Van. *Dwellers in Space.*
Rockwell, Carey. [pseudonym] *Danger in Deep Space.*
Smith, Robert. *Riders to the Stars.*
Vine, William. "Death Sentence."

1954 (25)

Asimov, Isaac. *The Caves of Steel.*
Bernard, Rafe. *The Wheel in the Sky.*
Brown, Fredric. *Martians, Go Home!*
Castle, J. [Jeffrey] Lloyd. *Satellite E One.*
Cooper, Edmond. [as George Kinley] *Ferry Rocket.*
Correy, Lee. [G. Harry Stine] "Amateur."
Courtney, Robert. "One Thousand Miles Up."
del Rey, Lester. [Walter Alvarez del Rey] *Step to the Stars.*
Duncan, David. *Dark Dominion.*
"The Dwellers of the Prime Galaxy." *Space Patrol.*
Elliot, E. C. [Reginald Alec Martin] *Kemlo and the Crazy Planet.*
Elliot, E. C. [Reginald Alec Martin] *Kemlo and the Martian Ghosts.*
Elliot, E. C. [Reginald Alec Martin] *Kemlo and the Sky Horse.*
Elliot, E. C. [Reginald Alec Martin] *Kemlo and the Zones of Silence.*
"The Exploding Stars." *Space Patrol.*
Fritch, C. E. "Many Dreams of Earth."
Galouye, Daniel F. "The Phantom World."
Gog.
Patchett, Mary E. *Adam Troy: Astroman.*
Sheckley, Robert. "Paradise II."
"Space Station of Danger." *Tom Corbett, Space Cadet.*
Steel, Mark. *Trouble Planet.*
"Terra, the Doomed Planet." *Space Patrol.*
Wilding, Philip. *Spaceflight Venus.*
Williams, Ralph. "Bertha."

1955 (19)

Anderson, Poul. *The Long Way Home.*
Appleton, Victor, II. [pseudonym] *Tom Swift, Jr., and His Outpost in Space.*
Ash, Alan. *Conditioned for Space.*

Asimov, Isaac. "Risk."
Asimov, Isaac. "The Talking Stone."
Brown, Slater. *Spaceward Bound.*
Chandler, A. Bertram. "Moonfall."
Correy, Lee. [G. Harry Stine] "The Plains of San Augustine."
Correy, Lee. [G. Harry Stine] "The Test Stand."
"Crash of the Moons." *Rocky Jones, Space Ranger.*
Elliot, E. C. [Reginald Martin] *Kemlo and the Craters of the Moon.*
Elliot, E. C. [Reginald Martin] *Kemlo and the Space Lanes.*
Elliot, E. C. [Reginald Martin] *Kemlo and the Star Men.*
Grant, Lee. "Signal Thirty-Three."
Ing, Dean. "Tight Squeeze."
Kornbluth, C. M. *Not This August.*
Lande, Irving W. "Slingshot."
Taylor, John Alfred. "Far from Home."
White, James. "Outrider."

1956 (18)

Appleton, Victor, Jr. [pseudonym] *Tom Swift on the Phantom Satellite.*
Bradbury, Ray. "The End of the Beginning."
Clarke, Arthur C. "Venture to the Moon."
Conquest of Space.
Dawson, Basil. *Dan Dare on Mars.*
del Rey, Lester. [Walter Alvarez del Rey] *Mission to the Moon.*
Elliot, E. C. [Reginald Martin] *Kemlo and the Gravity Rays.*
Jones, Tupper. *The Building of the Alpha One.*
Kelleam, Joseph E. *Overlords from Space.*
Knight, Damon. "Stranger Station."
Low, A. M. [Archibald Montgomery Low] *Satellite in Space.*
Moore, Patrick A. *Wheel in Space.*
Richardson, Robert S. *Second Satellite.*
Scortia, Thomas N. "Sea Change."
Shaara, Michael. "Four-Billion Dollar Door."
Space School. [television series]
Supergiant.
White, James. "Question of Cruelty."

1957 (8)

Asimov, Isaac. "Insert Knob A in Hole B."
Blish, James. *They Shall Have Stars.*
Bryning, Frank B. "For Men Must Work."

Clarke, Arthur C. "The Other Side of the Sky."
Elliot, E. C. [Reginald Martin] *Kemlo and the End of Time.*
Elliot, E. C. [Reginald Martin] *Kemlo and the Purple Dawn.*
Leinster, Murray. [Will Jenkins] *City on the Moon.*
Long, Frank Belknap. *Space Station #1.*

1958 (19)

Appleton, Victor, Jr. [pseudonym] *Tom Swift in the Race to the Moon.*
Appleton, Victor, Jr. [pseudonym] *Tom Swift and His Space Solartron.*
Blackburn, John. *A Scent of New-Mown Hay.*
Blish, James. *Earthman, Come Home.*
Blish, James. *The Triumph of Time.*
Clarke, Arthur C. "The Haunted Space Suit."
Elam, Richard M., Jr. [Richard Mace] "The First Man into Space."
Elam, Richard M., Jr. [Richard Mace] "The Ghost Ship of Space."
Elam, Richard M., Jr. [Richard Mace] "Mercy Flight to Luna."
Elliot, E. C. [Reginald Martin] *Kemlo and the Zombie Men.*
Fear, W. H. *Lunar Flight.*
Gunn, James. *Station in Space.*
Heinlein, Robert A. "Tenderfoot in Space."
Malcolm, Donald. "The Long Ellipse."
Mullen, Stanley. "Fool Killer."
Queen of Outer Space.
Silverberg, Robert. [as Ivar Jorgenson] *Starhaven.*
Thomas, Theodore L. "Satellite Passage."
White, James. "Tableau."

1959 (19)

"Asteroid." *Men into Space.*
Barr, Tyrone C. *The Last Fourteen.*
Battle in Outer Space.
"Building a Space Station." *Men into Space.*
Cooper, Edmund. *Seed of Light.*
Destination Space.
"Edge of Eternity." *Men into Space.*
Elliot, E. C. [Reginald Martin] *Kemlo and the Space Men.*
Ellison, Harlan. "The Discarded."
Harvey, Frank. *Air Force!*
Kuykendall, Roger. "All Day September."
Miller, Walter M., Jr. *A Canticle for Leibowitz.*
Nourse, Alan E. *Scavengers in Space.*

"Quarantine." *Men into Space.*
Silverberg, Robert, and Barbara Silverberg. "Deadlock."
Siodmak, Curt. *Skyport.*
The Sky Calls.
White, James. "Occupation: Warrior."
Wyndham, John, and Lucas Parkes. [John Beynon Harris] *The Out-*
ward Urge.

1960 (13)

Anderson, Poul. *Hunters of the Sky Cave.*
Appleton, Victor, II. [pseudonym] *Tom Swift and the Cosmic Astro-*
nauts.
"Dark of the Sun." *Men into Space.*
Elliot, E. C. [Reginald Martin] *Kemlo and the Satellite Builders.*
Leinster, Murray. [Will Jenkins] *Men into Space.*
Leinster, Murray. [Will Jenkins] *The Wailing Asteroid.*
Merak, A. J. *Barrier Unknown.*
"Mission to Mars." *Men into Space.*
"Sea of Stars." *Men into Space.*
Space Men.
"Verdict in Orbit." *Men into Space.*
"Voice of Infinity." *Men into Space.*
White, James. "Countercharm."

1961 (9)

Clarke, Arthur C. "Death and the Senator."
Clarke, Arthur C. *A Fall of Moondust.*
del Rey, Lester. [Walter Alvarez del Rey] *Moon of Mutiny.*
Elliot, E. C. [Reginald Martin] *Kemlo and the Space Invaders.*
Heinlein, Robert A. *Stranger in a Strange Land.*
Henderson, Gene L. "Tiger by the Tail."
Leiber, Fritz. "The Beat Cluster."
Lem, Stanislaw. *Solaris.*
Sutton, Jeff. *Spacehive.*

1962 (4)

Gorath.
Heinlein, Robert A. "Searchlight."
"Little Lost Robot." *Out of This World.*
White, James. *Hospital Station.*

1963 (8)

Appleton, Victor, Jr. [pseudonym] *Tom Swift and the Asteroid Pirates.*
Battle beyond the Sun.
Blish, James. *A Life for the Stars.*
Brunner, John. *Sanctuary in the Sky.*
Elliot, E. C. [Reginald Martin] *Kemlo and the Masters of Space.*
Leiber, Fritz. "Kindergarten."
Pohl, Frederik, and Jack Williamson. *The Reefs of Space.*
White, James. *Star Surgeon.*

1964 (7)

Bova, Ben, and Myron R. Lewis. "Men of Good Will."
Long, Frank Belknap. *The Martian Visitors.*
Pohl, Frederik, and Jack Williamson. *Starchild.*
Searls, Hank. *The Pilgrim Project.*
Silverberg, Robert. *Regan's Planet.*
"Specimen: Unknown." *The Outer Limits.*
Walters, Hugh [Walter Hughes] *Terror by Satellite.*

1965 (11)

Clarke, Arthur C. "The Last Command."
Dick, Philip K. *Dr. Bloodmoney.*
"The Love Affair." *The Man from U.N.C.L.E.*
McLaughlin, Dean. *The Man Who Wanted Stars.*
Mutiny in Outer Space.
Moorcock, Michael. *The Fireclown.*
Raphael, Rick. "The Mailman Cometh."
Snow Devils.
Vance, Jack. *Monsters in Orbit.*
War of the Planets.
The Wild, Wild Planet.

1966 (6)

Bova, Ben. "The Weathermakers."
del Rey, Lester. [Walter Alvarez del Rey; Paul Fairman] *Siege Peril-
    ous.*
Dick, Philip K. *The Crack in Space.*
Long, Frank Belknap. *This Strange Tomorrow.*
McCutchan, Philip. *Skyprobe.*

Neville, Kris. *The Mutants*.

1967 (8)

Bova, Ben. *The Weathermakers*.
Charbonneau, Louis. *Down to Earth*.
Clarke, Arthur C. "The Cruel Sky."
Clarke, Arthur C. "Love That Universe."
"The Faceless Ones." *Doctor Who*.
In like Flint.
The Terrornauts.
"The Trouble with Tribbles." *Star Trek*.

1968 (13)

Caidin, Martin. *Four Came Back*.
Clarke, Arthur C. *2001: A Space Odyssey*.
Del Rey, Lester. *Prisoners of Space*.
The Green Slime.
Janifer, Laurence M., and J. L. Treibich. *Target: Terra*.
Leiber, Fritz. *A Specter Is Haunting Texas*.
Martino, Joseph P. "Secret Weapon."
Panshin, Alexei. *Rite of Passage*.
Poyer, Joe. "Specialty."
Temple, William F. *The Fleshpots of Sansato*.
2001: A Space Odyssey.
"The Wheel in Space." *Doctor Who*.
White, Ted. *Secret of the Marauder Satellite*.

1969 (6)

Blish, James. "The Trouble with Tribbles."
Earls, William. "Jump."
Janifer, Laurence M., and S. J. Treibich. *The High Hex*.
Janifer, Laurence M., and S. J. Treibich. *The Wagered World*.
Martino, Joseph P. "Persistence."
"The Space Pirates." *Doctor Who*.

1970 (4)

Ballou, Arthur W. *Bound for Mars*.
Hoey, Edwin A. "Peace above Earth."
Ruben, William S. *Dionysus: The Ultimate Experiment*.

Silverberg, Robert. *World's Fair 1992.*

1971 (9)

Bova, Ben. *Exiled from Earth.*
Earth II. [unsold television series pilot]
Gernsback, Hugo. *Ultimate World.*
MacGregor, Ellen, and Dora Pantell. *Miss Pickerell and the Weather Satellite.*
Mason, Douglas R. *Satellite 54-Zero.*
Scott, Alan. *Project Dracula.*
Silent Running.
Solaris.
White, James. *Major Operation.*

1972 (13)

Anvil, Christopher. [Harry C. Crosby, Jr.] "Riddle Me This . . ."
Asimov, Isaac. "The Greatest Asset."
Bova, Ben. *Flight of Exiles.*
Buckley, Bob. "The Star Hole."
Chilson, Robert. "Truck Driver."
Clarke, Arthur C. *The Lost Worlds of 2001.*
Dickson, Gordon R. *The Pritcher Mass.*
Green, Joseph. "Three-Tour Man."
Hitchcock, Raymond. *Venus 13: A Cautionary Sex Tale.*
Kevles, Bettyann. "Mars-Station."
Martin, George R. R. "The Second Kind of Loneliness."
Tiptree, James P., Jr. [Alice Sheldon] "And I Awoke and Found Me Here on the Cold Hill's Side."
Vinge, Vernor. "Long Shot."

1973 (7)

Ball, Brian N. *Singularity Station.*
Bayley, Barrington J. *Collision Course.*
Clarke, Arthur C. *Rendezvous with Rama.*
Maxwell, M. Max. "Prisoner 794."
Plauger, P. J. "Epicycle."
Smith, George O. "The External Triangle."
White, James. "Spacebird."

1974 (7)

Benford, Gregory, and Gordon Eklund. "If the Stars Are Gods."
Bulmer, Kenneth. [as Tully Zetford] *Star City.*
Bulmer, Kenneth. [as Tully Zetford] *Whirlpool of Stars.*
Bulmer, Kenneth. [as Tully Zetford] *The Boosted Man.*
Pournelle, Jerry. "High Justice."
Scortia, Thomas N. *Earthwreck!*
Siodmak, Curt. *City in the Sky.*

1975 (14)

"The Ark in Space." *Doctor Who.*
Benford, Gregory. *Jupiter Project.*
Bova, Ben. *End of Exile.*
Brunner, John. *The Shockwave Rider.*
Bulmer, Kenneth. [as Tully Zetford] *The Virility Gene.*
Joseph, Franz. *Star Fleet Technical Manual.*
MacLean, Katherine. "The Gambling Hell and the Sinful Girl."
Niven, Larry. [Laurence van Cott Niven] "The Borderland of Sol."
Pedler, Kit, and Gerry Davis. *The Dynostar Menace.*
Pournelle, Jerry. "Consort."
"Revenge of the Cybermen." *Doctor Who.*
Reynolds, Mack. *Satellite City.*
"The Sontaran Experiment." *Doctor Who.*
Zebrowski, George. *The Star Web.*

1976 (16)

Bova, Ben. *Millennium.*
Cherryh, C. J. [Carolyn Cherry] *Brothers of Earth.*
Clarke, Arthur C. *Imperial Earth.*
Dicks, Terrance. *Doctor Who and the Revenge of the Cybermen.*
Haldeman, Joe. "Tricentennial."
Harrison, Harry. *Skyfall.*
Jackson, A. A., IV, and Howard Waldrop. "Sun Up."
Lucas, George. [Alan Dean Foster] *Star Wars.*
Martin, George R. R. "Nor the Many-Colored Fires of a Star Ring."
Pohl, Frederik. *Man Plus.*
Pournelle, Jerry. "Bind Your Sons to Exile."
Richmond, Walt, and Leigh Richmond. *Challenge the Hellmaker.*
Robinett, Stephen. *Stargate.*
Smith, George O. *The Complete Venus Equilateral.*

Vinge, Joan D. "The Crystal Ship."
White, James. "Custom Fitting."

1977 (14)

Benford, Gregory, and Gordon Eklund. *If the Stars Are Gods.*
Card, Orson Scott. "Ender's Game."
Cherryh, C. J. [Carolyn Cherry] *Hunter of Worlds.*
Golden, Frederic. *Colonies in Space: The Next Giant Step.*
Greenhough, Terry. *Thoughtworld.*
Kubaska, Theodore. "Univan and the Wheelies."
Marter, Ian. *Doctor Who and the Ark in Space.*
Petley, H. C. "And Earth So Far Away."
Pohl, Frederik. *Gateway.*
Robinson, Spider, and Jeanne Robinson. "Stardance."
Sheffield, Charles. "Dinsdale Dissents."
Space Academy. [television series]
Star Wars.
Watkins, William John. "Coming of Age in Henson's Tube."

1978 (21)

Bear, Greg. "The Wind from a Burning Woman."
Bova, Ben. *Colony.*
Cherryh, C. J. [Carolyn Cherry] *The Faded Sun, Kesrith.*
Cherryh, C. J. [Carolyn Cherry] *The Faded Sun, Shon'jir.*
Clarke, Arthur C. *The Fountains of Paradise.*
Cowley, Stewart. *Spacebase 2000.*
Dwiggins, Don. *The Asteroid War.*
Haldeman, Jack C., II. *Vector Analysis.*
Higgins, Bill, and Barry Gehm. "Home on Lagrange." [Song]
Hubert, Jean-Pierre. *Mort à l'étouffée.*
Kingsbury, Donald. "To Bring in the Steel."
Marter, Ian. *Doctor Who and the Sontaran Experiment.*
Niven, Larry [Laurence von Cott Niven]. "Flare Time."
Pournelle, Jerry. *Exiles to Glory.*
Randall, Marta. *Journey.*
Shaw, Bob. "Small World."
Sheffield, Charles. "Transition Team."
Simmons, Geoffrey S. *The Adam Experiment.*
Sullivan, Mark. *Station Zero-Zero.*
Verschuur, Gerrit L. "Contact!"
Vinge, Joan D. *The Outcasts of Heaven Belt.*

1979 (38)

Abels, Harriette S. *Forgotten World.*
Abels, Harriette S. *Green Invasion.*
Abels, Harriette S. *Medical Emergency.*
Abels, Harriette S. *Meteor from the Moon.*
Abels, Harriette S. *Mystery on Mars.*
Abels, Harriette S. *Planet of Ice.*
Abels, Harriette S. *Silent Invaders.*
Abels, Harriette S. *Strangers on NMA-6.*
Abels, Harriette S. *Unwanted Visitors.*
Bear, Greg. *Hegira.*
Benford, Gregory. "Dark Sanctuary."
Benford, Gregory. "Redeemer."
The Black Hole.
Bova, Ben. *Kinsman.*
Card, Orson Scott. "The Monkeys Thought 'Twas All in Fun."
Cherryh, C. J. [Carolyn Cherry] *The Faded Sun, Kutath.*
Dillingham, Peter. "House." [Poem]
Foster, Alan Dean. *The Black Hole.*
Girard, Dian. "No Home-Like Place."
Hogan, James P. *The Two Faces of Tomorrow.*
Ing, Dean. "Down & Out on Ellfive Prime."
Kingsbury, Donald. "The Moon Goddess and the Son."
Moonraker.
Niven, Larry [Laurence von Cott Niven], and Jerry Pournelle. "Spirals."
Reynolds, Mack. *Lagrange Five.*
Robinson, Spider, and Jeanne Robinson. *Stardance.*
Roddenberry, Gene. *Star Trek—The Motion Picture: A Novel.*
Rothman, Milton. "Prime Crime."
Sheffield, Charles. "Skystalk."
Sheffield, Charles. *The Web between the Worlds.*
Starstruck. [unsold television series pilot]
Star Trek: The Motion Picture.
Taylor, John Alfred. "Changeling."
Taylor, John Alfred. "Grave-11."
Webb, Sharon. "Itch on the Bull Run."
White, James. *Ambulance Ship.*
Wood, Christopher. *James Bond and Moonraker.*
Zebrowski, George. *Macrolife.*

1980 (31)

Asimov, Isaac. "For the Birds."
Blumberg, Rhoda. *The First Travel Guide to the Moon.*
Brin, David. *Sundiver.*
Cherryh, C. J. [Carolyn Cherry] *Serpent's Reach.*
Christensen, Kevin. "Bellerophon."
Correy, Lee. [G. Harry Stine] "Industrial Accident."
Cowley, Stewart. *Starliners: Commercial Spacetravel in 2200 A.D.*
Duntemann, Jeff. "Cold Hands."
Ford, John F. "The Wheels of Dream."
Goldstein, Stan, and Fred Goldstein. *Star Trek Spaceflight Chronology.*
Gottfried, Frederick D. "Hermes to the Ages."
Goulart, Ron. *Star Hawks: Empire 99.*
Heinlein, Robert A. "The Happy Days Ahead."
Ing, Dean. "Down & Out on Ellfive Prime."
Maynard, Jeff. *Introduction to Navigation: Star Fleet Command.*
Naha, Ed. *The Paradise Plot.*
Newman, Richard Louis. *Siege of Orbitor.*
Nicholson, Sam. [Shirley Nikolaisen] "Scrooge in Space."
Per Aspera ad Astra.
Pohl, Frederik. *Beyond the Blue Event Horizon.*
Randall, Marta. "Dangerous Games."
Randall, Marta. *Dangerous Games.*
"Rough Justice." [no author given]
"Shada." *Doctor Who.*
Silverberg, Robert. "Our Lady of the Sauropods."
Stiegler, Marc. "The Bully and the Crazy Boy."
Stone, Josephine Rector. *Green Is for Galanx.*
Swanwick, Michael. "Ginungagap."
Taylor, John Alfred. "Too Close to Home."
Vinge, Joan D. "Legacy."
Webb, Sharon. "Switch on the Bull Run."

1981 (22)

Appleton, Victor. [pseudonym] *The City in the Stars.*
Asimov, Isaac. "The Last Shuttle."
Cassutt, Michael. "The Free Agent."
Cherryh, C. J. [Carolyn Cherry] *Downbelow Station.*
Correy, Lee. [G. Harry Stine] *Space Doctor.*
Coulson, Juanita. *Tomorrow's Heritage.*

"The Dorian Secret." *Buck Rogers in the Twenty-Fifth Century*.
Gibson, William. "Hinterlands."
Gilliland, Alexis A. *Long Shot for Rosinante*.
Gilliland, Alexis A. *The Revolution from Rosinante*.
Goulart, Ron. *Star Hawks: The Cyborg King*.
Haldeman, Joe. *Worlds: A Novel of the Near Future*.
"Mark of the Saurian." *Buck Rogers in the Twenty-Fifth Century*.
Martino, Joseph P. "The Iceworm Special."
Oliver, Chad. "Meanwhile, Back on the Reservation."
O'Neill, Gerard K. *2081: A Hopeful View of the Human Future*.
Science Fiction. [no author given; John Silbersack]
Sheffield, Charles. "All the Colors of the Vacuum."
Sucharitkul, Somtow. [S. P. Somtow] *Mallworld*.
Tannehill, Jayne. "Last Words."
Tedford, William. *Silent Galaxy*.
Thunderbirds in Outer Space.

1982 (36)

Aldiss, Brian W. *Helliconia Spring*.
Android.
The Astronauts. [unsold television series pilot]
Ballard, J. G. "Report on an Unidentified Space Station."
Callin, Grant D. "The Turtle and O'Hare."
Carr, John F. "Shapes of Things to Come."
Cherryh, C. J. [Carolyn Cherry] *The Pride of Chanur*.
Cherryh, C. J. [Carolyn Cherry] *Merchanter's Luck*.
Cherryh, C. J. [Carolyn Cherry] *Port Eternity*.
Cohen, Barney, and Jim Baen. *The Taking of Satcon Station*.
Cole, Allan, and Chris Bunch. *Sten*.
Coulson, Juanita. *Outward Bound*.
Dulski, Thomas R. "My Christmas on New Hanford."
Farber, Sharon, and Correspondents [Susanna Jacobson, James Killus, and Dave Stout]. "Dr. Time."
Forbidden World.
Gibson, William. *Neuromancer*.
Gilliland, Alexis A. *The Pirates of Rosinante*.
Girard, Dian. "Invisible Encounter."
Heinlein, Robert A. *Friday*.
Holt, Paul F. "Good as Gold."
Johnson, Bill. "Meet Me at Apogee."
Killus, James, and Dorothy Smith. "High Iron."
Lupoff, Richard A. "Stomping Down Stroka Prospekt."

McIntyre, Vonda N. *Star Trek II: The Wrath of Khan*.
McKillip, Patricia A. *Moon-Flash*.
McNeil, Mark. "Scratches in the Dark."
Michener, James A. *Space*.
Naha, Ed. *The Suicide Plague*.
Nicholson, Sam. [Shirley Nikolaisen] "He Who Fights and Runs Away."
Niven, Larry [Laurence von Cott Niven], with Stephen Barnes. *The Descent of Anansi*.
Norwood, Rick. "IO."
Rohan, Michael Scott. *Run to the Stars*.
Star Trek II: The Wrath of Khan.
Sterling, Bruce. "Spider Rose."
Sterling, Bruce. "Swarm."
Young, Robert F. "The Moon of Advanced Learning."

1983 (26)

Aldiss, Brian W. *Helliconia Summer*.
Bischoff, David F., and Thomas Monteleone. *Day of the Dragonstar*.
Bishop, George. *The Shuttle People*.
Brin, David. "Tank Farm Dynamo."
Brin, David. *Startide Rising*.
Brunner, John. *The Crucible of Time*.
Cherryh, C. J. [Carolyn Cherry] *Forty Thousand in Gehenna*.
Correy, Lee. [G. Harry Stine] *Manna*.
Haldeman, Joe, and Jack C. Haldeman II. *There Is No Darkness*.
Haldeman, Joe. *Worlds Apart*.
Kahn, James. *Return of the Jedi*.
Langford, David. *The Space Eater*.
Lydecker, John. [Stephen Gallagher] *Doctor Who—Terminus*.
Oliver, Chad. "Ghost Town."
Return of the Jedi.
Rowley, Christopher. *The War for Eternity*.
Sheffield, Charles. *The McAndrew Chronicles*.
Slote, Alfred. *Omega Station*.
Sterling, Bruce. "Cicada Queen."
Sterling, Bruce, and William Gibson. "Red Star, Winter Orbit."
Sterling, Bruce. "Spook."
"Terminus." *Doctor Who*.
Trebor, Robert. *An XT Called Stanley*.
Vinicoff, Eric. "Blue Sky."
White, James. *Sector General*.

Wylde, Thomas. "The Nanny."

1984 (33)

Bova, Ben. "Isolation Area."
Brin, David. "The Crystal Spheres."
John Brunner. *The Tides of Time.*
Caidin, Martin. *Killer Station.*
Cherryh, C. J. [Carolyn Cherry] *Chanur's Venture.*
Cherryh, C. J. [Carolyn Cherry] *Voyager in Night.*
Cole, Allan, and Chris Bunch. *The Wolf Worlds.*
Diamond, Graham. "'Outcasts.'"
Gould, Stephen. "Rory."
Kube-McDowell, Michael P. "Menace."
Lambe, Dean R. "In a Cavern. . ."
Lorrah, Jean. *The Vulcan Academy Murders.*
Lupoff, Richard A. *Sun's End.*
Mason, Anne. *The Dancing Meteorite.*
McIntyre, Vonda N. *Star Trek III: The Search for Spock.*
Michaels, Melisa. *Skirmish.*
Place, Marian T. *The First Astrowitches.*
Pohl, Frederik. *Heechee Rendezvous.*
Pollack, Rachel. "Tree House."
Resnick, Michael. *Eros Ascending.*
Resnick, Michael. *Eros at Zenith.*
"Resurrection of the Daleks." *Doctor Who.*
Reynolds, Mack. *Chaos in Lagrangia.*
Robinson, Kim Stanley. *Icehenge.*
Sanders, Scott Russell. "Quarantine."
Sterling, Bruce. "Sunken Gardens."
Sterling, Bruce. "Twenty Evocations."
Supergirl.
2010: The Year We Make Contact.
Vinicoff, Eric. "Repairman."
White, James. *Star Healer.*
Zahn, Timothy. "Return to the Fold."
Zebrowski, George. *Sunspacer.*

1985 (36)

Aldiss, Brian W. *Helliconia Winter.*
Bear, Greg. *Eon.*
Bischoff, David F., and Thomas Monteleone. *Night of the Dragonstar.*

Brin, David. "The Warm Space."
Card, Orson Scott. *Ender's Game.*
Cherryh, C. J. [Carolyn Cherry] *Angel with the Sword.*
Cherryh, C. J. [Carolyn Cherry] *Cuckoo's Egg.*
Cherryh, C. J. [Carolyn Cherry] *The Kif Strike Back.*
Cole, Allan, and Chris Bunch. *The Court of a Thousand Suns.*
Di Filippo, Paul. "Stone Lives."
Fish, Leslie. "Carmen Miranda's Ghost." [Song]
Haldeman, Joe. "More Than the Sum of His Parts."
Heinlein, Robert A. *The Cat Who Walks through Walls.*
Holmes, Robert. *Doctor Who—The Two Doctors.*
Kelly, James Patrick. "Solstice."
Kotani, Eric, [Yoji Kondo] and John Maddox Roberts. *Act of God.*
Leiber, Justin. *Can Animals and Machines Be People?*
Michaels, Melisa. *First Battle.*
Oltion, Jerry. "The Getaway Special."
Park, John. "The Software Plague."
Resnick, Michael. *Eros Descending.*
Reynolds, Mack, with Dean Ing. *Trojan Orbit.*
Robinson, Kim Stanley. *The Memory of Whiteness.*
Rowley, Christopher. *The Black Ship.*
Sheffield, Charles. *Between the Strokes of Night.*
Shirley, John. *Eclipse.*
Shirley, John. "Freezone."
Star Trek III: The Search for Spock.
Sterling, Bruce. *Schismatrix.*
"The Two Doctors." *Doctor Who.*
Watkins, William John. *The Centrifugal Rickshaw Dancer.*
Webb, Sharon. *The Adventures of Terra Tarkington.*
Wightman, Wayne. "In the Realm of the Heart, In the World of the Knife."
Wylde, Thomas. "Space Shuttle Crashes!"
Yates, W. R. *Diasporah.*
Zebrowski, George. *The Stars Will Speak.*

1986 (33)

Asimov, Isaac. *Foundation and Earth.*
Barnes, John. *The Man Who Pulled Down the Sky.*
Bujold, Lois McMaster. *Ethan of Athos.*
Bujold, Lois McMaster. *Shards of Honor.*
Bujold, Lois McMaster. *The Warrior's Apprentice.*
Byers, Edward A. *The Babylon Gate.*

Card, Orson Scott. *Speaker for the Dead*.
Cherryh, C. J. [Carolyn Cherry] *Chanur's Homecoming*.
Clarke, Arthur C. *Arthur C. Clarke's July 20, 2019*.
Clarke, Arthur C. *The Songs of Distant Earth*.
Farren, Nick. *Vickers*.
Forstchen, William R. *Into the Sea of Stars*.
Gibson, William. *Count Zero*.
Innes, Evan. [Zach Hughes] *America 2040*.
Innes, Evan. [Zach Hughes] *The Golden World*.
Killough, Lee. *Spider Play*.
Kingsbury, Donald. *The Moon Goddess and the Son*.
Maddox, Tom. "Snake-Eyes."
McIntyre, Vonda N. *Barbary*.
McIntyre, Vonda N. *Enterprise: The First Adventure*.
Michaels, Melisa. *Last War*.
Moon, Elizabeth. "ABCs in Zero-G."
Morris, Janet, and Chris Morris. *Medusa*.
Resnick, Michael. *Eros at Nadir*.
Sheffield, Charles. *The Nimrod Hunt*.
Silverberg, Robert. "Blindsight."
Snodgrass, Melinda M. *Circuit*.
Stith, John E. *Memory Blank*.
"The Trial of a Time Lord." *Doctor Who*.
Varley, John. "Tango Charlie and Foxtrot Romeo."
Watkins, William John. *Going to See the End of the Sky*.
Williams, Walter Jon. *Hard Wired*.
Wodhams, Jack. "Station 2152."

1987 (38)

Banks, Iain M. *Consider Phlebas*.
Beason, Doug. "Lifeguard."
Beebee, Chris. *The Hub*.
Benford, Gregory. *Great Sky River*.
Brin, David. *The Uplift War*.
Claremont, Chris. *FirstFlight*.
Clarke, Arthur C. *2061: Odyssey Three*.
Cooper, Tom. *War Moon*.
Coville, Bruce. *Space Station ICE-3*.
Dicks, Terrance. *Doctor Who—The Faceless Ones*.
Drake, David. *Fortress*.
Goulart, Ron. *Daredevils, Ltd*.
Goulart, Ron. *Starpirate's Brain*.

Gould, Steven. "Poppa Was a Catcher."
Heinlein, Robert A. *To Sail beyond the Sunset.*
Hodgman, Ann. *Galaxy High School.*
Hogan, James P. *Endgame Enigma.*
Innes, Evan. [Zach Hughes] *City in the Mist.*
Kotani, Eric, [Yoji Kondo] and John Maddox Roberts. *The Island Worlds.*
Lupoff, Richard A. *The Forever City.*
McDonough, Thomas. *The Architects of Hyperspace.*
McKillip, Patricia. *Fool's Run.*
Mixon, Laura J. *Astropilots.*
Morris, Janet, and David Drake. *Kill Ratio.*
Packard, Edward. *Space Vampire.*
Pelletier, Francine. "La migratrice."
Pohl, Frederik. *The Annals of the Heechee.*
Preuss, Paul. *Breaking Strain.*
Snodgrass, Melinda M. *Circuit Breaker.*
Spaceballs.
Star Cops. [television series]
Star Trek IV: The Voyage Home.
Swanwick, Michael. *Vacuum Flowers.*
Tomino, Yoshiyuki. *Awakening.*
Tomino, Yoshiyuki. *Confrontation.*
Tomino, Yoshiyuki. *Escalation.*
White, James. *Code Blue: Emergency.*
Williams, Walter Jon. *Voice of the Whirlwind.*

1988 (36)

Allen, Roger MacBride. *Farside Cannon.*
Asimov, Isaac. *Prelude to Foundation.*
Baker, Pip, and Jane Baker. *Doctor Who—Terror of the Vervoids.*
Baker, Pip, and Jane Baker. *Doctor Who—The Ultimate Foe.*
Banks, Iain. *The Player of Games.*
Bear, Greg. *Eternity.*
Bova, Ben. *Peacekeepers.*
Brown, Dale. *Silver Tower.*
Bujold, Lois McMaster. *Falling Free.*
Cherryh, C. J. [Carolyn Cherry] *Cyteen.*
Clarke, Arthur C. with Gentry Lee. *Cradle.*
Cole, Allan, and Chris Bunch. *Fleet of the Damned.*
Dicks, Terrance. *Doctor Who—The Mysterious Planet.*
Dicks, Terrance. *Doctor Who—The Wheel in Space.*

Dorsey, Candas Jane. "Sleeping in a Box."
Duane, Diane. *Spock's World.*
Farren, Nick. *The Long Orbit.*
Gear, W. Michael. *The Warriors of Spider.*
Gibson, William. *Mona Lisa Overdrive.*
Goulart, Ron. *Everybody Comes to Cosmo's.*
Gunnarsson, Thorarinn. *The Starwolves.*
Harris, Raymond. *Shadows of the White Sun.*
Hellfire.
Hinz, Christopher. *Liege-Killer.*
Innes, Evan. [Zach Hughes] *The Return.*
Innes, Evan. [Zach Hughes] *The Star Explorer.*
King, T. Jackson. *Retread Shop.*
Lattimer, Dick. *Space Station Friendship: A Visit with the Crew in 2007.*
Lupoff, Richard A. *Galaxy's End.*
Michaels, Melisa. *Pirate Prince.*
Michaels, Melisa. *Floater Factor.*
Morris, Janet, and Chris Morris. *Outpassage.*
Murdock, M. S. *et al. Arrival.*
Preuss, Paul. *Maelstrom.*
Shirley, John. *Eclipse Penumbra.*
Snodgrass, Melinda M. *Final Circuit.*

1989 (39)

Asimov, Isaac. *Nemesis.*
Banks, Iain. *The State of the Art.*
Beebee, Chris. *The Main Event.*
Benford, Gregory. *Tides of Light.*
Bischoff, David F., and Thomas Monteleone. *Dragonstar Destiny.*
Bujold, Lois McMaster. *The Borders of Infinity.*
Bujold, Lois McMaster. *Brothers in Arms.*
Cherryh, C. J. [Carolyn Cherry] *Rimrunners.*
Clarke, Arthur C., with Gentry Lee. *Rama II.*
Cole, Allan, and Chris Bunch. *Revenge of the Damned.*
Coulson, Juanita. *Legacy of Earth.*
Coulson, Juanita. *The Past of Forever.*
Cover, Arthur Byron. *Stationfall.*
Dillard, J. M. *Star Trek: The Lost Years.*
Flynn, Michael E. "The Washer at the Ford."
Gear, W. Michael. *The Way of Spider.*
Gear, W. Michael. *The Web of Spider.*

Gibson, Edward. *Reach.*
Gunnarsson, Thorarinn. *Starwolves: Battle of the Ring.*
Hinz, Christopher. *Ash Ock: The Paratwa Saga, Book Two.*
Martin, Philip. *Doctor Who—Mindwarp.*
McCaffrey, Anne. "If Madam Likes You."
McDevitt, Jack. *A Talent for War.*
McIntyre, Vonda N. *Starfarers.*
"The Measure of a Man." *Star Trek: The Next Generation.*
Moon, Elizabeth. "Welcome to Wheel Days."
Murdock, M. S. *Armageddon off Vesta.*
Murdock, M. S. *Hammer of Mars.*
Murdock, M. S. *Rebellion 2456.*
Mystery Science Theater 3000. [Television series]
Niven, Larry. "The Return of William Proxmire."
Perry, Steve. *The 97th Step.*
Preuss, Paul. *Hide and Seek.*
Prisoners of Gravity. [Television series]
Quick, W. T. "High Hotel."
Rowley, Christopher. *The Founder.*
Simmons, Dan. *Hyperion.*
Star Trek V: The Final Frontier.
Steele, Allen. *Orbital Decay.*

1990 (51)

Allen, Amanda. "Rolling Down the Floor."
Allen, Roger MacBride. *The Ring of Charon.*
Anderson, Kevin J., and Doug Beason. *Lifeline.*
Banks, Iain. *Use of Weapons.*
Barnett, Bruce B. "Basket Case, or, The Grapes of Wraith."
"The Best of Both Worlds." *Star Trek: The Next Generation.*
Bisson, Terry. *Voyage to the Red Planet.*
Blackburn, Eric. "The Entertainer."
Bloom, Britton. *Matrix Cubed.*
Brin, David. *Earth.*
Bujold, Lois McMaster. *The Vor Game.*
Cherryh, C. J. [Carolyn Cherry] "Wings."
Clarke, Arthur C. *The Ghost from the Grand Banks.*
Clough, B. W. [Brenda] "Provisional Solution."
Clough, B. W. [Brenda] "La Vita Nuova (The New Life)."
Cole, Allan, and Chris Bunch. *The Return of the Emperor.*
Dicks, Terrance. *Doctor Who—The Space Pirates.*
Ecklar, Julia. "Carmen Miranda and the Maracas of Death."

Feeley, Gregory. *The Oxygen Barons.*
Fish, Leslie. "Bertocci's Proof."
Friesner, Esther. "In the Can."
Gear, W. Michael. *The Artifact.*
Gear, W. Michael. *Starstrike.*
Hoover, H. M. *Away Is a Strange Place to Be.*
Kato, Ken. *Yamato—A Rage in Heaven, Part One.*
Lewitt, S. N. "That Souse American Way."
Mand, Mary L. "The Pigeon Sisters on Space Station Three."
Marks, Betsy, and Anne G. DeMaio. "And Now the News:"
"A Matter of Perspective." *Star Trek: The Next Generation.*
McCaffrey, Anne. *Pegasus in Flight.*
McCaffrey, Anne. *The Rowan.*
Miller, John. *First Power Play.*
Murdock, M. S. *Prime Squared.*
North, Rick. *Ready for Blastoff.*
North, Rick. *Space Blazers.*
North, Rick. *The Young Astronauts.*
Pohl, Frederik. *The Gateway Trip: Tales and Vignettes of the Heechee.*
Preuss, Paul. *The Diamond Moon.*
Preuss, Paul. *The Medusa Encounter.*
Robinson, Ron. "Shadows on the Wall."
Sakers, Don, editor. *Carmen Miranda's Ghost Is Haunting Space Station Three.*
Sakers, Don. "The Man Who Traveled in Rocketships."
Sakers, Don. "Tarawa Rising."
Scott, Melissa, and Lisa A. Barnett. "The Carmen Miranda Gambit."
Shirley, John. *Eclipse Corona.*
Shwartz, Susan. "Confessional Booths."
Steele, Allan. *Clarke County, Space.*
Stewart, Ian. "Curlew's Choice."
Stirling, S. M. *The Stone Dogs.*
Williams, Walter Jon. "Elegy for Angels and Dogs."
Woeltjen, L. D. "The Never-Ending Battle."

1991 (39)

Barnes, John. *Orbital Resonance.*
Baxter, Stephen. *Raft.*
Boston, Bruce. "When Silver Plums Fall." [poem]
Bova, Ben. "The Long Fall."
Bujold, Lois McMaster. *Barrayar.*
Card, Orson Scott. *Xenocide.*

Cherryh, C. J. [Carolyn Cherry] *Heavy Time.*
Claremont, Chris. *Grounded!*
Clarke, Arthur C., and Gentry Lee. *The Garden of Rama.*
Dietz, William C. *Drifter.*
Donaldson, Stephen R. *The Gap into Conflict: The Real Story.*
Donaldson, Stephen R. *The Gap into Vision: Forbidden Knowledge.*
Duane, Diane, and Peter Morwood. *Space Cops: Mindblast.*
Fancher, Jane S. *Groundties.*
Gunnarsson, Thorarinn. *Starwolves: Technical Error.*
Hinz, Christopher. *The Paratwa.*
Ingrid, Charles. [Rhondi Vilott] *Radius of Doubt.*
Lerner, Edward M. *Probe.*
Maddox, Tom. *Halo.*
McIntyre, Vonda N. *Transition.*
Melton, Henry. "The Christmas Count."
Morris, Janet, and Chris Morris. *Threshold.*
Nighbert, David F. *The Clouds of Magellan.*
Niven, Larry [Laurence von Cott Niven], Jerry Pournelle, and Michael
    Flynn. *Fallen Angels.*
North, Rick. *Destination Mars.*
North, Rick. *Space Pioneers.*
North, Rick. *Citizens of Mars.*
Preuss, Paul. *The Shining Ones.*
Robinson, Spider, and Jeanne Robinson. *Starseed.*
Simmons, Dan. *The Fall of Hyperion.*
Stabenow, Dana. *A Handful of Stars.*
Stabenow, Dana. *Second Star.*
Star Trek VI: The Undiscovered Country.
Steele, Allan. *Lunar Descent.*
Sykes, C. J. *Red Genesis.*
Vinge, Joan D. *The Heaven Chronicles.*
Watkins, William John. "The Lagrange League Stationary Habitats."
    [poem]
White, James. *The Genocidal Healer.*
Zebrowski, George. *Stranger Suns.*

1992 (46)

Bova, Ben. *Mars.*
Bova, Ben, and Bill Pogue. *The Trikon Deception.*
Brennan, C. M. *The Genesis Web.*
Cherryh, C. J. [Carolyn Cherry] *Chanur's Legacy: A Novel of Com-
    pact Space.*

Cole, Allan, and Chris Bunch. *Vortex.*
Conly, Judith N. "Gung Ho." [poem]
Davis, Margaret. *Mind Light.*
Dietz, William C. *Drifter's Run.*
Dietz, William C. *Drifter's War.*
Donaldson, Stephen R. *The Gap into Power: A Dark and Hungry God Arises.*
Downing, Paula E. *Fallaway.*
Drake, David, and Bill Fawcett, editors. *Battlestation, Book 1.*
Drake, David. "Facing the Enemy."
Duane, Diane. "Killer Cure."
Duane, Diane, and Peter Morwood. *Space Cops: High Moon.*
Duane, Diane, and Peter Morwood. *Space Cops: Kill Station.*
Fancher, Jane S. *Harmonies of the Net.*
Fancher, Jane S. *Uplink.*
Forward, Robert L. *Timemaster.*
Graf, L. A. *Death Count.*
Gibson, Edward. *In the Wrong Hands.*
Haldeman, Joe. *Worlds Enough and Time.*
Harper, Tara K. *Lightwing.*
Ingrid, Charles. [Rhondi Vilott] *Path of Fire: The Patterns of Chaos #2.*
Kato, Ken. *Yamato—A Rage in Heaven, Part Two: The Way of the Warrior.*
Keith, William H., Jr. *Nomads of the Sky.*
Lewitt, S. N. "The Eyes of Texas."
McCaffery, Anne. *Damia.*
McCollum, Michael. *The Sails of Tau Ceti.*
McIntyre, Vonda N. *Metaphase.*
Morris, Janet. "A Transmigration of Soul."
Morris, Janet, and Chris Morris. *Trust Territory.*
Nye, Jody Lynn. "Starlight."
Perry, Steve. "Blind Spot."
Pohl, Frederik. *Mining the Oort.*
Randle, Kevin, and Richard Driscoll. *Star Precinct.*
Randle, Kevin, and Richard Driscoll. *Star Precinct 2: Mind Slayer.*
Randle, Kevin, and Richard Driscoll. *Star Precinct 3: Inside Job.*
Resnick, Michael, and Barbara Delaplace. "Trading Up."
Robinson, Kim Stanley. *Red Mars.*
Sheckley, Robert. "The Stand on Luminos."
Sheffield, Charles. *Cold As Ice.*
Stasheff, Christopher. "Globin's Children."
Steele, Allan. *Labyrinth of Night.*

Stirling, S. M. "Comrades."
Williamson, Jack. *Beachhead.*

1993 (74)

Anderson, Kevin J., and Doug Beason. *Assemblers of Infinity.*
Asimov, Isaac. *Forward the Foundation.*
"Babel." *Star Trek: Deep Space Nine.*
Babylon 5. [pilot film]
"Battle Lines." *Star Trek: Deep Space Nine.*
"Birthright." *Star Trek: The Next Generation.*
Brin, David. "What Continues, What Fails."
"Captive Pursuit." *Star Trek: Deep Space Nine.*
"Cardassians." *Star Trek: Deep Space Nine.*
Cherryh, C. J. [Carolyn Cherry] *Hellburner.*
"The Circle." *Star Trek: Deep Space Nine.*
Clarke, Arthur C. *The Hammer of God.*
Clarke, Arthur C., and Gentry Lee. *Rama Revealed.*
Cole, Allan, and Chris Bunch. *Empire's End.*
Conly, Judith N. "Imperatives." [poem]
Crandall, Melissa. *Shell Game.*
David, Peter. *The Siege.*
"Dax." *Star Trek: Deep Space Nine.*
Dillard, J. M. *Emissary.*
Drake, David, and Bill Fawcett, editors. *Battlestation, Book 2: Vanguard.*
Drake, David. "Failure Mode."
"Dramatis Personae." *Star Trek: Deep Space Nine.*
"Duet." *Star Trek: Deep Space Nine.*
Duane, Diane. "The Handmaiden."
Dugas, Don John. "Joint Ventures."
"Emissary." *Star Trek: Deep Space Nine.*
Feeley, Gregory. "The Mind's Place."
Friesner, Esther M. "You Can't Make an Omelet."
"The Forsaken." *Star Trek: Deep Space Nine.*
Gunnarsson, Thorarinn. *Starwolves: Dreadnought.*
Haldeman, Jack II, and Jack Dann. *High Steel.*
Hand, Elizabeth. *Icarus Descending.*
"The Homecoming." *Star Trek: Deep Space Nine.*
"If Wishes Were Horses." *Star Trek: Deep Space Nine.*
"In the Hands of the Prophets." *Star Trek: Deep Space Nine.*
"Invasive Procedures." *Star Trek: Deep Space Nine.*
Jeter, K. W. *Bloodletter.*

Keith, William H., Jr. *Warlords of Jupiter.*
Kirby, William S. *Iapetus.*
Kurtz, Katherine. "Battle Offering."
Lackey, Mercedes, and Mark Shepherd. "Medic."
Lewitt, S. N. "Charity."
Living and Working in Space: The Countdown Has Begun.
Lois and Clark: The New Adventures of Superman. [pilot film]
MacMillan, Scott. "Deadfall."
"A Man Alone." *Star Trek: Deep Space Nine.*
McCaffrey, Anne, and S. M. Stirling. *The City Who Fought.*
McCaffrey, Anne. *Damia's Children.*
"Melora." *Star Trek: Deep Space Nine.*
Moon, Elizabeth. *Hunting Party.*
Morris, Janet, and Chris Morris. *The Stalk.*
Morwood, Peter. "Taken to the Cleaners."
"Move Along Home." *Star Trek: Deep Space Nine.*
"The Nagus." *Star Trek: Deep Space Nine.*
"Necessary Evil." *Star Trek: Deep Space Nine.*
Nye, Jody Lynn. "Shooting Star."
"The Passenger." *Star Trek: Deep Space Nine.*
"Past Prologue." *Star Trek: Deep Space Nine.*
"Progress." *Star Trek: Deep Space Nine.*
"Q-Less." *Star Trek: Deep Space Nine.*
Robinson, Kim Stanley. *Green Mars.*
Rowley, Christopher. *To a Highland Nation.*
"Rules of Acquisition." *Star Trek: Deep Space Nine.*
"Sanctuary." *Star Trek: Deep Space Nine.*
Schofield, Sandy. *The Big Game.*
"Second Sight." *Star Trek: Deep Space Nine.*
Sheffield, Charles. *One Man's Universe.*
"The Siege." *Star Trek: Deep Space Nine.*
Stasheff, Christopher. "Hearing."
"The Storyteller." *Star Trek: Deep Space Nine.*
"Vortex." *Star Trek: Deep Space Nine.*
Weber, David. *The Honor of the Queen.*
Weber, David. *On Basilisk Station.*
Zebrowski, George. *Behind the Stars.*

TIMELINE

1869 ■
1870 ■
1871
1872 ■

=====

1894 ■
1895 ■
1896
1897 ▬

=====

1920 ■
1921
1922
1923
1924
1925
1926 ■
1927
1928 ■
1929 ▬▬
1930 ■
1931 ▬▬
1932 ▪
1933 ▪
1934 ▪
1935
1936 ■
1937 ■

Year	
1938	
1939	
1940	
1941	
1942	
1943	
1944	
1945	
1946	
1947	
1948	
1949	
1950	
1951	
1952	
1953	
1954	
1955	
1956	
1957	
1958	
1959	
1960	
1961	
1962	
1963	
1964	
1965	
1966	
1967	
1968	
1969	
1970	
1971	
1972	
1973	
1974	
1975	
1976	
1977	
1978	
1979	
1980	

1981

1982

1983

1984

1985

1986

1987

1988

1989

1990

1991

1992

1993

PART E.

OTHER WORKS CITED

This section provides data for some items referred to in the introduction or individual entries, including nonfictional works about space stations, bibliographies and reference books about science fiction, and anthologies of science fiction stories not deemed sufficiently unified in theme or relevant to space stations to be listed in the main bibliography.

E1. Asimov, Isaac, Martin H. Greenberg, and Charles G. Waugh, editors. *Space Shuttles: Isaac Asimov's Wonderful Worlds of Science Fiction #7*. New York: Signet, 1987. 384 p.

E2. Australian Science Fiction Association. *Index to British Science Fiction Magazines, 1934-1953*. Compiled by Graham Stone. Two volumes. Sydney: The Association, 1977. [Pagination irregular; by my count, 95 p.; 145 p.]

E3. Barron, Neil, editor. *Anatomy of Wonder: A Critical Guide to Science Fiction*. Third Edition. New York: R. R. Bowker Co., 1987. 874 p.

E4. Benford, Gregory, and George Zebrowski, editors. *Skylife: Space Habitats in Story and Science*. New York: Harcourt, Inc., 2000.

E5. Clarke, I. F. [Ignatius Frederick] *The Tale of the Future, from the Beginning to the Present Day*. London: Library Association, 1978. 357 p.

E6. Clute, John, and Peter Nicholls, editors. *The Encyclopedia of Science Fiction*. New York, St. Martin's Press, 1993. 1370 p.

E7. Day, Donald B. *Index to the Science Fiction Magazines 1926-1950*. Revised. Boston: G. K. Hall, 1982. 289 p.

E8. Di Fate, Vincent, and Ian Summers. *Di Fate's Catalog of Science Fiction Hardware*. New York: Workman Publishers, 1980. 157 p.

E9. Finger, Bill, story. Sid Greene and Joe Giella, art. "The Last Television Broadcast on Earth." [comic book story] In *Mysteries in Space: The Best of DC Science Fiction Comics*. Edited by Michael Uslan. New York: Simon and Schuster, 1980, p. 104-109. Story originally published in *Mystery in Space*, No. 22 (November, 1955).

E10. Gerrold, David. [Jerrold David Friedman] *The Trouble with Tribbles*. New York: Ballantine, 1973. 272 p.

E11. Goldberg, Lee. *Unsold TV Pilots: The Almost Complete Guide to Everything You Never Saw on TV*. New York: Citadel Press, 1991. 149 p. Revised and abridged edition of *Unsold Television Pilots*, published in 1990.

E12. Hardy, Phil. *The Encyclopedia of Science Fiction Movies*. Minneapolis, MN: Woodbury Press, 1986, 1984. 403 p.

E13. Harrison, Harry. *Spacecraft in Fact and Fiction*. Baltimore, MD: Octopus, 1980. 126 p.

E14. Hirsch, David, Gary Gerani, David Houston, Mike Cotter, and Bill Clark, compilers and authors. *Starlog TV Episodes Guide, Volume 2*. New York: Starlog Press, 1982. 98 p.

E15. Lofficier, Jean-Marc. *Doctor Who: The Programme Guide*. Revised and Updated. London: W. H. Allen and Co., 1989. 177 p.

E16. Malone, Robert. *Rocketship*. New York: Harper & Row, 1977. 127 p.

E17. Maltin, Leonard. *TV Movies*. 1981-1982 Edition. New York: Signet, 1980. 886 p.

E18. Metcalf, Norman, compiler. *The Index of Science Fiction Magazines, 1951-1965*. El Cerrito, CA: J. B. Stark, 1968. 249 p.

E19. Moskowitz, Sam. "The *Real* Earth Satellite Story." In *Explorers of the Infinite: Shapers of Science Fiction*. Cleveland: World Publishing Co., 1963, p. 88-105.

E20. Moskowitz, Sam. *Seekers of Tomorrow: Masters of Modern Science Fiction*. Cleveland: World Publishing Co., 1066. 433 p.

E21. New England Science Fiction Association. *Index to the Science Fiction Magazines, 1966-1970*. Cambridge, MA: The Association, 1973. 82 p.

E22. Nicholls, Peter, editor. *The Science Fiction Encyclopedia*. Garden City, NY: Doubleday and Company, 1979. 672 p.

E23. Nicholls, Peter. *The Science in Science Fiction*. New York: Alfred A. Knopf, 1983. 206 p.

E24. O'Neill, Gerard. *The High Frontier: Human Colonies in Space*. 1977. New York: Bantam, 1978. 344 p.

E25. Pournelle, Jerry, with John F. Carr, editors. *Cities in Space: The Endless Frontier, Volume III*. New York: Ace, 1991. 259 p.

E26. Pournelle, Jerry, editor. *The Endless Frontier, Volume I*. New York: Ace, 1979. 376 p.

E27. Pournelle, Jerry, with John F. Carr, editors. *The Endless Frontier, Volume II*. New York: Ace, 1982. 429 p.

E28. Schow, David J. and Jeffrey Frentzen. *The Outer Limits Companion*. New York: Ace, 1986. 392 p.

E29. Shwartz, Susan, editor. *Habitats*. New York: DAW, 1984. 220 p.

E30. Spinrad, Norman. "Dreams of Space." In *Science Fiction in the Real World*. Carbondale, IL: Southern Illinois University Press, 1990, p. 122-135. Originally published in *Isaac Asimov's Science Fiction Magazine* in 1987.

E31. Stanley, John. *Revenge of the Creature Features Movie Guide. Third Edition*. San Francisco, CA: Creatures at Large Press, 1988. 420 p.

E32. Sterling, Bruce, editor. *Mirrorshades: The Cyberpunk Anthology*. 1986. New York: Ace, 1988. 239 p.

E33. Tuck, Donald Henry. *The Encyclopedia of Science Fiction and Fantasy through 1968*. Three Volumes. 1974. Chicago: Advent Press, 1982. 286 p., 530 p., 370 p.

E34. Wehmeyer, Lillian Biermann. *Images in a Crystal Ball: World Futures in Novels for Young People*. Littleton, CO: Libraries Unlimited, 1981. 211 p.

E35. Westfahl, Gary. *Islands in the Sky: The Space Station Theme in Science Fiction Literature*. Preface by Gregory Benford. San Bernardino, CA: Borgo Press, 1996. 224 p. Second Edition. Rockville, MD: Borgo Press/Wildside Press, 2009. 265 p.

ABOUT THE AUTHOR

GARY WESTFAHL received a B.A. in Mathematics and English from Carleton College and a Ph.D. in English from Claremont Graduate University. Recipient of the Science Fiction Research Association' Pilgrim Award for lifetime contributions to science fiction scholarship, he has to date written, edited, or co-edited more than twenty books on science fiction and fantasy, including the Hugo-Award nominated *Science Fiction Quotations: From the Inner Mind to the Outer Limits* (2005) and the three-volume *The Greenwood Encyclopedia of Science Fiction and Fantasy: Themes, Works, and Wonders* (2005). He has also contributed over two hundred articles and reviews on science fiction and fantasy to scholarly journals and anthologies, the British science fiction magazine *Interzone*, the Locus Online and Internet Review of Science Fiction websites, and numerous reference works, including *The Oxford Companion to the History of Modern Science* and *The Cambridge Companion to Science Fiction*. He now lives in Claremont, California, with his wife Lynne and son Jeremy, and he teaches at the Learning Center of the University of California, Riverside, and for the University of LaVerne's Educational Programs in Corrections.

www.ingramcontent.com/pod-product-compliance
Lightning Source LLC
Chambersburg PA
CBHW021213090426
42740CB00006B/194